THE PATRIOTIC CONSENSUS

THE PATRIOTIC CONSENSUS
Unity, Morale, and the Second World War in Winnipeg

JODY PERRUN

UMP
University of Manitoba Press

University of Manitoba Press
Winnipeg, Manitoba
Canada R3T 2M5
uofmpress.ca

Printed in Canada
Text printed on chlorine-free, 100% post-consumer recycled paper

18 17 16 15 14   1 2 3 4 5

Cover design: Frank Reimer
Interior design: Karen Armstrong Graphic Design

Library and Archives Canada Cataloguing in Publication

Perrun, Jody, 1971–, author
The patriotic consensus : unity, morale, and the Second World War
in Winnipeg / Jody Perrun.

Includes bibliographical references and index.
Issued in print and electronic formats.
ISBN 978-0-88755-749-1 (pbk.)
ISBN 978-0-88755-462-9 (PDF e-book)
ISBN 978-0-88755-464-3 (epub)

1. World War, 1939-1945—Manitoba—Winnipeg. 2. World War,
1939-1945—Social aspects—Manitoba—Winnipeg. 3. Community life—
Manitoba—Winnipeg—History—20th century. 4. Winnipeg (Man.)—
Social conditions—20th century. I. Title.

FC3396.4.P47 2014   971.27'4302   C2014-903285-4
                                            C2014-903286-2

This research was based in part on source materials accessed through the courtesy
of the Government of Manitoba. The views, opinions, and conclusions contained in
this work are those of the author, and have not been endorsed
or approved by the Government of Manitoba.

The University of Manitoba Press gratefully acknowledges the financial support
for its publication program provided by the Government of Canada through the Canada
Book Fund, the Canada Council for the Arts, the Manitoba Department
of Culture, Heritage, Tourism, the Manitoba Arts Council,
and the Manitoba Book Publishing Tax Credit.

FSC
www.fsc.org
MIX
Paper from
responsible sources
FSC® C016245

To Emily and Elise, my little ones, for whom I have such high hopes . . .

CONTENTS

Illustrations and photographs follow pages 84 and 196

TABLES

ILLUSTRATIONS

Following page 84

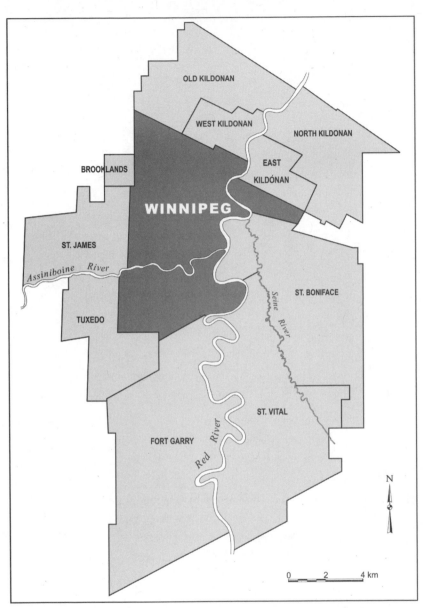

Map 1. Greater Winnipeg Metropolitan Area. Source: Canada, Dominion Bureau of Statistics. Census of the Prairie Provinces, 1946, vol. 1 (Ottawa: KP, 1949–51), Appendix C. Map design by Weldon Hiebert.

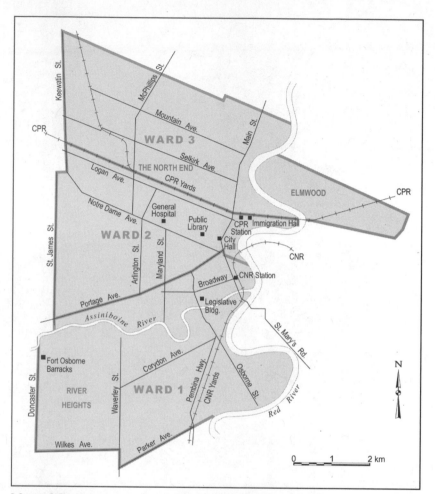

Map 2. Winnipeg, 1939–1945. Map design by Weldon Hiebert.

THE PATRIOTIC CONSENSUS

INTRODUCTION

At 1:18 a.m., on the morning of 1 September 1939, the first news despatches arrived in Winnipeg, announcing the German bombing of Polish cities. Residents of Warsaw, six hours ahead, awoke to the sound of air raid sirens. A crowd numbering in the hundreds held a night-long vigil in front of the Winnipeg *Free Press* building, where the bulletin boards delivered the latest updates. A thunderstorm broke over the city that night, drenching these "grim-faced spectators" with driving rain.[1] It was an appropriate harbinger of the six years to follow and a war that would claim 50 million lives across the globe. Cheering throngs had greeted the advent of the Great War twenty-five years earlier, but the "war to end all wars" had disabused most Winnipeggers of any notions about gallantry or glory. For most of them, this new war meant a sombre job to be done if the rule of law was not to be supplanted, throughout the world, by gangsterism.

* * *

A year into Canada's war effort, Mark S. Watson of the Baltimore *Sun* observed the growth in Canada's armed services and general public support for the mobilization of manpower and resources, and concluded that the country was more united than it had been between 1914 and 1918: "One cannot see all these [military] camps, filled with men of English, Scotch, Irish, Welsh and French descent, the factories, and the unexcited civilians of city and farm without being aware of an intense unity.... One is tempted to say that Hitler has seemingly done more than Canadian statesmanship to weld English and French Canada into one united nation."[2] Watson may have exaggerated, but national unity in wartime was obviously an issue of crucial importance, and it was Prime Minister William Lyon Mackenzie King's overriding concern during the Second World War. Although much of the written history of Canada's war focuses on such national issues, the home-front struggle was waged by people carrying out their daily activities in smaller communities where issues other than French-English relations determined the character of their war effort. How united was the response to war in a city as socially and ethnically diverse as Winnipeg? The question defies easy answer, given the potential social and ideological fault lines among the city's population.

Winnipeg was the second largest city in western Canada (after Vancouver) according to the 1941 census, with 221,960 people; if we include the suburban areas now incorporated in the city, the total was 290,540. The city was a conglomeration of ethnic origins, a microcosm of an emerging Canadian mosaic. The majority of residents of Winnipeg proper (58.7 percent) claimed British ethnic origin and the economic, social, and political elite – as well as much of the general population – celebrated Winnipeg's British character.[3] The foreign-born population made up 35 percent (77,523) of the city's total, with nearly half that number (34,037) coming from countries other than Great Britain or the United States. Despite the dominance of the British elite, 38.1 percent (84,597) of Winnipeggers claimed an ethnic origin other than British or French. There were large communities of Ukrainians (22,578), Jews (17,027), Germans (12,170), Poles (11,024), and Scandinavians (9,177), with a variety of other ethnic groups living in the city.[4]

These groups inhabited a city that in the nineteenth century had been the administrative centre of the fur trade from Hudson Bay to the Pacific Ocean, a frontier boomtown that evolved around the turn of the twentieth century into the western gateway for Canadian transcontinental economic and political expansion. With the construction of the Canadian Pacific Railway (CPR), Winnipeg became the metropolitan centre of a prairie hinterland that included the rest of Manitoba, Saskatchewan, and Alberta. The trains that carried the multitudes of eastern Canadian and European migrants who settled in the prairies all passed through the "gateway to the West," and so did the produce they later shipped back east. Winnipeg merchants made their fortunes supplying these settlers, prospering in light of the city's spectacular growth from 25,639 residents in 1891 to 136,035 in 1911. The pace of expansion was welcomed by the city's leaders but it occurred without adequate planning to ensure balanced and healthy urban development. The routing of the CPR's main line through Point Douglas prompted uneven growth, as immigrants and the working class were drawn mainly to the North End. By 1906, the peak of immigration to the city, the North End was home to 43 percent of Winnipeg's residents but accounted for less than one third of its geographical area.[5]

August 1914 marked a watershed after which the pace and optimism of Winnipeg's early growth gradually declined. The Panama Canal's opening deprived "the Chicago of the North" of its advantage as the trans-shipment point for all goods moving to or from western Canada, though Winnipeg remained an important industrial, commercial, and financial centre as the hub of the prairie grain trade. When war came that same month, Winnipeg responded by raising six infantry battalions for service in the Canadian Expeditionary Force overseas. More than 66,000 Manitobans served in Canada's armed forces, representing 10 percent of the province's total population and over 50 percent of those eligible for military service. Manitoba boasted the highest proportion of enlistments to population in the Dominion, and nearly 8,000 were killed overseas.[6] The Great War increased demand for labour and farm produce—and good weather improved the wheat crop in 1915—all of which helped to end the recession that had gripped the economy since 1913. Rising prices were good for farmers but inflation hurt everybody, especially the working class, since wages did not keep pace: while the cost of living had jumped 75 percent by war's end, wages had only increased 18 percent. Workers organized to fight for better conditions but employers refused to recognize their unions. Nonetheless, the location in Winnipeg of three transcontinental railways, their attendant yards and repair shops, and the spin-off industries they fostered depended on a growing work force that became more militant in 1918 and 1919.

Demands for union recognition, higher wages, and improved working conditions prompted the 1919 General Strike, but the legacy of the strike's defeat was the crippling of organized labour in Winnipeg. The arrest of the strike's leaders and the blunt use of force during the "Bloody Saturday" riot effectively ended labour's economic power, and a 1920 gerrymander of the city's ward system ensured the perpetuation of a firm grip on political power by the right-wing Citizen's League. Between 1914 and 1945, there were only two occasions when labour aldermen held as many seats as the Citizen's League, and they never held a majority.[7] But the strike's significance went beyond the position of organized labour; it laid bare the divisions between Winnipeg's socio-economic classes. The demands of labour leaders had long been ignored by employers and the General Strike represented "the latest and most serious manifestation of a lack of unity of economic or political purpose among the city's residents."[8] This rift in the city's social character had important ramifications for public life during the ensuing two decades.

Winnipeg enjoyed a brief period of prosperity in the late 1920s, but it fell between the book ends of the post-war economic slump and the Great Depression. The stock market crash in October 1929 ushered in the darkest decade in Canadian history. By 1932, one quarter of the city's work force (14,254 wage earners) was unemployed, the second highest rate in Canada. The number of individuals supported by relief peaked in April 1933 at 43,886. The Depression's lowest point for the province as a whole was reached in March 1937 when one in six Manitobans was on relief, a total of 115,155 people. Current revenues were insufficient to pay the costs of social assistance; so, despite the government's preference for balanced budgets and low taxation, Manitoba soon raised taxes to a level unmatched in any other province. Government debt still spiralled out of control: by 1935 both the city and the province hovered on the edge of bankruptcy even though government intervention to improve socio-economic conditions was minimal. Premier John Bracken's political approach made thrifty administration a priority and he preached a doctrine of non-partisan coalition government to negate effective opposition.[9] In practice, such tactics stunted political debate and precluded a creative response to the crisis. The government cracked down instead, deporting the foreign-born unemployed to reduce relief costs and cutting expenditures on social programs like orphan's allowances.

Protest from the Left was ineffectual, split as it was between the Co-operative Commonwealth Federation, the communist Party, and the Independent Labour Party. It was no more effective at City Hall, owing to the Citizens' League's control of City Council. Labour initiatives to offer more generous relief benefits were repeatedly blocked, and the Citizens opposed suggestions to meet the crisis by raising income and business taxes despite the fact that the latter were substantially lower than in other cities.[10] Given labour's inability to influence the dominant political institutions, it is perhaps not surprising that some among Winnipeg's working class advocated more radical solutions. Throughout the mid-1930s, Market Square was the meeting place for a variety of restless groups that blamed social problems on the dominant Canadian political and economic institutions. Michael Korol was a young communist who described the meetings in which he participated as "revolutionary," with speeches advocating the overthrow of the established order.[11] Fascist groups were also active in Winnipeg, including William Whittaker's Canadian Nationalist Party and Howard Simpkin's Canadian Union of Fascists. Whittaker's members styled themselves after the National Socialist *Sturmabteilung*, or SA, wearing brown shirts and swastikas, while Simpkin's wore black shirts in the fashion of Oswald Mosley's British Union of Fascists. Both groups spouted propaganda and disseminated antisemitic hate literature received from Nazi Germany. Winnipeg's communists were active in opposing their right-wing counterparts. They heckled fascist meetings and, on one occasion in June 1934, 2,000 communists instigated a brawl that broke up a rally of several hundred brown-shirts at Market Square.[12] German aggression in Europe resulted in the evaporation of local support for National Socialist ideology by 1938, and Canadian fascist groups gradually faded into obscurity. Communists were not much more successful in effecting significant social change, but they nonetheless maintained a radical presence on the local political spectrum.

*   *   *

The conflict between competing political ideologies—capitalist democracy, fascism, and communism—that was thus manifested in Winnipeg during the interwar period reflected, of course, a much wider struggle that would soon escalate on the international stage. The spectrum of public opinion in Winnipeg regarding the gathering storm was similar to that in other cities and towns across Canada. Manitobans watched the march of events overseas with a concern that was stoked by the persistence of influential Winnipeg *Free Press* editor John W. Dafoe's critique of the abandonment of collective security by the member states of the League of Nations, Canada in particular. Dafoe and other observers could see the war coming from a long way off, but it took public opinion some time to see the dangers as Dafoe did. In the early 1930s, there was still much sympathy for German revisionism. The editor of the Baldur *Gazette* argued in November 1932 that since the Allies had failed to effectively implement general disarmament, Germany should be allowed to re-arm despite the terms of the Treaty of Versailles. Others sympathized with German aims because they saw fascism as a buttress against the spread of communism. The *Country Guide* (formerly the *Grain Growers' Guide*) in April 1936 excused Germany's remilitarization of the Rhineland on the grounds that she could not be "forced to accept forever a position of inferiority among the nations." The Winnipeg *Tribune* also tended to look the other way, since Versailles was "a bad treaty." In March 1936, the *Tribune* suggested taking "Hitler at his word, accept[ing] Germany into the family of nations on the basis of real equality.... Peace can be based on the new conditions Germany has created." At the same time, the *Free Press* presciently observed that as long as "Germany confines her actions in contempt of treaties to her own territory she will probably get away with it. The guns will begin going off when Germany carries her violations outside her own territory." Few yet felt that war was imminent or necessary. A poll of Wesley College students in early 1936 indicated that a majority would rather secede from the British Empire than be drawn into another war because of Canada's imperial connection.[13]

Nazi aggression became increasingly blatant over the next three years: it included the forced annexation of Austria in March 1938; the bullying that prompted the Sudetenland's surrender at Munich in September 1938; *Kristallnacht*, the Jewish pogrom in November of that year; and the seizure of rump Czechoslovakia that marked Munich's repudiation in March 1939. In the wake of these events, especially the occupation of Prague, public opinion shifted. To the *Globe and Mail*, *Kristallnacht* had shown that Germany "could not be trusted." The world had now seen "the viciousness and uncompromising spirit of Nazi philosophy." After Prague, a majority of students at McMaster University, the University of Western Ontario, and the universities of New Brunswick, Saskatchewan, Alberta, and British Columbia all favoured intervention "to check the expansion of the totalitarian states," particularly if Britain were involved.[14] According to studies of public opinion in Manitoba and Ontario, the German occupations of Czechoslovakia and Memel in mid-March 1939 made it clear to most English Canadians that nothing short of war would suffice to stop Hitler.[15]

As international tensions mounted throughout the latter half of the decade, English Canadians became increasingly committed to standing beside Britain if war came. Conservative papers like the Brandon *Daily Sun* and the Winnipeg *Tribune* agreed that collective security and moral obligation to the Empire made Canada's path clear. As the *Eye-Witness* of Birtle, Manitoba, explained in a 31 March 1936 editorial, "should some overt act cause a repeat of Aug. 4th, 1914, Canada as an Empire Dominion could no more remain out of it than 22 years ago. Popular feeling would force any government in power to take quick action."[16] Historians disagree about the relative importance of the British connection to Canada's decision to join the war once it came. Some have argued that imperial sentiment was the determining factor. According to J.L. Granatstein, "Canada went to war because Britain went to war. Not for democracy, not to stop Hitler, not to save Poland."[17] Terry Copp argues, largely on the basis of editorials in Ontario newspapers, that public resolve to bend no further was galvanized in Canada as in Britain after Hitler's occupation of Prague and Neville Chamberlain's abandonment of appeasement in March 1939.[18] The range of sentiment in Manitoba and across Canada undoubtedly reflected both positions. In any case, Canadians greeted the declaration of war not with enthusiasm but with "a spirit of determined resignation."[19] The editor of the Neepawa *Press*, another rural Manitoba newspaper, was under no illusions about what the war would mean to Canadians, writing on 5 September 1939 that "if we do not fight it means eventual annihilation. If we win the millennium will not have started. The world will be in as bad or worse a mess as at the end of the last war. There will be suffering and unemployment. The world will not be made any 'safer' for democracy," but the prospect of "German domination would be unacceptable to all.... If we lose we know our state would be worse, not better."[20]

Winnipeggers held their breath as they read the news throughout the last month of peace before the Second World War. Throughout the first half of August the international news was dominated by the dispute between Germany and Poland over the port city of Danzig, reports of Japanese aggression against the British concessions in China, estimates of the armed strength of the European powers, and various predictions playing down the likelihood of war. On 22 August, readers were stunned by news of the Russo-German non-aggression pact, which seemed to signal the inevitability of war. Sir Edward Beatty, president of the Canadian Pacific Railway, announced in Winnipeg that the CPR's shops were preparing to manufacture war materials for the government. The federal government ordered a partial military mobilization a few days later. The Non-Permanent Active Militia was called out to guard railway bridges, the airport at Stevenson Field, and other crucial infrastructure in Winnipeg. Sailors and airmen passed through Winnipeg's train stations en route to postings in eastern Canada. The *Free Press* ran photos of military aircraft, soldiers in training, and civilians preparing trenches in London. It was reported on 31 August that Britain had ordered the complete mobilization of its armed services along with the evacuation of women, children, and invalids from major cities. Across Europe, 12 million armed men massed along the frontiers in preparation for the war that most everyone knew was coming.[21]

Britain and France declared war on 3 September when Germany ignored an ultimatum to withdraw its forces from Poland. In Canada, editorial opinion and even the governor general discussed the measures necessary to defend the country, even before Parliament voted to make Canadian participation official. The full story of Canada's declaration of war ran on page twelve of the 11 September edition of the Winnipeg *Free Press*. It was a foregone conclusion, not even worthy of the front page.[22]

*   *   *

We know relatively little about how Winnipeggers experienced the Second World War on the home front apart from what we can glean from other, more general works.[23] Yet the nature and depth of the Second World War's impact on other Canadians is not fully recognized either. Previous histories have established the framework of Canada's general political, economic, and military participation in the war,[24] but there has been relatively little research into the ways that the national war effort affected individuals or local communities. Jeffrey Keshen's *Saints, Sinners, and Soldiers* is a recent exception that acknowledges the extensive use of propaganda and social pressure to build what I call the "patriotic consensus," but does not see them as fundamental determinants of people's responses. Keshen argues that despite incidents of discrimination, antisemitism, or black marketeering, Canadians "proved unbounded in the generosity of their contributions of volunteer labour, money, material, and, at least outside of Quebec, willingness to serve militarily.... Such responses provided substance and longevity to the image of the Second World War as a conflict uniting people in a common and noble cause."[25] In tracing these themes, Keshen details the relationship between national war policies and their impact on the general population. Since each community has its own unique characteristics, Canadian historians have lately begun to examine individual cities to better understand the local nuances of a history dominated by the national narrative. Both Ian Miller's *Our Glory and Our Grief: Torontonians and the Great War* and Serge Durflinger's *Fighting from Home: The Second World War in Verdun, Quebec,* like Keshen's work, emphasize the unity of the citizens behind the war effort.[26]

This image of a nation united in defence of a just cause has had fairly wide currency, yet the home-front war experience in Winnipeg raises some intriguing questions about its validity. The Ukrainian community is a case in point: while all factions declared their loyalty to Canada, those with communist or Ukrainian nationalist sympathies spent as much effort and rhetoric opposing each other as they did the common Axis enemy.[27] And despite voluminous propaganda about fighting a war in support of liberal democratic values, the treatment of ethnic minorities and ideological dissidents devalued the concept of civil liberties, which is at the heart of most definitions of democratic freedom. Just how inclusive was the patriotic consensus that supposedly united Canadians? How did they demonstrate their commitment to the common cause?

The central themes informing this book are therefore not political, economic, or military.[28] Instead, the book focuses on human activity at the community level, on the way that people responded to the state's efforts to foster compliance with federal policies. In considering the reasons why people fight wars, what motivates them to endure wartime hardships, and what wartime tensions do to civil relations between different groups on the home front, an important distinction emerges between the non-state institutions of civil society and those of the state itself. Exploring this distinction is one way to integrate local and national history, to better understand the significance of local responses to national policies.

John Keane defines civil society as the "realm of life *institutionally separated* from territorial state institutions."[29] The concept often refers to private organizations outside state control, such as families, charitable groups, clubs and voluntary associations, churches, publishing houses, or newspapers. It is through these associations that people contribute to the life of their communities and put flesh on the bones of democratic society. Most people's daily routines are not conducted as members of this abstraction we call the state, but are experienced most directly as members of smaller communities, either individually or in the voluntary associations of civil society. This is the level at which the majority experienced war on the home front.

The dominant narratives of Canada's Second World War suggest that the main role in determining the nature of the war effort was played by the federal government, and the two great wars of the twentieth century are taken together as the cause of the progressive expansion of the apparatus of the state from the laissez-faire model of small government to the centralizing, intrusive institutions of the post-1945 welfare state. But the chapters that follow are filled with activities by people at the level of the local community and as members of the non-state institutions they created, like the Canadian Legion, the Imperial Order Daughters of the Empire, the Young Men's (and Women's) Christian Association, Winnipeg's Council of Social Agencies, the Winnipeg Civil Liberties Association, or the Young Men's Section of the Winnipeg Board of Trade. Canadians acting outside of officialdom significantly influenced the character of the home front war. Popular opinion, as expressed in the newspapers or letters to political leaders, demanded participation in 1939, and then called for an increased effort and "total war." Many groups advocated conscription, organized or participated in Victory Loan drives, pressured people to support them, helped provide auxiliary services to troops or voluntary community service, and demanded internment of enemy aliens. Shedding light on such local initiatives by the voluntary associations of civil society is therefore crucial to a more complete understanding of Canada's war effort.

The key to a voluntary, participatory national effort as opposed to one driven by fear or coercion is popular motivation. As Alexis de Tocqueville pointed out in his study of pre-Civil War America, voluntary associations both "fuse personal interest [with] the common good" and constitute the intermediate organizations that serve as a buffer between the state and the people, moderating the state's power and guarding against the excesses of strong interests within the polity.[30] My effort to understand how Winnipeggers linked their personal interests to the common good—victory—grapples with the relatively intangible themes of unity and morale that partly inform the studies of Keshen, Miller, and Durflinger, while building on their work to relate federal policies to the members of civil society who made them effective. My aim is to explore two general questions. The first pertains to unity, and the extent to which Winnipeggers pulled together in a time of national crisis given the ethnic and ideological divisions that separated people.[31] The second concerns morale: specifically, what gave people the will to fulfill the various demands placed on them by the exigencies of the national war effort, and persevere despite problems like family separation, housing shortages, or war weariness?

The concept of morale is an obvious abstraction, so before attempting to evaluate its effect on the home front in the pages to follow we must consider a definition.

In discussing morale, psychologists emphasize the behaviour of group members who are prepared to accept shared deprivations and who actively work to achieve shared goals. A high incidence of participation in the group's activities is taken as evidence of high morale. Nazi propaganda minister Josef Goebbels distinguished between the separate concepts of "*Haltung* (bearing, conduct, behaviour) and *Stimmung* (feeling, spirit, mood)" in assessing German morale.[32] There is thus an emotional or psychological element that influences one's willingness to accept hardship for the good of the group. Webster's dictionary combines these two aspects—behaviour and attitude— in defining morale as "a confident, resolute, willing, often self-sacrificing and courageous attitude of an individual to the function or tasks demanded or expected of him by a group of which he is part that is based upon such factors as pride in the achievements and aims of the group, faith in its leadership and ultimate success, a sense of fruitful personal participation in its work, and a devotion and loyalty to other members of the group." Minimizing social barriers is central to creating the group cohesion necessary for wide acceptance of shared goals. Maintaining cohesion during a prolonged conflict like the Second World War depends, according to psychologist Kurt Lewin, on the degree to which group members "keep clearly in view the total task and the final objective."[33] Propaganda can play a key role by establishing and reiterating that objective.

There is an obvious link between morale and unity in this relationship between the individual and the group. Neither concept lends itself to precise measurement, yet we can develop a sense of the strength of popular morale by looking at how people responded to the needs of the moment. Did they rise to the challenges posed by appeals to perform voluntary war work, for example, or give in to pessimism brought on by economic hardship or fear for the loss of a loved one? Unity is equally difficult to evaluate, but we can examine popular and government efforts to define common wartime goals in contrast to the treatment of minorities or disagreements over issues like military service. Investigation of these issues suggests that there was an evident divide in Winnipeg between those who comprised the patriotic consensus and those who were excluded or rejected it by choice, although the latter were a relatively small minority.

This research is geographically centred on the City of Winnipeg but it should be obvious that this is not strictly a history of Winnipeg during the Second World War. It is, rather, a history of the way Canadians experienced the war in Winnipeg. The distinction is important, because although I have chosen to focus on my hometown, there is much in the pages to follow that will apply equally to other cities. Winnipeg was, in many ways, representative of other urban areas on the Canadian home front, but there are some fascinating ways in which it was unique.

1

THE LIMITED CONSENSUS

There would never be a moment, in war or in peace, when I wouldn't trade all the patriots in the country for one tolerant man.

E.B. White, quoted in Sidonie Gruenberg, ed.,
The Family in a World at War

The Second World War is almost universally regarded among the Western democracies as "the good war." Given the brutal nature of the Nazi regime, with its police-state terror and genocidal racial doctrine, it is easy to see why, and a large number of witnesses have given precedence to patriotism, unity, and the feeling of an important duty accomplished in their memories of the conflict.[1] But why did Canadians enter the Second World War? A 1952 study of Manitoba public opinion determined that it was not Adolf Hitler's brutal treatment of German minorities that prompted calls for war, but his unilateral repudiation of international treaties and his challenge to the balance of power.[2] Winnipeggers knew from the war's beginning that they were fighting against National Socialist totalitarianism and resisting an aggressive German posture that aimed to redraw the map of Europe. Few opportunities were lost to decry Nazi "tyranny" or to reiterate that the Allies were fighting for freedom and democracy, though these abstract concepts left room for interpretation. Some spoke out against the repugnant Nazi racial policies, and the plight of Germany's Jews was apparent to those who cared to look. As early as May 1936, the *Presbyterian Record* recognized that Germany's aim was not just to "rob Jews of their human rights but actually to destroy the Jewish population."[3] Still, it was not until 1943 that widely publicized graphic descriptions of Hitler's concentration camps triggered a significant reaction among the

Canadian public. Canadians, therefore, did not enter the fight to safeguard human rights. Rather, they accepted the necessity of war to prevent a radical shift in the existing world order; and that meant, at least in part, preserving British power. A constant theme of editorial opinion throughout the late 1930s insisted that if Britain were attacked, Canada must stand by her. As J.L. Granatstein argues, once Britain declared war on 3 September 1939, Canada was certain to follow suit.[4] From that moment, Canada's leaders shaped the war effort in accordance with their Anglo-centric world view and in response to the demands of a developing patriotic consensus emphasizing the justice of their cause and citizens' duty to support it.

Having declared war, belligerent governments had to communicate to their populations a clear vision of what they were fighting for and motivate them to unite in the shared cause. In August 1941, American President Franklin D. Roosevelt and British Prime Minister Winston Churchill agreed to general war aims that were expressed in the Atlantic Charter. Although the United States was not yet at war, the Charter subsequently became the basis for the formal alliance between the various powers opposing the Axis. Its terms acknowledged the right of people everywhere to choose their own form of government, and reflected the Four Freedoms that Roosevelt had articulated in his address to Congress the previous January: freedom of speech and expression, freedom of worship, freedom from want, and freedom from fear. It was an idealistic proclamation that could not be completely fulfilled, either on the home fronts of the democratic Western Allies or in the post-war international order. Yet these were the principles Allied leaders said they were fighting for; and in general, they resonated with Canadians just as they did with Americans or Britons.

Roosevelt had told Congress that those who would oppose the dictators "must have the stamina and the courage which come from unshakable belief in the manner of life which they are defending."[5] Most Winnipeggers and their various organizations certainly preferred their way of life to the Nazi alternative, but unity was not absolute. For example, whether the 50.32 percent of Canadians who were not of British descent—according to the 1941 census—shared an unshakable belief in an Anglo-centric society that relegated them to the status of "foreigners" or, at best, minorities, is questionable. Nevertheless, the patriotic consensus would not permit forces of friction, such as ethnic disharmony or political dissent, to interfere with the war effort. Majority opinion—shaped by popular patriotic attitudes, media messaging, censorship, and propaganda—backed by the state's coercive legal power, discouraged dissent and created significant pressure to conform.

The tensions resulting from this pressure revealed fissures in the unity of a diverse population and occasionally undermined the principles Canadians believed they were fighting for. Freedom of expression was compromised as people became caught up in their own patriotism and condemned others who were not sufficiently zealous in their support for the war effort. Discrimination against ethnic-minority volunteers for the military showed that racial hierarchies existed in Canada as well as Germany. Canadian democracy itself was challenged when civil liberties were set aside because dissidents were deemed by public opinion to be threats to national security. Winnipeggers were united with people across the world in their resistance to the Axis powers, but the principles they agreed to fight for were not always honoured in the treatment of ethnic and ideological minorities at home.

A United Patriotic Response?

The onset of war in September 1939 was met, in Winnipeg as elsewhere, with a rush to the recruiting stations. The Department of National Defence ordered a partial mobilization of Non-Permanent Active Militia units in Manitoba for home defence on Friday, 1 September. As observers speculated on the likelihood of sending an expeditionary force overseas, unit headquarters at Minto and McGregor Armouries and Fort Osborne Barracks began to enlist volunteers for active service. Prospective soldiers could choose to serve in a light tank regiment, the Fort Garry Horse; a machine-gun unit, the Winnipeg Grenadiers; the infantry, with the Queen's Own Cameron Highlanders, Royal Winnipeg Rifles, Winnipeg Light Infantry, or Princess Patricia's Canadian Light Infantry; or they could join one of the artillery, signals, or engineer units. Many adventurous souls hoped to join the Royal Canadian Air Force (RCAF) or the Royal Canadian Naval Volunteer Reserve (RCNVR), but most were turned away as these services quickly filled their limited initial establishments. Some of the disappointed would-be sailors and pilots joined the army instead, while the more patient put their names on a waiting list. No one knew it then, but there would be room for them soon enough. It took a little longer to bring the army up to its authorized strength. One news report said that there were too many Great War veterans trying to enlist who could not pass the medical exam, and too few younger men who could. The veterans were said to be angry at the "lack of response from the young men." Their reaction was unjustified. More than 1,000 Winnipeg men joined up during the month's first weekend, before Canada had formally become a belligerent.[6]

The impulsive and the earnest wasted no time in offering themselves for military service. Premier John Bracken received numerous letters requesting him to intercede with military authorities in favour of applications to enlist, particularly regarding commissions in the navy and air force. Some of Winnipeg's employers were similarly caught up in the patriotic enthusiasm. A number, including Eaton's department store, Canadian Press, Great-West Life, City Hall, and the Winnipeg School Board, announced that they would preserve seniority and make up the difference between service pay and 75 percent of regular salary for any employees who volunteered. Some companies even continued employees' benefits.[7] A shared sense of duty, and perhaps a desire to escape the routine, encouraged a steady flow of recruits from the workplace to the parade ground. A survey of 347,900 Canadians on active service as of 30 June 1942 found that 85 percent had left their jobs to enlist. Only a relatively small proportion was propelled by unemployment, since many among the remainder were youths who had not yet joined the permanent work force when they volunteered.[8]

What motivated the more than 1.1 million Canadians who enlisted in the armed services? According to a 1943 army survey of 900 men, 64 percent said they were fighting for "freedom" while 23 percent said they were fighting for "democracy." In a similar survey, 91 percent said they were fighting for either democracy, freedom, or "security." When women began to join the armed services after 1941, many, according to historian Jeffrey Keshen, "sought to emulate a male family member in uniform" or to avenge the death of a loved one. Others joined to release men for active service.[9] These are small samples but the sense of duty was widely shared. One American who came to Canada in 1941 to join the RCAF and trained in Winnipeg described his reasons for enlisting: "I was sorely discouraged, disappointed, and fed up with the head-in-the-sand attitude of the United States and was convinced that once Hitler had taken over Britain and the rest of Europe, we would be next on his menu, and it was our duty to ... save civilization from ... the whole foul Nazi apparatus. I was deeply moved by the terrible abuses and the killings and the bombings of Britain and I wanted to DO something."[10] There were other motives. While many young men went looking for adventure in exotic places, some succumbed to popular pressure from peers or advertisements urging them to do their duty. Others volunteered later because they were subject to compulsory service for home defence and would have been called, eventually.[11]

The pace of voluntary enlistments was more than satisfactory to fill out Canada's limited mobilization of the armed services during the so-called Phoney War. Requirements increased dramatically after the fall of France and the Low Countries, prompting the federal government to take a firmer hold on the country's war effort. The National Resources Mobilization Act (NRMA) became law on 21 June 1940, and it gave Ottawa authority to use Canadian human and material resources as it best saw fit for the prosecution of the war. Prime Minister Mackenzie King had promised not to implement conscription for overseas service, but the NRMA permitted compulsory training and service for home defence. A national registration of all residents over sixteen years of age was carried out in August to determine which Canadians would be of most use to the country, and records were updated periodically throughout the war. Every registrant was required to carry a registration certificate at all times, and failure to produce it on request could result in a twenty-dollar fine and a mandatory appearance before a justice of the peace. The National War Services Regulations were promulgated that same month under the NRMA, specifying that all single or widowed male British subjects resident in Canada aged 21 to 45 years were liable for compulsory military training. Certain essential groups were exempted, including peace officers and the clergy, while students and conscientious objectors requesting deferment were to receive "special consideration." The regulations were subsequently amended to extend the age range subject to compulsory service, and to include married men. The initial thirty-day period for which they would be obliged to serve was also prolonged in February 1941 to four months. In April, liability was extended to the duration of hostilities. As a counterpart to this military mobilization, in March 1942 the federal cabinet established National Selective Service under the Department of Labour, to control mobilization of the civilian work force.[12]

The NRMA provided legal authority for an intensified government-directed war effort, but Ottawa did not exercise this authority to the extent desired by many patriotic individuals and groups. From the war's earliest days, the Canadian Legion had called for complete mobilization of manpower, wealth, industry, and resources.[13] By the summer of 1941, the Winnipeg *Tribune* was demanding compulsory military service for overseas and reallocation of labour from non-essential work. One editorial argued that "the Dominion government must have power to send any Canadian anywhere to do any-thing" as part of an "all-out war effort."[14] The *Tribune* continued to hammer away on this point in subsequent months, and argued against taking men out of essential industry and wasting time, money, and military training on them if they were to be used only for home defence. The Manitoba Legislature echoed the Legion and unanimously urged Ottawa, on 16 December 1941, to move to a "total war" footing and remove the restriction on compulsory service for home defence only.[15]

As Canada became more deeply engaged in the war, friction developed between over-zealous patriots and others who failed to meet their standards of commitment to the national crusade. After the Legion's May 1942 convention in Winnipeg again called for compulsory service, former president Brigadier Alex Ross exclaimed, "I have been outraged by the realization that there are young fit men, who do not seem to think they have any responsibility.... [E]very man between 18 and 60 belongs to his country."[16] Winnipeg lawyer E.K. Williams, later president of the Canadian Bar Association and Chief Justice of the Court of King's Bench in Manitoba, agreed. In a January 1942 speech, he condemned any "shirkers" who did not make sufficient sacrifices for the war effort, or did not conserve scarce materials. Williams lashed out at young, fit men who chose not to enlist, media stories and advertising that were not sufficiently focused on the war effort, politicians too concerned with their own power, and above all, the communist "Quislings ... [who] have been disloyal to Canada.... They have no place in this country. We should place the mark of beasts on them and put them where they belong."[17]

Deferment of military service for university students was heavily crit-icized. Justice J.E. Adamson, chairman of Winnipeg's mobilization board, favoured deferments only for medical, science, and engineering students. Regina's chairman, Justice J.F.L. Embury, categorically opposed all student deferments, and believed that "if we had less so-called higher education we would have more courage and public spirit.... Let's hope the Russians win the war for us. The way we are going we'd never manage our share for ourselves." University of Manitoba President Sidney Smith countered such criticism by stressing society's need for educated professionals and making it clear that any student failing to meet strict academic standards would be expelled.[18] Nevertheless, the popular cry for a more intensive war effort was widely heard and generated significant pressure on the segment of the male population at the age appropriate for military service.

Because the war grew out of a struggle between conflicting ideologies—democracy, fascism, and communism—one's personal beliefs might be subject to the judgment of over-zealous patriots. The exemption of conscientious objectors from military training antagonized the more belligerent segment of the general population that saw them as shirkers, but the issue of participation in the war effort was a source of division among some conscientious objectors themselves, the Canadian Mennonite community in particular. Leaders of the various Mennonite denominations had been at odds over their community's position as the war approached in the summer of 1939. The *Kanadier* Mennonites were pacifists who had immigrated to western Canada from Russia in the 1870s, and they distrusted the *Russlaender* faction, more recent arrivals who had fled the Soviet Union in the 1920s. Because the latter had taken up arms to defend their villages during the Russian Revolution, the *Kanadier* Mennonites feared that the *Russlaender* would compromise their exempted status as pacifists. While the *Kanadier* leaders rejected any form of service, others wanted to find some accommodation. C.F. Klassen of the Mennonite Central Relief Committee in Winnipeg, for example, pressed for the employment of conscientious objectors in a field ambulance corps, though other Mennonite leaders continued to balk at any form of service under military supervision. After a series of meetings with officials of the Department of National War Services, a compromise was worked out in December 1940 whereby conscientious objectors would accept alternative service at civilian work camps. Those holding pacifist views were required, when called, to serve on projects in Canada's national parks, including Riding Mountain in western Manitoba. The war did not pass easily for conscientious objectors; although the terms of alternative service were broadened in 1943 to include essential agricultural or industrial work, all were deprived of the right to vote and forced to contribute part of their wages to the Red Cross. They retained only twenty-five dollars per month above the costs of subsistence, which led to hardship for those with dependents or medical problems.[19]

Those who were willing to find an acceptable compromise on the issue of service were viewed more favourably than other pacifists, like the Doukhobors and Jehovah's Witnesses, who often refused to cooperate or report to work camps unless they were prosecuted. Some conscientious objectors went overseas with the Civilian Corps of Canadian Firefighters, commanded by Winnipeg Fire Chief D.A. Boulden, to help fight fires and carry out rescue and salvage operations in British cities hit by German bombers. Other conscientious objectors were finally permitted to join the Royal Canadian Army Medical Corps and the Canadian Dental Corps in September 1943. By the war's end, over 10,000 Canadian conscientious objectors had been granted a deferral of military service, including 3,021 in Manitoba, more than in any other province. Mennonites accounted for 2,453 of the total number, though almost as many—about 2,000—joined the armed forces.[20]

Still, there was a very small measure of sympathy for the views of conscientious objectors and the plan for alternative service did not preclude controversy. Regina mobilization board chairman J.F.L. Embury complained that labour in the national parks contributed nothing to the war effort and wasted the talents of educated workers and those Mennonites who wished to serve Canada's armed forces in some non-combatant capacity. Winnipeg's chairman, J.E. Adamson, "actively sought to undermine the pacifist position" and, in a speech before a large group of Mennonites in Steinbach on 7 May 1941, urged their leaders to let prospective soldiers "go as regular Canadians and come back as heroes." Many would prefer to enlist but for the obstruction of their clergy and elders, he insisted, since "your Mennonite boys are not slackers and cowards."[21] Despite the obvious implication of his argument, Adamson apparently did not believe that conscientious objectors were cowards, since he told a Winnipeg audience that "there need be no fear of young men from cowardice or selfishness developing conscientious objections. It takes courage to plead such a conviction.... If young men such as I mention ... are called up, they will refuse to obey and the upshot will be sending out police to arrest them, then disobedience at the camps, all involving cost to the Government and tribulation at the Training Centres, without advancing the war effort." That said, Adamson maintained that the pacifist position was untenable because Canada was engaged in a war of defence rather than aggression—a war to protect the weak from Nazi brutality—and he cited a number of clerical authorities who had asserted that such a war was morally justifiable. According to the Reverend Canon J.O. Murray of St. John's College, for one, Christians were "not merely justified in fighting," but were "bound to fight."[22]

Some constituencies of public opinion were less than tolerant of the pacifist position. The Canadian Legion, for example, was viewed by at least one observer as harsh in its criticism. The Reverend David Toews, chairman of the Canadian Mennonite Board of Colonization in Rosthern, Saskatchewan, complained to Howard W. Winkler, Liberal Member of Parliament for Lisgar,

Manitoba, about the public criticism of Mennonite conscientious objectors. He felt that "the militarists in our country, [such] as the legion [sic], ... will not be satisfied with anything that is granted to our people, short of full military combatant service." When Mennonites claimed "our rights as conscientious objectors, the press and the public make so much fuss."[23] Winkler, for his part, expected the May 1942 Legion convention in Winnipeg to produce "some pretty hot-headed resolutions."[24] Legion members could be uncompromising, and so could others who were concerned about pacifist influence eroding Canadian support for the war. Adamson harboured such fears and he objected to the practice of Alternative Service officers permitting Mennonite conscientious objectors to teach school, on the grounds that their pacifist doctrine would result in a "failure to inculcate citizenship" among pupils.[25]

When Alternative Service officials proposed to adjust payment regulations to benefit thirty conscientious objectors working in Manitoba mental hospitals in early 1945, hospital administrators objected. As explained by L.E. Westman, the federal government's Chief Alternate Service Officer, the provincial government seemed to be "unduly alarmed about the possibilities of public criticism" over its employment of conscientious objectors. It was especially hesitant about the prospect of paying them "a little more money" because "there is quite a little witch hunting still about conscientious objectors in Manitoba." As Westman noted, the workers concerned were "among the better educated" of those who received postponements of military service, and they had admittedly done a good job at work generally seen as undesirable. On a wage of twenty-five dollars a month plus subsistence, Westman felt that it was "getting to be a long war for these men," some of whom had families to feed. National Selective Service head Arthur MacNamara, previously a long-time official in Manitoba's departments of Labour and Public Works, subsequently advised Premier Stuart Garson that he might want to make some "adjustments" to their working arrangements if he wanted "satisfactory continuing employees" rather than a group of disgruntled workers who would have to be forced to do their jobs.[26] Manitobans made liberal donations of time and money to benefit war charities (see Chapter 4), but their attitudes towards those who were less committed to the national cause could be uncharitable.

In contrast to the case of conscientious objectors, some volunteers who tried to enlist were not welcome. As in the First World War, military authorities after 1939 preferred not to accept volunteers from certain ethnic minority groups, particularly those of African or Asian descent. Eugenics theory was widely accepted at the time, and many people believed that these groups "lacked the valour, discipline, and intelligence to fight a modern war."[27] In 1940, the question arose in Ottawa about the desirability of calling Canadians of Japanese, Chinese, or East Indian origin for military service under the NRMA. The Cabinet War Committee decided that they should not be called, but "should be asked to make their contribution to the war effort in other ways." Opposition to accepting volunteers from these groups stemmed, in part, from fears that minorities might use military service to buttress their claims for enfranchisement. In any case, acceptance of these volunteers was left to the discretion of individual unit commanding officers. Few got through because, as Under Secretary of State for External Affairs Norman Robertson explained, "in some branches of the services a 'pure European descent' or 'pure white race' rule exists which excludes men of Chinese, Japanese and East Indian races."[28]

The issue was revisited in Ottawa following the declaration of war with Japan in December 1941. As public opinion in British Columbia pressed for the forced evacuation of residents of Japanese origin in early 1942, government officials received numerous messages from Japanese Canadians demonstrating their loyalty by offering themselves for military service. A meeting of representatives from the departments of National Defence, National War Services, External Affairs, and the Royal Canadian Mounted Police (RCMP) considered the question of enlisting men of Asian origin in the forces. One RCAF officer related his belief that "Japanese are not trustworthy and the popular sentiment is unfavourable to them. Their presence in the Armed Forces would be a cause of friction and ill-feeling." The meeting bluntly noted that the question of employing Asians for military service was strictly an army problem since "there exists a colour bar in the Air Force." Although the participants agreed that "no service, no branch of a service, no rank in a service should *in principle* be closed to any Canadian on grounds of race or colour alone," the conference concluded that "the *practical* difficulties of mixing races should receive full recognition; and neither fighting efficiency nor civilian morale should be sacrificed to the principle of racial equality" (emphasis in original). Further, it recommended that no unit "should be obliged to accept a volunteer of any of these races if it is felt that this would not conduce to the advantage of the service."[29]

The divisional registrar in Winnipeg, responsible for calling men under the NRMA, fully shared this view, and a minor controversy arose concerning the willingness of officers in Military District 10 to accept non-white recruits. In November 1942, Lieutenant-Colonel C.D. McPherson, the registrar, requested the Department of National War Services (DNWS) to clarify whether the exclusion of Asians extended to Black Canadians as well, since he had recently come across "two or three cases, one a colored porter and one a Chinese," and wanted to know if they should be called up or not. He had earlier been told that in the absence of formulated policy, he should simply avoid calling certain names when they came up on the rolls. Chinese continued to be excluded from NRMA call-up, though volunteers could be accepted if "found suitable," but McPherson was advised that "negroes" were to be called up in the same way as anyone else.[30]

The issue did not end there. A year later, McPherson told the Mobilization Section of the National Selective Service (NSS), which had taken over responsibility for mobilization from DNWS, that the authorities at Military District 10 refused to accept Black recruits, either as general service volunteers or for home defence. When a story broke in the newspapers in December 1943 about the refusal to call Black Canadians for service, McPherson claimed that military authorities had asked him not to call such men. Officers at Military District 10 promptly denied this claim, saying "they had no objection to the call-up of Negroes" and no knowledge of the request to which McPherson had referred. They subsequently told McPherson to call up any Blacks on his list, and officers now said they had no objection to calling Blacks. Neither National Defence Headquarters nor National Selective Service officials would admit to knowledge of any such request. Arthur MacNamara, head of the NSS, sent McPherson a sharp rebuke two weeks later, after determining that the exclusion of certain men had resulted from a private agreement between McPherson and a senior officer at Military District 10, of which the commanding officer apparently had no knowledge. MacNamara made it clear that such a policy contravened NSS regulations.[31]

Blacks and Asians were not the only minorities deemed unacceptable by Winnipeg's military authorities. Mobilization regulations and government policy confirmed that Aboriginals were liable to be called for training despite their ambiguous citizenship status, and despite the precedent of their exemption from compulsory service during the First World War. Although many Aboriginals resisted compulsory training for these reasons, the position taken by the government was that they were in fact British subjects and the same regulations applied to them as to other Canadians. And yet in Winnipeg, responsible military officers still refused to enlist Aboriginals, ostensibly on grounds of language or medical barriers. The military district's recruiting officer, Major Maris Garton, expressed the view that "Indians" should not be accepted as volunteers nor called for compulsory training because they could not "stand confinement to camp or barracks for long periods," nor could they cope with the "nervous demands incidental to modern warfare."[32] According to historian Emily Arrowsmith, such generalizations were "based on the assumption that Aboriginal people had 'inherent' racial traits that made them prefer the 'nomadic' lifestyle."[33]

J.E. Adamson, chairman of Winnipeg's mobilization board, objected that certain ethnic groups could not be excluded under the current regulations, but a compromise was managed whereby natives would be granted unlimited deferment as essential "agricultural" labour.[34] Some Aboriginals managed to enlist in the army anyway, and proved the blanket application of racial stereotypes to be unjustified. One of them was Tommy Prince, from Manitoba's Brokenhead Ojibway Nation, who served with distinction in Italy as part of the elite Canadian-American First Special Service Force. Prince became one of Canada's most-decorated Aboriginal soldiers in the process, winning the Military Medal and the American Silver Star.[35] By 1944, Aboriginal soldiers had been decorated seventeen times for bravery in action.[36] Despite such accomplishments, the Second World War was a "white man's war" as much as the First, and the colour bar remained in place until 1943 in the air force and 1944 in the navy.[37]

Anglo-Canadian prejudice hampered a united war effort. Polls later in the war showed a continuing dislike and mistrust of all "foreigners." In fact, many refused to believe that "foreigners" would ever become "good Canadians."[38] But English Canadians of that era made it more difficult for minority groups to develop the same attachment to their new home. They hardly welcomed the ethnic immigrant, complaining that non-British newcomers, especially eastern Europeans, were unassimilable, ignorant, dirty, and immoral. Immigrants apparently took jobs from Canadians, forcing the native-born to emigrate, and tended to create foreign enclaves in urban areas and throughout the west by settling together in large blocks. Many English Canadians wanted to preserve a Canada of British character and ethnic stock, and saw in immigration a threat to their vision of the country's future.[39] The

Wartime Information Board recognized that there would be little surprise if "foreigners" did not exhibit the same commitment to the war effort as "real" Canadians, "for numbers of these people, naturalized or not, have suffered years of humiliating discrimination because of their names, accents or appearance." Such discrimination "cuts its victims off from the only experience which can make them feel like Canadians. And until they feel like Canadians they can have little urge to fight for Canada."[40] There was much truth in such conclusions and racism was manifested in various ways. One veteran recalled searching for a friend at a Winnipeg army base when:

> mistakenly I walked into another barracks, and a guy asked my name and I said, 'Pawliuk.' And he said, 'Oh, a bohunk.' That's what he said, right off the bat. And I said, well, what could I say? I was just one among the whole barracks full of them. But I recall little things like that very clearly, because it did hurt me. I felt, gee, I am as much Canadian as anybody else. I spoke no other kind of language except English, I did all the things that everybody else did, and why should I be called something different?[41]

Winnipeggers of non-British origin may have felt the sting of discrimination but it did not prevent them from joining the armed forces or participating in the war effort through voluntary work (see Chapter 4). They responded like others to a national crisis that was brought home to them daily in a patriotic tone that was shaped by the government's information management apparatus.

Ottawa sought to control the character of the information transmitted to the public to ensure that it was sufficiently patriotic and promoted recognition of Canadians' duty to make the sacrifices necessary for victory. The Defence of Canada Regulations permitted censorship of anything deemed prejudicial to the efficient prosecution of the war or likely to cause disaffection. To facilitate the flow of information, Ottawa created the Censorship Coordinating Committee in the war's first month. This committee included representatives drawn from the Department of National Defence, the Post Office, the Canadian Broadcasting Corporation, and the Canadian Press Association. It advised journalists, editors, publishers, broadcasters, and filmmakers about acceptable material, and it had the authority to fine transgressors or ban publications it considered subversive. Later, in December 1939, the Bureau of Public Information (BPI) was set up to inform the press and public about the government's war policies. The BPI was then reorganized in 1942 into the Wartime Information Board (WIB). The WIB had a wider mandate to sell measures like tax hikes, rationing, and increased control of labour to Canadians as part of an intensified war effort. It worked closely with advertising agencies, journalists, academics, the Canadian Institute of Public Opinion, and the National Film Board to craft the most effective propaganda. Censorship officials argued that the main purpose of censorship was to prevent useful information from reaching the enemy but, as Keshen states, "they also heavily excised information or opinions they judged potentially damaging to morale and recruitment."[42]

The media generally complied voluntarily with censorship regulations and played an important role in encouraging patriotically correct attitudes. Radio news reports about the war reached approximately 75 percent of adult Canadians every day, and both newspapers and the film industry were very influential.[43] Although the media generally retained their right to criticize specific government policies, the righteousness of Canada's war effort was seldom questioned and, as Timothy Balzer notes, "the vast majority of the Canadian news media fully supported the war effort."[44] At the battle front, correspondents like Matthew Halton usually stressed the heroism of Canadian fighting men, and Ross Munro later admitted: "I was committed to the war completely and utterly, right from the start.... Maybe it was jingoism, chauvinism, and stupidity, but we felt that the Germans were going to wreck this world of ours and that we would have to stop them."[45]

On the home front, too, there was no shortage of publicists eager to do their bit by influencing public opinion. According to Madge MacBeth, president of the Canadian Authors' Association, Canadian writers had a "clear and definite duty" to publicize democratic ideals: "Our duty is to keep telling our heroic youth—and those who stay at home—what they are fighting for."[46] One group of prominent Winnipeg residents, including Lieutenant-Governor R.F. McWilliams, George V. Ferguson of the Winnipeg *Free Press*, and University of Manitoba President Dr. Sidney Smith, formed a Manitoba War Speakers' Committee to publicize measures citizens could take on the home front. The committee published "Facts for Victory," a newsletter that offered tidbits of information to encourage conservation of food and scarce goods, contribution to salvage and War Savings drives, reduction of absenteeism, and general self-sacrifice for the war effort. Readers were encouraged with numerous catch phrases to bolster resolve, such as: "Price of Victory in Canada's War

... Plainer Living, Harder Work"; or "Stop those rumours! Don't you be an enemy block-bomb in your neighborhood!!" If patriotic sentiment was not enough, guilt could be used effectively to get the message through. Ten days after the failed Dieppe raid of 19 August 1942, the newsletter asked, "Would you give a soldier wounded at Dieppe a bed?" His suffering could be eased by the purchase of twenty-five dollars in War Savings Certificates.[47] Local newspapers, for their part, often published congratulatory positive reinforcement during and after salvage or War Savings drives. One article asserted that "every community in Manitoba is taking part in this [rubber] drive." The appeal to participate was universal: "Our local Canadian Legion Branch is arranging for collection depots...and all that remains to make it a real success is the co-operation of you and you and you!"[48] Such messages, whether delivered through newspapers, radio, cinema, street-car advertising, or announcements in church, created significant pressure to conform to the war effort.

Honing the message required a deft hand. Writers recognized that audiences would be suspicious of falsehoods or "uniformly positive copy," but even bad news could serve the national purpose if presented in the correct light.[49] Misleadingly optimistic interpretations of events overseas still caused skepticism, especially early in the war, and blatantly partisan spin naturally raised ire. Some members of the media took issue with uncritical acceptance of sanitized war information. A Toronto *Telegram* editorial of 26 July 1940 stated that newspapers in democratic countries had a dual responsibility in wartime: to decide what news can be published and what might be likely to aid the enemy, and to keep the people informed about public affairs. It observed that "in Germany and Italy the rulers destroyed the free press of their countries and set up a gigantic propaganda machine ... to guide public opinion along the paths they desired." Canada, it argued, was in similar danger because Ottawa had engaged "corps of writers to turn out propaganda which officialdom wants the people to read." Press liaison officers, tasked with releasing government announcements to the papers, were of dubious value to the public because their reports "are often prepared in a manner which makes them simply a boost for the department concerned."[50]

Some publications retained their right to offer a dissenting opinion, such as *Canadian Forum*, on the left of the political spectrum, or *Saturday Night* on the right.[51] The former ran an article by Earle Birney in January 1940 that scorned the moral crackdown on freedom of thought and expression resulting from government information control. Later, Carlton McNaught was

moved to warn readers of *Canadian Forum* about the biased news copy published during the "conscription clamour" in October 1941. Some newspapers,
he argued, aimed to "befog public thinking" by printing "articles camouflaged
as news," emphasizing news favourable to their position, and loading their
pages with letters to the editor virtually all in support of compulsory service.[52]

The Winnipeg *Free Press*, for its part, was openly friendly to Mackenzie
King's Liberal government. The editor, John W. Dafoe, enjoyed such a considerable reputation that the *Free Press* was judged by intellectuals like University
of Toronto historian Frank Underhill to be the only newspaper in Canada that
exercised national influence.[53] It was the only daily in Canada with a regular
circulation outside of its own province.[54] Dafoe had made no secret of his
disdain for King's isolationist foreign policy throughout the 1930s, but he was
inclined to give Ottawa the benefit of the doubt on most issues once the war
began. Dafoe's successor as *Free Press* editor, George Ferguson, later wrote that
Dafoe "had laid it down as a major principle in 1939 that, in wartime, editorial
policy should be confined to supporting whatever the Government did until
such time as we could stomach it no longer."[55] Dafoe had told him on the day
Britain declared war that "I fancy we are in for some pretty black weeks [and]
perhaps months [and] we'll have to learn to gloss them over enough not to
break popular morale.[56]

If carried to extremes, such a stance could erode the credibility of a newspaper, even one as influential as the Winnipeg *Free Press*. Arthur Lower was a
contemporary of Dafoe's who participated with him in the Canadian Institute
of International Affairs, meetings of the Learned Societies, and a local study
group on Pacific relations. Lower commented upon Dafoe's death in 1944:
"Since I have known him, he has been overtaken by the timidities of old age....
He has been increasingly uncritical of this present government, notably the
damage inflicted on Canadian liberty by its ... institution of ... the Defence [of
Canada] Regulations and the equally great damage inflicted on parliamentary
government by the cabinet's cavalier method of announcing important decisions by order in council."[57]

Dafoe's soft editorial policy was consistent with the goal of encouraging
national unity and support for the war effort, but it might be seen as an
abdication of public responsibility. A healthy parliamentary system of government depends upon probing analysis of public affairs and the weighing of
competing ideas through vigorous political debate. By offering that analysis,
newspapers could play an important role in maintaining effective democratic

institutions in wartime. That role was undermined when the attempt to encourage a united patriotic response to the war effort stifled debate and allowed the majority perspective to become normative. Marginalization of those holding dissenting opinions was carried to the extreme when dissent came to be seen as a threat to the state's war effort and prompted the curtailment of civil liberties.

Sacrificing Democratic Freedoms

To minimize any such threat, Ottawa wasted no time in laying out the legislative framework for wartime internal security. When Germany invaded Poland on 1 September 1939, Ottawa invoked the War Measures Act, permitting the cabinet to issue any orders or regulations deemed necessary "for the security, defence, peace, order and welfare of Canada." The War Measures Act thus conveyed authority to govern by order-in-council without the necessity for parliamentary scrutiny. The Defence of Canada Regulations (DOCR) were proclaimed under its authority two days later, a full week before Canada declared war. Together, these two pieces of legislation afforded the federal cabinet "almost unlimited authority."[58] The sixty-four Defence Regulations overrode fundamental legal rights and civil liberties in order to preclude acts of subversion. Regulation 21, for example, authorized detention without trial in order to prevent suspected persons from committing acts harmful to national security. *Habeas corpus*, the requirement for authorities to produce a detainee in court and give cause for detention, was suspended along with the right to legal counsel for those being held. Regulation 39 compromised the freedoms of speech and the press by making it "an offence to print, publish, or circulate any document or material intended or likely to cause disaffection to His Majesty, or to prejudice recruiting, or to be prejudicial to the safety of the state or the efficient prosecution of the war." It was likewise an offence to utter statements having the same effect, and more than 100 people were prosecuted for making remarks considered unpatriotic or disloyal. Freedom of association was infringed for members of thirty-four groups, made up mainly of communists or fascists but also including Jehovah's Witnesses. All were banned under Regulation 39C. Like the War Measures Act, the DOCR were not subject to parliamentary review apart from the work of a select committee of the House of Commons that occasionally met to consider amendments to the regulations. Moreover, because action under the DOCR was left to the provinces, enforcement was not always consistent.[59] There was thus scant legal protection during the war from the arbitrary exercise of state power. In one case, a Binscarth, Manitoba, resident was convicted on three charges under the DOCR for refusing to let his children salute the flag or stand for the national anthem, "God Save the King," both acts he considered "idolatry." He was sentenced to three months in jail and fined $100 plus costs.[60]

Public reaction to these measures, in certain quarters, was animated. Citizens concerned with the anti-democratic character of Ottawa's wartime powers formed civil liberties associations in Montreal, Toronto, Winnipeg, and Vancouver to press the government to relax the tightest restrictions. G.M.A. Grube, a member of the Toronto group, warned *Canadian Forum* readers in November 1939 about Ottawa's assumption of unnecessary, dictatorial powers, the stifling of criticism by making illegal any unfavourable statement, and the resort to government by order-in-council. Grube and others pointed out the contrast with Britain's Emergency Powers Act, under which every order was subject to parliamentary approval and had to be renewed annually, as was the Act itself.[61] That same month, a group of Winnipeggers wrote Mackenzie King to ask for the repeal of Regulation 21 and restoration of *habeas corpus*. The authors, United College history professor Arthur Lower, his colleague David Owen, United Church minister Lloyd Stinson, and a future Co-operative Commonwealth Federation member of Parliament for Winnipeg North, Alistair Stewart, formally instituted the Winnipeg Civil Liberties Association the following spring. They were ultimately joined by a score of others, including University of Manitoba historian W.L. Morton and economist Mitchell Sharp, later a federal civil servant and cabinet minister.

Apart from letters to King and other politicians, the group made its arguments in public addresses and in the newspapers. Lower addressed a meeting of the Native Sons of Canada in February 1940, condemning the DOCR because they gave the impression of widespread disloyalty among sections of the population. He argued that the British defence regulations better protected individual freedom because they laid out specific offences and penalties and clearly defined the scope of government power, while the DOCR gave Ottawa unlimited powers of arrest and detention. Public acceptance of these laws was "a sign of political adolescence, our lack of knowledge of what liberty in an ordered society really is."[62]

The Winnipeg Civil Liberties Association sent an open letter to the prime minister which was published in the *Free Press* a week later. It contended that the powers assumed by the federal government amounted to "virtually as much authority as the German Reichstag in 1933 surrendered to ... Hitler." The government's assumption of such powers, ostensibly to ensure "the safety of the state," was "virtually equivalent to the complete abrogation of the law." In proclaiming the War Measures Act and the DOCR, Ottawa had created "all the legal framework for a dictatorship." The letter admitted that the government had wielded its new power with restraint thus far, so that "we have not yet got the dictator." But, it cautioned, "neither have we got to the end of the war. We do not know which will arrive first."[63]

During the 1940 federal election, the civil liberties associations sought support from candidates for a parliamentary committee to review and suggest amendments to the Defence Regulations. After the election, Lower and the Winnipeg group sent another rebuttal, a "Memorandum on Canadian Freedom in Wartime," that was published in the newspapers and signed by seventy-seven prominent Canadians. This was a more detailed critique with the central argument that in a war to preserve freedom abroad, it must also be protected at home.[64] Although the cabinet approved the inter-parliamentary review committee that Lower and his associates demanded, events in Europe and public opinion at home shortly precluded the possibility of any reduction in Canada's internal security measures. The DOCR remained in full force for the duration.

Citizens put up their guard against enemy agents and other subversives when Canada joined the war. The day before Parliament made its official declaration of war, a North End woman raised an alarm after sighting saboteurs at the McPhillips Street railway underpass. Police investigation confirmed their identity as surveyors from the city's engineering department.[65] The RCMP immediately moved to cut off any threat of sabotage by interning known Nazi sympathizers, about 200 in all. This may have been sufficient during the period of the Phoney War, but there was widespread panic about enemy agents across Canada following the German conquest of western Europe in the spring of 1940. Amid rumours that the German army had been aided by fifth columnists in Europe and fears that Canada could be the next target, citizens held rallies in Vancouver, Calgary, Toronto, and Montreal calling for the internment of enemy aliens. The police were swamped with calls from people reporting suspect behaviour.[66]

The Legion and other groups criticized the government for not taking adequate measures for home defence as a measure of paranoia set in. One veteran labelled Winnipeg "one of the centres of the fifth column in this country." A meeting of Legion members from various city branches expressed the belief that Czechoslovakian refugees who fled their country after the Sudetenland was ceded to Germany in 1938 were "deliberately exported ... to become members of the fifth column in Canada." The members went so far as to urge a survey of the entire province, followed by internment of all who could not give "a satisfactory account of themselves."[67] Similar fears were shared in other parts of the country. A particularly shrill group of 3,500 veterans in Windsor, Ontario, claimed that there were at least 7,500 enemy reservists just across the American border, men "who have regularly drilled and trained and who await the word of our enemy's leader to act according to a long pre-arranged plan."[68]

Premier John Bracken received a number of letters endorsing the registration of aliens and persons of "enemy origin," the surrender of all firearms and ammunition by same, and internment of all enemy aliens. The Legion was particularly vocal in this regard. It called for the organization of a home defence force to protect against sabotage. President L.D.M. Baxter of the Legion's Manitoba Command wrote Bracken that recent "press reports of subversive activities" necessitated immediate attention to the creation of a home guard force. A Winnipeg branch of the National Union of Railwaymen offered to help "cope with [this] 'fifth column' menace." They claimed that "certain subversive groups" had recently increased their level of activity, and feared that the railways might be targeted for sabotage, a claim echoed by the Legion.[69]

Ottawa's response did not entirely satisfy advocates of more vigorous local action. The militia was initially called out to guard federal properties, and Bracken argued in a letter to Mackenzie King that Ottawa should be responsible for maintaining troops at provincial power plants since they provided electricity for essential services under federal jurisdiction in Manitoba. Bracken was informed that the federal government considered protection of private property a local responsibility. Although Ottawa had furnished guards for a few selected points, like the Ontario hydro plants near Niagara Falls, their proximity to the American border made them a special case.[70] Military properties were to be defended by a new Veteran's Home Guard, composed of ex-servicemen, but it was up to local authorities to guard other facilities.[71]

To answer a popular clamour to help with home defence, wartime emergencies, and the "curtailment of subversive activities," Manitoba Attorney General W.J. Major set up a provincial committee to organize men ineligible for either active or Home Guard service into voluntary rifle associations.

Major proposed to accept all citizens who were fit, whether or not they had military experience, and he had 3,000 registered volunteers in Winnipeg alone by June. Training would be carried out only as needed to make them effective when called upon, though supplementary training would be optional.[72] Ottawa did not see the need for these rifle associations. C.G. Power, acting Minister of National Defence, told Bracken that the Canadian Active Service Force (the active army), the Non-Permanent Active Militia (the reserve), and the Home Guard were sufficient to meet any contingencies. He argued that the creation of civilian rifle associations would lead to wastage of arms and ammunition, and it would be impossible to guard these weapons if they were dispersed across the country. If Ottawa would not authorize the rifle associations, Bracken replied, the province would create a "volunteer constabulary" under its own authority in order to "satisfy local demands for opportunity of service" from those unable to join the military.[73]

The Manitoba Volunteer Reserve duly became operative on 1 August 1940. It formed companies across the province, organized by judicial district, with six in Greater Winnipeg. Training through 1940–41 focused on special constable duties, drills, target practice, first aid, and methods of assembly and transportation. The creation of the Manitoba Volunteer Reserve may have been a mere political expedient designed to placate excited citizens, since the provincial government appears to have neglected it once the fifth-column hysteria passed. In April 1941, the commanding officer advised Bracken that the provincial government would have to show an active interest in the reserve "so that the volunteers will feel that they are carrying out a useful purpose in doing this unexciting duty." By the end of the year, interest had waned in some companies in the absence of any emergency to validate their existence, though at least one company evolved into a functional reserve unit for the Fort Garry Horse fighting overseas.[74]

Ottawa's main reaction to the fifth-column hysteria was to tighten restrictions under the DOCR. The federal government amended Regulation 39 on 5 June 1940 to ban fascist and communist groups and permit seizure of their property. It made registration requirements more stringent in response to calls for action against enemy aliens, and the RCMP began to arrest Italians as well as Germans after Italy attacked France on 10 June. Police conducted searches without warrant, detained "foreigners" and communists without laying charges, and sent hundreds to internment camps.[75] In its move to intern enemy aliens, the Canadian government was acting in step with its allies and public opinion. The British government had arrested more than 6,000 suspected enemy agents and sympathizers during the war's first week, and both Britain and France rounded up large numbers of enemy aliens as the crisis escalated in mid-May 1940.[76]

The internments had a significant impact in Winnipeg because they affected a variety of constituencies. In a city shaped by immigration, with a strong tradition of labour radicalism—the most obvious example being the Winnipeg General Strike of 1919—the DOCR seemed to those on the Left like a tool wielded by the establishment to keep ethnic minorities, opposition politicians, and organized labour in their places. Only a handful of the province's 41,000 ethnic Germans were interned,[77] but all things German came under popular suspicion for the war's duration. The Winnipeg unit of the Army and Navy Veterans called for closure of all German clubs, which it saw as "hives of Nazi activities." The government Liquor Commission was even criticized for selling off a stock of German beer it had purchased before the war.[78] The small Italian community in Manitoba did not draw much attention, but members of other ethnic groups, especially Ukrainians, were a matter of concern because of their ties to the communist Party.

Canadian communists were put in an impossible position by the party's policy reversal during the remarkable events of August and September 1939. In spite of the German-Soviet non-aggression pact, aldermen Jacob Penner and M.J. Forkin both spoke out against the Nazis at a mass meeting in Market Square on 26 August, organized by the communist Party's provincial executive.[79] Tim Buck, the party's leader in Canada, had even telegraphed his support for the government's foreign policy to the prime minister. But upon the Soviet invasion of eastern Poland on 17 September, Buck and the party decided that Canada was actually involved in "an imperialist war, between imperialist powers, for imperialist aims on both sides."[80] Party members began to argue that Canada should withdraw from the war, and some communist and foreign-language newspapers carried on a subtle propaganda campaign to that effect. For example, Winnipeg's pro-communist Ukrainian-language daily, *Narodna hazeta*—the only Ukrainian daily in Canada—wrote on 25 November 1939 that "the ruling classes [presumably of the Allied powers] ... are restricting the democratic rights of the people and intensifying fascism in their own countries" while the people bore the burdens of the war effort.[81]

Some local communists were prosecuted even before party membership became illegal. A high-profile case involved Annie Buller, business manager of the communist *Mid-West Clarion*. Buller went into hiding after a warrant was issued for her arrest in March 1940, in response to articles in the paper that were deemed subversive. She was arrested in February 1941 and sentenced to twelve months in prison for distributing material "likely to be prejudicial to the efficient prosecution of the war"—the *Clarion*—and for continuing to be a member of the Communist Party of Canada, a contravention of Regulations 39A and 39C. There was also a concurrent internment order against her that was intended to be put into effect after her release.[82]

Other communists got the same treatment. The Winnipeg business agent for the United Garment Workers of America, Louis Guberman, was arrested along with Buller, her husband, Harry Guralnick, and John (Jock) McNeil, and charged with continuing membership in the Communist Party. While Guberman awaited trial, an internment order was signed by the Minister of Justice on 8 April. When the case was dismissed in October for lack of evidence, the RCMP acted on the internment order and confined Guberman at Headingly jail. As a brief prepared by the union complained, the Guberman case indicated that "if the investigators failed to produce evidence that would justify his conviction in a court of the land, they were determined to see that he was detained, regardless."[83] The Canadian Labor Defense League protested the arrest of Buller and other staff members of the *Clarion* as an attack against the freedom of the press, under the "anti-democratic and fascist-like [DOCR]," the application of which "can only result in the suppression of all democratic freedom in Manitoba and the destruction of the civil liberties of the people of our Province."[84]

B.K. Sandwell, the editor of *Saturday Night* and a member of Toronto's Civil Liberties Association, explained how internment orders permitted authorities to do an end-run around the legal safeguards normally provided by the courts. Police could take action against someone under the DOCR in two ways. The first was through the courts, which would require making public the evidence against the accused and would thereby allow a defence to be made. This method was not favoured if evidence against someone was furnished by undercover agents, because making evidence public would risk identifying the operatives and thus ending their usefulness. The second method was through an internment order signed by the justice minister, which "involves no court proceedings, no notice to the person interned, no pleadings of any kind, and no publicity. The police, armed with the order, which has been issued without the knowledge of the person against whom it is directed, simply call for him and take him away. It is often impossible for his family to find out where he is for a considerable time. His neighbors [sic] and the press are not encouraged to be inquisitive about him."[85]

There was little mystery surrounding Jacob Penner's internment. Penner, a sitting alderman, was interned in June 1940 under Section 21 of the DOCR after publicly advising "true Socialists" to oppose the war.[86] Such public statements incurred the wrath of government and patriots alike, and encouraged the party's ban as a subversive organization. Penner was not the only prominent communist politician in Winnipeg when the ban became law. His colleague M.J. Forkin was also a member of City Council; James Litterick was a member of the provincial Legislature; and there were two members of the Winnipeg School Board, Bill Ross and Andrew Bilecki, a former alderman. Police raids following the ban rounded up over twenty members of the party in Winnipeg, most of whom were interned at Kannanaskis, Alberta, along with German prisoners of war and Canadian fascists. Bilecki was interned along with Penner; Ross and Litterick went into hiding. More than 100 Canadian communists were interned by 1942.[87]

The city's economic and political elite, as represented by the Civic Election Committee (CEC), joined the chorus pressing Ottawa to rein in subversives during the spring and summer of 1940. But while the Legion set its sights on anyone impeding the war effort, the CEC focused on the ones that challenged its grip on political power. The CEC called a public meeting on 18 June, inviting "all ... groups interested in civic affairs" to consider a resolution to be sent to federal and provincial authorities, urging amendment of the DOCR to prevent members of outlawed organizations from standing for, or holding, public office. The CEC sought wide public representation at the meeting to give the resolution the weight of united public opinion. A significant number complied, and the resolution was adopted by representatives of 135 community organizations with a combined membership of 38,000 people. The committee's secretary argued that the resolution represented "considerable feeling" in Winnipeg concerning the "insufficient enforcement" of the Defence Regulations and the requirement for Canada to "do all in her power to protect herself from enemies within or without, and more particularly from within."[88]

These public articulations of concern over an imagined fifth-column menace were, to a certain extent, spontaneous; but sensationalized news reports did nothing to mitigate the paranoia. Articles in the *Free Press* referred to a "drive" or "campaign" to stamp out fifth columnists, during which a "close watch [was] being maintained on all suspects." Meanwhile, the actions of a Manitoba school district advertising for a teacher able to speak German was considered worthy of investigation by the provincial Department of Education.[89] When the paper endorsed the internment of "elected civic representatives" following the Communist Party ban, and attacked Forkin personally in the context of the pending civic elections, he responded in a letter to the editor: "One is driven to the conclusion that the Free Press is willing to defend democracy anywhere, except in Canada and Winnipeg in particular."[90] The irony must have been bitter for Forkin; he had served with the British Army during the Great War, a war supposedly fought to make the world safe for democracy, and yet he was now being persecuted for his political views.

Forkin and other communist politicians faced other opposition. At an Independent Labour Party meeting during the fall 1940 civic election, Mayor John Queen denounced Forkin as "an agent of Stalin" and argued that "North Winnipeg would be everlastingly disgraced if Forkin were re-elected." Queen recalled that Forkin and Penner were the only members of city council to vote against a resolution supporting the war effort, and went on to claim that "if Forkin is re-elected it will be the fault of those who stay at home on election day.... Don't let it be heralded over Canada that a Nazi-communist could be elected in North Winnipeg." Another speaker, J. Steinberg, "declared that North Winnipeg must 'eradicate the poison of Communism'" by defeating the communist candidates in the upcoming elections.[91] The anti-communist backlash was enough to defeat Forkin in the November 1940 civic election, and the provincial Legislature soon moved to enact the principle behind the CEC's June resolution. On 11 December, members debated a bill to prevent anyone convicted or detained under the DOCR from holding public office. Although the Public Office Disqualification Act was passed, among those opposing it was John Queen, a member of the Legislative Assembly as well as the mayor of Winnipeg. Queen's respect for democratic practice overrode his hatred of communism and his animosity toward Forkin. He argued that "members of the legislature were not there by the good graces of the other members, but by the voice of the people who elected them. That was the essence of democracy. The electors, not the legislature, should deal with members who did not give satisfactory service."[92]

The radical Left in Winnipeg found little sympathy among those with more conservative political views, and communists carried on their fight against the DOCR in isolation from mainstream civil libertarians, although they often used similar language. Like the members of the Winnipeg Civil Liberties Association, they wrote letters to the newspapers and sent petitions to the politicians, but they also organized more direct demonstrations of the popular will. In March 1940, for example, a Ward 3 Unemployed Association meeting, attended by 500 people, passed a resolution in favour of repealing the War Measures Act. They argued that the Act was generally "undemocratic and savoring [sic] of fascism," and permitted the infringement of the rights to freedom of speech, freedom of assembly, and freedom of association.[93] A number of similar groups were formed, such as the Committee for Release of Labor Prisoners. This committee sent a delegation of wives of interned labour leaders to present a brief to the special House of Commons committee reviewing the DOCR in April 1941, and later petitioned Ernest Lapointe, the federal justice minister, for the repeal of Regulation 21 and release of those interned under its terms. Meetings of these groups were routinely attended by hundreds.[94]

The rationale for continuing to detain Canadian communists evaporated after a surprise German attack in June 1941 brought the Soviet Union into the war as Canada's ally. Ottawa was in no hurry to amend its policy, and agitation increased for a repeal of the Communist Party ban and the release of its interned members. The preceding April, William A. Kardash, a Ukrainian-Canadian who had lost a leg in the Spanish Civil War, was elected to the provincial legislature. Kardash was a dedicated communist—he had earlier been arrested under Regulation 39 but not convicted—and he worked to keep the plight of the twenty-seven interned Winnipeg "anti-Fascists" in the public eye.[95] Kardash and other party members never lost an opportunity to label themselves "anti-fascists" rather than communists; they emphasized the new tag in public statements and letters to the editor from men like Norman Penner, son of the interned Winnipeg alderman. In a speech to the Legislative Assembly in December 1941, Kardash stressed the fact that he and three others who were now interned had "fought ... against the Nazi and Fascist forces" in Spain. What sense did it make to lock up men who shared the same enemy as the rest of the Canadian people? When five of the interned men (including Penner and John Navis) had sons already serving in Canada's armed forces, how could the government continue to question their loyalty?[96] Local communists also formed the Winnipeg branch of the Council for Democratic Rights to work toward the release of internees. Joe Zuken, a lawyer and school trustee, was elected chairman. The executive included, among others, William Kardash, Jock McNeil, Andrew Bilecki, Mrs. Jacob (Rose) Penner, and Mrs. John (Mary) Navis.[97] The council repeated demands throughout 1942 for the release of Penner and the other communists. It held a large public meeting at the Winnipeg Auditorium in February, sent a resolution to the federal cabinet, and selected delegates for a national meeting of the organization in Ottawa.[98] Andrew Bilecki and Jock McNeil, both recently released, spoke at a Walker Theatre rally on 23 April 1942, as did Kardash and Zuken. These rallies drew other members of the political Left along with the communists. Lewis St.G. Stubbs, an independent member of the Legislature and former provincial judge, also spoke, claiming that the Defence Regulations had "set Canada back to the pre-Magna Carta days, stripping citizens of every vestige of civil rights and liberties."[99] The Council sponsored the publication, in July, of an open letter to Ralph Maybank, Member of Parliament for Winnipeg South Centre and a member of the parliamentary committee reviewing the DOCR, repeating its demands and calling for the prosecution of "all pro-Fascist, fifth-column saboteurs and their organizations which are still permitted to carry on their defeatist, divisive, pro-Hitler and pro-Vichy activity." The letter was printed in the *Free Press* and readers were asked to sign their names before forwarding it to Maybank.[100] Another meeting in July protested the internment of Harry Guralnick. Kardash chaired the meeting, at which Zuken, Stubbs, and Alistair Stewart also spoke.[101]

In fact, the federal government was already taking steps towards the release of some interned communists. On 5 March 1942, a large crowd met Andrew Bilecki at the Canadian Pacific Railway station upon his release from internment. Bilecki, a "Canadian-born Ukrainian" and former alderman, had been held for nineteen months. He now supported the war effort, endorsed the pending plebiscite on conscription, and expected the release of his comrades to follow.[102] Jacob Penner was released from his internment in Hull, Quebec, in early September. On his return to Winnipeg after two years and three months, Penner, who had earlier opposed Canada's participation in the war, now stated "that he was glad to be in a position to help the Canadian people to defend the country against the Axis powers. He said he felt that it is the duty of Canadians to stand united until victory is won." Harry Guralnick was also finally released in September, though his wife, Annie Buller, remained in custody in Portage la Prairie.[103]

Communist rhetoric may have delayed the results they sought. Certain public statements helped to alienate those of more moderate opinion and reinforced suspicions about their loyalty to Canada. Kardash's speeches, for example, often descended into propaganda for the Soviet war effort. Speaking in Toronto in May 1942, Kardash argued for the opening of a second front in Europe. Timing was critical, he said: an invasion of western Europe could greatly shorten the war, but unless it was mounted immediately, the Allies risked total defeat. Kardash made his speech at a time when the Germans were near their deepest penetrations into Russian territory and the USSR's need for a second front was desperate. Once the Soviets were in the war and in trouble, Kardash and other communists began to demand conscription and an increase in the Canadian army's strength to two fully-equipped army corps. He suggested that all of the vast resources of men and *matériel* building up since the United States joined the Allied war effort should be used to "defeat [Hitler's] armies now, when the entire strategical [sic] and tactical situation in Europe favors an Allied invasion." Kardash argued that the Allied armies were sitting idle "while the future of the world is being decided," and went so far as to say that only "cowards, or appeasers, or fifth columnists" would favour allowing the Soviet people to bear the brunt of the fighting while the Germans were free to concentrate their might on the eastern front.[104]

Kardash and his comrades were conduits for communist propaganda that exaggerated the accomplishments of the Soviet Union. In December 1941, after the Wehrmacht had advanced to the gates of Moscow and Leningrad, he claimed that "the Soviet people and the heroic Red Army have been delivering death blows to the Nazi hordes for almost six months," while Canadian communists languished in internment camps.[105] Later, he argued that Canada should honour the anniversary of Hitler's attack on Russia, 22 June, a day that marked "the beginning of the end of his easy victories." He suggested that it would be fitting to offer a national day of tribute to "the efforts of the great Soviet people and their warrior leader Stalin," and fly the Soviet flag "from every public building in Canada."[106] Kardash's colleague Leslie Morris, editor of the communist paper *Canadian Tribune*, thought it was fortunate that the Allies could rely on the Soviet Union. "For the first period of the war against the USSR," Morris wrote, "Hitler had the advantage of surprise, and unreadiness in Britain and the USA. Had that been coupled with any weakness on the part of the USSR, the war might have been lost in 1941. But the power of the Red Army, the unity of the Soviet home front and the magnificent strategy of the Soviet command, frustrated Hitler's military plan."[107]

Spouting such partisan propaganda, it is little wonder that others questioned the loyalties of Canadian communists. During debates in the Manitoba Legislature in late March 1942, J.R. Solomon, the member for Emerson, commented on Kardash's appeal for the release of interned "anti-Fascists." Solomon said "he would endorse the plea were he satisfied that the communists had definitely changed their minds." But after their early flip-flop on support for the war, he said they had done "everything possible to hamper the war effort" including issuing a manifesto to the people of the Dominion in May 1941, "asserting that it was a lie that our war was against Fascism or that Britain was fighting for democracy." They did not decide to support the war effort until Germany invaded Russia. While Solomon was not "questioning the sincerity of their support now," he still wondered if they were "supporting the war effort because they believed in the democratic principles for which Canada is fighting, or was it only because Russia was an ally by circumstances? Would the communists ... cease supporting the war effort if Russia dropped out of the war?"[108] Solomon's skepticism was probably shared by many who remembered the first two years of the war but, like Kardash, he was Ukrainian and his opposition to the communist position was influenced in part by internal divisions within that community, which will be explored in the next chapter.

There was a substantial degree of unity behind Canada's war effort, as Winnipeggers' response to all manner of patriotic appeals showed—from recruiting to salvage collection to War Savings drives. But the consensus was far from total. It was manipulated in part by government information control, though many jumped on the patriotic bandwagon of their own accord. Those who did not share in the consensus, like conscientious objectors and communists, were harassed or prosecuted. Some civil libertarians recognized the fundamental contradiction between fighting for freedom abroad while restricting it at home, but their protests were largely drowned out by more belligerent voices. Other Canadians who belonged to ethnic minorities were not fully admitted into the national crusade, but were expected to play whatever part was assigned to them by society's elite. In some cases, wartime insecurities could prompt certain groups to lash out at those on the other side of the perceived divide between "us" and "them." Our attention now turns to the effects of this tendency on three groups: Ukrainian Canadians, anti-conscriptionists, and the Japanese in Manitoba.

2

US AND THEM

Shortly after the war began, G.M.A. Grube, a professor of classics at the University of Toronto and member of Toronto's Civil Liberties Association, wrote in *Canadian Forum* that "war, by its very nature, tends toward repression, rouses primitive passions, and thus creates an atmosphere in which reasonableness, free discussion, and a spirit of toleration are difficult to maintain. War is therefore a dangerous weapon for democracy to use, even in its own defence."[1] The experience of some minority groups in Winnipeg and southern Manitoba confirms the accuracy of Grube's observation. Within a split Ukrainian community, opposing groups of communists and nationalists fought their own propaganda war and sought to impugn the loyalty of the other faction at every turn. Anti-conscriptionists found little appetite among the patriotic majority for truly free discussion, along with a distinct unwillingness to respect dissenting opinions. And for the Japanese Canadians sent to work on Manitoba's sugar beet farms, the spirit of toleration was in short supply. These examples show that there were impediments to Canadian unity apart from French-English relations, and that persecution of racial minorities and the erosion of democratic freedoms were consequences of Canada's war effort, regardless of liberal-democratic war aims.

Ukrainians

Winnipeg was a nexus for political, ethnic, and religious divisions, and the city's Ukrainian community was affected by all of them. Manitoba was home to the largest group of Ukrainians in Canada—89,762 in 1941—and

Winnipeg was their cultural centre. The seats of their two major church-es—Greek Catholic and Greek Orthodox—were located here, as were the main Ukrainian newspapers, leading businesses, and important cultural and educational institutions. The community was concentrated in the North End, where most of the city's 22,578 Ukrainians lived. They were an important electoral group, with 10 percent of the city's population. In 1942, politicians of Ukrainian origin held seven seats in the provincial Legislature and one seat on City Council. There was also one school trustee.[2] But the Ukrainian community was hopelessly divided by political and religious differences, many of which had been exported to Canada from Europe along with the approximately 240,000 immigrants who arrived between 1892 and 1939. The split between Ukrainian communists and nationalists precluded any measure of unity, and the rivalry had repercussions that threatened the community's morale and commitment to the war effort.

To make sense of the Ukrainian-Canadian community's complex politics requires some understanding of their homeland's recent history. Ukraine had been divided and ruled by a succession of regimes since before the First World War. The largest extent of Ukrainian territory was ruled by the Russian Empire until 1917, but the western provinces of Galicia and Bukovyna were part of the Austro-Hungarian Empire. An independent Ukrainian state was briefly established after Russia and Austria-Hungary were defeated in the Great War, but Ukraine was again partitioned following a series of unsuccess-ful wars with Poland and the new Union of Soviet Socialist Republics between 1918 and 1921. Ukrainians found themselves living under Polish, Romanian, and Czechoslovakian rule in the west, while the eastern territories were in-corporated within the USSR. The conflicts of this chaotic period resembled a civil war, as some Ukrainians subscribed to Bolshevik ideals and fought for a socialist Ukraine, while a "white" faction eventually allied with the Poles and forces assembled by the Western Allies in an attempt to suppress the Russian Revolution. The important city of Kiev changed hands eight times within a three-year period, and events produced a tangle of allegiances: nationalists fought communists within Ukraine, and Poles and Russians without. A period of relative stability set in during the mid-1920s, but the Soviet plan for agricultural collectivization after 1929 prompted resistance from the "nationally-minded" government of the Ukrainian Soviet Socialist Republic at Kiev. In response, the Soviet dictator, Joseph Stalin, ordered a program of repression that included confiscation of produce and a purge of the Ukrainian intelligentsia and Communist Party.[3] Soviet law required government quotas to be filled before produce from collective farms was given to the peasants who grew it, and the quotas were inflated so drastically in 1932 that starvation became widespread. Farmers who "hoarded" or refused to give up their grain were exiled or executed. The famine induced by Moscow's policies in 1932 and 1933 was responsible for the deaths of between 5 million and 7 million Ukrainians, thus making the USSR the greatest enemy of Ukrainian nationalists.

The Ukrainians who settled on the Canadian prairies brought their political and religious rivalries with them. They came in two major waves: the first, from roughly 1892 to 1914, encompassed approximately 170,000 from Galicia and Bukovyna. These immigrants were divided by religion—the Galicians were mostly Greek Catholics while those from Bukovyna were Greek Orthodox—and the two groups tended to segregate themselves though they settled in proximity to each other. The second wave, from 1919 to 1939, brought about 68,000 from Galicia and Volhynia, both provinces under Polish rule.[4] Ukrainian minorities in these territories were culturally and economically oppressed, as were those in the parts of Bukovyna and Carpatho-Ukraine incorporated within Romania and Czechoslovakia, respectively. As a result of the repression in the western provinces and in the Ukrainian Soviet Socialist Republic, some new Canadians from these regions subscribed to a militant nationalism and held as their goal the re-establishment of an independent Ukrainian state. The Left was equally committed to preserving a communist Ukraine. Others, particularly among the earlier immigrants, were concerned mainly with improving conditions for Ukrainians in Canada. Since Ukrainian Canadians constituted the fourth largest minority in Canada by 1940,[5] the community's internal politics and competing organizations posed a significant obstacle to a united war effort.

One of the two major non-communist groups, the Ukrainian Self-Reliance League (USRL), was an Orthodox lay organization devoted to fostering cultural development of the community in Canada. It thoroughly subscribed to democratic practices, with allegiance to Canada holding first claim on its loyalties. Its adherence to the Orthodox church, however, alienated Catholic Ukrainians. The Ukrainian National Federation (UNF), on the other hand, was a secular, authoritarian, and revolutionary group devoted, above all, to securing Ukrainian independence. It was linked to the Organization of Ukrainian Nationalists (OUN), a "quasi-fascist" militant group active in Europe that used terrorist tactics in its fight to free the western Ukrainian provinces from Polish control. As a result of its affiliation, the UNF was "tainted with fascism," in the words of historian Oleh Gerus, and the leaders of the USRL feared that this militant brand of nationalism would erode the moderate, respectable image that they sought to project.[6] The non-communist groups were therefore splintered, but pressure from Ottawa contributed to a semblance of unity after the creation, in November 1940, of the Ukrainian Canadian Committee, an umbrella organization that sought to coordinate Ukrainian support for the war effort and to maximize the Ukrainian community's influence on government policy by speaking with one voice.[7] On one issue, the rival nationalist organizations found easy agreement: their antipathy for Ukrainian communists.

The pro-communist Ukrainian Labour Farmer Temple Association (ULFTA) was the strongest secular Ukrainian organization, according to historian Thomas Prymak. Its membership in 1940 was estimated at 20,000— although as many as 50,000 Ukrainians may have participated in its cultural activities—and it published the only Ukrainian-language daily newspaper in Canada, Winnipeg's *Narodna hazeta* (The People's Gazette). The ULFTA had five labour temples and its headquarters in Winnipeg, with perhaps 200 branches and eighty temples across Canada. Although the secretary of the central committee claimed the ULFTA to be "strictly a cultural and educational organization" and "an absolutely non-political body,"[8] Prymak writes that it "supported the Soviet Union and glorified the achievements of the Soviet Ukrainian Republic." At the same time, it was "very critical of affairs in Canada."[9] Economic conditions offered much to criticize during the 1930s, whatever one's political stripe, and the ULFTA grew during the Depression by attracting urban unemployed with propaganda about the Soviet workers' paradise. At the organization's tenth convention in Winnipeg in July 1931, members passed a resolution accepting their duty to defend the Soviet Union. The convention enumerated its immediate goals, the first of which was "unity with all revolutionary labour movements in the field of economic and political struggle under the ideological leadership of [the] Communist Party of Canada." It also aimed to assist in the liberation of Western Ukraine from Polish rule.[10] The ULFTA, like the Communist Party of Canada, clearly took its orders from Moscow.

Ukrainian-Canadian communists, led by John Navis, represented one of the largest and most important factions in the party. Subordination to

Moscow led them to completely accept Soviet propaganda. They denied the truth behind the famine, which Stalin's policies induced, and the persecution of comrades and kinfolk in Europe during the brutal purges of the 1930s.[11] All this fuelled an internecine feud among politically conscious Ukrainians in Winnipeg during the war; and what it lacked in bloodshed, it made up in vitriol. The two factions, communists and nationalists, fought a propaganda war amongst themselves even as their adopted homeland entered the struggle against Hitler, and it played out in Winnipeg's newspapers and in the politics of the rival Ukrainian organizations.

This feud was, of course, influenced by events overseas. If the period encompassing the Second World War counts among the most brutal and tragic in human history, it was certainly bleak and confusing for Ukrainians in Europe and in Canada. The fluidity of events overseas heralded dark times and shifting allegiances for groups on both the Left and the Right. Some Ukrainian nationalists in the mid-1930s sympathized with German intentions to redraw the map of central Europe, believing that Hitler would support their aspirations for an autonomous Ukraine. The Munich agreement of 1938 that began the dissection of Czechoslovakia granted a form of autonomy to the provinces of Slovakia and Carpatho-Ukraine, encouraging Ukrainian nationalists to look towards the consolidation of a homeland free from foreign control. After Hitler seized Prague in March 1939, Germany permitted Hungary's absorption of Carpatho-Ukraine and any Ukrainian support for Hitler's foreign policy evaporated with what they considered a betrayal.[12] A second blow fell with the Anglo-French guarantee of Polish territorial integrity at the end of March 1939. As the *Kanadiiskyi farmer* (Canadian Farmer) put it, "herein lies the tragedy of our situation. On the one hand, a sense of duty towards Canada prompts us to defend it. On the other hand, the prospect of dying in defense of Poland is a horrible thing, and would be still more horrible because, by our sacrifice, we would be helping to enslave the Ukrainians living in Poland."[13]

The same sentiments were expressed in other nationalist papers, though some were equally appalled at the prospect of a British alliance with the Soviet Union. The editor of Toronto's nationalist weekly *Ukrainskyi robitnyk* (Ukrainian Toiler) wrote on 5 May 1939 that "if Britain had concluded a military alliance with the.... [USSR], then the Ukrainian-Canadians would have been placed in a most pitiable situation in being compelled to help the Soviets, the worst enemies of their national aspirations." The communist daily *Narodna hazeta*, on the other side of the spectrum, was suspicious of British imperialism and Western plots against the USSR. It later praised Allied support for Poland, once the Germans attacked "defenceless Ukrainian and White Ruthenian towns" there, and urged readers "to stand in defence of their democratic Canada and their brothers in the Western Ukraine against the bloody Nazi aggressor!"[14] But the communist position was about to change again.

The conflict between the Ukrainian Left and Right intensified when communists abruptly rejected the "imperialist" war and welcomed the Soviet occupation of eastern Poland, with the resultant annexation of Galicia and Volhynia to the Ukrainian Soviet Socialist Republic. For the nationalist factions, this move represented the perpetuation of Ukrainian oppression, an uncertain fate for their European leaders and the Ukrainian churches, and can only have fuelled their hatred for the communists.[15]

Ottawa's reaction to the communist denunciation of the war was, of course, to outlaw the party, intern its leaders, and seize its properties, including the ULFTA halls. In a move that can hardly have been thoroughly considered, the federal government then resold some of the buildings to rival groups. The Ukrainian Labour Temple in Winnipeg, at 197 Euclid Avenue, for example, was sold to the UNF over the ULFTA's protests, sparking a riot involving "several hundred persons" and a barrage of eggs, frozen vegetables, bottles, and bricks outside the building on 28 December 1941. Twelve people were arrested, though proceedings were stayed.[16] Hostility between the two sides flared up again in August 1943, when UNF members changed the name on the building's cornerstone, prompting a disturbance involving an estimated crowd of 400. The fight spread to City Hall when Council debated the granting of a dance-hall licence in December 1943. Amid "warnings of violence and bloodshed by opposing Ukrainian factions," alderman Jacob Penner accused the UNF of fascism. Despite his protest, the licence was duly granted.[17]

While some Ukrainian nationalists may have privately opposed the war and welcomed the reduction of Poland, all of the right-wing organizations immediately proclaimed their loyalty to Canada and their support for the war effort. Because the Soviets were viewed with suspicion by the Western powers before 1941, Ukrainian nationalists' anti-communist position did not cause any inconvenience. Commitment to the Allied cause was assured as long as there was no alliance with the USSR.[18] The non-communist newspapers and organizations encouraged Ukrainians to enlist, support War Savings drives, and contribute through the Red Cross and other voluntary work. Ukrainian Canadians responded to these appeals like other Canadians. There was even a UNF initiative, though it came to naught, to raise Ukrainian units to serve alongside the Canadian army overseas.[19]

Hitler's invasion of Russia in June 1941 dramatically altered the situation for Ukrainians in Winnipeg. Wasyl Swystun of the UNF claimed that Ukrainian-Canadian loyalty to Canada and the British Empire had not been affected, and urged an intensification of efforts in support of the war, particularly in recruiting for the armed forces.[20] But according to Prymak, the UNF's enthusiasm slackened significantly. They could not openly criticize Britain's alliance with the Soviets, and Britain's war aims offered little hope for Ukrainian post-war independence. Ukrainian communists, on the other hand, could now forget their earlier proclamations and go all-out in support of a just war in defence of freedom, Great Britain, and Canada.[21]

With the Communist Party ban still in effect, they acted through a new organization, the Ukrainian Association to Aid the Fatherland. Its first national convention was held in Winnipeg in early June 1942, with 400 delegates representing Ukrainian communities across Canada. The conference stressed the need for unity among Ukrainian Canadians if victory were to be achieved, and now echoed nationalist appeals to join the armed forces, increase war production, and provide support for war charities.[22] The convention also favoured direct financial aid to the USSR for the Red Army and conscription for overseas service. Perhaps, in order to preclude continuing questions about its ultimate loyalty, the convention decided to change the organization's name to the generic Association of Ukrainian Canadians.[23]

Though both factions were now committed to the war, their partisan rhetoric continued unabated. Their spokesmen and their presses took turns casting aspersions on the loyalties of the other: the communists claimed that nationalist support for German revisionism before the war equated to fascism, the nationalists in turn accused them of obeying the directives of foreign dictators while "trying to spread Communism and confusion in Canada."[24] Despite paying lip service to the need for unity, the Association of Ukrainian Canadians convention resolved to "unsparingly expose before the people and the government Canada's internal enemies, the fifth-columnists, Hitler agents, saboteurs and spies operating in the Ukrainian Canadian environment." In this, they were taking direct aim at the member groups of the Ukrainian Canadian Committee. One writer for Toronto's *Ukrainske Zhyttia* (Ukrainian Life) spared no venom in claiming that "the leaders of the Ukrainian nationalist organizations ... understandably not only regard everyone who is fighting against the Soviet Union as a friend, and hate everyone who helps the Soviet Union, but they were and continue to be exponents of fascist ideology and haters of democratic ideas."[25] William Kardash launched similar attacks in the Manitoba Legislature. In March 1942, he alleged that the UNF had been closely linked with the Nazis, and that money collected by that organization had been sent to Ukrainian fascists in Berlin. In response, J.R. Solomon, a member of the USRL, said that "the great bulk of Ukrainians in this country were neither followers of Stalin nor of Fascist leaders, but red-blooded Canadians who do not take orders from outside sources."[26]

The nationalists were put in an awkward position by Canada's new alliance with the USSR, and they soon became something of an embarrassment to Ottawa. The Ukrainian Canadian Committee reaffirmed its loyalty to Canada and commitment to the war effort, but some of its members continued to advocate the creation of an independent Ukraine—which implied the end of Soviet control over their homeland. Following criticism of the USSR in the UNF paper *Novyi shliakh* (The New Pathway) throughout the summer of 1941, the government's press censors delivered a warning that open criticism of the USSR could potentially harm the alliance and therefore constituted a breach of the Defence of Canada Regulations. A congress of the Ukrainian Canadian Committee in June 1943 nonetheless cited the principles of the Atlantic Charter as it reaffirmed its desire for an independent Ukraine. But those principles were overridden by the simple reality that Allied solidarity was a necessary condition in the fight against Hitler. After the Soviet emissary to Canada complained to the Department of External Affairs about statements in the Ukrainian press that "advocated, in effect, the territorial dismemberment of an ally," the RCMP was directed to begin collecting intelligence concerning the nationalist organizations.[27] No evidence of subversion was uncovered, but the episode reveals the inconvenient truth that wartime expediency trumped the freedoms for which Canadians believed they were fighting.

It can hardly be said that the Ukrainian community in Winnipeg was united behind Canada's participation in the war—in fact, a significant body of opinion, represented by the communist faction, opposed it until June 1941 when Germany forced the Soviets into the conflict. Given the complicated politics behind the question of Ukraine's position in Europe, it is understandable that more than simple loyalty to Canada informed the respective stances taken by the rival organizations in Winnipeg. Yet, despite their internal conflict, Ukrainian Canadians on both sides of the national question ultimately got behind the war effort in its many forms. The Winnipeg *Free Press* estimated that there were 35,000 to 40,000 Ukrainian Canadian servicemen in uniform by February 1942, and other figures covering the entire course of the war estimate that 11.4 percent of the Ukrainian population in Canada enlisted, a higher proportion than the national average.[28] Ukrainian civilians supported War Savings drives like other Canadians. They contributed money and service to voluntary efforts in the city—for example, the Ukrainian Women's Association donated a pair of ambulances through their fundraising work, sent comforts to the fighting men overseas, and visited wounded veterans at Deer Lodge. The community also sponsored a Ukrainian Canadian Servicemen's Association in London.[29] Although nationalists and communists never resolved their differences, all eventually accepted the need to defeat Hitler, whatever their aspirations for their native land.

Conscription

The example of Winnipeg's Ukrainian community reveals some of the home front's unsavoury realities, such as the erosion of democratic freedoms as a result of political differences, and the contribution of partisan propaganda to conflicts between and within ethnic groups. The less virtuous side of the "good war" was also exposed, on the local and national stages, by the debate over conscription.

The previous chapter suggested that some newspapers helped to marginalize minority opinion by overzealously promoting a patriotic response to wartime demands, thereby abdicating their responsibility to offer objective analysis of public affairs. *Free Press* editor John W. Dafoe recognized the importance of offering a balanced treatment of the conscription debate. Dafoe wrote, in a 1941 editorial, that "the issue of conscription is so serious and raises questions of such magnitude that it ought, in the interests of national unity...to be discussed in terms of studious moderation and with careful regard for the feelings and sentiments of those holding different views."[30] During the Great War, he had seen how much the uncompromising advocacy of conscription could undermine national unity and the morale that was so necessary to the war effort. When the debate broke out once again, Dafoe's clear intention was that, despite his preference for conscription, the *Free Press* would not "rock the boat and make it more difficult for the government to maintain a facade of unity in the prosecution of the war effort." Dafoe's position was that once the government decided on conscription the paper would openly support the policy, but not before.[31] The *Free Press* would abandon Dafoe's "studious moderation," however, in a series of editorials analyzing the April 1942 conscription plebiscite results that pointed the finger at Winnipeg's ethnic minorities. The Winnipeg *Tribune*, meanwhile, was so uncompromising in its advocacy of conscription that it hardly admitted the legitimacy of opposing views on the matter. A rather one-sided conscription debate thus boiled over in the pages of Winnipeg's newspapers with heated editorial opinion portraying opponents of the preferred policy as disloyal to Canada's war effort.

The details of the conscription debate have been fully treated elsewhere, so a brief outline will suffice.[32] All political parties had rejected conscription throughout 1939, but the disastrous turn of events in western Europe in the spring of 1940, along with continuing setbacks in the Balkans, North Africa, and Russia throughout 1941, led to widespread support in much of Canada for an intensified military contribution. In late 1941, the federal cabinet debated a program to expand the army to two corps comprising three infantry divisions, two armoured divisions, and two independent armoured brigades, plus ancillary troops. Although Major-General Kenneth Stuart, Chief of the General Staff, assured the government that conscription would not be necessary to sustain such a force, the figures on available manpower he cited were dubious.

King and the federal government were caught in a vise: they had promised Quebecers, in 1939, not to enforce conscription in order to secure Quebec's support for Canada's entry into the war. Quebec expected Ottawa to keep that promise. Meanwhile, English Canadians complained ever more loudly about inefficient use of manpower and the need to put Canada on a total war footing. They objected to a minority holding the rest of the country hostage, and trotted out the usual clichés about majority rule in a democracy.[33] During the battle for Hong Kong, the Manitoba Legislature passed a resolution in favour of total war and conscription for overseas service. During the debate, Conservative member H.D.B. Ketchen, a Great War veteran, declared that "Canada was ready for conscription of every man and woman whose services could be used.... Certain political pledges against conscription had been given in an election campaign and were now held out as an excuse for avoiding the issue."[34] Faced with potential rifts in cabinet and in the country, Mackenzie King settled upon a plebiscite to free the government from its earlier pledge not to impose conscription for overseas service. The Throne Speech that opened Parliament on 22 January 1942 announced King's plan. The plebiscite would ask: "Are you in favour of releasing the Government from any obligations arising out of any past commitments restricting the methods of raising men for military service?"[35] It did not refer directly to the implementation of conscription, but there was hardly a doubt among Canadians about what was at issue.

Some constituencies of opinion flayed the government for stalling and trying to avoid the responsibilities it had been elected to exercise. Premier Bracken had warned Ottawa that to settle the issue this way would be the "crowning indignity" of our history. The Montreal *Gazette* adapted Churchill's famous line about the Royal Air Force in the Battle of Britain: "Never were so many people humiliated by so few." The Ottawa *Journal* believed that "the majority of the people of this country don't give a tinker's curse about Mr. King's so-called pledge, but are concerned only with the best means of winning the war." The *Globe and Mail* similarly called it a "cowardly evasion of leadership." The *Tribune* was more moderate. While not approving of the policy, it argued that since the issue was to be decided by a plebiscite, the duty of Canadians was to "vote to remove the dead hand of the past from the urgent necessities of the present." The *Free Press*, meanwhile, could not understand all the outrage over what it called "a promise kept."[36] Regardless of the criticism, the plebiscite was a deft political move. It allowed the government and its supporters to profess responsiveness to the demands for total war from English Canada even as they put off the moment when King would be forced to betray his pledge to French Canada.

Pro-conscriptionists expected that a "Yes" vote would prompt swift action to increase the forces available for overseas duty. Once the plebiscite campaign commenced, they marshalled their forces. University of Manitoba President Sidney Smith chaired a non-partisan group called the Affirmative Vote Committee, representing a number of Winnipeg organizations, which ran a "Yes" campaign in the city. Support was widespread, and a parade of groups publicized their position in favour of a "Yes" vote when Canadians went to the polls on 27 April 1942. One of these groups, the Ukrainian Canadian Committee, arranged sixteen meetings—all in one day—in church and community halls. The communists were on side too, and they seized the opportunity to bring their movement into the open and generate popular support. A group of "women relatives" of interned men, including Ruth Penner and Mary Navis, sponsored a radio broadcast in support of the "Yes" side. Even James Litterick, a former member of Manitoba's Legislative Assembly who had gone into hiding, argued for an affirmative vote and offered himself for military service.[37]

The Affirmative Vote Committee organized a rally at the Auditorium on 9 April, in which all political groups participated. William Kardash even represented the communists, now working alternately under the name of the United Workers Party or the Workers Election Committee. Sidney Smith chaired the meeting and music was supplied by the Canadian Legion band. The keynote speaker, introduced by Premier Bracken, was Murdo MacPherson, former attorney general of Saskatchewan. Canadians, he said, were fighting for freedom of speech, freedom of the press, freedom of worship, freedom of association, and freedom to join labour unions. He argued that exercising the franchise by voting—and voting "Yes"—was another of the democratic rights they were fighting for. A "Yes" vote was imperative in order to back up those already in uniform and sustain their morale. John Queen, one of the speakers who followed, went so far as to suggest that it would be a "national calamity" if the plebiscite did not pass by an overwhelming majority.[38] As voting day approached, the newspapers expressed similar sentiments and drummed up pressure to vote correctly. The *Tribune*—and some federal cabinet ministers—equated those who might vote "No," or even fail to vote, with Quislings, while a true "Canadian will go to the polls, and make sure his friends go and he will vote 'yes.'"[39] The *Free Press*, which had earlier downplayed the need for conscription in its support for federal policy, now also urged a "Yes" vote, calling it "an opportunity for service, a proof of earnestness, a badge of honor."[40] Such pronouncements belied the freedoms MacPherson referred to, since they equated voting "No" with disloyalty. As journalist André Laurendeau reflected, "it was only the enemy or the traitor then, a Quisling, a turncoat, or a filthy collaborator ... who would dare vote anything but Yes."[41]

Canadians went to the polls on 27 April 1942. An overwhelming 80 percent voted "Yes" in English Canada, but 73 percent voted "No" in Quebec. The vote freed the government from its manpower pledges, but concern for the large opposing minority prompted King's classic obfuscation: in his interpretation, the result of the plebiscite meant "not necessarily conscription, but conscription if necessary." In Manitoba, the results of the vote showed a large affirmative majority in both the city and the province as a whole. With a voter turnout of about 70 percent, Winnipeggers voted more than seven to one in favour of releasing the federal government from its pledge not to implement conscription. Across the province, the majority was four to one. But the tally betrayed a measure of division that partially reflected the spacial grouping of ethnic minorities. The south end of the city, largely Anglo-Saxon in ethnic composition, delivered a huge affirmative vote. Two polls in North Winnipeg—home to most Ukrainians, Poles, and Germans—had a majority in the negative, the only ones in the city proper. Outside Winnipeg, the constituency of Provencher, with a large French-Canadian population, had the only "No" majority in Manitoba, though the constituencies of St. Boniface, Dauphin, Springfield, and Selkirk had large "No" minorities. Within the constituency of St. Boniface, nearly all the Transcona polls and all but one Norwood poll had large "Yes" majorities, but in the City of St. Boniface itself—with 6,922 residents of French ethnic origin and 7,005 of British origin, out of a total population of 18,157—only two polls out of ten voted "Yes." Other Franco-Manitoban communities also voted "No," including La Broquerie, Lorette, Ile des Chenes, St. Pierre, Ste. Agathe, and St. Jean. In Ste. Anne and St. Norbert, "No" votes more than doubled the number of "Yes" votes.[42]

Despite the huge majority in favour of conscription, ultra-patriots and those who believed Canada had to do more to defeat the Axis powers appear to have felt that their city's honour was impugned by the proportion of "No" votes, and some had little doubt who was to blame. A series of *Free Press* editorials blamed the "No" vote primarily on Germans and Ukrainians, though the Poles and French were also singled out. Those who voted "No," one article claimed, were "Nazis at heart" who "do not want Canada to win the war." The writer claimed that Winnipeg's Ukrainians were victims of bad leadership within their community and supposedly put their hatred for Russia above their duty to Canada: "Anybody who fights Stalin is their friend," the *Free Press* wrote. The editorial concluded that "Winnipeg has a large number of potential fifth columnists loose in the North End."[43] A follow-up editorial asked: "Who were these people who voted against releasing the Government from its pledges?" After breaking down the "No" vote by individual polls, the paper's conclusion was simplistic and inflammatory: "Wherever the people of British stock predominated the affirmative vote carried overwhelmingly, and wherever Canadians of French, German, Ukrainian and Polish origins were predominant the negative vote generally triumphed."[44] The paper was not alone in coming to this conclusion, which was echoed by a study prepared for the federal government by the Canadian Institute of Public Opinion in March 1943.[45]

Ukrainian communists, whose loyalty was legitimately suspected because of their earlier opposition to Canada's war effort, used the episode as a club to beat their Ukrainian Canadian Committee rivals. At a Walker Theatre rally on 1 May 1942, Andrew Bilecki accused Ukrainian nationalists of distributing leaflets urging people to vote "No." He suggested that the release of interned Ukrainian leaders would have made a difference in the relative proportion of votes.[46] William Kardash tried to capitalize on the suspicion aroused by the *Free Press*, labelling the Ukrainian National Federation as "openly pro-Nazi" and calling for the internment of its members.[47] Some readers agreed with the paper's assertion that the problem could be blamed on poor leadership within the ethnic communities. One resident of Magnus Avenue wrote in to reveal that a "No" campaign had been conducted in the North End, including the distribution of pamphlets urging a negative vote. Apparently, this was enough to signify that "the true patriots of this country should take steps against potential fifth columnists." Another resident was also disturbed by "the large negative vote in the Ukrainian and Polish districts," which could be attributed to "the kind of leadership which allowed Hitler to grab half of the European continent without a struggle."[48] These letters, and the *Free Press* editorials, ignored the fact that both communist and nationalist Ukrainian leaders had strongly urged their communities to vote "Yes."

Protests from other readers soon had the editorial page backpedalling. According to one letter, "in the west, as in Ontario, there has been witnessed a hysterical press campaign which made it impossible for the negative opinion to express open opposition, it dared not do so, and accordingly adopted the only remaining vehicle of expression." The writer was part of a group of six Scottish- and Irish-Canadians who all voted "No" in Norwood.[49] Another condemned the "brutal insult" that had been offered to Ukrainian Canadians and reminded readers that over 100 Ukrainians had served at Hong Kong.[50] Beatrice Brigden, a social activist and organizer for the Co-operative Commonwealth Federation in Manitoba, was "amazed and aroused ... to protest" by the tone of the editorials: "Is Canada headed for a time when it will be Verboten to differ from some self appointed authority? For what are over 300,000 Canadians fighting? Is not the very essence of democratic government, the core of the right to vote on public issues to be found in recognition of the fact that there are always two sides to a story [sic]."[51]

The Ukrainian Canadian Committee, of course, wasted no time in protesting what it regarded as spurious charges laid in the *Free Press*. They reminded the editors of both daily papers that "during the whole course of the war the Ukrainians have acted loyally, and have supported Canada's war effort by large voluntary enlistments. Imputing Nazi sympathies to them is an injustice and an insult. It has caused a great deal of resentment and is not conducive to national unity which is paramount at this critical time of war."[52] The authors of the UCC's letter, Wasyl Kushnir and J.W. Arsenych, explained the incidence of "No" votes as a result not of sympathy for Nazism or hatred of Russia, but an "intense dislike of conscription which they believed they had left behind in Europe." Voters had been instructed to vote according to their conscience, and were reminded that exercising the franchise was one of the democratic freedoms Canada was fighting for. To suggest now that anyone who voted "No" was disloyal, they argued, implied that the plebiscite had hardly been a free vote. The UNF paper *Novyi shliakh* declared that the vote was not a test of loyalty but a protest against the government's handling of the war effort, against discrimination by civil servants, and against the military's refusal to promote qualified Ukrainian servicemen to positions of authority.[53] The Ukrainian Women's Council also objected, writing that "you have done a great injustice to innocent people [and] created discords in many loyal hearts." The editorials, it said, did nothing but breed suspicion and foster intolerance.[54]

Observing the developing embarrassment of the *Free Press*, the conservative Winnipeg *Tribune* could smell blood and its editors pounced. The *Tribune* argued that Winnipeg had made a very favourable showing with its proportion of "Yes" votes, one of the highest among Canadian cities. It blamed the "No" vote largely on Manitoba's federal ministers, T.A. Crerar and J.T. Thorson, and on its rival newspaper. The *Free Press* had spread the word "for many long months ... day in and day out, that conscription was unnecessary." The *Tribune*, meanwhile, had warned its readers of "the necessity for all-out conscription and has urged the government to go to the people and frankly state the urgency of this need. We received no help from the *Free Press*—indeed, nothing but cold water, until it was too late, until the idea had been firmly fixed in many minds that conscription for overseas was unnecessary. The *Free Press* should examine its own conscience and decide whether its own editorials over a long period were not a factor in the 'No' vote."[55]

The *Free Press* ultimately conceded a partial retraction. The paper admitted that its conclusions were less than completely sound. Moreover, "the ready response of many Canadians of non-Anglo-Saxon origin to the appeals for men issued by the armed services has been among the most cheering tokens of a steadily growing solidarity among the diverse peoples that make up this country."[56] It still implied, however, that there was only one way for loyal, clear-headed Canadians to have voted. Those who voted "No" either "[refused] to face issues," failed to understand those issues, or were politically backward.[57]

The *Free Press* appeared distinctly confused on the issue. The paper's editors, Dafoe in particular, supported conscription in principle, but would not publicly come out in its favour until the federal government adopted it as policy. Until the plebiscite was announced, the paper's editorial page maintained that while the utmost war effort was desired, the government could best determine how to use Canadian manpower and the necessity for conscription to reinforce Canada's army overseas. Once the cabinet decided on the need for a free hand regarding the method of raising reinforcements, the paper became fully committed to the "Yes" campaign. After various pronouncements about the need to act in accordance with the will of the majority but cautioning against alienation of a dissenting minority,[58] it then published reactionary editorials portraying the North End as a haven for fifth columnists because a large minority voted "No." Meanwhile, on the same page containing the initial impeachment of Winnipeg's minorities, another editorial chastised the pro-conscriptionists for "declaring, against official evidence to the contrary, that immediate conscription was necessary" and for failing to recognize the national division that would result from concerted opposition to their preferred policy. The course of action urged by conscription advocates, it judged, was not in the public interest, but neither was the discord the *Free Press* had created by its skewed analysis of the plebiscite results. That analysis was inconsistent with the position the senior editors had reiterated on numerous occasions and certainly contributed nothing to national unity or to a resolution of the conscription issue.[59]

In the plebiscite's aftermath, the *Tribune* initially took a moderate position in the ongoing debate. It urged the abandonment of inflammatory terms like "conscript," which could only harm the morale of those called up. The NRMA men, like active service volunteers, were soldiers who would be glad to serve as long as the measure of sacrifice was equally shared. About one-third of all men called under the NRMA between 1941 and 1944, in fact, "went active," though many were subject to considerable pressure to do so. "The greatest lesson of the war in Canada," the *Tribune* professed, was the people's willingness "to respond to every strong measure." Even with compulsory service, it argued with a touch of sophistry, "Canada is still going to be a nation of cheerful volunteers."[60]

This argument was predicated on the belief that the adoption of compulsory service for overseas would be immediately carried out, now that the plebiscite was settled and the government had received what pro-conscriptionists considered a clear mandate. But although the government moved to amend the National Resources Mobilization Act without delay, the cabinet was split between those like King who wanted to return to Parliament for approval before any NRMA men were actually sent overseas, and those like J.L. Ralston and Angus Macdonald who felt that further debate would render the plebiscite worthless.[61] After a full month had passed without action, the *Tribune* blasted Ottawa's dithering. It clearly felt that Canadians had been "promised [an] all-out manpower program of which conscription for overseas would be just a part." Instead, the "Canadian Appeasers," the cabinet faction led by King, wanted to use the "weasel method" of requiring yet another new bill—even after the NRMA was amended—authorizing conscription whenever it was finally deemed necessary. To the *Tribune*, this was a time-wasting redundancy that would merely serve to prolong the nation's division over the debate. Despite the plebiscite result, the government still "has no intention of introducing conscription for overseas in the near future, if at all." While Britain had just marked the thousandth day of "the bloodiest war of all history," three years which had seen "the fall of Poland, Norway, France, Greece, Hong Kong, Malaya, Singapore and Java," Canada continued to wait.[62]

The pro-conscriptionist position represented by the *Tribune* expected the government to fully rationalize its direction of Canada's human resources in order to truly move to a total war footing. Advocates called for an end to the "home defence" restrictions on conscription as well as "manpower selection," the direction of workers into those forms of employment with greatest benefit to the war effort. They remained unsatisfied with the government's persistent efforts to wage war on a limited liability basis even after what they considered a resounding verdict in the plebiscite, and frustration mounted as the months passed without the total mobilization they expected. In a March 1943 editorial, the *Tribune* condemned Ottawa's "political cowardice" in continuing to hold the NRMA men in North America. Instead of sending them to places like

Jamaica and Newfoundland to relieve active service troops for duty in Europe, the government should use the "Zombies" wherever they were needed.[63] As the argument went, this limitation on service required additional volunteers to fill out the army overseas, which bled the farms of agricultural workers and industry of skilled labour. Ottawa's refusal to send the "Zombies" overseas thus contributed to a manpower crisis that was made worse when the situation in Europe escalated in the summer and fall of 1944.

As Canadian troops grappled with the Germans in Normandy and Italy, the *Tribune* attacked Mackenzie King's manpower policy with increasing vehemence.[64] The *Free Press* continued to defend the government, quoting J.L. Ralston's explanation that casualties overseas had been lower than expected, the reinforcement pool was up to strength, and there were 50,000 active service men in Canada waiting to go over.[65] It thus appeared that recruiting was yielding an adequate supply of men. The *Tribune* remained unsatisfied with the justification of the government's "puppet press" and decried the "essential injustice of the failure to apply conscription. Put baldly, it means killing off our finest Canadians ... while pampering and carefully preserving these young men who are unwilling to sacrifice their lives for Canada."[66]

The bitterness informing the war of words between Winnipeg's two major dailies over the need for conscription also permeated the general population and the army itself. There were a number of violent clashes involving substantial numbers of volunteers and conscripts at training centres in Calgary and Petawawa in July 1944, and Shilo on 18 September. The Shilo altercation occurred when, according to the *Tribune*, general servicemen became "enraged that they had to live in the close proximity of hundreds of men in the same uniform as they, but unwilling to fight for Canada." Using a "score of manly fists," the volunteers "put on a demonstration to the N.R.M.A. personnel" in objection to the latter's "lack of proper principles."[67] Such clashes were sometimes spurred by taunts to "go active," and on occasion, even members of the Canadian Women's Army Corps (CWAC) got into it. A witness to the riot at Shilo observed that "some of the C.W.A.C.'s cause a lot of the trouble.... [A] C.W.A.C. will yell at an N.R.M.A.: 'Zombie! Yah, Zombie! Why don't you join up?'" Another riot was sparked in Fort Frances, Ontario in early December, when high school students and air cadets similarly harassed NRMA men in a café.[68]

Throughout the autumn of 1944, the *Tribune* continued to hammer away on its editorial page at "the Zombie disgrace" and "the unfair, wasteful and cowardly methods of handling our priceless manpower."[69] The paper intensified its attacks after Major Conn Smythe returned from France and declared that the army was sending inadequately trained men into combat. Reports soon began to arrive of artillerymen, engineers, and other specialist troops being remustered to meet the shortage of trained infantry reinforcements.[70] Ralston visited Canadian troops in Europe to investigate these reports, and he returned home committed to sending the NRMA men overseas in order to bring combat units up to strength. Instead, a recalcitrant King forced his resignation. When Ralston's successor as Minister of National Defence, former army commander A.G.L. McNaughton, proved unable to persuade the Zombies to volunteer, King finally bowed to the inevitable and ordered 16,000 conscripts overseas on 23 November.

The *Tribune* nevertheless continued to heap scorn on King and McNaughton for their new policy of "converting" the Zombies into volunteers "by the simple process of telling them that they are going overseas and that they might as well give the nod," a procedure it called "compulsory volunteering."[71] Once the conscription issue was finally settled, the *Tribune*'s editor, John Bird, assessed the episode in these terms: "What is so hurtful is that we had to go through this filthy political mill" in order to fulfill the government's basic duty to provide adequate reinforcements for the troops overseas. "That is why the country is so angry. It does not like the taste of politics where Canadian lives are at stake."[72]

The conscription crises of 1942 and 1944 showed little evidence of the "studious moderation" Dafoe had advised in 1941. Instead, they revealed a jingoistic constituency of opinion ready to frame a public debate in such terms that dissenters appeared disloyal. They also exposed the limitations of the public consensus behind Canada's participation in the war. Canadian unity could only be undermined by the majority's willingness to ignore opposing points of view, whether through blunt "majority rules" arguments, by pointing the finger at ethnic minorities, or by efforts to make life so uncomfortable for prospective soldiers that they felt compelled to volunteer. Mackenzie King understood the need to retain the consent of the minority if the country were to be governed and its war effort made effective. The *Free Press* did too, for the most part, though its inconsistency in analyzing the plebiscite results alienated many who refused to accept the erosion of their freedom to disagree.

Table 2.1. Conscription Plebiscite Results, 27 April 1942

Constituency	"Yes" Votes	"No" Votes
Winnipeg (total)	108,252	15,026
North Winnipeg	24,205	6,987
Winnipeg North Centre	24,071	3,482
Winnipeg South Centre	34,221	2,412
South Winnipeg	25,755	2,145
St. Boniface*	8,086	5,627

Source: Winnipeg *Tribune*, 30 April and 26 June 1942.
* Included Transcona, Norwood, Springfield, Ste. Anne, and St. Norbert.

Japanese Canadians

No other theme in Canada's Second World War history reveals a greater contradiction of the principles the Allies purported to stand for than the forced evacuation of Japanese Canadians from the west coast in 1942. In a move motivated by long-standing anti-Japanese sentiment and the same sort of fifth-column hysteria that prompted earlier round-ups of Germans and Italians, the federal government dispossessed 22,000 residents of Japanese origin—13,000 of whom were Canadian-born or naturalized—and sent them to resettlement camps in the British Columbia interior or work projects in Alberta, Manitoba, and Ontario. Some local residents protested settlement of evacuees in their communities, and Japanese Canadians continued to endure discrimination and racial animosity in their new homes. The story of the government's acquiescence to popular demands for the evacuation has been thoroughly investigated elsewhere.[73] Most accounts rightly emphasize the injustice of the decision to rescind the civil rights of an entire community for reasons which bore an uncomfortable resemblance to the treatment of Jews in Hitler's Germany.[74] In order to fully understand the local repercussions of these events, we must consider the reception accorded Japanese evacuees who came to Manitoba within the context of the Hong Kong debacle, a tragedy for countless families in the host society that influenced the way they received the newcomers.

The residents of Winnipeg and southern Manitoba were intimately connected to the battle for the British colony of Hong Kong. One of the two Canadian infantry battalions sent to reinforce the colony's defences in the autumn of 1941, in response to a British request, was the Winnipeg Grenadiers.

The regiment's 1st Battalion had been mobilized as a machine-gun unit in September 1939, but it converted to a rifle battalion after it was posted to Bermuda and Jamaica for garrison duty in May 1940. The battalion returned to Winnipeg in September 1941 before leaving for Hong Kong, via Vancouver, on 27 October. The Canadian force, which also included Quebec's Royal Rifles of Canada, arrived on 16 November. It was not fit for combat because its state of training was incomplete, but British military intelligence—and therefore the Canadian army's general staff, which did not perform an independent analysis—did not consider war with Japan to be imminent. By sending the Canadian brigade to augment Hong Kong's garrison, the respective governments hoped to deter Japanese aggression. Brigadier J.K. Lawson, the force commander, therefore did not expect to have to fight, and intended to bring his men up to standard following their arrival in Hong Kong. The Canadian force would have three weeks to carry out further training before the Japanese attack on the morning of 8 December, though it was to little avail. The island was admittedly indefensible without further reinforcement, which became impossible given the control of the western Pacific that Japan won by its surprise attack on the United States Navy at Pearl Harbor and its sinking of the British capital ships *Prince of Wales* and *Repulse* a few days later. Still, Hong Kong's defenders held out for 17 days before surrendering to superior Japanese forces on Christmas Day, 1941. The two Canadian battalions lost 290 killed during the battle, including a number who were butchered by their captors after surrendering. Nearly 500 more had been wounded, while 267 later succumbed to the brutal conditions in Japanese prisoner of war camps and died in captivity.[75]

The fall of Hong Kong meant disaster for a thousand Manitoba families and a joyless Christmas. As the battle's end drew near, the *Tribune* reported that "grievous news from Hong Kong lies heavily upon all Manitoba." Once news of the surrender broke, the newspaper honoured the members of the battalion along with their wives and families, who now faced "almost unbearable grief and anxiety as their men faced death."[76] A feature in *Maclean's* magazine described the atmosphere:

> This province has learned the meaning of tragic suspense. It started when Hong Kong was besieged. Everybody seemed to know someone in the Winnipeg Grenadiers, and all Canada knew that the Grenadiers were in Hong Kong along with the Royal Rifles from Quebec. When Hong Kong surrendered the tensions increased.

Soldiers' relatives started at every step on the porch, every telephone ring. Rumors flashed everywhere. One, that the casualty lists were being delayed so homes wouldn't be saddened at Christmas. Another, that the newspapers already had the lists. A third, that some relatives had already been notified.[77]

Casualty lists were not available but the numbers were expected to be high. The newspapers reassured relatives that they would be notified as soon as the government received word. In late December, both Canada and the United States informed the Japanese government that Japanese prisoners of war would be treated humanely, in accordance with the 1929 Geneva Convention, even though Japan had not signed it. Citing officials in Ottawa, the *Tribune* speculated that the Japanese government would reciprocate. No doubt the paper hoped to encourage the next-of-kin and allay their fears.[78]

Winnipeggers mourned, but they were also determined to rebuild the battalion and continue the fight. As members of the regiment's reserve battalion offered to go active to fill the gap left in the army's order of battle, the government announced that the 1st Battalion would be reconstituted and recruiting began immediately.[79] When British Foreign Secretary Anthony Eden later announced that the Japanese had bound and bayoneted fifty members of the Hong Kong garrison and raped and murdered captured nurses, Lieutenant-Colonel J.N. Semmens, the new battalion's commander, said the news would "act like a wild tornado to fan the flame of anger that burns within us now.... That anger is not alone aimed at the Japanese but at anything that impedes or hampers the all-out effort of this country.... To the Winnipeg Grenadiers it means grim preparedness."[80] In May 1945, Lieutenant-Colonel E.S. Russenholt, commander of the Grenadiers' reserve unit, requested that a battalion from the regiment be included in any Canadian force put together to fight in the Pacific theatre, since it had a score to settle with the Japanese. After Japan's surrender, the reserve battalion "volunteered, almost to a man," for the occupation force, though they were to be disappointed as most reserve members were unfit for active duty.[81]

Japanese atrocities had fuelled this desire for revenge. In mid-February 1942, the *Tribune* reported charges that the Hong Kong prisoners were being mistreated, based on reports from a missionary in Chungking claiming that they were denied food, water, and sanitary facilities. Three days earlier, the Japanese government had announced it would observe the Geneva convention and feed and clothe prisoners fairly. Preparations commenced in

Canada to ship relief supplies to the prisoners in Hong Kong, and one of the five Canadian Red Cross parcel-packing plants opened in Winnipeg for this purpose in late 1942. The prisoners in Hong Kong did occasionally receive Red Cross food parcels, but the Japanese would not accept such shipments with any regularity so most of the Winnipeg parcels ultimately went to Europe.[82] One member of the Winnipeg Grenadiers later wrote of the value of those parcels that made it through:

> I feel incompetent to express the gratitude that is ours towards the ... Red Cross.... We are more than conversant with the difficulties presented by the indifference of the Japanese. The much needed food and gifts were certainly welcome. Although they were not always available it was not the fault of the Red Cross, but the attitude of the Japanese. It can be truthfully said, however, that what we did receive, came at the most critical period of our incarceration. Hope was revived and many who might easily have gone under were saved by the foods that were sent in to us.... Sufficient to say, that those of us who were spared to return, will never forget the good work of these messengers of God.[83]

Besides blocking the shipments of Red Cross parcels, the Japanese refused to release complete lists of the prisoners of war they held. They also delayed the transmission of mail: one shipment of letters written in the summer of 1942 did not arrive in Canada until September 1943. The wife of one Grenadier, Sergeant Robert Manchester, received word that he was alive in a camp near Tokyo only in mid-October 1943, almost two years after he was captured. She had received no definite word of his condition since the fall of Hong Kong.[84] Inspection reports of prisoner of war camps by the International Red Cross and neutral powers—Argentina, for Canadian prisoners, or Switzerland, for the British—typically did not say much except that the treatment of prisoners was improving. Other reports indicated that the Japanese had executed Allied prisoners, and it became widely known later in the war that the Japanese also tortured and worked them to death on projects like the Thai-Burma railway. In January 1944, Anthony Eden told the British House of Commons that thousands of British troops had died as prisoners of the Japanese while being forced to perform slave labour and live without adequate shelter, food, clothing, or medical attention.[85] Eden warned Japan that Britain would not forget the atrocities perpetrated against these prisoners; neither would Canada, whose servicemen had endured the same mistreatment.

Canadians of Japanese ethnic origin were hardly responsible for the fate of Hong Kong's defenders. The people who agitated for the forced evacuation of British Columbia's coast did not distinguish between the Japanese in Asia and those in Canada, however, regardless of naturalization or even Canadian birth. Animosity towards British Columbia's Japanese minority was the product of a long-standing racial cleavage that dated back to the mid-nineteenth century. It sprang from the white majority's xenophobic reaction to cultural differences, economic competition, and a perceived inability to assimilate the Japanese into Canadian society. Hostility flared up in the late 1930s in response to Japanese aggression in China and fears that the west coast would be vulnerable to attack in case of war with Japan.[86] Prejudice fuelled additional fears about potential Japanese fifth columnists after Canada's declaration of war on 7 December 1941.

Repression of the Japanese minority proceeded in stages. The federal government immediately interned a handful of enemy nationals and seized all Japanese fishing vessels, which deprived many of their livelihood. A curfew was imposed. Cameras, firearms, and automobiles were seized. Radios, liquor sales, and long-distance telephone calls were prohibited. In mid-January, Ottawa announced that all enemy aliens would be removed from as-yet undefined protected areas of British Columbia. None of these measures satisfied an increasingly shrill public demand for the complete removal of all persons of Japanese origin, to which the prime minister finally bowed on 24 February 1942 in ordering their evacuation from the coastal region to temporary settlements in the interior.[87] No distinction was made between Japanese nationals, naturalized immigrants, and Canadian-born *Nisei*, which meant that the citizenship rights of the latter groups were effectively negated. The British Columbia Security Commission (BCSC) was subsequently established to direct the relocation and exercise responsibility for the evacuees. Evacuees were permitted to carry possessions to a maximum of 150 pounds per adult and seventy-five pounds per child—everything else had to be stored, sold, or given away. Orders-in-council authorized the government to turn their belongings over to the Custodian of Enemy Property for disposal, as it had done with property seized from the Ukrainian Labour Farmer Temple Association. Various historians of the evacuation have professed the community's innocence and desire to demonstrate its loyalty.[88] According to Peter Ward, the RCMP concluded that the Japanese population posed no threat, though J.L. Granatstein and Gregory Johnson have questioned the competence of the

RCMP's intelligence service.[89] In any case, the Japanese were forcibly removed from the coast, despite the lack of any solid evidence to the contrary.

Since economic opportunities were limited in the interior settlements and the cost to maintain evacuees was offset by liquidation of their assets by the Custodian of Enemy Property, many families elected to relocate to Alberta, Manitoba, and Ontario for agricultural work. Some single men went to join road-work camps, and others left their families to do so. The cooperation of Manitoba's government was requested in the winter of 1942 in relation to two work projects. One proposal sought to employ 500 "Japanese nationals" on road building between Flin Flon and The Pas. They would be closely guarded, or so Premier Bracken understood, and would be moved away as soon as work was completed. Bracken's cabinet was "not enthusiastic about the proposal," he told T.A. Crerar, federal Minister of Mines and Resources, but "we feel it is our duty to assist the Government" with necessary war measures, and so would offer no objection.[90] Popular sentiment in The Pas did not welcome the Japanese and the Board of Trade spoke for the community in expressing the preference that they should not be permitted to settle there. Opposition also came from the Hudson Bay Mining and Smelting Company, whose officers were concerned about sabotage to the vulnerable wooden trestles on the Flin Flon railway. The project was ultimately rejected, to the disappointment of the people living in those communities who regretted the loss of the road.[91] Bowing to anti-Japanese sentiment in Manitoba, Bracken's public position on the project had been to stress that the province had not requested the use of Japanese labour but had been asked to cooperate as a war measure, and he made it clear that the costs would be borne by Ottawa.[92]

Bracken adopted a similar line regarding the Department of Labour's request to permit the movement of as many as 500 Japanese families to work on sugar beet farms. He reiterated his willingness to cooperate, again providing that Ottawa assumed full responsibility for costs and protection against sabotage, and agreed to remove them once the need subsided.[93] The project went ahead, with the BCSC offering strict terms to pacify any local opposition to the influx of Japanese: it undertook to send only agricultural labourers, to be responsible for their transportation, medical needs, and financial support in cases where they could not meet their expenses, to provide any necessary security, to restrict their movement within the province, and to remove them after the war. Most of the evacuees who came to the province would work for independent farmers, though almost 200 were employed by the Manitoba

Sugar Company. According to one account, the Security Commission gave the Manitoba Beet Growers Association a curious guarantee that any evacuees moved to the province would remain on the farms to which they were assigned, in essence forming a pool of captive labour. The guarantee does not appear to have been upheld, nor was it offered to the Manitoba Sugar Company.[94]

Before the West Coast evacuees arrived, the Japanese population of Manitoba was minuscule. It numbered less than twenty people the day after Canada joined the Pacific war, including seven "red caps"—porters working for the Canadian National Railway—a technician in the Canadian Army Dental Corps, an elevator operator at the Royal Alexandra Hotel, a tailor, a lamp shade manufacturer, their wives and children. One red cap, Mr. K. Himuro, called December 7th "the most unhappy day in his life." He had volunteered in Regina during the Great War but was medically unfit. He had lived in Winnipeg since 1921, and proclaimed that "Canada is my home now.... I want to do anything to help win—I'll work in a munitions factory, or anywhere else ... the government wants me to work."[95] Such patriotism did not stop the railway from immediately firing all of its Japanese red caps.[96] Alice Nakauchi was five years old when she came to Winnipeg from Moose Jaw in the late 1920s, and nineteen when the war started. She recalled no harsh treatment after Hong Kong, even from people who had relatives there. She expected difficulty later, when the veterans returned, but remembered meeting some on a street car who were friendly and tried to speak Japanese with her.[97]

Experiences of discrimination varied, some feeling it keenly while others were largely unaffected. None could escape being identified with a visible minority group obviously distrusted by other Canadians, since the government had required them to submit to registration regardless of their citizenship. There were other, more personal, reminders. Sadako Mizobuchi had immigrated to Vancouver in 1937 and was living in Winnipeg with her husband by 1941. Both went to work in a Jewish nursing home in Middlechurch, where they were boarded. Living conditions and food were relatively poor, prompting her husband to see the manager, who asked, "what are you complaining about? You are an enemy alien."[98]

Farmers who employed evacuee beet workers were to provide suitable furnished housing with garden plots, clean water, and payment at market rates. Newspaper advertisements stressed that farmers accepting Japanese workers would not only be easing their own labour shortage but also assisting with the resolution of the evacuation problem in British Columbia; thus, they would be supporting the war effort.[99] As Peter Nunoda concluded in his study of the Japanese-Canadian community, the project was "both ill-conceived and incompetently administered."[100] Farmers were led to believe that the workers they accepted would be thoroughly experienced agriculturalists, but in many cases they were either fishermen or had only peripheral experience. Harold Hirose, who brought his family to Manitoba, had been an accountant for the Surrey Berry Growers Association.

The first group of evacuees—twenty families comprising 118 people—arrived in Winnipeg on 13 April 1942 and were initially billeted in the Canadian Pacific Railway's immigration hall. A group of workers from the Young Women's Christian Association met evacuees at the train station to welcome and help them upon arrival. By the end of the month, there were hundreds of new arrivals to join those still awaiting placement. The last group had arrived at the beginning of June, swelling the total number to over 1,000.[101] Conditions in the immigration hall were primitive by today's standards, but perhaps not unlike those in armed forces training facilities. The floors were sex-segregated, so families were split, with little privacy. Inhabitants were subject to curfew and slept on bunk beds furnished with one blanket and one sheet, not quite warm enough for Winnipeg in the early spring. They queued up to use the single bathroom at the end of each floor and to receive their meals. Ken Nishibata, as an adventurous eleven-year-old, learned to eat unfamiliar "Canadian" food like macaroni and cheese, and enjoyed sneaking out of the hall on trips to Eaton's department store.[102]

Evacuees remained at the immigration hall until selected by host farmers. Those with little children had a difficult time finding a placement; farmers passed them over because children could not work. Some were lucky in this human lottery, finding new homes with decent living and working conditions. Many were not. Akira Sato's family was placed in Headingley, where the people were friendly and made them welcome at church. But his mother became ill after the first season and could not work, so the family sought permission to move to Winnipeg to find other employment. The city was officially off-limits to evacuees, who had to secure permission to travel there, even for such basic necessities as doctor's appointments. Ken Nishibata wound up in Emerson, where the teachers were "really nice" to him and the farmers treated them well.[103]

Kanaye (Connie) Matsuo's family was not so lucky. After two days at the immigration hall, they were placed near Lockport, where three couples and two children shared an uninsulated sugar beet house measuring about twenty by twenty-four feet. They had to draw water from the Red River and boil it for the first month, until they got access to a well. Despite the stipulation requiring fresh water supplies, this was not an isolated example among beet workers. A few other families were placed in nearby St. Andrews, and they met concerted hostility from local residents. Some of the Winnipeg Grenadiers had come from the area, and emotions ran high in the aftermath of the Hong Kong disaster. Residents complained to municipal officials and the BCSC, ostensibly because of their proximity to several "major war industries" and a school. The St. Andrews municipal council protested the location of Japanese families "anywhere within the municipality," and 102 area residents petitioned Manitoba's BCSC representative to this effect.[104] Matsuo and the others remained in the area for about a month; as she later recalled, "that month was a nightmare."[105] The few families that had been placed in the area were relocated, and Matsuo moved to Fannystelle, where the farmer was friendly.

Work on the sugar beet farms was a hard way to make a living, and many families could not earn enough to support themselves. The problem was recognized by BCSC officials but neither they, nor officials in the provincial Public Works department responsible for administering relief to evacuees with insufficient income, showed much sympathy. The BCSC's Manitoba representative admitted, in correspondence with one Public Works official, that government policy was largely responsible for evacuees' necessitous circumstances. It could have been concluded from the tone of the letter that the beet workers merited more favourable consideration than other "destitute people," since "many of them are confined to beet areas where there is insufficient remuneration to sustain their families." Moreover, the commission restricted their ability to move in search of better arrangements, "in order to keep harmonious relations with the various municipalities."[106] Yet the BCSC's local Welfare Officer, the government's liaison with individual Japanese experiencing difficulty, exhibited evident distaste and a profound lack of empathy with his charges.

Public Works officials kept case files on those applying for relief. A fair proportion of the evacuees who came to Manitoba—eighty-nine in all—required some relief. Some were single men but most were families with children. The pattern that developed usually saw recipients go on relief in the spring after their earnings from the previous season ran out; most of the payments were for food during the months before beet wages started to come in. Many of the relief applicants had been fruit farmers, and more than a few were over fifty years of age. Sugar beet harvesting must have been very hard work for older people unused to what one man called "back-breaking" labour, yet even those families where the adults were younger or had children old enough to help with chores could not succeed, like one forty-four-year-old carpenter, his thirty-four-year-old wife, and their three children aged thirteen, twelve, and seven years. This family had owned a house and fifty-three acres in British Columbia, where they worked as market gardeners. In Manitoba, they depended on a parsimonious government for their maintenance.[107]

Many of the beet workers were not the experienced agriculturalists the BCSC had advertised, and many of them were scarcely equipped for the work. Relief recipients in the spring of 1943 included a fifty-nine-year-old widow with gall stones and her sixteen-year-old daughter. A fifty-nine-year-old man, whose family was in Japan, was hampered by the loss of the thumb and two fingers from his right hand. In another family, the fifty-eight-year-old husband was unable to do hard work due to rheumatism. His wife, age forty-eight, was also ill, and his adult son was blind. It was a very long, lonely war for an elderly man of sixty-nine years who had not been naturalized and whose wife remained in Japan. He worked seven to eight acres for Manitoba Sugar in an area where the nearest other Japanese person was fourteen miles away.[108]

Comments written by responsible officials show that the relief assistance they provided was inadequate and grudgingly given. One father on relief, who had to spend ten dollars to take his two sons to Winnipeg for dental treatment, "was advised not to make any more trips to Winnipeg, and use his money for food only." The anonymous writer of one case memo balked at issuing a grocery order "which apparently is intended to re-imburse this jap [sic]." The man in question had incurred unbudgeted expenses in moving his family to Winnipeg. Relief for another family with four children under the age of six amounted to $35.88 per month.[109] According to Leonard Marsh's landmark *Report on Social Security for Canada*, the minimum food budget necessary for subsistence in a family of five averaged $43.20 per month in urban conditions in 1941.[110] Lower costs may have been seen in the rural setting, particularly if the family had a garden plot; but the discrepancy remains significant since this family was larger than average and there were undoubtedly additional budgetary requirements for clothing and sundries. Still, relief officials considered them a "problem family" because the husband owed for medical bills in British Columbia prior to evacuation, and the BCSC had to pay for further medical expenses related to the wife's pregnancy and other family illnesses since arrival in Manitoba. In the assessor's opinion, the husband was "none too anxious to support his family."[111]

The BCSC Welfare Officer described another family head, whose wife was hospitalized, as "a very thriftless person. Were it not for the fact that three young children are concerned, we would have been inclined to have them do without relief for another month or so." The officer had concluded some months earlier that this family's debt problems resulted from a simple failure to live within the relief allowance. He apparently believed that other families made do and so should this one, in spite of the hardships imposed by the wife's illness. Some of the farmers who supervised the beet workers were even less charitable. One farmer in the Emerson area told the BCSC that "he was averse to granting relief to any Japanese families." Another expressed the same objection, since he believed that granting relief would "have a demoralizing effect on the Japanese ... and would tend to undermine the farmers [sic] authority over them."[112]

Evacuees who were unwilling to accept their powerless position without speaking up for themselves were seen as troublemakers. A report on one family's situation stated that the man in question had refused to sign the beet contract with his host farmer until he was assured of continued support for his wife and four children. The man asserted that his earnings as a single worker would not be enough to provide for them, and that "relief would have to be granted them while he supported himself on his earnings. We pointed out that his wife and children were his responsibility, not that of the Commission." Another man was judged a "smart aleck" who "has all the answers" and would likely be found at the bottom of any trouble arising in his district, because he argued that the relief food allowance was inadequate and questioned the provisions for medical expenses.[113]

Some evacuees sought improvement in a change of scene or employment. A group of evacuees, led by Harold Hirose and Shinji Sato, formed the Manitoba Japanese Joint Council to represent the interests of beet workers to the BCSC. They hoped to secure better work and housing conditions, and access to alternative employment. Men could get off-season work in bush camps or peat farms, but employment in Winnipeg was not initially permitted.[114]

Winnipeg City Council restricted employment of Japanese evacuees for fear of sparking a drop in wage levels, and an October 1942 bylaw prevented them from accepting work for less than forty-five cents an hour at a time when the minimum wage was only about twenty-five cents. It was not until July 1943 that the bar against residence in the city was lifted in response to a general labour shortage.[115] Many of the evacuees would relocate to the city with the BCSC's permission, though conditions did not always improve greatly. Connie Matsuo's family could not make enough money to survive in Fannystelle without using up their savings, so they went to work for a St. Vital market gardener who treated them like slaves.[116] As an accountant, Harold Hirose had secured early permission to settle in Winnipeg, but there were few office jobs for Japanese and he was refused work as a taxi driver since there would be contact with clients. He was forced to take a job as a dishwasher at the nursing home in Middlechurch for thirty-five dollars a month with room and board, while his wife earned thirty dollars making beds. Most of the other employees were also Japanese, including a number of former railway red caps.[117]

Hirose's difficulties were common and most jobs remained closed to the Japanese. The work available was often hard, dirty, and undesirable, at places like Dominion Tanners or the abattoirs, though these were preferable to beet work. They gradually entered a number of manufacturing companies, some of whom had military contracts. Hirose was eventually hired as an auditor at bus maker Western Flyer, and he recruited a number of others to join him. Some of the women were able to find work in the needle trades with Winnipeg garment factories.[118] A number of girls had also been permitted to enter the city at an early date for placement with Winnipeg homes as domestic help, in return for room and board while they attended school. Nobu Sato recalled her time as a "schoolgirl": "It wasn't an easy life. You had to get up early and get everything done before you went to school." She helped look after two little boys and fixed meals, attending to her studies in the evenings. She was well received by the host family and at Kelvin High, where she was the only Japanese girl.[119] Others attended the University of Manitoba, which accepted eight Japanese students in the 1942–43 term, the only Canadian university to do so. At the request of the Department of Labour, the YWCA assumed responsibility for screening domestic placements to ensure the schoolgirls' welfare, and the "Y" also became a meeting place for the city's young Japanese.[120]

Evacuation from British Columbia did not put an end to the racism that confronted most Japanese Canadians, and it imposed both emotional and practical difficulties. Many people and some patriotic organizations were hostile to their presence. The May 1942 Canadian Legion convention at Winnipeg's Royal Alexandra Hotel unanimously urged Ottawa "to send all people in Canada of Japanese race back to Japan after the war," and to ensure "that no peace treaty should be entered into with Japan without the provision for such repatriation."[121] The Manitoba Chapter of the Imperial Order Daughters of the Empire (IODE) wrote to Errick Willis, the provincial Minister of Public Works, arguing against permitting any Japanese to "enter any business, or fill any position," since all jobs would be needed once Canadian servicemen started to return home. They later declared their opposition to allowing the Japanese to hire or drive taxis in Winnipeg, along with their support for both a 9:00 p.m. curfew and post-war "repatriation" to Japan.[122] The Winnipeg and District Trades and Labour Council opposed the importation of Japanese labourers from British Columbia to Manitoba's towns and farms as a "cheap labor [sic] scheme." One member "contended that the Japs constituted as great a menace here and that the proper place for them was the internment camp."[123] St. Boniface City Council sent a resolution to the BCSC registering its opposition to any Japanese settlement there.[124]

The most pressing needs when moving into the city were finding employment and accommodation. Finding anything other than the least desirable jobs was complicated by racism, as Hirose learned. And while securing housing in Winnipeg was difficult for everyone because of the shortage (discussed in Chapter 5), it was even harder for the Japanese. Hirose tried to rent one suite from a landlady whose other tenants threatened to leave if she took him in. Connie Matsuo recalled walking for miles in search of a vacancy. Shizuko Miki found that houses with "to rent" signs were not available to her family. Tom Mitani and his wife were advised to tell prospective landlords that they were Chinese. Some were refused by people who advertised a vacancy but then claimed that their premises were already rented and they had forgotten to remove the sign. Because of the discrimination they had experienced in British Columbia, Hirose recalled, the Japanese moving into Winnipeg were advised to spread out and avoid settling in the same area. But it was obviously difficult when choices were so limited. By October 1944, there were 230 evacuees living in Winnipeg, but with the housing shortage and the increasing return of veterans, the Department of Labour's Japanese Division, which had succeeded the BCSC in February 1943, once again closed the city to Japanese migration.[125]

The department's policy at this time was to disperse the Japanese throughout the country, and it established placement centres in a number of cities that worked closely with the National Selective Service to assist evacuees in finding acceptable work. Some agreed that dispersal would be a favourable solution to the racial animosity they had experienced. Yet evacuees remained under the control of the department's Japanese Division, required permission to travel within Manitoba or across provincial boundaries, were not permitted to buy land, and were ineligible to vote. Despite the federal government's preference for eastern settlement, it would not give any guarantees about the freedom of evacuees to settle anywhere permanently until after the war.[126] The Japanese were thus constrained from exercising so many of their basic rights that a sizeable proportion would consider the drastic step of emigration to Japan, a country many of them had never seen.

The prime minister had stated his government's policy regarding Japanese settlement on 4 August 1944 in the House of Commons. It had four principles: concentration of Japanese in British Columbia would not be permitted; disloyal individuals would be deported; there would be no immigration in the early post-war period; and finally, those loyal Japanese-Canadian citizens who remained would be justly and fairly treated. Individual Japanese Canadians would be called before a judicial committee created for the purpose of determining their loyalty. This further humiliation could be avoided by those who "voluntarily applied to return to Japan." The government called it "repatriation."[127] In the spring of 1945, the evacuees were required to signify their intentions regarding repatriation on questionnaires administered by the RCMP. It was supposed to be an impartial process, with no pressure applied to secure a preferred result. There was, nonetheless, a certain measure of coercion, though at least one family in Manitoba was advised by a sympathetic RCMP officer not to choose repatriation because Japan was being devastated by Allied bombing.[128]

Japanese Canadians faced a difficult choice. Those who planned to stay in Canada knew they were expected to resettle east of the Rockies. Failure to comply, some suggested, might be seen as evidence of disloyalty. For those who remained in British Columbia's interior settlements, moving east would be a gamble at best. Financial security had evaporated with the evacuation and it was uncertain where they might be permitted to live and work. In Greater Winnipeg, groups like the IODE and the Civilian Committee for Rehabilitation of Veterans demanded the termination of all Japanese employees to free up jobs for returned men. Others, like Transcona's town council, wanted all people of Japanese origin removed from the country. Pressured by the government, confronted by often hostile public opinion, and no doubt frustrated by the prevalence of racism in wartime Canada, it is not surprising that many Japanese signed for repatriation. By August 1945, over 10,000 Japanese—representing more than 43 percent of their population in Canada—had requested to leave the country. In Manitoba, 405 made the same decision.[129]

As the war's end approached and peace returned, the tide of repression began to recede. Perhaps this was due to the revelation of the full horrors of the Nazi regime and widespread revulsion against its doctrine of racial hierarchy. It simply may be that, as the tension caused by a war of such magnitude finally began to ease, Canadians stopped to reflect on the values they professed to stand for. Opposition to proposed legislation that would have disfranchised anyone whose forebears originated in a country at war with Canada had developed in the summer of 1944, and it was magnified in 1945. Protests against Ottawa's plans to deport and revoke the citizenship of Japanese Canadians came from groups like the Co-operative Commonwealth Federation, the Canadian Welfare Council, the Toronto-based Cooperative Committee on Japanese Canadians (CCJC) and its branches across the country, the United Church, the Church of England, the Young Men's and Young Women's Christian Associations, Winnipeg's Civil Liberties Association, the Winnipeg *Free Press* and the *Tribune*. The CCJC, for example, was committed to the repeal of the orders-in-council which conferred Ottawa's authority to deport and revoke the citizenship of the Japanese Canadians. It included many of the same people who had spoken out on civil liberties issues throughout the war, such as *Saturday Night* editor B.K. Sandwell in Toronto or, in Winnipeg, maverick politician Lewis St. G. Stubbs and Monarch Life Assurance president Edgar Tarr.[130]

Meanwhile, the United Church mounted a grassroots letter-writing campaign that bombarded Manitoba Premier Stuart Garson with resolutions urging the removal of any legal or economic barriers to settlement in Manitoba and protesting involuntary deportation or exclusion of Japanese residents from any province in Canada.[131] The Reston branch of the church's Women's Missionary Society wrote Garson to articulate what it saw as a fundamental issue for "Canadian democracy at home and our reputation abroad. Democracy is not a reality in any country where it is denied to some of its citizens. Either we have it or we are all in danger of losing it."[132] Even the IODE and some Canadian Legion branches had come to believe "that Canada's signature to the Atlantic charter, which pledged itself to abolish racial discrimination, should mean something, that our professions of democracy [and] ... our naturalization laws should mean something."[133]

Manitoba's premier was unwilling to take a stand based on strong principles in this context of amorphous public opinion. When University of Manitoba historian W.L. Morton suggested that the Government of Manitoba take a lead against Ottawa's repatriation plans and declare that it had "no objection to any loyal Japanese Canadian residing within its jurisdiction," Garson was non-committal. Since any conclusive move to deport the Japanese awaited establishment of the loyalty tribunal, he felt that the federal government's course was not yet clear. Garson acknowledged that some of the repatriation applications may have been signed under duress, but he did not wish to interfere with those who truly wished to leave Canada. Finally, Garson insisted that since immigration and citizenship were areas of federal responsibility under the constitution, Manitoba had no power to exclude any Canadians from residency. Any public statement he might make would therefore achieve nothing except to criticize the federal government. Garson reiterated this position in replies to other correspondents and in a public statement on 20 December 1945. This statement disclaimed any responsibility over the settlement of Japanese Canadians in Manitoba, though he did offer the opinion that those with Canadian citizenship should have the same mobility rights within the Dominion as any other Canadian.[134] He thus evaded any moral responsibility or leadership and remained content to pass the buck to Ottawa.

Garson's position was somewhat disingenuous but sensitive to public opinion. It is clear from public and private statements by his predecessor, dating back to 1942, that Bracken had fully expected Ottawa to remove any Japanese placed in the province. In March 1945, Garson reminded readers of the *Tribune* that Manitoba had accepted the evacuees on the "understanding that when the emergency was over the Dominion would remove them."[135] The province ultimately made no effort to enforce this condition of the agreement because the winds of public opinion shifted at the end of the year. As the National Emergency Powers Act (Bill 15) was moving through Parliament in November 1945, a *Free Press* editorial expressed the sentiment informing the growing opposition to a clause that would confirm the cabinet's power to deport the Japanese Canadians: "This clause by which the Government seeks to give its action against Canadian-born Japanese some legal basis should come out of Bill 15. It is reminiscent of the Nurnberg laws passed by the Nazis, and is one of the things the United Nations fought against in the war with Germany. Civilized countries do not deprive people born within their borders of their citizenship, and then deport them to the land from whence their fathers came."[136] The *Tribune* later demanded a Supreme Court ruling on the constitutionality of the orders-in-council authorizing the proposed deportations,[137] and though the federal government's power to act was eventually upheld by the Judicial Committee of the Privy Council, the public support underpinning its willingness to use that power had steadily eroded.

Even as the debates over Japanese disfranchisement and deportation unfolded, some members of the *Nisei* community offered the ultimate expression of loyalty to a country that was considering revoking their citizenship. After repeated requests by Australian and British officers for Japanese Canadians to serve on loan with their forces in the Far East as interpreters and translators, the Cabinet War Committee finally authorized *Nisei* enlistment into the Canadian Army in January 1945. Some had already enlisted in the British Army rather than wait out the delays in Canada, and a handful of others had managed to enlist for general service in various regiments across Canada as early as October 1939.[138] This passage clearly meant a great deal to the men concerned. Akira Sato, who had been rebuffed in his attempt to join the air cadets—because of a hernia, not because he was Japanese—was inspired by the Honour Roll of students from Gordon Bell High School who had been killed in action. He realized that, at some point, he had "cross[ed] that line, where you become more Canadian than Japanese." When he learned that he was now eligible to join the army, his "eyes lit up." He later remembered meeting a chaplain who, in addressing his unit, "never mentioned that we were Japanese." They were simply good Canadians doing their bit for their country. This was the first time anyone had ever referred to Sato this way, and it was a proud moment that left him with "tears running down my face."[139] Sato was still training in Vancouver when the Pacific war ended, so he never made it overseas.

Eichi Oike did, and after training in India he was posted to Shamshuipo Camp in Hong Kong. The camp, which had formerly held Canadian prisoners of war, now held the Japanese, and Oike worked there as an interpreter until his return to Winnipeg in June 1946.[140] Hozumi (Bill) Sasaki was another who enlisted in Winnipeg and served as an interpreter in India, Rangoon, and Singapore. His unit fought a guerilla war, penetrating enemy lines in search of information.[141] Harold Hirose was also accepted, after trying to join the army repeatedly since 1939. He hoped that military service would hasten the achievement of suffrage and open occupations like law or public service that were closed to Japanese Canadians. Hirose served with a Field Broadcasting Unit of the Indian Army in Malaya, engaged in translation and dissemination of propaganda.[142] Minoru Tanaka, one of the general service volunteers, was not from Winnipeg—he enlisted in Wymark, Saskatchewan, in April 1941. He served, however, with Winnipeg's Fort Garry Horse in northwest Europe. He was carrying on a family tradition begun by his father, who had served with the 10th Battalion at Vimy Ridge in 1917. On 19 February 1945, Tanaka's tank was hit near Calcar, Germany. He succumbed to his wounds the next day and was buried at Groesbeek Canadian War Cemetery.[143]

By the time Canada's Japanese servicemen returned home, the deportation debate had largely been resolved. Of the more than 10,000 who had applied for repatriation, 4,720 changed their minds by the end of 1945, and the proposed loyalty tribunal never materialized. In the end, the Government of Canada did not deport any Japanese residents against their wishes. Still, a bad taste lingered for many of Manitoba's Japanese, 118 of whom went ahead with repatriation.[144] Some were bound to go not by the government but by family obligations. Toshiko Sasaki was an eighteen-year-old girl who had spent the last five years in Letellier, where she received her education. She left Winnipeg in September 1946, a sense of duty prompting her to accompany elderly parents who had decided to return to Japan. She hoped to return as soon as her parents were settled in Japan but doubted that either government would allow her to do so. "'I was born in Westminster, B.C. and know no other country.... Two of my sisters are engaged and will be married soon,' she said. 'I'll miss their weddings.'" Her three older sisters saw them off at the train station, and were devastated by the splitting of their family. One of Toshiko's sisters "fell alongside the train when it was leaving the east coach yards. Despite pleadings ... the girl would not move. She was carried away."[145] This family's separation epitomized part of the tragedy that the war brought down on Japanese Canadians.

Edgar Iwamoto experienced an equally devastating side of that tragedy. Born in Vancouver, Iwamoto was sent to Japan at age four to be raised by an aunt in Hiroshima. He completed his elementary education there before returning to Vancouver in 1931 for high school. Iwamoto was serving with a Field Broadcasting Unit in India when an American B-29 Superfortress dropped the atomic bomb on Hiroshima. As Roy Ito explains, "it was a terrible shock. His aunt's home was located almost in the centre of the city, and he knew it was almost certain she had died in the holocaust. The school he had attended, the neighbours he had known, friends and relatives, had all been obliterated in one terrible moment.... Hiroshima would never leave his mind."[146] For Iwamoto and all the Japanese in Canada with family in the home islands or serving with the enemy's military forces, Japan's fate must have engendered an indescribable inner conflict.

Table 2.2. Japanese Evacuees from British Columbia

Born in Canada	6,727
Naturalized Canadians	7,011
Japanese nationals	9,758
U.S. citizens	16
Total	23,512

Source: British Columbia Security Commission, "Removal of Japanese from Protected Areas," March 4, 1942 to October 31, 1942, 28, copy in AM, GR 43, Premier's Correspondence, G113, file 112 (1945), War – Japanese Nationals.

Toleration and the "Good" War

For some Canadians, the "spirit of toleration" that G.M.A. Grube had written about in *Canadian Forum* was a casualty of war. Most would now agree that the Second World War was a just war, though we must concede that there were dark moments both in battle and on the home front. Some groups did not fit into the patriotic consensus, and were marginalized for failing to think, vote, or look like the majority. Opposing Ukrainian-Canadian associations sought to influence the state to suppress their ideological rivals. Newspapers, veterans, the Affirmative Vote Committee, civilians, and soldiers accused and scorned opponents of compulsory military service. Ordinary citizens and their associations demanded the forced relocation of the Japanese Canadians, petitioned the government against settlement of evacuees in their municipalities, and discriminated against Japanese who sought work or accommodation. Deportation of citizens was considered a war crime at Nuremberg;[147] but while Allied prosecutors were working to build their case against Nazi leaders, the Canadian government considered a similar measure against its own citizens of Japanese descent. When we pause to remember these events, it is clear that although some may recall the Second World War as "the good war," for many others it was an unmitigated tragedy.

3

INVESTING IN VICTORY

Wars are always expensive. From 1939 to 1945, the Dominion government in Ottawa spent approximately $22 billion to fight the Second World War. Without accounting for the cost of pensions, this figure was still more than four times greater than cumulative federal expenditures in the entire preceding decade.[1] The increase in government spending was astonishing for an industrially under-developed country of 11 million citizens but it was made possible by an unprecedented expansion of Canadian industry which saw Canada's Gross Domestic Product increase by 50 percent from 1939 to 1946.[2] With virtually full employment a product of wartime economic growth, Canadians were earning more money than ever before and Ottawa siphoned off record amounts in income and other taxes—about $14 billion worth. This still left a sizeable portion of wartime budgets to be found by borrowing Canadians' disposable income through a variety of voluntary savings plans. Canada's war finance program was a distinct success, raising another $13 billion,[3] but how was it accomplished? What machinery was set up, what motivators were used, to persuade Canadians to part with even more of their hard-earned money than the taxman was already taking?

To tackle this assignment, the federal government created a group of new organizations, most importantly the National War Finance Committee (NWFC), which drew on the talents of some of the nation's most successful financiers, advertising companies, and public figures to execute a series of drives with one shared goal: to convince Canadians to buy Victory Bonds and War Savings Certificates, and then to buy more of them. Winnipeg, like other cities across the country, was assigned ever-increasing quotas for sub-scriptions. To inspire citizens to meet these objectives, the NWFC undertook sophisticated national publicity campaigns, comprising advertising and cere-monial events designed to play on a complex variety of themes which evolved in response to the changing climate of opinion as the war progressed.

Since Victory Loans were the centrepieces of Ottawa's war finance public-ity, this chapter concentrates on local Victory Loan campaigns, although the publicity measures adopted were also applied to a lesser degree in War Savings drives. The publicity campaigns can be seen either as focal points for the co-alescent patriotic consensus, or as mechanisms of psychological compulsion, disseminating propaganda to facilitate achievement of state objectives. The great success of the nine Victory Loan campaigns leaves little doubt that the government was successful in persuading Winnipeggers that it was their duty to buy bonds. The most effective propaganda reflected popular values, and a study of the barrage of messages directed at Winnipeggers during the loan drives offers a glimpse of what motivated them to join the economic war effort. In doing so, they joined in a national consensus that was crucial to sustaining home front morale.

Creating the Instruments of Wartime Finance

Convincing Canadians to save for victory was not as pressing a need in the war's first year as it would become later. Ottawa's war finance policy was ini-tially based on two principles: equal sharing of the war's burdens, and "pay as you go."[4] In practice, equal sharing meant that taxation would spread the burden among Canadians on the basis of ability to pay. "Pay as you go" meant that the cost of the war would be paid out of current revenues as much as possible, not put off for later generations to face as the government had done during the Great War. This would be possible only because the government of Prime Minister William Lyon Mackenzie King was committed to a "lim-ited liability" war effort that would not see Canada bleed itself dry to save European civilization for a second time within twenty-five years. Rather than raising huge armies for service overseas, King and his ministers would send only one division to the United Kingdom. They would invest in home defence instead, building up naval and air forces to defend Canada's coastlines and air space. These forces would not be susceptible to the same high casualty rates the Canadian Corps had suffered from 1915 to 1918, so conscription would be unnecessary. It was a politically safe choice for a country still divided by the

Great War's legacy. Emerging from the budgetary crises of the Depression, Ottawa's bottom line was the overriding consideration during the fall and winter of 1939–40, a period which C.P. Stacey characterized as the "reign of the dollar."[5]

The fall of France and western Europe in the spring of 1940 brought that reign to an end. With Britain and the Commonwealth standing alone in a fight which had been transformed, thanks in part to British Prime Minister Winston Churchill's rhetoric, into a crusade to save the world from Nazi barbarism, budgetary concerns became secondary. Canada, until 1941 Britain's most important ally, dramatically increased her military commitments. Besides bearing much of the cost of the British Commonwealth Air Training Plan, Canada would raise an overseas army of five divisions plus ancillary troops, a bomber group and tactical air squadrons, and substantial naval forces. Shipments of food and material assistance were sent to allies, especially Britain and the Soviet Union, and the munitions and supply program was accelerated to fulfill the logistical requirements of total war.

Paying for this increased war effort would require a drastic revision of the "pay as you go" policy. The solution advocated by British economist John Maynard Keynes in his 1940 treatise *How to Pay for the War* combined steep tax increases with compulsory savings.[6] Canadian Finance Minister J.L. Ilsley's revised policy combined obligatory and voluntary approaches. On the one hand, personal and business income taxes were increased dramatically, a flat-rate National Defence tax was levied, and a compulsory savings plan was introduced. On the other hand, Canadians would be persuaded to lend their after-tax income to the government through the purchase of War Savings Certificates and Bonds. Combined, these measures were expected to generate the necessary revenues and, equally important, prevent large-scale inflation in an expanding economy by absorbing civilians' surplus spending power, thereby reducing demand for resources needed for war production. Enforced curtailment of goods for civilian consumption was one step held in reserve, in case additional measures became necessary.

In the meantime, Ottawa began building up the machinery responsible for eliciting funds voluntarily. The early War Savings program solicited subscribers for two main products. Investors could buy government bonds in a series of two War Loans in January and September, 1940. Objectives for these loans were modest, compared to later issues—$200 million in federal government bonds for the first, $300 million for the second—and were met largely

Figure 1.1. Winnipeg Grenadiers Parade on Memorial Avenue, 8 October 1939.

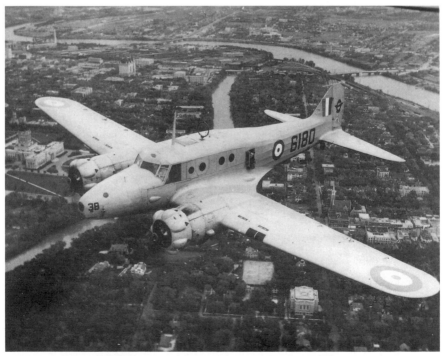

Figure 1.2. British Commonwealth Air Training Plan aircraft flying over Winnipeg.

Figure 1.3. Queen's Own Cameron Highlanders Depart for Training, 24 May 1940.

Figure 1.4. Eaton's Decorated for VE-Day.

Figure 3.1. *To Have and to Hold!*

Figure 3.2. *Save to Beat the Devil!*

Figure 3.3. *All Canada is United*

Figure 3.4. *Help Finish the Job*

Figure 3.5. *"Some Chicken…Some Neck!"*

Figure 3.6. *"Mr. Churchill Himself"*

Figure 3.7. *Keep These Hands Off!*

Figure 3.8. *"You'll Have to Do the Signing, Mister"*

Figure 3.9. *Choose Your "Bonds"*

Figure 3.10. *For Victory*

Figure 3.11. Canada Got it First!

Figure 3.12. "I'm dreaming of a modern kitchen . . . !"

Instructions for Proceedure During
BLACKOUT

Wednesday, June 4, 10 to 10.30 p.m.

AUTHORITY:

The city council have approved of a "Blackout" of the downtown area of the city on the night of Wednesday, June 4, from 10 p.m. to 10.30 p.m. with a preliminary Alert Signal at 9.55 p.m.

BOUNDARIES:

1. C.P.R. tracks on the north.
2. Red river on the east.
3. Assiniboine river on the south.
4. Sherbrook street on the west.

IF YOU ARE AT HOME, IN A HOTEL ROOM OR APARTMENT:

1. Turn out all external lights.
2. See that no lighting in your house is visible from the outside.
3. If you cannot obscure your windows with dark materials, turn off your lights, but do not use the main switch.
4. Listen in on your radio for the happenings all over town.
5. Managements of hotels and apartment houses are responsible for exterior lighting.

DRIVING YOUR CAR OR MOTOR VEHICLE:

1. Immediately pull over to curb or roadside and turn off your lights and motor. This includes bicycles.
2. Do not try to drive on with your lights out.
3. Do not park in front of fire exit, fire plug, hospital entrance or at a street intersection.
4. Do not block centre of street as fire engines and police cars may have to answer emergency calls.

STORES, MANUFACTURING COMPANIES, INDUSTRIAL PLANTS AND OFFICE BUILDINGS:

1. Have someone on duty during the Blackout.
2. Be sure all external lights are out, including Neon signs.
3. See that internal lights are not visible from the outside.
4. Your presence on the premises will aid materially in protecting your property and making the Blackout a success.

PEDESTRIANS:

1. Remain on sidewalk—do not cross street.
2. Do not smoke or expose any light.

MAIN SWITCHES:

Will not be turned off—it is up to you individually to make this test a success.

IMPORTANT:

Do not forget your skylight if you have one.

Figure 3.13. Blackout Instructions, June 1941.

through direct appeals from banks and securities brokers to their clients.[7] Less wealthy Canadians, including children and housewives, were encouraged to buy War Savings Stamps and Certificates. Certificates were available in smaller denominations, from five to $100; a certificate purchased for four dollars would be worth five dollars at maturity, typically seven and a half years later. Subscribers could buy them directly or through the collection of stamps. Pass books filled with sixteen stamps (at twenty-five cents each) could be redeemed for one five-dollar certificate. War Savings Stamps and Certificates were available year round, and regular purchases were encouraged. Bonds, whether for the War Loans or later Victory Loans, were only offered during the specific periods of the drives.

The relatively small amounts raised by these means may have seemed adequate for immediate needs during the reign of the dollar; but once Canada was drawn into the fighting, it was quickly recognized that it would not be a short war, and the government's conservative budgetary estimates would therefore have to be overhauled. A new strategy was clearly necessary to tap the spending power of the wage-earning masses. In a letter to Ilsley, written in the fall of 1940 after the Second War Loan, John Imrie, chair of the Canadian Daily Newspapers' Association, urged the finance minister to "put Canada's war loan promotion on a popular, mass-appeal basis with an intensive selling organization in every city, town and village."[8] Ottawa did exactly that, instituting a new Victory Loan program that would make use of mass sales techniques, including advertising blitzes, door-to-door canvassing, payroll deductions, celebrity testimonials, public ceremonial events, and not-so-subtle propaganda. The organization set up to manage the new drives evolved from the *ad hoc* National War Loan Committee chaired by Bank of Montreal General Manager George Spinney, which had overseen the first two loans in 1940. It re-emerged as the first Victory Loan Committee in the spring of 1941.

The Victory Loan Committee's mandate to conduct mass appeals would bring it into direct competition with the War Savings Committee. Beginning with the sale of War Savings Stamps and Certificates in May 1940, the latter committee's goal was continuous sales to the general public. To this end, stamps and certificates were offered at banks, post offices, and retail stores. Employers cooperated by establishing payroll deduction plans. The War Savings Committee coordinated a large voluntary sales organization and mounted a series of patriotic drives "that appealed for support to people of all ages and circumstances." The new Victory Loan Committee would invade

all of these areas, but because Victory Loans were only available during limited drive periods it was thought that the two organizations could co-exist.
By the end of the first Victory Loan campaign in June 1941, it was clear that
they could not. Unwillingness to coordinate advertising campaigns and the
decision by the Victory Loan Committee to compete for payroll deduction
subscriptions exacerbated the rivalry. Ultimately, Finance Department officials assigned greater priority to the loans, and the War Savings Committee's
days were numbered. It was clearly losing momentum through the summer of
1941, with sagging sales and the resignation of its chairman, and it was amal-
gamated in December with the loans organization into a new National War
Finance Committee. With Spinney as chairman, the new committee would
direct both operations.[9]

The NWFC's membership included sixty representatives drawn from
trade and commerce, industry, organized labour, agriculture, the professions,
and women's groups to provide advice on how to appeal to these disparate
sectors of society.[10] A Finance Department background memo set out the
rationale for the committee's operations. While much of the NWFC's advertising for War Savings dwelled on themes that would evoke an emotional
response—such as patriotism, the sacrifice of armed forces personnel, or the
threats posed by the Axis powers—the memo was informed by more rational
economic motives. It focused on a number of related goals: generating revenue to fund the war effort was the most obvious; reducing civilian demand for
consumer goods would husband necessary war materials, control inflation,
and stabilize the cost of living; and, finally, creating a reserve of savings would
help to kick-start the consumer economy again after the war. If low- and
middle-income earners had savings with which to buy consumer goods once
they became available in quantity again, production and employment would
be sustained despite the flooding of the job market that would follow demobilization of service personnel and munitions workers. War Savings would
thereby help prevent a recurrence of the recession that had followed the Great
War. To achieve these goals, the NWFC would "conduct a continuous and
forceful educational programme" to convince Canadians that lending money
to the government was not only the patriotic thing to do, it would also preclude more direct government intervention in the form of stricter rationing
and measures to control inflation.[11]

The NWFC needed to sell Canadians the idea that it was not enough
simply to buy bonds or certificates once in a while, using their past savings.

Setting aside current income to make regular purchases was the desired practice because the government's objective was to reduce civilian consumption so that scarce resources could be redirected to "war purposes."[12] This amounted to asking people to subsist on the "minimum expenditure required to maintain civilian health, efficiency, and morale."[13] The hard part would be to convince Canadians that a reduction in their standard of living would be in their best interests, and to foster voluntary compliance.

To broaden the public appeal for bond sales, Spinney's Third War Loan Committee (soon to be renamed) chose to follow the example of the three Victory Loan drives of the Great War, which raised approximately $1.7 billion between 1917 and 1919.[14] Flexibility and a varied approach were the means to the end. To persuade Canadians to divert their savings and present earnings from personal use to government use, the committee devised an instrument for virtually all contingencies in order to sell bonds, stamps, and certificates through "every possible channel." Ilsley sent letters to individual homeowners during the first five Victory Loans. Salesmen went door-to-door. Bank customers, employees in the workplace, and even children were solicited. Newspapers were filled with ads and colourful posters were widely used. The goal was to make "every person in receipt of income in any form ... feel obligated to divert part of such income to war purposes."[15]

One mechanism that brought maximum persuasive pressure to bear on wage earners was the payroll savings plan—a device instituted during the First World War to solicit employee contributions to the Canadian Patriotic Fund, and eagerly resurrected for the Second.[16] The War Savings Committee had initiated the payroll program for companies with at least ten employees, and the NWFC extended it to bond sales prior to the Second Victory Loan. The program's terms specified a schedule of instalments on a minimum fifty-dollar bond purchase—for example, seven monthly payments of $7.22 each during the Third Victory Loan, later changed to $8.40 per month for six months. When the program commenced, Ilsley sent out a circular to employers throughout the country, urging them to institute payroll deduction plans. He suggested that employers arrange interviews with workers to convince them to increase their pledges to 5 percent of income, to display posters to push the message, and even to have new employees sign War Savings pledges when taken on the payroll.[17] The NWFC's structure later included a payroll savings division to focus on penetrating the workplace more efficiently. It advised workplace organizers to appoint payroll savings committees to coordinate appeals. To generate enthusiasm and provide information, mass meetings were held, replete with decorations, films, music, speakers delivering addresses prepared by the NWFC, and other publicity materials to encourage bond sales. Afterward, these meetings were usually followed up by an internal canvass of each worker, done by other employees or sometimes by management.[18] One poll of prairie respondents who bought bonds through their place of employment during the Fifth Victory Loan revealed that 39 percent had been canvassed by a fellow employee, 26 percent by a foreman, and 31 percent by a company executive, so more than half had been pressured by a superior.[19] A routine tactic was to arrange for a firm's general manager to send letters to each employee, stressing the importance of participating in the plan. Ethel McKnight, an employee at Bulman Brothers, a Winnipeg printing company, received one such letter from her boss. It read: "You all know how tremendously important it is to put this loan over the top in no uncertain way. Manitoba's quota is $53,000,000. That means that every one of you must give your support to this Third Victory Loan in order to make it a real success. If we cannot personally fight the least we can do is to let our dollars work to support those who are fighting for us."[20] The letter did its job: McKnight bought a bond for the Third Loan, and most of the others as well.

To introduce a prize to work towards, a symbol of recognition, and to stimulate competition with other firms, the NWFC provided "V" flags to businesses investing a certain proportion of their total payroll in bonds or certificates with a specified quota of participants. This practice parallelled the award of honour pennants to cities and provinces meeting their loan quotas. "V" flags were awarded during the Seventh Victory Loan, for example, to those firms with 90 percent of employees subscribing at least 15 percent of the payroll. As a motivational tool, the "V" flag was apparently a great success in Manitoba. The provincial representative in the NWFC's payroll savings division stated that the flag was considered their most effective workplace sales inducement. Eligible firms received their flags with much fanfare and ceremony, and the newspapers printed the names of Manitoba winners throughout the loan drive.[21]

Manitoba's provincial government first instituted its payroll deduction plan to encourage regular purchase of War Savings Certificates and Stamps within the civil service, and it was later extended to bonds. The element of competition was evident, as government employees were pressed to contribute under the plan and forego "outside undertakings" in order to "make a better showing."[22] A memo sent to members of the provincial Department of Education in July 1943 "pointed out that the percentage of subscriptions in industry is much higher than is the case with the Civil Service." Provincial employees were urged to supplement their bond purchases with War Savings Certificates, and a list was circulated, showing the percentage of employees from each department who were contributing. This provided ready recognition for the Treasury Department, then the runaway leader with 100 percent compliance, but it also made clear which other departments were not measuring up.[23] Many employers also posted lists naming contributors, which had the same effect.

All of these measures must obviously have placed great pressure on employees to conform and buy bonds or certificates. Some undoubtedly felt coerced. One clerk working for the federal government recalled that "when a ... drive was on, we were given to understand that we were to buy and if we did not ... we were brought into the chief's office [who] mentioned love of country, duty ... and ... the error of trying to hold out."[24] There was a backlash against this sort of pressure from some Canadians who decided to sell bonds from earlier issues in order to buy new ones and maintain a facade of compliance. A Wartime Information Board correspondent in Ottawa wrote that "people are already beginning to talk about the projected October Loan and on all sides one hears criticism of the system which coerces people in firms into subscribing in order to maintain 100 percent participation of the firm. It is obviously the reason why there are so many re-sales, and does create resentment on the part of a large number of people against the Loans."[25] There were similar complaints from Edmonton about the amount of pressure applied at Royal Canadian Air Force stations to "compel men to take bonds and make the station quota look high."[26] The NWFC was "perturbed" over the scale of the redemption problem. For example, statistics showed that 448,000 fifty-dollar bonds and 161,000 $100 bonds had been re-sold in the last three months of 1943 alone.[27] The committee therefore devoted special attention to the issue in its print, film, and radio advertising (see Figure 3.1). Still, the payroll deduction plan greatly facilitated bond purchases and succeeded in the NWFC's goal of diverting progressively larger amounts of current income to government use. Compared to the Second Victory Loan total of roughly $60 million, payroll subscriptions jumped by 43 percent in the Third Loan, and by another 53 percent in the Fourth. By the end of the Seventh Victory Loan, payroll savings had accounted for $947 million, or about 25 percent of bond sales to individuals. And the national payroll savings objective, 15 percent of employers' payrolls, was being routinely exceeded, with 17.5 percent on the Sixth Loan and 17.75 percent on the Seventh.[28]

Payroll deduction was one of the mechanisms used by the NWFC to facilitate purchases by those with modest incomes. At the opposite end of the income scale were the so-called "special names," those wealthy individuals, banks, trust and insurance companies, or large corporations capable of buying bonds worth $25,000 or more at each issue. Ultimately, more than two thirds of the total amount subscribed in Winnipeg for Victory Bonds, and slightly more than half of the provincial total, came from the few hundred members of the special names category, including notable firms like James Richardson and Sons or Great-West Life. These proportions were similar in the rest of the country, where special names accounted for a little more than half of the totals raised.[29] The special names group was obviously instrumental to the success of the Victory Loans, but to achieve the goal of absorbing wage earners' surplus spending capacity required the NWFC to present its message in ways that would reach the majority of ordinary Canadians. To do so, it would build on techniques developed by one of its predecessor organizations.

Before it was blended into the NWFC, the War Savings Committee established precedents for the mass public appeals that would make the Victory Loan program such a huge success. A 1940 drive saw over one million workers sign up for payroll savings, though these were mostly one-time rather than ongoing purchases. A "Smash Hitler" campaign aimed to sign up "2,000,000 regular War Savers." The Committee sponsored a booth at Toronto's Canadian National Exhibition, with martial displays intended to stir patriotic citizens to the desired end. Special appeals were made to women, because it was estimated that they did the vast majority of household shopping. Women's groups and voluntary organizations were encouraged to appoint War Savings committees to promote sales, to hold special meetings where stamp purchases were the price of admission, or to form "16" clubs in which members would each contribute one stamp with the completed pass book then being raffled off. Individuals were asked to shop in stores that sold stamps and certificates, to take their change in stamps, to give certificates as Christmas or birthday presents, and to avoid unnecessary spending in order to "Serve by Saving." Women's maternal roles were also called upon; they were urged to "inculcate in children a desire to help Canada—and at the same time teach them thrift through investment in War Savings Certificates."[30] Despite these efforts, sales fell off in the latter half of the year. To bolster them, an "all-out national appeal" was launched early in 1941.[31]

Although it was not intended as such, Winnipeg's February 1941 War Savings drive appears, in retrospect, as something of a dry run for the larger Victory Loan efforts that followed. The sales effort, advertising, involvement of eminent local figures, and public spectacles devised to support the drive foreshadowed the publicity barrage developed later by the National War Finance Committee. The drive opened on Friday, 7 February with a massive canvass of Winnipeg homes and businesses. Approximately 400 volunteers targeted downtown businesses that were too small to operate the payroll deduction scheme. Another group focused on businesses outside the downtown core. Hundreds more visited suburban areas and individual homes. Because the great majority of volunteer workers across the country were women, the Winnipeg *Free Press* recognized that "the success of the drive will depend largely upon the way the women do their share."[32]

At noon that same Friday, Winnipeggers crowded downtown to witness "one of the most spectacular sights seen on the prairies since the start of the war."[33] The "Battle of Portage and Main," as it was called, was staged to promote the drive, and the novelty of the event was clear from the tone of news reports. Beginning at 11:45 a.m., sirens along the two main thoroughfares warned of approaching enemy aircraft. Police redirected automobiles, and streetcars came to a halt. As soldiers from the 13th Field Regiment, Royal Canadian Artillery, lined the intersection, the band from the Royal Canadian Air Force began to play. Soon, motorcycles leading an advancing mechanized column arrived, followed by gun tractors towing 18-pounder field guns. Upon arrival in the square, "with lightning-like speed the helmeted riders of the units dismounted and threw the guns into firing positions, pointing south and east." Pairs of soldiers "threw themselves on the ground behind their anti-tank rifles" to cover them. An officer kept the crowd informed about the action over a loudspeaker. Next, a gas rattle warned the troops to don their gas masks, and in the words of a Winnipeg *Free Press* reporter, "the men in the street became ghouls—strange fierce-looking men of another world." The denouement was provided when aircraft from the RCAF's No. 2 Training Command "blazed overhead." By 12:20 p.m., the "battle" was over and a well-entertained crowd watched as the guns were hooked up again and the soldiers paraded back to barracks.[34]

One of the drive's goals was to educate people about their part in supplying the country's financial requirements. The War Savings Committee's newsletter proclaimed that "$120,000,000 Annually is Canada's War Savings Need! Every Canadian family must pledge and sacrifice."[35] Manitoba's provincial target was $520,000 monthly. In case one's duty was not sufficiently clear, a series of speeches by provincial leaders like Premier John Bracken, Lieutenant Governor R.F. McWilliams, and Winnipeg Mayor John Queen spelled it out. McWilliams, for example, appealed to those who perhaps did not feel the need to get involved:

> There is but one way that the sinews of war can be provided.... The money that pays for them must come out of our pockets.... There is no man or woman, boy or girl, whose pocket is so small, or whose means of earning is so slight that he or she cannot buy a certificate and keep on buying week by week.
>
> The challenge hits every one of us in the face. We cannot escape our responsibility. We cannot miss the chance to do what we can in this fight. We cannot face the man who is risking his life in our defence unless each and every one of us is able to say 'I did my bit.'[36]

Following the institution of regular Victory Loan drives, NWFC officials continued to press the public to buy stamps and certificates. In 1943, for example, the committee estimated that stamp sales alone would reach $12 million. Schools were a major target for marketing efforts. Since children represented one of the main sources of regular sales, a "25¢ Club" stamp booklet was promoted to encourage students to buy at least one stamp each week.[37] The general public was not neglected, however. Some campaigns equated War Savings with the purchase of necessary weapons and war equipment. Advertising methods were often colourful, as one visiting Toronto reporter observed: "A unique piece of war finance publicity in Winnipeg this fall was the street car completely painted in red, white and blue, with huge block letters along either side advising the public to Stamp Out the U-Boat and to Buy War Savings Certificates Regularly. First sight of the strange Winnipeg electric tram which operated on the main line made one think it was a stunt promoted by a circus or carnival."[38] Such imaginative publicity and the themes articulated by McWilliams became familiar in the coming years as they were applied in increasing measure to new campaigns, particularly to support the Victory Loans.

Pushing the Message

The NWFC's publicity efforts would combine public spectacles such as the Battle of Portage and Main with varied forms of advertising. NWFC advertising constituted a pervasive domestic propaganda campaign, confronting Canadians seemingly at every turn and generating a lot of pressure to support the war effort by buying bonds and certificates. Popular notions of propaganda often envision a tool of deception wielded abroad by governments and militaries as a means to confuse the enemy and weaken his will to fight, or used domestically to deceive or control the public. The concept of propaganda has thus acquired a somewhat sinister image, though scholarly definitions cover a broader range of communication. To Victoria O'Donnell and Garth Jowett, for example, propaganda is "the deliberate and systematic attempt to shape perceptions, manipulate cognitions, and direct behavior to achieve a response that furthers the desired intent of the propagandist."[39]

American political scientist Harold Lasswell defined propaganda in 1934 as "the technique of influencing human action by the manipulation of representations." Such representations might encompass any of the means used to communicate ideas. They might include spoken or written language, imagery, music, or other art forms. The task of a propagandist "is to intensify attitudes favorable to his purposes, to reverse obstructive attitudes, to win the indifferent or at least to prevent them from becoming antagonistic."[40] That task was facilitated by seven commonly used devices that were identified by the Institute for Propaganda Analysis, an American organization active from 1937 to 1942. These devices included: "name-calling" to induce the formation of negative judgments; "glittering generalities," essentially the reverse of "name-calling," using positive images; the "transfer" of authority, sanction, or prestige from someone held in respect to something the propagandist would have the audience accept; "testimonial," or endorsement, often by celebrities; "plain folks," the attempt, usually by politicians, to appear as ordinary people and therefore trustworthy; "card-stacking," the use of deception to win support; and the "band-wagon," a suggestion that everyone else feels a certain way or knows something to be true.

Most of these seven devices were used in loan publicity, both in ads commissioned by the NWFC and those contributed independently by newspapers. A common example of "name-calling" was to demonize Hitler. One NWFC poster portrayed a worried *fuhrer* wearing horns, with the caption "Save to beat the Devil!" (Figure 3.2). Editorial cartoonists followed suit, sometimes with less subtlety, as in one example of a wanted poster that reviled him as a mere "house painter" and "killer."[41] Another frequently used device was the "transfer" of authority, particularly Churchill's, and sometimes devices could be used together: one poster for the first Victory Loan drive, featuring Churchill, combined transfer with the "bandwagon" claim that "ALL CANADA is United in this Single Purpose" (Figure 3.3). "Testimonials," such as film spots with Bing Crosby or other Hollywood stars, were a frequent resort, just as they are today. Messages emphasizing how wonderful the post-war consumer economy would be, filled with new homes, cars, washing machines, and other conveniences, offered numerous "glittering generalities."

The key tactic of successful propaganda, however, was the manipulation of emotions. According to the Institute for Propaganda Analysis, "emotion is the stuff with which propagandists work. Without it, they are helpless; with it, harnessing it to their purposes, they can make us glow with pride or burn with hatred, they can make us zealots in behalf of the program they espouse.... Without the appeal to our emotion—to our fears and to our courage, to our selfishness and unselfishness, to our loves and to our hates—propagandists would influence few opinions and few actions."[42] This observation was borne out by a study of Canadian war posters commissioned by the U.S. Office of Facts and Figures, devoted to domestic propaganda, which suggested that the main reason many of these ads and posters so successfully resonated with the public was because they appealed to an emotional response—such as anxiety over the need to protect one's family, love of country, or hopes and fears for the future.[43]

The NWFC's publicity campaigns were intended to reach Canadians on a variety of levels: they could appeal to the emotions, use rational argument, or even entertain. The publicity for each Victory Loan reflected a few central themes, such as patriotism, duty, family, or the enemy threat. Patriotic or duty-based themes dominated throughout much of the war, with messages that referred to Canada's financial need, ties to the mother country and aid to allied nations, or doing one's bit to help win the war. Patriotic symbols and images, including such mainstays as the British lion, the Union Jack, or the maple leaf, were prominent in print advertising and other media. Other patriotic themes borrowed heavily from Churchillian rhetoric (see Figures 3.4 and 3.5). The slogan for the first Victory Loan was "Help Finish the Job." It derived from Churchill's famous plea to the Americans to "give us the tools and we will finish the job," delivered in a radio address on 9 February 1941.

Churchill had sought to reassure his audience that the British would not cave in to Hitler, as long as they had the means to fight. Another featured a resolute Churchill and proclaimed: "There is not a home in all Canada, not a fireside or family gathering that does not quicken into rapt attention when the voice of Churchill, the articulate voice of the Empire, comes rumbling over the air waves. To Canadians his great inspiring messages ring with pride, confidence and persuasion."[44] While there were very few, if any, ads featuring Mackenzie King, Churchill's image was widely circulated. Another ad portrayed a smiling Churchill tipping his hat at the door of a Canadian family he visits in order to personally explain the importance of buying Victory Bonds (Figure 3.6).

Family themes allowed exploitation of emotional ties as well as Canadians' sense of duty. One oft-reproduced Victory Bond poster featured a young mother and baby threatened by grasping claws marked with the German swastika and the Japanese rising sun, with the injunction to "Keep These Hands Off!" (Figure 3.7). Other ads and posters depicted family reunions with returned servicemen, or protection of children or Canadian life in general. A related group of patriotic appeals focused more directly on the enemy threat and the battle against the Axis. There were numerous antagonistic portrayals of German and Japanese leaders, or graphic depictions of the hardships faced by conquered civilians in occupied countries. Many ads urged support for Canada's servicemen who were fighting for their country. Sacrifice themes were common, with ads often referring to servicemen laying down their lives as part of the price to be paid for victory, or suggesting the debt of obligation owed to those who had shed their blood. A poster for the Ninth Loan focused on a wounded Normandy veteran telling the viewer that "You'll have to do the signing, Mister," because he had lost his right arm between Caen and Falaise (Figure 3.8). This sort of "guilt trip" was a common theme echoed in much war finance propaganda, including Ilsley's personal letters to Canadians, the Victory Loan dedication pledges (discussed below), and even a film cartoon called "Home Front" that showed "a soldier wondering if the home front people are doing what they can" to support their fighting forces.[45] By providing the money to buy the equipment they needed, according to the slogan for the Fifth Loan, ordinary people on the home front could "Speed the Victory." A number of images presented Canadians with a choice between freedom and slavery, and the way to ensure the former was obvious (Figure 3.9).

The themes of war finance publicity evolved in response to the war's changing circumstances. Victory Loan slogans like "Come on Canada" or

"Back the Attack" urged civilians to get behind the war effort during the first four loan drives in the period before Canadian forces were committed to battle in great numbers. Later campaigns asked Canadians to increase their financial commitment in order to "Put Victory First" as the fighting intensified overseas and tension built leading up to the invasion of Normandy on D-Day. As Canadian troops became more involved on European battlefields, advertising continued to dwell on the increasing financial need for weapons and equipment, and the responsibility of the home front to support those at the battle front. As the Seventh Victory Loan approached in the summer of 1944, there was some concern that people would feel less inclined to buy bonds because the invasion had begun and the end was in sight.[46] Increasing emphasis was therefore placed on themes of self-interest to give people another reason to buy bonds. The slogan for the Seventh Loan, accordingly, was "Invest in Victory." As the war neared its climax in the spring of 1945, the Eighth Loan sales campaign put more stress on the value of saving for the post-war reconstruction period. Almost 80 percent of all Victory Bond salesmen polled (and 72.5 percent on the prairies) reported that the main reason people bought bonds during the Eighth Loan was because they were a good investment, whereas most had hitherto bought bonds to help win the war.[47] NWFC public opinion research indicated a responsiveness among Canadians to the theme of consumer self-interest, and the committee tailored an increasing proportion of new advertising to exploit this theme during the final campaigns. One broadsheet made the connection between a housewife and her husband in action overseas, "Two minds with but a Single Thought": they were "Both saving for their future Home and Happiness" by buying bonds. Another newspaper ad featured a housewife proclaiming, "I'm dreaming of a *modern* kitchen" filled with new appliances (see Figure 3.12). Victory Bonds, apparently, would make her dream a reality.

The NWFC had the cooperation of newspapers in promoting its message. Winnipeg newspapers ran numerous articles and editorials supporting the loan campaigns. They reported daily on a loan drive's progress, routinely describing highlights of the daily noon-gun ceremony (described below), followed by stories of notable bond purchases by individuals and groups. The progress of various businesses toward their own objectives was regularly noted, especially awards of "V" flags. Many of these stories were written with intent to persuade others to do their share, as in the following excerpt from the *Free Press*: "In Emerson, a man who earned only $225 from Jan. 1 to May 1,

Table 3.1. Victory Loan Slogans and Symbols

Loan	Period	Slogan	Symbol
1st War Loan	15-19 January 1940		
2nd War Loan	9-21 September 1940		
1st Victory Loan	2-21 June 1941	Help Finish the Job	Victory Torch
2nd Victory Loan	16 February - 7 March 1942	Come on Canada	Maple Leaf
3rd Victory Loan	19 October - 7 November 1942	Nothing matters now but Victory	Dagger
4th Victory Loan	26 April - 15 May 1943	Back the Attack	Roman numeral IV
5th Victory Loan	18 October - 6 November 1943	Speed the Victory	Winged V
6th Victory Loan	24 April - 13 May 1944	Put Victory First	Winged VI
7th Victory Loan	21 October - 11 November 1944	Invest in Victory	Flaming Sword on Arabic 7
8th Victory Loan	23 April - 12 May 1945	Invest in the Best	
9th Victory Loan	22 October - 10 November 1945	Sign Your Name for Victory	Fountain pen through Arabic 9

Source: LAC, RG 19, vol. 592, file 155-30-0, NWFC; BCA, NWFC file 2-2, Victory Loan Slogans & Symbols.

marched into loan headquarters recently and put $200 cash on the line for a bond. Later when he heard that sales in his district were lagging he again entered the campaign rooms and bought a $300 bond on the instalment plan."[48] During the Sixth Loan, the *Tribune*'s daily front page included a photo of a different soldier, sailor, or airman along with a description of his job. By doing his duty, the captions advised, "he puts victory first." The obvious implication was that the civilian's duty was to put victory first by buying bonds.

Like the newspapers, film companies cooperated in the publicity effort and their productions were often sponsored by business concerns. As with much sponsored print advertising, this was a means for manufacturers to keep their brand names in the public consciousness despite the depleted wartime consumer goods market. To promote the Seventh Loan, Coca-Cola sponsored "an inspirational slide film" entitled "If You Marched By," General Motors provided a short film called "In All Thy Sons Command," and Hollywood studio MGM produced a ten-minute feature starring Spencer Tracy as a professor of history in a Canadian university.[49] Other publicity was incorporated in the newsreels. More films were to be produced for the next loan, including a twenty-minute film by 20th Century Fox featuring Fibber McGee and Molly, Bob Hope and Bing Crosby, Frank Sinatra, Carmen Miranda, Harry James, and Betty Grable. Besides making promotional films, entertainers and other celebrities frequently lent their support directly by making public appearances during loan campaigns.[50]

Radio, of course, was a popular medium of the masses and the NWFC made much use of its capabilities for persuasion. It sponsored a series of programs like "The Victory Loan Hour," that mixed music, humour, drama, and direct appeals in order to encourage bond sales. Celebrities like film stars and musicians contributed by performing pieces with war-related themes. "The Victory Loan Hour," hosted by Lorne Greene, could be heard on Wednesdays over the Canadian Broadcasting Corporation's network, which included Winnipeg stations CJRC and CKY. "Highlights for Today" aired for thirty minutes on Sundays, and listeners could catch "They Tell Me" five times a week for fifteen minutes. The latter program was "directed to a large but specific audience—namely women, the person [sic] in the home who directs the spending of the family budget." The intention of all these programs was to be entertaining but still motivational. One episode of "Highlights for Today" closed with the narrator tackling the problem of Victory Bond redemptions:

> here's a thought to carry into the new week. If one of our airmen were to fly almost to his objective in Germany and then decide he would rather be back in London seeing a show or dancing in a supper club—and if he turned back to England for that very reason— well, it would be mighty serious and his superior officers wouldn't hesitate to speak our condemnation. But suppose the tables were reversed. Suppose that grand bunch of flyers of ours, who never have turned back from any task, were to learn that some of us had purchased Victory Bonds and War Savings Certificates to help them over there—and then a few weeks or a few months later, without any real need or emergency to force us to do so, we had cashed them in! Turned back on our pledge ... walked out on our part of the job! Well—there it is—let's think it over.[51]

The NWFC thus used all available media to persuade Canadians to buy securities, though newspaper advertising received priority in the committee's publicity budgeting. The Second Victory Loan provides a typical example. The NWFC spent almost $700,000 on advertising of all types: approximately

$543,000 on publications, including daily and weekly newspapers, foreign language papers, magazines, religious, labour, and trade papers, veterans' publications, and the financial press; added to that was $154,000 for other media, including radio ads, posters and broadsheets, street car ads, and other printed materials.[52] Expenditures were roughly similar during other loan drives.[53]

Fostering Consensus

The NWFC used another publicity method that was integral to the success of the Victory Loans. Public ceremonies and stunts presented a series of propagandized public spectacles that deserve special attention because they generated a level of excitement that made people receptive to the message the NWFC disseminated through its advertising. Patriotic spectacles would contribute significantly to the success of all nine Victory Loans through to November 1945, partly by generating popular pressure in support of voluntary war finance mechanisms, but also by creating an atmosphere of consensus and shared purpose.

Mass public spectacles had evolved in the nineteenth century to shape, in new ways, the nature of popular engagement with symbols of state power. Historian David Cannadine has explained that the nineteenth-century Great Powers tended to compete in staging elaborate state ceremonials that exhibited their power or stressed the longevity of traditions associated with their ruling houses. Such rituals marked the centennial of the American Revolution in 1876, the 1878 funeral of King Victor Emmanuel II in Italy, the 1880 inauguration of Bastille Day in France, the 600th anniversary of the Austrian Habsburg monarchy in 1882, the 1896 coronation of Tsar Nicholas II in Russia, and the Silver Jubilee of Kaiser Wilhelm II in 1913, to cite just a few examples. Cannadine notes two schools of thought regarding the significance of popular experiences of royal ceremonials in twentieth-century Britain which are relevant to this study of Victory Loans. Some research has suggested that such ceremonial events had an integrative influence, reflecting and reinforcing "deeply rooted, widely held popular values." Other findings have indicated not "a publicly articulated expression of consensus," but rather a "'mobilization of bias'—an example of the ruling elite consolidating its ideological dominance by exploiting pageantry as propaganda."[54] Other works have shown that such ceremonials could serve both the integrative and propaganda functions.[55]

Canadians shared in British spectacles like Queen Victoria's 1897 Diamond Jubilee and also staged some of their own. In July 1908, the 300th anniversary of Quebec City's founding was marked by a series of historical pageants that "gathered warships from three navies to the river below Quebec and featured processions, illuminations, fireworks, parades, reconstructions, a massed military tattoo, regatta, sail-pasts, ... concerts, ... a solemn open-air mass, church services, state dinners, balls, garden parties, and, crowning the occasion, the presence of the heir to the throne, His Royal Highness the Prince of Wales."[56] More recently and closer to home, Winnipeg had experienced similar excitement during the Royal Tour of King George VI and Queen Elizabeth during the summer of 1939. Preparations had been laid months in advance for events connected with the 24 May visit, which included a parade with floats commemorating the history of Manitoba, an official reception at Government House, and decoration of public buildings.[57] The Royal Tour had a unifying effect on Canadians as the country drifted toward the Second World War, and Victory Loan spectacles would similarly foster an integrative, patriotic consensus. Like the royal rituals studied by Cannadine, they simultaneously created an element of popular pressure to conform to state goals that proved difficult to resist.

The first step in fostering that consensus was to create a unifying discourse to which Canadians would relate. Part of that discourse involved selecting central themes and slogans for the Victory Loan campaigns. The national committee chose the slogan "Help Finish the Job" for the first mass drive. Chairman Spinney felt that the slogan's origin, Churchill's appeal to the Americans, would be obvious.[58] The first Victory Loan also had a stirring symbol, the Victory Torch, and an innovative promotional program that involved Canadians across the country. The Victory Torch campaign was conceived by Mr. W.H. Goodman, Managing Editor of the Canadian Publishers War Finance Publicity Committee. His idea was to "fashion a symbolic torch... fly it from coast to coast on a bomber accompanied by men of the three armed services, and then fly it over for presentation to The Rt. Hon. Winston Churchill." In making the Victory Torch the centrepiece of the loan's publicity campaign, Goodman had selected an icon with an implicit motif that would be recognizable to most Canadians. The torch icon has been used variously as a symbol of life, enlightenment, truth, and love, among other abstractions. More specifically, torch iconography is a distinct feature of much imagery connected with themes of war and remembrance, partly as a result of John

McCrae's famous poem, "In Flanders Fields," which implores Canadians:

> *Take up our quarrel with the foe:*
> *To you from failing hands we throw*
> *The torch; be yours to hold it high.*

McCrae's torch was incorporated in numerous Great War memorials erected by Canadians during the inter-war period. Many community memorials either paraphrased or directly quoted his poem, and two notable national monuments prominently feature torch symbols: the Vimy Memorial, unveiled in 1936, and the National War Memorial, completed in 1939.[59] The torch image had also been used in Victory Bond posters during the Great War, so its pedigree was firmly established by the time Goodman adopted it.

The Victory Torch created for the loan drive was a substantial icon in its own right: five and a half feet tall, it was covered in gold leaf and weighed fifty-five pounds.[60] Inscribed with the message "PART OF THE TOOLS—CANADA'S VICTORY LOAN 1941," it would stop at thirty cities, beginning in Victoria and concluding in Halifax. Cities receiving the torch would inaugurate their drives by staging "elaborate patriotic ceremonials with a note of consecration ... imbued with a spiritual quality" designed to arouse "patriotic emotions." The RCAF would supply a bomber and crew to carry the torch across Canada and then to Britain. An "illuminated scroll" would accompany the torch, signed by each city's mayor, the lieutenant governors and premiers of all provinces, the governor general, the prime minister, and the leader of the opposition. Miniature scrolls would be signed by officials in cities not visited by the bomber. Once the loan's $600 million objective had been reached, the bomber and crew would fly to London to present the torch and scrolls to Churchill on Dominion Day, 1 July 1941.[61]

What did Goodman mean by "elaborate patriotic ceremonials?" The national Victory Loan Committee suggested that local dedication ceremonies across the country should include participation by local military units, bands, veterans, police, fire departments, religious and school groups, local organizations including Boy Scouts, Girl Guides, and cadets, in a "semi-patriotic, semi-religious ceremonial of the highest possible dignity." Those assembled would be led in prayer by a "local church dignitary," there would be patriotic songs ("O Canada," "The Maple Leaf Forever," "There'll Always Be an England") and religious hymns, and a "Torch Day" address would be made by a featured speaker, followed by a mass Victory Torch dedication pledge. The ceremonial should conclude with "the biggest parade that each community has ever put on."[62] To further the "spiritual quality" of the campaign, the committee also decided to name June 8th "Victory Loan Sunday," when church leaders would be asked to speak on behalf of the loan during their services.[63]

Morale was one "spiritual" consideration, and official policy for promotion of the first Victory Loan drive was geared to boost morale even as it sought to boost sales. The national committee intended to make the spectacles so impressive that reports would both give the people of Britain cause to take heart and warn the enemy that Canada was in the fight until "glorious victory" would be won.[64] Publicity policy was shrewd and manipulative. Advertising during the three-week drive was managed "so as not to give Canadians the idea that success was easy—nor that failure was in sight. Announcing too great a volume of subscriptions in the first two or three days might, it was felt, cause over-confidence among the public and result in slackening interest and slackening subscriptions. Conversely, to announce a vast volume in the first few days and a slump in the next few, would ... generate unreasoning fear that the loan was in a tailspin and foredoomed to fail—thereby bringing about public discouragement and reluctance to subscribe."[65] Control was exercised by rationing the provision of figures to the papers through daily morning and evening press releases.

General publicity policy for the campaign, and those to follow, was thus determined at the national level by the Victory Loan Committee and later by the NWFC. But much of it was to be implemented locally by provincial and civic subcommittees. The provincial publicity committees functioned by organizing distribution of publicity materials they ordered from the national committee, contacting local groups and service clubs for cooperation, and making suggestions for local press coverage. Municipal committees were responsible for similar areas, including arrangements for special events like parades, stunts, or prominently displayed graphic progress charts.[66] The promotional materials available to the Manitoba committee included flags, honour pennants and certificates, bumper stickers, posters, street car and billboard ads, envelope "stuffers," and speaker's manuals with suggested speeches of varying lengths.[67] The Manitoba committee made appropriate use of these items and, during the first Victory Loan, it also requested that the province's municipalities issue proclamations urging all businesses and householders to fly flags and decorate their premises during the period of a campaign. Mayor John Queen accordingly issued a proclamation to that effect on 22 May 1941.[68]

Public Victory Loan events normally coincided with the periods during which bonds were available for purchase, though the first drive was an exception. The nominal drive period was from 2 to 21 June 1941, but, in this case, events were scheduled to accommodate the special logistical requirements of the Victory Torch plan, as well as the symbolism that would be associated with two major patriotic holidays, Victoria Day and Dominion Day. The torch therefore began its journey on 24 May in Victoria, and was scheduled to arrive in Winnipeg on 1 June. The local campaign was to be kicked off on the evening of Saturday, 31 May, by a series of eleven bonfires in parks around the city. Other communities would have their own bonfires. The idea was to hold a party in each location, complete with bands playing, to "weld all citizens of the province together in a mighty effort" to meet Manitoba's Victory Loan objective, set at \$43 million. Winnipeg's bonfires were ultimately postponed due to rain until the following Saturday, though they were held on schedule elsewhere in the province.[69] The highlight of the Winnipeg campaign, in any case, was the torch dedication ceremony on Sunday, 1 June.

Upon the bomber's arrival at Stevenson Field, the torch was conveyed to the Legislative grounds by a parade of local military, naval, and air force units, Winnipeg Police, and Royal Canadian Mounted Police. Bands from Princess Patricia's Canadian Light Infantry and the RCAF played as the parade passed along Memorial Boulevard, lined with a Canadian Legion honour guard. A platform was erected on the steps of the Legislature for assembled dignitaries, including Premier Bracken, Lieutenant Governor McWilliams, Mayor Queen, and senior officers of the armed services in Manitoba. According to the Winnipeg *Free Press*, "a dense crowd blotted out the northern lawns of the legislative building ... to take part in the dedication of Canada's golden Torch of Victory." Conspicuous among the crowd were the Norwegian, Icelandic, Greek, American, Polish, Swedish, Dutch, and Danish flags, borne by members of Winnipeg's various ethnic communities.[70]

The dedication ceremony was a paroxysm of warlike British patriotism that left little doubt about Winnipeggers' enthusiasm for the war effort or their affinity for the mother country. Reverend W.G. Martin opened the ceremony with a prayer and the Salvation Army band played "Onward Christian Soldiers" as the crowd sang along with the 400-voice choir. Bracken then made a rather pedestrian address that nonetheless played on the crowd's loyalties: "We meet here today ... at a critical time in the history of the British Empire. In this central province of Canada, we have gathered together once

Table 3.2. War and Victory Loan Drives, National Totals, 1940–1945

Loan Drive	National Objective	Number of Subscribers	Amount Subscribed
1st War Loan	$200 million	178,363	$250,000,000
2nd War Loan	$300 million	150,890	$324,945,700
1st Victory Loan	$600 million	968,259	$836,820,250
2nd Victory Loan	$600 million	1,681,267	$996,706,900
3rd Victory Loan	$750 million	2,032,154	$991,389,050
4th Victory Loan	$1.1 billion	2,668,420	$1,308,716,650
5th Victory Loan	$1.2 billion	3,033,051	$1,570,583,750
6th Victory Loan	$1.2 billion	3,077,123	$1,405,013,350
7th Victory Loan	$1.3 billion	3,327,315	$1,659,906,200
8th Victory Loan	$1.35 billion	3,178,275	$1,563,619,350
9th Victory Loan	$1.5 billion	2,947,636	$2,022,473,800
Total Subscribed			$12,930,175,800

Source: NWFC, *Statistics and Information on Dominion Government Public Borrowing Operations*, 20.

again, to pledge ourselves anew to the Cause of Britain, and the principles for which she stands—we are here to give our answer, in deeds not wishes, to the challenge of the Mother Land." He went on to evoke Britain's sacrifices in the war to date, and to urge the people of Manitoba to meet their Victory Loan target of $43 million so it could not be said "of us by later generations, 'They failed their Empire at the hour of its greatest peril.'"[71] Chief Justice E.A. McPherson next led the crowd in reciting the pledge of affirmation, which thundered across the Legislative grounds, carried on the voices of a crowd 10,000 strong: "I hereby declare my belief in Almighty God and re-affirm my loyalty and allegiance to His Majesty the King, and further declare my support of British institutions. I pledge myself and my all to hold the Torch high and to march shoulder to shoulder with the United Kingdom and our allies in our righteous cause to victory and enduring peace." Bracken, McWilliams, and Queen then signed the scroll and returned it to the torch immediately afterwards.[72]

The Victory Loan campaign comprised a number of events that allowed the public to participate and exhibit their patriotism in a variety of ways. The first week of the drive included, among other events, a rally at the Auditorium; another parade to the Legislature, featuring the military, bands, Boy Scouts, and cadets; a cadet review at Osborne Stadium; a bicycle decoration contest at the Legislature; and special church services on Victory Loan Sunday. Another event that would become a loan drive institution was the daily "noon gun" ceremony at Portage and Main. Following a flag-raising ceremony, an 18-pounder field gun, installed beside the Great War memorial statue outside the Bank of Montreal, would fire once for each million dollars subscribed since the last day, and a giant thermometer marked the progress towards the provincial target. On the second day of the drive, the gun fired four times.[73]

There was one other spectacle elaborate enough to rival the torch dedication. On Wednesday, 4 June, the city staged a half-hour blackout of the downtown area. The Winnipeg *Tribune* did its best to stir Winnipeggers' enthusiasm for the event. That night, it reported on the 4th, "all the bedlam and fury of total war will be loosed on the heart of the city. It will be like London, Rotterdam, or Belgrade at their worst—without the bloodshed."[74] The action got underway at 10:00 p.m. Warning "sirens wailed and then 75,000 people saw the lights flicker out in downtown Winnipeg." Aircraft passing over the city dropped flares while thunder flashes "like giant fire crackers" were set off at dozens of points to simulate the effect of falling bombs. Searchlights deployed on building tops swept the sky and ten anti-aircraft guns fired a "barrage" at the hostile air force. Organized city sportsmen fired gunshots from the roofs of downtown buildings to simulate machine guns. Four 4.5-inch howitzers in Provencher Park and troops of two 18-pounder field guns at the Old Exhibition grounds, Legislative Building, and Minto Armoury, fired specific tasks. Women apparently shrieked at the "terrifying" din created by the artillery and thunder flashes, which "split the night with noise and flame." In the midst of the artillery programme, soldiers "equipped with Bren gun carriers, motorcycles and armored cars" advanced east from Sherbrook Street, under cover of smoke, to wipe out a body of "enemy" parachute troops barricaded behind sandbags on Portage Avenue between Fort and Smith Streets. "Through rolling smoke clouds and flame, the carriers rolled relentlessly ahead, straight at the barricade," which they crushed, driving the defenders away. The force then reorganized and set up posts at the Bridge of the Old Forts and the intersection of Main Street and Higgins Avenue. In all, 3,500 active and reserve troops, some coming in from Shilo, Manitoba, "battled grimly along Portage and Main in the most realistic fight they'll see until the real thing."[75]

Apart from the military presence, other groups also participated. St. John Ambulance set up fifty-two First Aid posts manned by 285 volunteers to treat the "wounded," and they were put to the test. There were thirty minor casualties that night, including a heart attack, women fainting, soldiers with "gunshot burns," and one soldier taken to hospital with severe neck burns after being struck by a flare from a Very pistol. When it was all over, a number of young boys helped the soldiers clear the sandbags from Portage Avenue. City police, RCMP, and hundreds of volunteers from the Royal Canadian Naval Volunteer Reserve, the Manitoba Volunteer Reserve, and the Legion of Frontiersmen all assisted in maintaining order and ensuring compliance with blackout regulations.

Winnipeggers apparently observed most of the rules, as there was no "blackout crime," though a few who did not fully comply would "be amazed if they knew how far a burning cigarette is visible in the dark." One man was singled out for "irresponsible" behaviour that "betrayed himself and his fellow citizens." Despite warnings in the paper, radio, and a loudspeaker truck on the street, he peered out an office window with a lit cigarette: "One man's failure to do his duty threatened the blackout. If the test had been real, if Nazi bombers had been raking the sky, his act would have menaced the lives of thousands." Others ignored warnings to stay off the street or move their cars. The *Tribune* waxed melodramatic in response: "From such as these does fate choose the first tragic victims of war. They did not do what they were told. Only expert planning and their own good fortune kept them safe."[76] The blackout exercise thus had both practical and propaganda value. It was, in part, a test of the responsiveness of civil defence measures, and also an occasion to practice some impressive military manoeuvres. The activities provided a unique opportunity for residents to empathize with the struggles faced by their allies in Europe, for authorities to stimulate the impulse to do one's duty and buy bonds, and even to preach conformity with the war effort.

Manitoba passed its $43-million target with more than a million to spare on Thursday, 19 June, and hoisted an honour pennant during the noon ceremony at Portage and Main, accompanied by a three-gun salute.[77] The total raised by the end of the drive was over $53.5 million, and Winnipeg's quota of $23.2 million was also surpassed with nearly $29.7 million in bonds sold. Across the Dominion, Manitoba ranked fourth in value of subscriptions per capita, and third in ratio of Victory Bond applications to population. Manitoba was first in percentage of quota achieved. Ultimately, one out of every thirteen Manitobans—and one out of every nine Winnipeggers—bought a bond, and the average subscription was $50.51.[78] The national objective of $600 million was likewise oversubscribed by a substantial margin. The federal Minister of Pensions and National Health, Ian Mackenzie, flew the Victory Torch to the United Kingdom at the end of the drive and presented it to Winston Churchill on Dominion Day. His speech on the occasion, like the one Bracken delivered in Winnipeg during the dedication ceremony, paled in eloquence compared to the one made by Churchill that had inspired the campaign.[79] The loan drive had been, nonetheless, a resounding success.

"If" Day

In its program for the first Victory Loan, the National War Finance Committee built a template that proved very successful in motivating Winnipeggers, like other Canadians, to lend their money to the government. The national publicity committee's report on the campaign recommended that each subsequent loan drive should contain "a special feature of dramatic interest" like the Victory Torch, "calculated to make strong emotional and dramatic appeal."[80] Heeding this advice, the NWFC executive appointed a Dominion Ceremonials Committee to organize a program along similar lines, to ensure a continuing high level of interest and participation in the upcoming Second Victory Loan, scheduled to begin in February, 1942.[81] The Ceremonials Committee published bulletins with suggestions to guide provincial and municipal committees in their loan drive preparations, and to coordinate them to accord with the overall theme of the campaign.

The plan for the Second Victory Loan was to light a series of "Beacon Fires of Freedom" in all communities, starting in eastern Canada and moving west across the country. The committee wanted to launch the program with a similar ceremony in the United Kingdom, involving Winston Churchill. The Canadian ceremonies were to extend over a nine-day period, starting in Prince Edward Island on the drive's opening day, 16 February, and reaching Manitoba on the 21st. There was to be a huge bonfire to mark the main ceremony, plus a smaller beacon that would burn continuously throughout the campaign near the principal civic office building in each community. The ceremonies were to mirror the Torch Day events from the preceding spring, with parades, choirs, bands, participation by community groups, patriotic addresses by prominent citizens, and a rededication pledge similar to the first one. Mayors were asked to issue a proclamation, requesting all businesses and households again to fly the Union Jack throughout the loan campaign, and to proclaim 22 February "Second Victory Loan Sunday," for which special church services would be organized. The Ceremonials Committee further suggested that all clubs, organizations, or other groups that held regular meetings should be prevailed upon to devote the principal meeting held during the campaign period to the Second Victory Loan, and obtain a speaker "to fully cover the need for a full response to the loan and participation by all members of the organization being addressed."[82]

The responsibility for coordinating the local ceremonials program and any other publicity events fell first upon the National War Finance Committee, Manitoba Division. The Manitoba committee's members included some esteemed local businessmen: H.E. Sellers, president of Federal Grain Ltd., was chairman, and sat on the NWFC's Executive Committee. He was also involved in fundraising campaigns for Canadian war services. E.J. Tarr, president of Monarch Life Assurance, was vice-chairman for a short period, and had been chairman of the provincial War Savings Committee before the NWFC was created. Other members included Ralph D. Baker of James Richardson and Sons, who later took over from Tarr as vice-chairman; W.J. Parker, president of Manitoba Pool Elevators; the Hon. J.C. Dryden; Judge W.J. Lindal; and a dozen others. Premier Bracken acted as honorary chairman of the provincial committee. The Manitoba organization had a publicity committee to "bring before our citizens the need of vigorous effort to put this Second Victory Loan across successfully." There was close cooperation with the Winnipeg committee, chaired by J.D. Perrin, which in turn formed subcommittees for Special Events and Public Relations.[83] These committees decided to veer away from the national plan to light large bonfires, perhaps because they were not considered appropriate given February temperatures. The main event of the Second Victory Loan campaign in Winnipeg, and perhaps in the entire country, was not so much a ceremony as a stunt—and it was a stunt that garnered major media attention across Canada and even the United States. It was called "If Day," and in the words of Winnipeg *Tribune* reporter Vince Leah, it was "the biggest and most important publicity stunt" ever attempted in the city.[84]

If Day originated in the Manitoba Division's belief that special measures were required to induce ordinary wage-earners to subscribe to the limit if the Second Victory Loan were to be a success. A report written by the division's Public Relations Committee reveals the strategy it believed would best persuade Manitobans to comply, and it is worth citing in some detail. The report suggested that most people had not yet made the level of sacrifice in their daily living standard that would be required to meet the objectives of the NWFC:

> To properly reach the individual, the work of the Public Relations Committee must ... make the average man and woman realize that our way of life can only be retained through personal sacrifice.
>
> In previous loans the thrifty people bought bonds because they had savings. To a limited extent, people have purchased War Saving Certificates through salary deduction. Now people must be sold the idea of reducing their personal standard of living in order to buy bonds and at the same time to release their available savings bank deposits, for purchase of bonds.
>
> The most difficult task before us seems to be in the field of promoting commitment of current earnings of the large mass of salaried employees and wage earners, to buy Victory bonds on deferred payments. This is a grim business and the public relations committee face up to it as such. No ordinary publicity measures would seem to meet this need.
>
> We therefore propose to develop the theme of "Freedom" throughout the period of the campaign.... [S]uccessive events will be devoted to each element of freedom as we know it, in turn. Schools, churches, business, government, labor, sport, all the channels of democratic activity will be appropriately promoted on a scheduled day.

To cast these elements in sufficiently stark relief to make clear the value of that freedom, it was necessary to show Manitobans what they stood to lose if the Axis powers were not defeated. The Public Relations Committee therefore proposed "a preparatory event which we believe is without precedent on this continent": a Nazi invasion of Winnipeg.[85]

If Day, like the June 1941 blackout, presented the military with an opportunity to conduct a unique exercise in urban warfare. A simulated "blitz" would begin with RCAF aircraft representing German dive-bombers flying over Winnipeg, Brandon, Dauphin, and other Manitoba cities. Active and reserve army troops would then conduct a fighting withdrawal through Winnipeg as the "Wehrmacht" conquered and occupied the province and its capital. Once in control, the occupation forces would stage a series of events calculated to leave a strong impression with the public of the ways that life would change "if" the Germans were victorious. There would be a book-burning outside the public library by the Gestapo, churches would be closed down, and the premier, lieutenant governor, mayor, and city aldermen would be arrested and interned. George Waight, in charge of the Special Events section of the Winnipeg committee, wrote Bracken that when Manitobans "actually see our prominent leaders and business men in a situation which *might* arise 'if' they fail in their efforts, the urge to go 'all out' is more likely to be manifest."[86]

Winnipeg's If Day began late on Wednesday, 18 February 1942, when German aircraft were sighted over Norway House. Air raid sirens sounded at 6:00 a.m. the next morning. Defence troops under the command of Colonel D.S. MacKay assembled at Fort Osborne Barracks and the Minto and McGregor Armouries for the largest manoeuvres in the city's history to that date. The weather that morning was a chilly −24°C, but the cold did not stop soldiers or civilians from playing their parts. All local reserve army units participated, with support from the Artillery Training Centre in Shilo, the Infantry Training Centre at the University of Manitoba, and ancillary troops. By 7:00 a.m. a defence perimeter was established on a three-mile radius from City Hall, and a blackout was imposed over the city. Soldiers from the 5th Field Brigade took up positions in St. Boniface, the Queen's Own Cameron Highlanders in Fort Rouge, the Veterans' Guard of Canada in River Heights, the reconstituted Winnipeg Grenadiers in St. James, the Winnipeg Light Infantry in the city's North End, and the Royal Winnipeg Rifles at the Canadian Pacific Railway's Weston Yards. Civilians also got involved. The Patriotic Salvage Corps operated mobile canteens to feed participants in the manoeuvres, and members of St. John Ambulance operated first aid posts downtown. Meanwhile, 1,000 members of the Manitoba Volunteer Reserve acted as air raid wardens, fighting simulated fires and operating ambulances before ultimately taking up defensive positions on the left bank of the Red River.[87]

The battle commenced at 7:03 when field guns firing blank artillery rounds from positions in East Kildonan engaged imaginary enemy forces advancing on the city. Other gun positions were located at River Park, St. Ignatius Church, and Polo Park. Universal carriers patrolled through Tuxedo, River Heights, St. Boniface, St. Vital, St. John's, and Brooklands. Anti-aircraft units were established at the Mall (Memorial Boulevard), the Canadian National Railways depot, City Hall, Osborne Stadium, and the Paris Building. Supposedly "under pressure from Nazi panzer forces," the city's defenders withdrew at 7:45 into their second-line positions along a perimeter two miles from City Hall, under covering fire from the artillery.[88] Mobile anti-aircraft cars were operated by thirty five-man crews, all members of the Manitoba Fish and Game Association, who fired blank shotgun shells at imaginary enemy aircraft as railway "torpedo-tracks" exploded in the streets to simulate falling bombs. As the mock battle reached its climax, the 10th Military District Engineers received orders to blow up the city's bridges as the troops retreated to the city's core for a last stand. The engineers placed dynamite charges on the ice under the nine bridges, and used smoke generators and coal dust to simulate their demolition. The Norwood, Main Street, Osborne, Maryland, St. James, Provencher, Elm Park, Louise, and Redwood bridges were all "destroyed." By 9:30, the battle was over. The defenders having "surrendered," the German occupation was about to begin.[89]

The men portraying the invaders were members of the Young Men's Section of the Manitoba Board of Trade, and the forty field-grey uniforms they wore had been rented from Hollywood. Some had painted battle scars on their faces for dramatic effect. George Waight, one of the main planners of If Day, also got into the act by impersonating a Gestapo agent. As they took control of the city, the "steel-helmeted Nazis in captured Bren gun carriers and commandeered cars and buses" patrolled the streets and blocked roads to search motorists and passengers.[90] They sand-bagged and surrounded Eaton's department store, the Hudson's Bay Company, and other downtown buildings, and set up anti-aircraft searchlights. Police headquarters, City Hall, and the Legislative Building were captured and high-ranking officials arrested. Mayor John Queen and aldermen William Scraba, C.E. Simonite, R.A. Sara, and John Blumberg, as well as the mayor's secretary and the city clerk, were taken to Lower Fort Garry for internment. Premier John Bracken and Lieutenant Governor R.F. McWilliams were also interned in the fort's "concentration camp," along with a number of cabinet ministers, including Errick Willis, J.S. McDiarmid, James McLenaghan, and Ivan Schultz.

The new order would be a harsh one for Winnipeg residents—though it only lasted one day—thanks to the realistic and detailed preparations made by If Day's planners.[91] Clergymen, as well as politicians, were arrested. Religious and ethnic associations were disbanded. Notices "proclaiming the death penalty for all who in any way resisted the army of occupation were posted everywhere, to be read by an incredulous populace."[92] Food stocks were subjected to austere rationing limits,[93] and all wheat was to be sent to Germany. Authorities would permit a buy-back scheme in case of starvation.

Automobile owners were required to surrender their vehicles. Other supplies were confiscated for use of the occupation army, including clothing and metals. A start was made at one Winnipeg apartment block, where Nazi thugs ransacked residences and carted off their booty. The pillaging did not stop with material goods. Winnipeggers would pay the costs of the occupation, and Canadian currency was to be replaced with German. The transition began when "early-morning customers at coffee counters" were forced to take their change in "worthless paper Reichmarks." The bullying continued at noon, when two dozen German soldiers barged into the cafeteria at Great-West Life, "forced men and women from their luncheon tables and stole their food."[94] Commuters could also expect a rough ride. Passengers on the Winnipeg Electric Company's street cars received special transfers instructing them in the new etiquette: "Verboten! It is forbidden to remain seated in the presence of a German officer. By order. Erich von Neurenberg. Gauleiter."[95] Some were roughed up and required to show their registration papers.

Intellectual conformity replaced freedom of expression for Winnipeg residents. A bonfire outside the Carnegie Library on William Avenue burned all books deemed contrary to Nazi philosophy—or at least those superfluous copies already destined for the incinerator. School children would be properly indoctrinated by the new authorities. All those from six to sixteen years of age would be forced to join the Hitler Youth. In the meantime, storm troopers took over Robert H. Smith school, arrested the principal, and insisted that students would learn, henceforth, only the Nazi "truth." Other children were dismissed from school early so they could listen to the radio play "Swastika Over Canada" on the Canadian Broadcasting Corporation's network.[96]

Winnipeggers were forced to endure the ignominy of having their city renamed "Himmlerstadt," and Portage Avenue became "Adolf Hitler Strasse." But other Manitoba cities also suffered German occupation. In Brandon, field guns had fired on the approaching enemy, who subsequently "captured" strategic points before rounding up prominent civilians. Members of city council were seized, and Mayor F.H. Young was required to broadcast a message to citizens to keep calm and obey the instructions of their conquerors. Portage la Prairie, Carberry, Russell, Flin Flon, The Pas, and Killarney also staged If Day theatrics. Civic officials from Selkirk, like those from Winnipeg, were interned at Lower Fort Garry. Virden was forced to accept the name "Virdenberg."[97]

The simulation was over in Winnipeg by 5:30 p.m., when a parade down Portage Avenue featured signs urging residents to "Buy Victory Bonds" because "It Must Not Happen Here." As a graphic indicator of the effort to ensure it did not, a huge forty-foot map of the province was hung outside the Bank of Montreal building at Portage and Main. It was divided into forty-five sections, each representing $1 million in Victory Bond sales. One Union Jack was added to the map for each million subscribed during the loan drive, until Manitoba's target of $45 million was reached and the entire province was symbolically liberated. Later in the evening, the Norwegian minister to the United States, Wilhelm de Morgenstierne, spoke at a Winnipeg Auditorium rally about conditions in his home country under the occupation, providing the climax to If Day.[98]

The sight of coal-scuttle helmets, jack boots, and the swastika flag, flying from public buildings in place of the Union Jack, had been a shock. Despite numerous warnings that the invasion and military manoeuvres were staged, some Winnipeg residents were fooled by If Day's realism. People outside of Manitoba took notice, and the stunt brought Winnipeg international recognition. Newsreel coverage was expected to reach an audience of 40 million, the average number of weekly moviegoers.[99] The story was covered by *Life*, *Newsweek*, *Time*, scores of papers in New York, Minneapolis, Boston, and even a local paper in Whangerei, New Zealand. Of course, papers across Canada carried the story, as did the CBC. According to the *Globe and Mail*, Manitoba "deserves a special word of commendation in the Victory Loan campaign because of the unique effort made to show what failure would mean. Winnipeg was in the hands of Hitler and his ironclad gangsters for a day, figuratively speaking.... Winnipeg had a day of it, in imagination, with enough real adventure to make the imagination work." The U.S. Office of Facts and Figures and the U.S. Treasury asked for details pertinent to their own bond drives. Vancouver followed Winnipeg's example and bought the surplus Reichsmarks for its own If Day.[100]

The Manitoba Division's publicity campaign in support of the Second Victory Loan was a great success. Special events did not altogether ignore the NWFC's ceremonials program, but Manitoba's campaign was, in the main, conceived locally. Instead of bonfires, the Winnipeg committee arranged a rally at the Auditorium on Second Victory Loan Sunday, featuring a large replica of the Victory Torch that was lit during a "rededication" ceremony to stand as a "beacon of freedom."[101] The rally included a patriotic address by University of Manitoba President Sidney Smith, a 200-voice choir, the Salvation Army Band, and another pledge administered by Mr. Justice A.K.

Dysart. The event was billed as a "Freedom of Worship" service in connection with the overall theme the Manitoba Division had selected for the loan drive, and the Winnipeg *Tribune* supplement to its If Day edition, "Das Winnipeger Lügenblatt," provided examples of the kind of censorship that could be enforced if freedom of the press were lost under a National Socialist regime (see Appendix 1). There was also a "Freedom to Play" event at the Auditorium on 23 February, featuring figure skating, a junior hockey game, and national radio broadcaster Foster Hewitt.[102] Other events promoted the loan on a smaller scale: the daily noon-gun ceremony was continued though it was moved from Portage and Main to the Legislative grounds; the American consul general for Winnipeg, A.W. Klieforth, stationed in Austria and Germany from 1924 to 1941, spoke to a luncheon crowd at the Fort Garry Hotel on If Day about German methods of Nazification and plans for world conquest; and renowned American newspaper columnist Dorothy Thompson visited the city to speak at an Auditorium rally on 26 February.[103]

Collectively, these events inspired Winnipeggers, and other Manitobans, to put the loan drive "over the top." The map at Portage and Main was covered in Union Jacks by Tuesday, 3 March, as Manitobans exceeded their quota and "liberated" the province with four days to spare. The amount raised was nearly $65 million, and the number of people who bought bonds—105,038—was almost double the number from the first Victory Loan. Of these totals, 69,713 Winnipeggers bought almost $37 million in bonds.[104] Canadians together oversubscribed the national objective of $600 million by more than a third.

Tightening Belts

By the opening of the Third Victory Loan in October 1942, Canadian forces had seen action at Dieppe as well as Hong Kong. NWFC publicity adopted an increasingly grim and determined mood in the aftermath of these two disasters. Canada's military stake in the war was increasing and a corresponding financial commitment was needed from ordinary Canadians. The new gravity of the situation prompted a subtle change in the tone of bond appeals. Federal Finance Minister J.L. Ilsley had previously called on Canadians "to buy bonds to the limit of your capacity" in order to support their servicemen and safeguard their freedom.[105] The argument now advanced had a new character that reflected the desperate nature of the fight facing the Allies and let Canadians know that they would have to further tighten their belts. Premier Bracken, as honorary chairman of the Manitoba Division, gave a radio address a few days in advance of the loan drive's opening, which played on the theme of greater personal sacrifice and self-deprivation that the NWFC was trying to sell. It is worth noting in some detail since it clearly spells out what the government expected of Canadians and the measures that could be taken if they did not comply.

Bracken hinted that unless Manitobans and other Canadians increased their subscriptions, manufacturing of civilian goods would probably have to be curtailed. Restrictions could mount to the point where only the barest "necessities of life" would be available. Perhaps other peacetime activities, such as sports and entertainment, would also have to be curtailed along with consumer spending, reduced to the lowest level "consistent with national health and morale." The premier explained that the federal government had only two possible courses of action to finance the war, either to arbitrarily "close down thousands of enterprises and ration everything," or to tax and borrow from Canadians to the limit in order to pay the costs of military mobilization and industrial production. In choosing the latter option, Ottawa *"has preferred to rely on the loyalty and self-determination of every Canadian citizen"* (emphasis added). Bracken acknowledged that "our taxes have been multiplied until they seem almost unbearable," but "if the loan fails in its objective ... the Dominion will then have no choice but to adopt even more vexatious rates of taxation and even stricter rationing."[106] Bracken's references to curtailment of civilian consumer goods, services, and leisure activities was no doubt calculated to suggest that civilians did not yet have it so bad, but that greater austerity could soon be required. He framed Ottawa's preference for taxing and borrowing as an almost beneficent course of action, and his reference to the loyalty of citizens implied that those who did not comply were disloyal and unpatriotic.

The national objective for the Third Victory Loan in October-November 1942 was set at $750 million, and Ilsley estimated that half of that total would have to come from individual subscribers as opposed to corporations. In answer to complaints that people had little money for bonds because taxation was now so high, another NWFC message argued: "the plain facts are that Canada *needs* the money and the people of Canada *have* the money. If our present level of living makes it impossible for us to contribute to the Victory Loan, then *it is our bounden duty to lower that level, to eliminate all luxuries and to come down to the bed-rock of the necessities of life*" (emphasis in original).[107] To win their cooperation, the finance minister wanted Canadians to identify, on a personal level, with the sacrifices made by the troops overseas. By saving, Ilsley suggested, they could make that connection: "We have a serious and grim business in hand—a struggle which calls for the best that is in us. Our best includes the ultimate which every one of us can do in the matter of saving and lending to our country. This is the only direction in which most of us can attempt to match the valorous performance of our Armed Forces."[108]

The NWFC therefore chose a theme for the Third Victory Loan that sought to capitalize on the public interest generated by Canadian combat operations and the prospect of more action to come: the Commando Dagger. It was a timely symbol. British Commandos had captured public attention with amphibious raids such as those against the Norwegian Lofoten Islands in December 1941 and the French port of St. Nazaire in March 1942, and they had joined the 2nd Canadian Infantry Division in the Dieppe raid in August. Lieutenant-General A.G.L. McNaughton, meanwhile, had recently put his own public relations spin on the build-up in Britain of his First Canadian Army, calling it a "Dagger pointed at the Heart of Berlin." In explaining its choice of the Commando Dagger, the Dominion Ceremonials Committee explained that this symbol would permit "a direct tie-up between individual communities throughout the Dominion and men from these communities who are now serving in the fighting forces overseas. Thus will every Canadian be put in position to participate personally with General MacNaughton [sic] in 'pointing the Dagger at the heart of Berlin.'"[109]

The plan for the main ceremonials in the Third Loan called for a repetition of the Victory Torch proceedings, substituting for the torch a large replica of the dagger issued to Britain's Commandos. The Ceremonials Committee suggested that communities feature the replica dagger outside their main public building, along with a graphic to chart the progress of the loan drive. It recommended using a large outline map of Europe with Berlin clearly marked, toward which a dagger would move from Britain as subscriptions mounted. Another option—the one used in Winnipeg—was to mount a large heart labelled "Berlin" beneath a dagger which would be lowered by steps as the quota was approached, finally to plunge in up to the hilt when it was surpassed. Apart from the replicas, the NWFC was to supply each municipality with an actual commando dagger, obtained from British supplies, that would be featured in campaign events and about which a constant honour guard would be maintained. The daggers would be sent overseas to a military unit representing each respective community at the loan's completion. To assist in making the personal connection, subscribers would receive a lapel pin with a design of the dagger.[110]

The drive opened in Winnipeg on Sunday, 18 October 1942, with the Commando Dagger ceremonial. A parade of military units conveyed the dagger to the Legislature, where the general pattern established during the first Victory Loan was followed. Bracken, H.E. Sellers, and Winnipeg *Free Press* editor John Dafoe made suitable speeches; a flight of twelve aircraft flew past in a V-formation to add dramatic effect; two members of the Queen's Own Cameron Highlanders just back from Dieppe, Captain William E. Osler and Company Sergeant-Major George Gouk, a winner of the Distinguished Conduct Medal, were introduced; and the dagger was dedicated by 18,000 spectators and 2,000 military personnel. Following the main event at the Legislature, drive organizers arranged secondary "Dagger Parades" at Winnipeg schools on subsequent days of the campaign, in order to spread the message to a greater proportion of residents. The dagger was presented to a local community leader at each of these ceremonies, to be retained until the next event.[111]

While the pledge given during the Torch dedication in June 1941 included generalities and abstractions like loyalty to the King and support for the Allied cause, the pledge for the opening dagger ceremonial in front of the Legislative Building was more sophisticated. It suggested a greater weight of personal responsibility and shrewdly echoed the phrasing of the Atlantic Charter signed by Churchill and U.S. President Franklin D. Roosevelt in August 1941, in order to emphasize citizens' individual stake in the war aims for which the Allies were fighting:

> With a faith that shall live, I hereby reaffirm my trust in God and my allegiance to His Majesty, The King. I accept this war as my personal war requiring strenuous self-denial. I appreciate the privileges of our way of life. I look forward to a world in which freedom of worship, freedom from want and fear and freedom of opportunity are fully realized. I believe that right shall triumph and that a victory of justice is assured. Therefore, I solemnly pledge myself to earnestly fulfill, to the limit of my power, each wartime duty that faces me and so stand shoulder-to-shoulder with those of my fellowmen [sic] who are defending with their lives our mutual cause.[112]

Captain Osler read the pledge to the crowd, and the pressure to conform to its sentiments must have been great. Here were two war heroes who had risked their lives at Dieppe, asking the crowd to fulfill a few minor, and largely symbolic, home front duties. How could anyone in the crowd help but feel that, by comparison, buying bonds or collecting salvage was the least they could do?

The other focal point for the drive, apart from the dagger ceremonies, was a second "Freedom to Play" night. This one featured a football game at Osborne Stadium on 23 October between the Winnipeg All-Stars, chosen from Winnipeg's three senior football teams, and the U.S. Naval training team from Wahpeton, North Dakota. The game also included marching bands, a Royal Canadian Naval Volunteer Reserve (RCNVR) honour guard, a precision drill demonstration by RCAF airwomen from No. 5 Bombing and Gunnery School in Dafoe, Saskatchewan, and a parade of flags from the Allied nations. There was a salute at half-time to armed forces "heroes" from Hong Kong and Dieppe by the Queen's Own Cameron Highlanders pipe band, the local unit of the Veterans Guard, and Winnipeg city police. George Gouk of the Camerons was again introduced, along with H.E. Sellers and former Blue Bombers coach Reg Threlfall, who spoke on behalf of the loan. The Winnipeg team won, 27–5.[113]

Manitoba was the first province in the Dominion to reach its loan target of $53 million, after which the province's dagger was presented along with a special message to General McNaughton in England.[114] Financially, the campaign was another success. But the ceremonial theme seems to have failed to resonate with people the way that the Victory Torch had, and the campaign could not capture the same energy generated by If Day.[115] The NWFC decided to "dispense with nationally organized ceremonials" after the Third Victory Loan. Future drives would make do with a single national ceremony on Parliament Hill in Ottawa, and each province would be free to stage its own individual promotional campaign.[116]

Although there would be no more grand national ceremonials or stunts to rival If Day, many of the elements from earlier drives were nonetheless retained in future campaigns. Winnipeggers continued to observe Victory Loan Sunday and adorn their homes, businesses, and public spaces with patriotic displays or signs. The specially decorated red, white, and blue streetcar again urged people to "Get on the Bond Wagon" and "Buy Victory Bonds." There were more ceremonies and celebrity appearances. A "monster" rally at the Auditorium helped kick off the Fourth Loan drive in April–May 1943 with

Table 3.3. Victory Loan Drives, Manitoba Totals, 1941–1945

Loan Drive	Manitoba Quota	Total Subscribed	General Sales & Payroll	Number of Applications	Ratio Applications to Population
1st Victory Loan	$43 million	$53,547,400	$13,475,950	56,011	1 in 13
2nd Victory Loan	$45 million	$64,972,300	$17,034,150	105,038	1 in 6.9
3rd Victory Loan	$53 million	$74,169,150	$17,841,450	116,983	1 in 6
4th Victory Loan	$75 million	$89,366,400	$25,531,800	158,220	1 in 4.6
5th Victory Loan	$80 million	$99,872,650	$30,233,400	175,171	1 in 4.5
6th Victory Loan	$80 million	$102,912,850	$32,735,100	180,832	1 in 4.4
7th Victory Loan	$90 million	$110,125,850	$41,904,800	173,664	1 in 4.2
8th Victory Loan	$95 million	$109,851,700	$45,104,600	186,390	1 in 4.3
9th Victory Loan	$100 million	$141,789,850	$63,932,200	179,900	1 in 4.35

Note: The totals raised for each Victory Loan included contributions by "Special Names" and members of the fighting services stationed in Winnipeg and throughout Manitoba. Special Names totals were calculated both before and after "reallocations," which referred to subscriptions by national companies which were divided amongst the provinces according to population. The figures for "Total Subscribed" include reallocations. Various sources are difficult to reconcile since they often used different criteria in compiling statistics. For example, both the NWFC's Manitoba Division and contemporary newspapers reported the Manitoba quotas as above, but the NWFC's official statistical summary released in 1946 did not include reallocations in quota calculations. Quotas have been taken from the former sources because these figures were used to determine progress in public ceremonies; figures for number and ratio of applications come from the Manitoba Division. But because these sources were not always consistent in the manner of recording statistics, the figures under "Total Subscribed" and "General Sales & Payroll" have been taken from the NWFC's summary. The "General Canvass and Payroll" category offers the closest estimate of the contributions of average civilian Winnipeg residents. See AM, P5005, NWFC—Manitoba Division, "Analysis of Final Results, Canada's Ninth Victory Loan, October 22nd to November 10th, 1945," 19-19A; Winnipeg *Free Press* and Winnipeg *Tribune* coverage of various loan campaigns; NWFC, *Statistics and Information on Dominion Government Public Borrowing Operations.*

Winnipeg's own Bert Pearl of the Happy Gang as master of ceremonies.[117] Dignitaries and speakers for future Victory Loan events included representatives of organized labour as well as the usual politicians, military personnel, and more celebrities. The Sixth Loan, for example, featured appearances by Hollywood actresses Gail Patrick and Kay Francis. Winnipeg's own starlet, Deanna Durbin, was invited to participate in the Fourth Loan, though it is uncertain whether she actually made the trip.[118] Ilsley and other federal cabinet ministers, NWFC chairman George Spinney, and Graham Towers, Governor of the Bank of Canada and Spinney's successor after the Fourth Loan, all made regular visits to explain the reasons why Canadians should buy bonds.

Military demonstrations generated the most interest. The Fourth Loan drive opened with a parade and ceremony at Portage and Main that included 100 paratroopers from the 1st Canadian Parachute Battalion. The unit was training at Shilo and this was their first public parade, so it was a distinct novelty.[119] The Winnipeg committee chose a navy theme for its Fifth Loan campaign and erected a huge wooden battleship, the "Greater Winnipeg," at Portage and Memorial with a progress indicator running up the mast to the crow's nest. The other services were not left out. Canadian troops were now in action in Italy, and there was no shortage of interest in martial demonstrations. One of the highlights of the Fifth Loan was the first public "performance" by paratroopers in Canada, a drop on Assiniboine Park by thirty men on Saturday, 23 October 1943. The *Tribune* estimated that between 85,000 and 100,000 spectators squeezed into the park to watch the event. Also of interest was a pair of sixty-inch searchlights put on display at the Legislative grounds, along with a Bofors anti-aircraft gun. The searchlights lit the sky in a "V" for victory that could be seen for miles on Friday, 29 October, and they remained on display at various points around the city for the duration of the drive.[120]

The Sixth Loan, in April-May 1944, was opened at the Legislature by an 18-pounder artillery salute of eighty rounds, one for each million dollars of Manitoba's objective. A Spitfire was stationed in front of the Bank of Montreal for the loan period—apparently the first to be displayed in western Canada. Winnipeggers also witnessed a "Parade of Armed Might," featuring 200 armoured vehicles, artillery pieces, and transport vehicles. It was touted as the "largest mechanized convoy ever placed on the streets of a Canadian city." According to the *Tribune*, this would be "Winnipeg's chance to see some of the arms the United Nations have piled up along the British coasts ready for the thrust into Europe. Winnipeg streets will tremble to the powerful vibrations of the engines which will smash Germany into submission. More than ever Winnipeggers will understand why their dollars are required to keep this equipment flowing in a steady stream into Europe behind our men. These are the machines of victory bought by Victory Bonds."[121]

The Seventh Loan continued the trend of parades, returned to the idea of staging a mock battle, and added a pageant held on the steps of the Legislative Building. The program for the latter included music, flags, huge maps of the theatres of war, and representatives of the invaded countries (Figure 3.19). Norman Lucas of the CBC and Lieutenant C. Ellis, RCNVR, outlined the progress of the war from 1939. As each country fell, German swastikas and Japanese rising suns covered the maps, only to be removed as the tide turned in favour of the Allies. Other events prominently featured returned servicemen and those yet to go overseas. Major-General Rod Keller, a past Winnipeg resident and former commanding officer of the 3rd Canadian Infantry Division during the Battle of Normandy, was home to speak at the Auditorium, and a wings parade was held for British Commonwealth Air Training Plan graduates in connection with the loan.[122]

The noon-gun ceremony was a regular feature of the loan drives. While it oscillated throughout the war between the Mall and "Victory Square" beside the Bank of Montreal at Portage and Main, it was back at the latter location for the Fourth Loan and its general pattern had been established. A military band and gun crew would march down from the Mall (Memorial Boulevard) and form up at the square by 11:45 a.m. daily. Explanations for the live radio broadcast would be given to the crowd. The broadcast would begin at 11:55 with a "Fanfare of Trumpets," followed by an announcement of progress made in the loan drive. A special guest would speak on behalf of the loan for two minutes, and often a war worker or serviceman would be interviewed. The ceremony concluded with the firing of the gun and "God Save the King." An 18-pounder field gun was used up to the Sixth Loan; for the last three drives, it was replaced with a 25-pounder, which had become the Royal Canadian Artillery's standard gun.[123] The gun normally fired once for each million dollars raised on the previous day. The last wartime campaign, the Eighth, added a new ritual to the ceremony, the changing of the guard, and featured a German "doodlebug"—a V-1 flying bomb—that had fallen on London.[124]

What sort of return did the NWFC get for all of the advertising, programming, and public events and spectacles it arranged? Wartime Information Board reports on public opinion, based on correspondence from selected observers across the country, occasionally noted criticism about the high cost of publicity which some considered extravagant.[125] Yet the NWFC estimated that Victory Loan campaigns "cost less than 1 cent for each $1 of Bonds sold."[126] By the latter loans, there was more evidence of public weariness in the face of the government's constant propaganda bombardment. The Manitoba Division of the NWFC reported after the Seventh Loan that "all features [of the campaign] should have entertaining value as the guiding factor and loan messages

should take a very small part in actual billing. It was found increasingly difficult to obtain audiences for speakers such as [Major-General Rod Keller]
unless additional attractions were provided."[127] One Wartime Information
Board correspondent wrote, regarding the Eighth Loan, that "people seem
to be getting a little weary; many say they are willing to see this one through
because they hope it will be the last one."[128]

Nevertheless, publicity measures as a whole succeeded in catching the
attention of a majority of Canadians. Following the Third Loan, for example,
a public opinion poll of 2,337 respondents across the country found that 65.6
percent correctly identified the campaign slogan, 84.2 percent identified
the Commando Dagger symbol, and 92.1 percent knew whether the loan
objective had been met.[129] A larger poll of 5,275 people following the Fifth
Loan found that 73 percent knew the overall loan objective, 96 percent knew
the community's objective, and 83 percent knew the campaign slogan. Of
prairie respondents, 79 percent bought bonds.[130] The Wartime Information
Board believed that the need for the Seventh Loan was taken for granted
by Canadians and that they would continue to offer a high level of support.
One Winnipeg observer quoted a railroad worker's reaction to the abolition
of compulsory savings: "Seeing that the Government is taking less from me
this year I am going to try and give them more in the Loan." A later summary
suggested that reports "continue favorable [sic], and are remarkable for the
almost total lack of criticism of the Loan."[131]

The ultimate measure of the effectiveness of Victory Loan publicity campaigns, in any case, is the ever-increasing amounts that Canadians lent to the
federal government. The NWFC's main objectives were to raise revenue with
which to continue the fight, to absorb Canadians' surplus spending power in
order to curb inflation, and to create a savings reserve to fuel post-war reconstruction. The committee enjoyed real success in accomplishing these tasks.
Despite heavy tax increases, the savings rate of average Canadians reached
25 percent of disposable income.[132] War Savings securities helped absorb
that extra proportion of income in a booming war economy, and controlled
inflationary pressures that would have undermined Ottawa's price control
policies and driven up the cost of living. All of the NWFC's objectives were
successfully met because the committee engineered a very sophisticated campaign of domestic propaganda that emphasized values in which Canadians
fundamentally believed, such as patriotism, protection of loved ones, and the
need to defeat the Axis enemy. As loan objectives successively grew, so did

the totals subscribed. Each loan surpassed its objective, both nationally and in Manitoba. If one of the NWFC's additional goals was to have every person in receipt of income buy bonds, it largely succeeded in Winnipeg. From the first through the last Victory Loan, the number of bond purchase applications steadily rose and so did the ratio of applications to population until, on average, more than one in three city residents committed to buying a bond during the last four drives (see Table 3.4).

Spectacles, Morale, and Consensus

Spectacles like the Victory Torch ceremony, If Day, or the Parade of Armed Might were instrumental in mobilizing support for the loans. Some consideration of the nature of spectacles and the dynamics of crowd behaviour will help explain why the campaigns were so successful. Exploring these features of the ceremonials also helps to reveal their significance for understanding one set of popular reactions to Canada's war effort. John MacAloon's study of the Olympic Games offers a theoretical definition that assigns a number of notable characteristics to true spectacles. Derived from the Latin *specere* ("to look at"), the word refers to something that constitutes a remarkable sight. Spectacles must be public displays "of a certain size or grandeur" that "appeal to the eye by their mass, proportions, color, or other dramatic qualities." They institutionalize the mutually dependent relationship between performers and spectators; "if one or the other...is missing, there is no spectacle." Unlike rituals, especially religious ones, spectacles do not require active participation, but offer the option of merely observing. Some spectacles, nonetheless, may contain elements of ritual. Finally, "spectacle is a dynamic form, demanding movement, action, change, and exchange on the part of the human actors who are center stage, and the spectators must be excited in turn."[133] The Victory Loan ceremonials, stunts, parades, and military demonstrations clearly fit the definition.

Spectacles inherently involve crowd behaviour, and the Victory Loan events included masses of people demonstrating their support for the war effort through patriotic display. Cultural behaviour theorists Ralph H. Turner and Lewis M. Killian distinguish between an expressive mode of crowd behaviour and an instrumental mode. The crowds that supported Victory Loan events were examples of the expressive mode because they gathered merely to show off their patriotism, not to perform any concrete action. Expressive crowds, according to Turner and Killian, display an atmosphere

Table 3.4. Victory Loan Drives, Winnipeg Totals, 1941–1945

Loan Drive	Winnipeg Quota	Total Subscribed	General Sales and Payroll	Number of Applications	Ratio Applications to Population
1st Victory Loan	$23,200,000	$29,695,050	$8,896,700	33,657	1 in 9
2nd Victory Loan	$23,569,000	$36,933,600	$10,174,850	69,713	1 in 4.35
3rd Victory Loan	not recorded	$42,997,550	$10,653,000	77,974	1 in 3.8
4th Victory Loan	$14,319,000*	$53,629,400	$13,335,050	93,894	1 in 3.2
5th Victory Loan	$14,400,000	$55,700,550	$16,015,150	105,881	1 in 3.2
6th Victory Loan	$14,400,000	$57,456,350	$16,177,500	109,242	1 in 2.9
7th Victory Loan	$18,900,000	$60,627,550	$21,542,700	113,622	1 in 2.6
8th Victory Loan	$22,500,000	$63,730,450	$24,326,100	118,084	1 in 2.7
9h Victory Loan	$27,500,000	$84,252,000	$37,374,250	121,900	1 in 2.7

Sources: *Canada at War* 20, Jan. 1943, 29, copy in AM, GR 43, Premier's Correspondence, G76, files 112 (1942), War and 112 (1942) War—Loans; "Wartime Public Bond Issues in Canada", copy in GR 43, Premier's Correspondence, G129, file 23 (1946), War Loans; Canada, Dominion Bureau of Statistics, *Canada 1945: The Official Handbook of Present Conditions and Recent Progress* (Ottawa: KP, 1945), 198; *Canada 1946* (Ottawa: KP, 1946), 187; *Canada Year Book 1946* (Ottawa: KP, 1946), 989; AM, P5005, National War Finance Committee—Manitoba Division, Analysis of Final Results, Canada's Ninth Victory Loan, October 22nd to November 10th, 1945, 19-19A. Winnipeg *Free Press* and Winnipeg *Tribune* coverage of various loan campaigns.

*By the Fourth Victory Loan, the NWFC had begun separating the Special Names quotas from the rest of the city's and province's objectives, which accounts for the lower total. Of the $75 million objective for Manitoba in the Fourth Loan, $51 million was to come from Special Names, $24 million from the rest of the province, with $14,319,000 of that coming from Winnipeg.

of solidarity by assembling in large numbers, marching, and vocalizing common sentiments or goals, all of which might generate a shared sense of power. Expressive crowds might be manipulated, however, when their apparently spontaneous responses are, in fact, elicited by an appropriate stimulus.[134]

The Victory Torch dedication pledge described above can be seen as one way in which NWFC propagandists manipulated those gathered for the ceremony, through a discourse emphasizing loyalty to Canada's fighting men, the mother country, and the cause of victory. But the scale of popular interest and participation in the drives, and the sustained response to bond appeals over the course of four years from 1941 to 1945, suggests that if people were manipulated, they were, to a certain degree, willing participants. Why would this be so? Early scholarship on crowd behaviour tended to argue that crowds were driven by unconscious or subliminal impulses which would induce people who were caught up in the moment to act in impulsive or irrational ways. In recent decades, however, researchers have moved towards the view that crowds are more often motivated by "objectives that are consciously understood and generally shared." The crowds taking part in Victory Loan ceremonials participated in deliberate displays of patriotism and loyalty that in effect sanctioned the power of the state and the military. The influential work of anthropologist Victor Turner offers one theory to explain their motives. He defined the concept of *communitas,* a state supposedly experienced during festivals and other celebratory or commemorative events in which participants, temporarily joining together in a wider communion or consensus, are liberated from the constraints of their usual status or role in society by "a sense of wholeness and solidarity. Prior differences of class, ethnicity, gender, or other social constructs are momentarily displaced."[135] It is easy enough to imagine that crowds gathered for Victory Loan events in Winnipeg and elsewhere in order to experience the moral security that such a large group consensus would convey in a time of national crisis, when so many Canadians' lives and loved ones were under threat.

What, then, is the overall significance of this study of the Victory Loan drives and the national propaganda that fed them? It is much more than a simple investigation of the nuances of war finance, though the economic results are themselves important for what they reveal about the changes in Canada's economy during the war. From a popular point of view, the war finance programs had equally important effects. As historian Wendy Cuthbertson writes: "virtually every Canadian who could afford to buy a bond did."[136] If we recall that a high rate of participation was considered as evidence of high morale, the increasing ratio of bond applications to population in Winnipeg is indicative. Psychologists Goodwin Watson and Kurt Lewin argued, during the war, that morale could be maintained by setting shared goals to work toward, while encouraging a feeling that individual effort can make a difference in the effort to reach them. Knowledge that progress is being made could be fostered and morale enhanced if intermediate steps towards the goal could realistically be achieved, but not too easily, since a sense of accomplishment depends upon a certain level of difficulty.[137] When these factors are recognized, the Victory Loan campaigns can be judged as contributing to public morale by setting a significant challenge that Winnipeggers successfully overcame.

Ottawa's war finance program ultimately helped the patriotic consensus to coalesce. One American study has suggested that U.S. Treasury officials hoped to use War Bond drives as a way to foster national unity,[138] and the evidence presented here certainly suggests that Winnipeggers and other Canadians pulled together in support of this particular aspect of the war effort. Despite the coercive aspects of war finance programs, the loan campaigns ultimately succeeded because of a fundamental consensus that saw them as worthwhile and necessary. There is a wealth of evidence to support this conclusion. Payroll deduction subscriptions, perhaps the best indication of support among the mass of wage-earning Canadians, grew four-fold between the Second and Seventh Victory Loans.[139] A public opinion poll in May 1942 further revealed Canadians' commitment. A substantial proportion of the 3,000 respondents nationwide, four out of ten, said they would be willing to increase their amount of Victory Bond or War Savings subscriptions, even if it meant doing without goods they would normally buy. This proportion was even larger on the prairies, where nearly half were willing to make the sacrifice. Although there were some who bought bonds to save face only to redeem them soon after, 75 percent of prairie respondents and 70 percent nationwide indicated that they planned to hold their securities until the war ended, if not longer.[140] Another indication of consensus was the scale of voluntary support underpinning NWFC operations. Even after the war had ended, the Ninth Victory Loan campaign drew on a pool of at least 125,000 voluntary workers.[141] This sort of commitment was made by Canadians independent of any specific propaganda urging them to do so.

People's reasons for supporting the Victory Loan campaigns were heartfelt. According to a 1946 study of the psychology of American War Bond drives—and there is no reason to expect Canadian motives to have been significantly different—buying bonds was not just "an expression of patriotic sentiments." For some, it could be "a quasi-magical procedure for protecting sons or brothers exposed to danger," in response to ads suggesting that buying bonds would bring them home sooner or provide the equipment they needed to keep them safe. It was also "a symbol of participation in a significant joint endeavor with an indefinitely large number of like-minded members of one's in-group." For others, it could serve as "a device for allaying a cumulative sense of guilt" about not doing enough for the war effort.[142] NWFC publicity measures addressed these motives, and participation in campaign events permitted Winnipeggers to experience the sense of community so necessary for upholding home front morale.

It was established in the first two chapters that some minorities of ethnicity and opinion did not fully share in this patriotic consensus, and questions have been raised about the depth of their support for the war effort. One Wartime Information Board correspondent from Winnipeg wrote that "I have heard a good deal of criticism of the Slavic people. It was said that their lack of enthusiasm for the purchase of Victory Bonds proves that they have not accepted the responsibilities of citizenship in a democracy."[143] Ninette Kelley and Michael Trebilcock similarly claim, in their study of Canadian immigration history, that a supposed paucity of contributions from ethnic communities to Victory Loan drives was evidence of a relative lack of support.[144] This may have been the case in other parts of Canada and, in fact, the NWFC admitted the need for greater efforts to get its message out to foreign language groups, including those in rural Manitoba.[145] But there is scant evidence that any particular groups in Winnipeg exhibited a special reluctance to buy bonds. Another WIB correspondent wrote just before the Fifth Victory Loan, "I believe that when the drive gets under way people in this 'new Canadian' part of the city will measure up as well as they have in all previous drives."[146] In one early example of solidarity, local Ukrainians held a War Savings concert consisting of "musical and dancing entertainment" at the Auditorium in October 1940, "the receipts of which went to swell the sale of War Savings Stamps.... Admission was free to purchasers of two War Savings Stamps and a 10-cent programme."[147] The NWFC had included foreign-language and ethnic newspapers in its advertising blitzes, and many were based in Winnipeg.[148] The message appears to have been favourably received, since there were many instances where notable bond purchases by ethnic organizations were specifically mentioned in the Winnipeg papers. For example, the *Free Press* singled out the Holy Ghost Mutual Aid society, a Polish group, for its $5,000 subscription to the first Victory Loan drive. By the fourth day of the Third Loan drive, the head office of the Ukrainian Relief Association of Canada had already subscribed $10,000 in bonds. And fourteen members of the Hungarian Democratic Organization of Winnipeg bought $1,550 in bonds during the Eighth Loan.[149]

What does the Victory Loan story reveal about the relationship between the government, through its war finance apparatus, and the communities that it sought to engage? The government employed numerous mechanisms to persuade or coerce Canadians into supporting the drives, but people ultimately remained free to abstain if they chose. Popular pressure was overbearing, but those who objected could and did maintain a facade of conformity by subscribing and later redeeming their bonds. It is true that the patriotic consensus was not absolute, but enthusiastic responses to public ceremonials and the increasing subscription levels reveal a steadfast commitment to the community's war effort that suggests a basic belief in the justice of the Allied cause which even non-conformists recognized.

Articulating and reinforcing the patriotic messages that fuelled the Victory Loan drives was part of an important ideological process cementing social cohesion. As John Porter explains in his classic work *The Vertical Mosaic*, cohesion depends on the acceptance, by disparate groups, of society's dominant collective sentiments and values. This task of articulation, reinforcement, and legitimization falls on institutions like schools, universities, and churches, which carry out the indoctrination of the community's membership, as well as the newspapers and other media which disseminate or popularize the dominant ideology. Hence the importance to the NWFC of designating Victory Loan Sunday, of using schools to sell War Savings Stamps, and of co-opting newspaper publishers and advertising agencies in attempting to foster compliance with its savings policies. The staging of elaborate ceremonials clearly helped to enhance Winnipeggers' unity and morale. In Porter's view, "ritualistic ceremonies" serve to reduce tensions between social groups by using an emotionally charged discourse that appeals "to values which are 'above' a society's internal divisions."[150] Robert Rutherdale makes similar conclusions about recruiting campaigns or fundraising for the Canadian Patriotic Fund in three Canadian cities during the Great War. His comments about the impact of patriotic rituals, parades, and speeches are equally applicable here: Although "support for Canada's participation [in the war] was far from uniform ... when mayors, public officials, or other local elites addressed large audiences, they emphasized common goals, usually in terms of fighting for a moral ideal: a 'just cause,' [or] a 'fight for civilization.'"[151]

Just as Rutherdale singles out local elites, Porter suggests, in relation to philanthropic fundraising campaigns that had much in common with Victory Loan drives, that success depended on the support of prominent community leaders, especially business executives, who endorsed the drives, mobilized support from their friends and contacts, and recruited organizers, often from among their own firms' junior executives.[152] The process, which Rutherdale describes as "a dynamic engagement of local hierarchies ... served to reinforce an integrated, stratified, and stable model of local community."[153] We have seen this same process at work in Winnipeg, where business leaders from the commercial and financial sectors were mobilized to run the drives, and the "special names" subscribers accounted for more than half of the totals raised. While it was undoubtedly the elite groups that formed the local committees to run loan drives in cooperation with the NWFC, grassroots clubs and community groups were also pressed into service, whether it was women's clubs raffling off War Savings Certificates, St. John Ambulance participating in blackout exercises, or the Young Men's Section of the Winnipeg Board of Trade providing the realism that made If Day a success. In all of these ways it was the cooperation of non-state associations that made national policies effective at the local level.

4

THE SPIRIT OF SERVICE

The importance of morale in wartime is obvious and yet difficult to measure. In the Second World War, often described as a "total war," the lines between battle front and home front blurred as a result of the mobilization of civilian populations to provide the human and material resources required by the state's armed forces in their struggle with the enemy. Maintenance of high morale at home was necessary to ensure the continuing efficiency of all facets of the war effort. Failing morale or belief in the cause could lead to absenteeism, lower levels or quality of production, declining military enlistments, or excessive worry about loved ones, leading to distraction from one's duties. Given its importance and yet its intangibility, how can home-front morale be assessed? If high morale is exhibited by factors like a willingness to participate in furthering the community's goals, the enthusiastic response of Winnipeg residents to appeals for voluntary war workers—irrespective of their differences in ethnicity, sex, age, or class—provides one reliable indicator. Volunteer work providing community welfare and auxiliary services to the troops was an important way in which individuals showed their commitment to the national war effort.

Instituting Voluntary Services

The war greatly increased the profile of voluntary work in Winnipeg and across the country, and motivated a larger segment of the population to contribute their labour. The initial rationale was to contribute to the welfare of Canada's fighting men and their families. The government and other concerned parties recognized that maintaining servicemen's morale was essential to the creation of an effective military force, and that morale would suffer if the troops lacked facilities for relaxation and pleasant diversions from the hardships of training and combat, or if they were preoccupied by worries about family problems back home. It was also evident that civilian morale partly depended on opportunities to get involved and connect personally to the war effort. National service organizations like the Red Cross, the Young Men's and Young Women's Christian Associations, the Knights of Columbus, and the Salvation Army traditionally had been relied upon to fulfill most of these requirements for "auxiliary" or "war services" through voluntary work. At the war's outbreak, the Department of National Defence set up a directorate of Auxiliary Services to provide direction and oversight for this important work.[1]

The Red Cross was probably the most active of the national organizations, with a hand in various services for both civilians and armed forces personnel. Red Cross volunteers knitted socks, sweaters, and other field comforts for the troops, and shipped a variety of goods overseas for civilian relief. They packed parcels for prisoners of war and ran an Enquiry Bureau to help the families of prisoners seek information about their loved ones. There was also a blood donor service, and Red Cross blood banks meant the difference between life and death for many wounded soldiers, sailors, and airmen. The YM/YWCA and the Salvation Army offered their recreational facilities to men and women in uniform, operated hostels and other leave centres, Hostess Houses at military camps for men to visit their families and friends, and rooms registries to help service wives find accommodation in crowded cities. The Knights of Columbus, among other contributions, offered a flower service to make local deliveries for men serving overseas.[2] Other groups also participated in many forms of voluntary war work, most notably the Canadian Legion and the Imperial Order Daughters of the Empire (IODE). The Legion assumed significant responsibilities from September 1939, catering to the troops' requirements for sports and entertainment, educational services, and dependents' welfare.[3] The IODE continued a service it had provided during the Great War: donating reading material to both the Royal Navy and the Royal Canadian Navy, and furnishing libraries for military hospitals. This was an important contribution that compensated for the wartime shortage of paper, especially in Britain, "where the home supply of reading matter has been exhausted." The IODE also undertook the very special task of maintaining the graves of airmen killed in Canada while training under the British Commonwealth Air Training Plan.[4]

All of these organizations were active in Winnipeg and local residents contributed to their operations. But the lead role in providing voluntary services in Winnipeg was taken from the war's beginning by local rather than national organizations, and the work they did was not limited by any strict definition of auxiliary services. Rather, it expanded in a wide range of home-grown initiatives. Some of these initiatives were so successful in attracting the support of local residents that Winnipeg shortly became renowned for its level of voluntary war and community services.

The most outstanding success, and the initiative that established Winnipeg as a leader in the mobilization of volunteer services, was the creation of the Central Volunteer Bureau. It originated as a local response to a nation-wide call for volunteers. The outbreak of war in 1939 had led a group in Toronto to organize a national survey of women willing to contribute their time for voluntary war service. The Voluntary Registration of Canadian Women would be administered locally, so approximately 1,800 women gathered at the University of Manitoba's Broadway campus on 20 September 1939 to approve the creation of a volunteer registry for war or emergency service. The committee formed to administer the survey included leaders of social welfare organizations like Monica McQueen, executive secretary of Winnipeg's Council of Social Agencies. McQueen and her colleagues were concerned that momentary enthusiasm for war work might endanger consistent, long-term voluntary support for the city's social services. There was at that time little national war work to be done, however, so it was apparent that the most effective use of the registration would be at the local level. To capitalize on the wave of early enthusiasm for the war effort, the committee thus reinvented its mandate to include community service as well as war work.[5]

The relationship between the two types of voluntary work was clear, according to McQueen: "The women were quick to realise the urgency of keeping up community services so that the boys who were going overseas could have the peace of mind that comes from knowing that someone was looking after his family, and that definite thought and planning was under way to help him when the time came to return to civilian life."[6] The dual focus on community and war service made the Winnipeg organization a success, according to *The Survey*, an American journal for social workers. It wrote that "many women who previously had shown no interest in community work came to perceive the relationship of community welfare to total defence and soon were engaged in driving children to clinics, acting as hospital aids, ... and doing the various clerical jobs that social agencies ask of volunteers. Busy and useful, they felt themselves part of a whole community effort."[7]

Registration began on 10 October when the Greater Winnipeg Bureau for the Voluntary Registration of Canadian Women—later called the Central Volunteer Bureau (CVB)—opened its office at the corner of Portage Avenue and Hargrave Street. The Bureau's radio appeal to women over sixteen years of age stressed patriotic motives:

> Even if you can only give a few days a week of your time, or only a few hours every week, you will be helping your country.... There will be plenty of jobs to do—plenty of war work, don't forget that—but there will be other essential jobs which will require sacrifice and time: unpaid, inglorious jobs which are important if we want to keep Canada a free, democratic country. Any work which keeps Canada running at this time is war work. And it is up to the women of Winnipeg to do it. It is up to us to hold the Home Front.[8]

The registration effort initially generated a list of 7,000 volunteers and gathered information on their interests, training, experience, and availability. The immediate task was to organize an efficient file-card system to facilitate the process of matching volunteers with suitable skills to requested placements. It was a huge undertaking in itself, but there was no shortage of assistance. Unemployed stenographers and married women with office experience set up the filing system during the day, while others helped out in the evenings after their shifts at places like Great-West Life or the city libraries. It took seven weeks to get the system up and running. Material assistance was volunteered in addition to "manpower." With no cash on hand at their start-up, the Bureau received loans of office space, furniture, and equipment from local businesses, as well as printing and mimeographing services. The CVB made no public appeal for funds; it received initial support from the Junior League, supplemented by the Catholic Women's League, the Professional and Business Women's Club, and other groups.[9] A major sponsor after 1940 was the Patriotic Salvage Corps, which was operated by volunteers supplied from the CVB.

There was a lot of inter-agency cooperation. Many of the war and community service agencies in Winnipeg got volunteer help from the CVB, and many of the Bureau's members also belonged to these organizations. To cite one example, members of the Roman Catholic, Anglican, and United Churches and the ladies' auxiliaries of the Legion, Winnipeg Grenadiers, Fort Garry Horse, and Queen's Own Cameron Highlanders joined other CVB workers in the Red Cross prisoner-of-war parcel-packing plant on Lombard Avenue. There were about 800 volunteers in all. This plant opened at the end of 1942 and was the largest of five operations across Canada. The Winnipeg parcels were originally intended to be shipped to prisoners in Japan but, since the Japanese would not accept them, they went to camps in Europe. By 1944, the plant had produced more than a million parcels, averaging about 24,000 a week.[10] These parcels were a lifeline for prisoners. Two disabled Dieppe veterans attested upon their return from German captivity that, without the Red Cross parcels, "we would have died."[11]

The CVB benefited from weekly columns devoted to its activities in both daily newspapers, the *Free Press* and the *Tribune*, which kept readers informed and applied subtle pressure to contribute by showing people how much their neighbours were doing for the war effort. The scope of unpaid work done by its members was impressive. In 1940, 8,000 volunteers distributed ration books. They provided the "manning" pool for Women's Voluntary Services activities, such as First Aid courses and Air Raid Precautions blackout demonstrations. Other tasks included running a car service for the General Hospital; teaching art at St. Joseph's Vocational School, dance classes at the Jewish Orphanage, and golf for the YWCA; providing clerical assistance for the August 1940 National Registration of manpower; driving babies to the Children's Hospital milk depot and Children's Aid workers to visit unmarried mothers.[12] To enumerate the entire range of placements staffed by the CVB would require a very long list. Volunteers helped with community events and services, worked in health and welfare institutions, assumed administrative and clerical positions, provided auxiliary services for the troops in the service centres and hostels in Winnipeg, ran the salvage effort, and assisted federal bodies like the Dependents' Advisory Board and the Department of National War Services.

Winnipeg's CVB was the first in either Canada or the United States to combine voluntary war work with general community service. A 1941 National Film Board production, *The Call for Volunteers*, held up the "Winnipeg Plan" as a model for volunteer organizations. Winnipeg was also recognized by the American Association for Adult Education in a booklet entitled "Women in Defence." Margaret Konantz, the CVB's President, took requests in the autumn of 1942 from cities like Fort William, Regina, Saskatoon, and Edmonton to offer advice on creating similar organizations. The next year, she made additional trips to Vancouver, Victoria, and Calgary.[13] By 1942, according to the CVB's annual report, there were "literally hundreds and hundreds of volunteer offices" throughout the United States and Canada that were modelled on the Winnipeg Plan.[14]

The CVB had added 1,500 men to its register by 1942, and they filled an expanding array of volunteer placements. Still, the Bureau's core was its female members. Its officers were virtually all women, and a list of names reads like a Who's Who of Winnipeg's female population. Monica McQueen was the first chairman. Margaret Konantz became president and was later Manitoba's first female Member of Parliament. Her mother, Edith Rogers, the first female elected to Manitoba's Legislative Assembly (in 1920), was a member of the CVB's advisory board and had been active in voluntary services during the First World War. Mary Speechly, active in numerous women's organizations and wife of prominent physician and coroner Dr. H.M. Speechly, was also on the board. Other leaders included the local feminist, city alderman, and lieutenant governor's wife, Margaret McWilliams, and the wives of *Free Press* editor George Ferguson, Military District 10 commanding officer H.J. Riley, and Premier John Bracken.[15]

The Central Volunteer Bureau helped staff a wealth of projects that made distinct contributions to the war effort. One activity that was popular among many voluntary associations was the provision of clothing and relief supplies for shipment overseas. During its first year of operation, the CVB established a Refugee Clothing Bureau for victims of the fighting in Europe, with material assistance from the Red Cross.[16] Then, as people followed news of the blitz over Britain, the focus shifted there. In 1941, a joint endeavour united the many groups simultaneously collecting and shipping clothing to British victims of German bombing. The new organization, Victory Bundles of Manitoba, combined the efforts of hundreds of groups across the prairies and neighbouring areas of the United States, with fifty in Winnipeg alone.

V-Bundles, as it was often called, centralized the collection and shipment of relief contributions not only for Winnipeg, but for all three prairie provinces. As with the CVB, space for V-Bundles' workrooms was donated. Drycleaners, shoemakers, seamstresses, tailors, and hundreds of other volunteers, both male and female, helped repair and pack donated articles, with "only first-class goods" being shipped. The rule was "not just to give away what you did not want, but to give what you would appreciate most if you had lost everything."[17] The British Women's Voluntary Services was the official distributor of clothing relief supplies from abroad, and the Clothing Representative for the borough of Bermondsey wrote to Konantz in 1943 to express her appreciation. "We have been through some very tough times in this part of London," she wrote, "but the thrill of being able to clothe people with some good, clean clothes after having lost all they possess in one blow, is beyond describing ... nothing I write can describe the gratitude that has been shown, or the comfort that your clothes have given people."[18] As the war continued, clothing drives were also held on behalf of the Aid to Russia Fund and a Greek Clothing Relief campaign.

While some volunteers worked to furnish clothing supplies for the needy in Europe, others participated in another recycling activity common across the country but especially successful in Winnipeg. Salvage collection became an important activity as stocks of materials necessary for war production became stretched. Paper was in short supply and rags were sought for building materials, clothing, and industrial uses. Scrap metals were collected for the manufacture of weapons and equipment. Cooking fats and bones were needed to make explosives and aircraft glue. And after Japan's advance in the Pacific cut off Allied supplies of natural rubber, the call went out for old tires, hoses, and other rubber products. In February 1941, the Department of National War Services initiated a National Salvage Campaign to increase awareness of the need to conserve scarce materials, to involve average Canadians in the national war effort, and to provide a measure of leadership to local groups across the country that had already started to collect salvage.[19] One of the first had been organized in Winnipeg months before.

The city's overwhelming response to a Saint Boniface Hospital request for donations of used medicine bottles inspired the creation of one of the most successful and widely recognized salvage organizations in North America, the Patriotic Salvage Corps. Margaret Konantz led the initiative to organize collection of salvageable materials in the summer of 1940, well before their importance to the national war effort was generally recognized. The Salvage Corps experienced some growing pains with its first drive in August. Volunteers accepted everything that people dropped off at school collection points, only to realize that half the material was unmarketable after they spent a month sorting it. The Corps quickly refined its approach with specified categories of acceptable materials it could re-sell. Methods of collection evolved from school pickups and individual house-calls to a scheduled curb-side service. The new practice of "boulevard" pickups commenced on 1 March 1942 and greatly increased the amount of material received, but the organization had grown along with the demand for salvage. The Corps had moved from its original home in the fire station at Gertrude Avenue and Osborne Street to larger premises at 755 Henry Avenue west of Sherbrook Street, and it now called on sixty volunteer drivers operating a fleet of twenty trucks. While the Salvage Corps would add some male volunteers, women did the bulk of the work. News reports reflected contemporary concerns over acceptable gender roles, even as they celebrated the volunteers' achievements. The women wore white coveralls as their uniform, and one reporter reassured readers that it was "amazing ... how trim and feminine they can look even after a long, hard day out in the snow and slush."[20] Children were also crucial to the operation. They were initially pressed into service to bring their family's recyclables to the schools or go door-to-door in their neighbourhoods. Movie theatres encouraged them by offering free Saturday matinees where the price of admission was a bundle of rags, gramophone records, or tins of cooking fat.[21]

In 1943, a series of systematic drives was planned to collect materials especially needed for the war effort: fats in March, rags in April, rubber in May, ferrous metals in June, non-ferrous metals in July. Public events were held to generate publicity and support for such efforts, similar to Victory Loan spectacles if on a smaller scale. In the case of the metals drive, a large map of Germany was displayed at Portage and Main with an Allied bomber above. Enemy cities were figuratively blown off the map as the metals came in. The drive opened with a parade of school children, armed with scrap metal "weapons," marching to a ceremony at Portage and Main. In another event connected with a national Red Cross aluminum drive, Winnipeg housewives pelted an effigy of Hitler hung in the Hudson Bay's parking lot with a barrage of donated aluminum pots and pans. Other groups held similar "pot Hitler" events, one of which was put on by local Polish Canadians with the cooperation of the Polish consul. Advertising and news articles urged everyone to "Get in the Scrap," and post-office stamps on letters reminded Canadians to "Save metals, rags and waste paper."[22]

A huge number of volunteers contributed their time to the Salvage Corps. The total was estimated at over 33,000 by 1943, including teachers, students, truck drivers, sorters, and sales people. Their accomplishments were impressive. The Corps collected over 94 million pounds of material and operated four retail stores to sell re-usable clothing and household goods it collected along with the other salvage. Victory Shop No. 1 handled clothing and knick-knacks, No. 2 sold furniture and other goods, and there was also a general Salvage Shop and a Book Shop. A Treasure Ship project during the 1943 Christmas season collected silver, china, antiques, and other valuables, raising over $11,000 to help finance a hostel for merchant mariners in Halifax. For the next two Christmases, toys collected house-to-house by Girl Guides were repaired and sold in the Victory Shops. There was even a Salvage Corps Doll Shop. The Corps ultimately earned over $378,000, with profits donated to various war services.[23]

Winnipeg's salvage drives made a real contribution to the war effort at home and overseas. In addition to providing eight mobile kitchens for areas suffering under German bombing raids, they earned money to purchase wireless sets for searchlight crews defending British airspace. At home, the Patriotic Salvage Corps gave indirect aid to the war effort by discouraging waste, recycling necessary materials, and funding war service projects like the Central Volunteer Bureau. Its success prompted an article in the Philadelphia *Inquirer* which noted that Winnipeg's salvage corps was "one of the best known on the continent," largely because "Manitobans collect more than twice as much salvage as does the average Canadian." Ottawa agreed that Winnipeg furnished the "model for Salvage Corps across Canada."[24]

One element of the salvage effort that evolved to serve a much wider purpose was the Block Plan originally instituted to keep Winnipeg house-wives aware of pickup schedules and necessary materials. As it was expanded by the Central Volunteer Bureau in 1942, it divided the city into zones with block captains in order "to provide the quickest, most efficient method of mobilization of Winnipeg women for any worthwhile project of city wide scope." It had two routine tasks, canvassing for the Women's Division of the Red Cross and for the Community Chest, but it was put to use in other important ways. Block captains helped organize Victory Gardens, signed up 3,000 women for a vegetable canning project, found 4,500 blood donors, as-sisted the Department of Agriculture by conducting a Bread Survey, and later disseminated information on veterans' benefits. The basis of organization was simple: "A woman a block in every part of the city ... responsible for houses in her particular block," with block captains directed by zone and regional leaders.[25] According to one observer, the Block Plan allowed housewives who could not leave their areas to contribute their services, and it built "community solidarity and citizen participation in a very real and tangible fashion."[26]

Coordinating Service Provision

As a growing number of people got involved with voluntary work in the community or on behalf of armed forces personnel, the need arose to form a coordinating body to maximize the efficiency of their efforts. There was a great deal of overlap, especially during the war's opening stages. The national auxiliary service organizations were responsible, in theory, for providing services at military camps and bases. As needs escalated with the growing war effort, they gradually expanded their operations to include urban areas. This led to increased costs, competition for the public donations that funded war services, and duplication of programs. Minimizing competition for donations became increasingly important as war charities proliferated so, by the end of 1940, Ottawa mandated joint appeals. Then, in 1942, the government decided to fund directly the war services delivered by the national auxiliary service organizations, partly to prevent interference with solicitation for Victory Loan subscriptions. To keep costs down, Ottawa encouraged the national organizations to focus exclusively on services for troops in camps and overseas. Cities and towns were another matter. The Council of Social Agencies had already taken a lead in organizing Winnipeg's war services in June 1941, when it invited representatives of the auxiliaries and welfare agencies to participate in what became known as the Greater Winnipeg Coordinating Board for War Services. This was at first only an advisory body, but in April 1942 the Department of National War Services delegated to local citizens' committees the administrative responsibility for providing and funding auxiliary services to troops in urban areas.[27]

The Greater Winnipeg Coordinating Board was an inclusive body whose membership was open to any group working to provide war or welfare services in the city. The inaugural meeting on 11 June 1941 was attended by approximately 150 delegates, including the mayor, lieutenant governor, members of the provincial government, Department of National Defence, regimental or other unit associations and ladies' auxiliaries, the Canadian National Institute for the Blind, Children's Aid Society, Young Men's Hebrew Association, and the Board of Trade, to mention only a small cross-section of groups that took an active part in the Coordinating Board's work. Other members were added as circumstances dictated. For example, because the city became an important transit point for American troops and equipment en route to bases in the northwest or work sites for the Alaska Highway, the growing number of U.S. personnel in Winnipeg made it logical for the Board to add an American voice. A representative for American forces in the city joined the Board in January 1944, and another from the American Legion joined later in the spring.[28]

The Coordinating Board served as a mechanism for its member organizations to rationalize their efforts. It worked through a number of committees, each responsible for a different area of service. While it would be as ponderous to describe every function of the Board as it would be to list the work of every individual voluntary organization, a survey of some representative activities undertaken by its committees indicates the scale of cooperative effort invested by a diverse group of interested parties. Some services had already been consolidated under a single agency or umbrella group, as in the case of the Central Volunteer Bureau, which simply constituted the Board's corresponding Voluntary Services Committee. Similarly, the Regional War Services Library Committee became part of the Board's Education Committee. The Library Committee had been formed in the fall of 1940, comprising a number of local groups already working to supply the demand for reading materials for service personnel at home and overseas. Under this committee, the Canadian Legion's Educational Services division supplied educational and technical books, the Manitoba Library Association provided works of fiction, the IODE offered magazines, and the National Council of Jewish Women looked after newspapers. The committee collected donated reading materials in street bins, at schools, the Post Office, and Eaton's and Hudson's Bay department stores. It sorted, repaired, and packed books and periodicals for shipment at two central depots. The CVB contributed additional volunteers to help with collecting and sorting, as did the Red Cross and other groups like the Women's Club, the Whirlwind Club, Boy Scouts, Girl Guides, and cadets.[29]

The Entertainment Committee fulfilled a need that was as important as reading material to the maintenance of morale in the armed services, putting on live shows for the troops in Winnipeg and military bases throughout the province. This undertaking demanded a significant contribution of time and effort from committee members and performers. The committee formed nineteen troupes, each with thirty to forty members. They performed at military and air force bases across the whole of Military District 10, including weekly shows at Shilo that required regular travel from Winnipeg. During nine months in 1944, for example, the committee staged 210 shows, both in and outside the city, for audiences totalling more than 179,000 troops. They also entertained service personnel in Winnipeg at the Orpheum Theatre or the military hospitals at Fort Osborne Barracks and Deer Lodge, and made arrangements to bring in visiting troupes such as the Massey-Harris Company's "Combines," the "Army Show," "Meet the Navy," and the Royal Canadian Air Force's "Swing-time Revue."[30]

The Train Reception Committee carried a comparable workload. Its eighty members from sixty-four different Winnipeg organizations arranged receptions for troop trains that became famous across the country, in the process coordinating the work of thousands of volunteers. Because Winnipeg had no central station for passenger trains during the war, volunteers had to duplicate their work at both the Canadian National Railway and Canadian Pacific Railway stations. Train Reception volunteers met more than 500 trains and well over 100,000 servicemen and women between 1942 and 1945. Troops passing through were met between the hours of 8:00 a.m. and 11:00 p.m., but volunteers remained on call to meet men returning home at any hour. The committee routinely created an "aura of gaiety and expectancy" at the stations, which were adorned with flags and "Welcome Home" banners. Bands played to set a festive mood while hostesses passed out refreshments, souvenir packages, or magazines. Canadian Legion guides assisted relatives and led the returning men through the station to the reception. Often the mayor was on hand to deliver an official greeting. The most anticipated moments occurred in a quiet room away from the crowded rotunda, where long-separated family members awaited their reunion.[31] As word spread among servicemen about the amenities furnished at these receptions, Winnipeg gained such a reputation that the Department of National Defence recommended that other cities follow the Train Reception Committee's example.

The reunions at Winnipeg's train stations were not the only activities planned by the Board that concerned servicemen's families. Most of the armed forces units raised in the city had regimental associations or ladies' auxiliaries, and these groups were commonly concerned with ensuring the welfare of comrades on active service and their dependents. For some of these groups, fulfilling this role during the Second World War was simply a continuation of the work they had done for families of veterans of the Great

War during the 1920s and 30s. The Coordinating Board's Dependents' Welfare Committee served as a point of liaison between the many armed forces auxiliaries active in the city and representatives from welfare agencies. It was also a point of reference for those with questions about resources or problems related to family welfare, such as finances, housing, veterans' civil re-establishment benefits, or medical care. But the committee went beyond a simple problem-centred orientation; it also created a trust fund for dependents of the Winnipeg Grenadiers who fell at Hong Kong, and formed a sub-committee to welcome war brides to the city. These women greeted newcomers at the train station, provided introductions to members of their husbands' unit auxiliaries, and hosted a Welcoming Tea in the spring of 1945 to help them get acquainted. At a national conference of war service agencies in January 1945, the Winnipeg organization for welcoming British wives was singled out "as being the most satisfactory."[32]

Regimental associations and ladies' auxiliaries were unique in their direct connection to the men on active service. The welfare of servicemen's families was perhaps their most pressing concern, since almost everyone had a husband or son or brother in the army. The Fort Garry Horse Women's Auxiliary was one such group that did representative work. One of its members conveyed the spirit shared by these organizations: "In these grave days ... the ladies of the Auxiliary, recognizing the many opportunities for service, realize that there are many wives and friends of the Regiment to whom the word 'work' has taken on a new significance. To these we extend a very sincere invitation to join us." The war offered not only "a multitude of opportunities to assist in this great fight for democracy," but also provided the "opportunity for better acquaintance, grounds on which to build a splendid fellowship."[33]

The most common task undertaken by these fellowships was knitting donated wool into field comforts. For this purpose, the Hudson's Bay Company donated a "Wool room" that served as the Fort Garry ladies' headquarters. The auxiliary also raised funds to buy Victory Bonds or purchase medical equipment for Deer Lodge Military Hospital, sold cookbooks, and held numerous teas and raffles to raise money for "cigarettes and comforts for the Regiment."[34] The women shared in the Train Reception Committee's work and held summer picnics and Christmas parties for the children of the regiment. Hospitalized veterans or active servicemen were cheered by their visits, and by the Christmas presents and "ditty bags" containing toiletries, candy, and books they brought. The auxiliary's social welfare committee donated money and hampers to families in need, as did the regimental association itself, which maintained a Benevolent Fund for this purpose. Cooperation between these unit associations and other voluntary organizations, fostered by the Coordinating Board, was mutually beneficial. The Red Cross helped by shipping the auxiliary's parcels of food and comforts overseas, where they were stocked for camps and hospitals in the United Kingdom and other war zones. In return, Fort Garry ladies pitched in with work on Red Cross and other groups' projects. By the end of 1944, according to the Women's Auxiliary's secretary, twenty-six members were working at the prisoner-of-war parcel plant and 90 percent had received Red Cross pins for faithful service.[35]

One of the Coordinating Board's largest undertakings was to furnish a recreation centre for service personnel on leave. The United Services Centre was housed from 1942 to 1945 in the Annex of Eaton's downtown department store, and it offered troops a canteen, dance floor, lounges and reading rooms, a check room for baggage, uniform mending, and a games area with billiards, table tennis, and even slot machines. Visitors could send telegrams, buy cigarettes or a ticket to a hockey game, and arrange accommodations with local hostesses or the United Services Lodge, a hostel operated by the Coordinating Board. Some of these services were also offered at smaller locations like the Airmen's Club, run by the Winnipeg Women's Air Force Auxiliary for men training in the British Commonwealth Air Training Plan, but the United Services Centre was open to members of all the armed services.[36]

The response by both volunteers and patrons was outstanding. The Centre received donations of all the money and equipment needed to begin operation, including fire insurance, appliances for the kitchen, even the renovation work and decoration. Contributors included 189 different organizations and individuals from the military, commerce, industry, the arts, and service clubs. In 1943 alone, the Central Volunteer Bureau helped place over 8,000 volunteers at the United Services Centre.[37] The facility required a staff of 150 women per day, and it was no doubt a big job to keep that many volunteers satisfied and all of the positions filled, especially the less-glamorous ones, regardless of illnesses, vacations, personal problems, or other considerations. Yet as one Winnipeg resident told her soldier-husband, "Almost every woman I know goes down to the New United Service Centre, and feels for a time the thrill and interest of welcoming and serving service people from all over the world."[38] Visitors gratefully took advantage of the facility. The Centre's staff had planned, in 1942, for an average of 500 to 700 visitors per day, or about

21,000 per month. They grossly underestimated its appeal. The first month of operation saw over 55,000 visitors, and the number only increased as the war continued. Staff counted 9,000 patrons on New Year's Eve, 1943, and 7,603 on VE-Day. As Gertrude Laing wrote in 1948, "The United Services Centre remains the biggest single volunteer undertaking not only of the Co-ordinating Board, but of the City of Winnipeg."[39]

The Board's role in coordinating work on collaborative projects like the United Services Centre was vital because so many parties were active in providing war services and the enthusiasm of volunteers could sometimes produce minor problems. In the case of patient visiting at Deer Lodge Hospital, for example, the duplication of effort caused by a number of smaller groups working outside the framework of the Board's Joint Hospital Visiting Committee apparently caused confusion and some embarrassment for both patients and staff. Small difficulties like these notwithstanding, the Coordinating Board was proactive in fulfilling needs for different war services as they arose, and the level of success it attained was largely attributable to the perhaps unusual degree of cooperation among the various groups that comprised its membership. In Gertrude Laing's opinion, "the Board enjoyed the confidence of the member parties because it was organized on a very broad base. No one organization exercised more influence than any other, and membership was freely open to all the war service groups in Winnipeg that wished to join."[40]

This was not necessarily the case in all cities. During the war's first two years, disorganization resulted from jurisdictional competition between the Departments of National Defence (DND) and National War Services (DNWS), and overlap due to the expansion of work by the national auxiliary service organizations. There was some evidence by late 1941, according to one DNWS memo, that "voluntary civilian services are disintegrating."[41] The coordinating committee that had been set up in Calgary had already ceased to function and there were serious problems in Edmonton. The chairman of Edmonton's committee, T.H. Thomas-Peter, had written to the Minister of National War Services, J.T. Thorson, complaining about a lack of cooperation from DND's auxiliary service officers, appointed in each military district to provide liaison between armed forces units and war service groups. Thomas-Peter noted that the Edmonton Council for the Coordination of Auxiliary War Services was prepared to disband unless Ottawa confirmed its authority "to demand cooperation from the auxiliaries and their officers, and ... to control unauthorized war workers for the sake of lending maximum efficiency to their efforts."[42] Thomas-Peter's attitude may have contributed to the problems in Edmonton. His preoccupation with the council's authority to "demand cooperation" and enforce control stood in contrast to the disposition of Winnipeg's Coordinating Board as described by Laing. Ottawa's solution, as noted above, was to transfer direction of citizens' committees to DNWS and give it the responsibility for providing services in urban areas, thus simplifying the jurisdictional tangle, providing hitherto missing bureaucratic leadership, and ending much of the overlap with the national service organizations.

Other features of the DNWS plan were already in place in Winnipeg, such as the establishment of volunteer registration bureaus, affiliation with local salvage organizations, and liaison with the department's Women's Voluntary Services Division.[43] Winnipeg, in fact, led the way with a number of war service initiatives. By war's end, Ottawa had recommended the "Winnipeg Plan" for both the CVB and troop train receptions, and acknowledged the city's organizations for salvage collection and clothing relief as models for others to follow. The block plan, too, influenced plans in other cities for salvage operations and provision of wartime information.[44]

Pulling Together

In considering all of their activities, the aspect that truly stands out is the amount of sheer hard work that volunteers put in, year after year, and the broad base of women, men, and children who shared in it. The effort they expended was indeed considerable, but it was one indication of the debt they felt they owed to the men who had left home to fight for their country. This sentiment was apparently not universally held in other Canadian communities. According to army unit morale reports, some areas exhibited a cool or indifferent attitude toward service personnel. Where this was the case, it was usually in garrison towns like Halifax where they competed with civilians for access to local services like housing, pubs, or bowling alleys. Winnipeg, however, was "noted for its cordial attitude toward personnel of the Armed Forces." In Fort Garry, for example, residents extended more invitations for home hospitality to troops at the army's Basic Training Centre at the University of Manitoba than the soldiers could accept without compromising their training.[45]

There can be no doubt that the level of voluntary service performed by Winnipeg residents was exceptional. But how united were the city's various social groups in assuming these burdens? Did they offer their time and effort in equal measure? The short answer is that middle-class, Anglo-Protestant women usually took the lead in organizing voluntary organizations, partly because working women and mothers with young children were simply too busy caring for their families. "Well-to-do women," on the other hand, "were more likely to employ domestics at home, allowing them free time to devote to voluntary work."[46] Many leaders of the Central Volunteer Bureau fit this demographic. But it was not just wealthy, married housewives with little to do that took part in Winnipeg's voluntary work during the Second World War; working men and women also got involved. The Great-West Life Company formed a War Service Unit with a Variety Troupe that performed throughout the province to entertain servicemen, and the unit staffed other volunteer activities organized by the Coordinating Board. Employees of other Winnipeg companies also got into the act. There were numerous "Business Girls' Groups" formed at the city's banks, insurance houses, grain companies, and railways.[47]

Children also participated in a range of war service activities. Westminster United Church had a Wolf Cub pack that assisted with "patriotic deliverys [sic] of circulars" and collected salvage and magazines.[48] Girl Guides and Brownies sewed or knitted for V-Bundles, helped at the Blood Donor Clinic, the prisoner-of-war parcel plant, the magazine depot, or at a canteen they ran at the Winnipeg Auditorium for Red Cross workers. Schools participated in a number of projects. For example, Daniel McIntyre Collegiate Institute's grade eleven class raised money to buy wool for Red Cross knitting and held clothing drives, while Fort Rouge School children knitted for the IODE and helped raise money to provide milk for Britain. Meanwhile, fourteen-year-old *Free Press* carrier Paul Pelchuk and his thirteen-year-old helper, Allan Geddes, responding to appeals for the Aid to Russia Fund, organized a quiz contest and a schedule of movie nights. They used a projector Geddes received for Christmas, borrowed from the Department of Mines and Natural Resources some travel and nature movies to screen in addition to some of their own comedy shorts, sold tickets for three cents each, and gave out candy as quiz prizes. They donated $4.50 to the Red Cross.[49]

If voluntarism was not limited to housewives, was such service performed by various ethnic groups alike? We have seen in earlier chapters that some groups were not fully accepted into the patriotic consensus, whether because of ethnicity or political orientation. But if there had been any concerted reticence, one could expect that voluntary commitments to war services by minority groups would have been lacking. This was not the case. Some divisions within the volunteer community were perhaps natural, owing to the leadership exercised by a group of women that was not broadly representative of Winnipeg society as a whole. There was also a trend, noted by Serge Durflinger in his study of Second World War Verdun, by which religious, linguistic, or ethnic groups organized themselves separately but contributed to the same causes as that community's charter group. This trend was apparent in Winnipeg during the 1919 influenza epidemic when Jewish and other ethnic groups organized their own relief services to "take care of their own," in accordance with "notions of ethnic self-reliance."[50] The trend continued after 1939 with ethnic organizations supporting causes like Polish Relief or Aid to Russia.

There is some evidence that the leaders of mainstream voluntary service organizations, many of whom indeed came from Winnipeg's old stock British majority, may have been slow to reach ethnic minority residents early in the war. Monica McQueen, chair of the provincial board administering the Voluntary Registration of Canadian Women survey, noted in late October 1939 that "so far the response from the foreign born population has not been very good."[51] This was very early in the game, however, only two weeks after registration commenced in Winnipeg. The provincial board contained Polish, Ukrainian, and French representatives, and it was soon apparent that Winnipeg's ethnic groups were ready to serve.

For example, the CVB's file card system listing the skills of volunteers was cross-indexed "so that if we want a French speaking telegraph operator with car, and free any time, we can find out all about her in two seconds, or if we want a Polish woman who will have two soldiers to dinner any time, we will have her telephone number right away."[52] The CVB itself worked on behalf of those in need, regardless of ethnicity. It organized a Finnish Relief Tag Day early in the war, and its Refugee Clothing Bureau cooperated with Polish, Finnish and Jewish Relief Committees. According to Monica McQueen, it was staffed by "[m]ore than 200 volunteers of every race and creed ... working there every week for the victims of Nazi aggression."[53] The chairman of the Greater Winnipeg Coordinating Board for War Services, W.J. Major, also testified to the cross-cultural response of Winnipeg's volunteers: "It is no exaggeration to say that thousands of our citizens, particularly women, are working on the various committees of the Board.... The members of the committees come from all branches of our citizenry—from all nationalities and from all denominations."[54] To cite one final example, Community Chest contributions showed no signs of division based on ethnicity. Mr. F.R. Denne, director of the 1942 Community Chest drive in Winnipeg, described the campaign as "the smoothest running one we have ever had. I have been associated in some way with every drive since the Chest inception in 1922 but there never was one in which this City was so closely united. Everyone regardless of race or creed, were with us [sic]...." The campaign raised over $340,000, representing 108 percent of the objective.[55]

Many members of Winnipeg's ethnic communities had solid reasons to back the war effort because their families had immigrated from regions later overrun by the Axis powers. The Polish community was one of the most active, and it set up a Polish Defence Committee to collect relief supplies for refugees in the old country. Another of its activities, a tag day on 5 October 1940, drew about 300 volunteers and raised over $5,000 for the Polish government in exile. Polish Canadians with continuing ties to their ancestral land obviously had a deep interest in Allied victory given the decimation of Poland by the German invasion that started the war. Thousands of Poles fought alongside Allied troops and many of them served in the Royal Air Force. A visit to Winnipeg by the Duke of Kent in August 1941 was therefore noteworthy, since the Duke was inspector-general of the RAF. A garden reception was held at Government House on 15 August 1941, with Winnipeg's Polish community leaders invited to meet him. They represented groups such as the Polish Gymnastic Association Sokol, the Polish branch of the Canadian Legion, the Polish Veterans' Association, the Federation of Polish Societies, the Polish National Defence Committee, and various churches. Hundreds of other Poles turned up unofficially to catch a glimpse of the Duke, who was greeted by a group of young people wearing traditional Polish costumes.[56]

Likewise, there could be little doubt where Jewish Winnipeggers' sympathy lay. On 19 August 1941, the *Free Press* reported that a Winnipeg man had lost five brothers and a sister in Nazi-occupied Poland. Mr. J. Silverstein of Boyd Avenue received a letter from his niece that was smuggled out of the Warsaw ghetto, describing how three of the brothers apparently "left for Russia" after being bombed out of their homes, while another went looking for the fifth brother, supposedly in Lublin. None returned. The sister had been killed earlier in the war.[57] When the Dominion government held its conscription plebiscite in the spring of 1942, Winnipeg's Jews were among those calling for a Yes vote "as an important step in the direction of total war."[58]

Even small minority groups like Winnipeg's Chinese were conspicuous in supporting the war effort. At a special meeting of the Chinese National League's headquarters on Pacific Avenue in October 1940, members heard guest speaker Dong Yeu Wai of Victoria declare that "it was the patriotic task of every Chinese Canadian to carry on his duty in wartime." That duty apparently included supporting war service organizations. A few days earlier, the Chinese were specially mentioned in the Winnipeg *Free Press* for donations to the Red Cross Drive.[59] Like the Poles, they had a particular interest: although Canada was not yet involved in the Pacific war, the Chinese had already been fighting Japan for nine years. Members of Winnipeg's Chinese community sustained their commitment to the war effort over the long term; in June 1943, the Winnipeg *Tribune* profiled a group of Chinese women who met every Friday at the United Church's Chinese Mission on Logan Avenue. They not only worked for the Red Cross, they also donated sewn and knitted articles to the IODE for shipment to Britain. They were currently holding a tea with proceeds going to the Chinese Refugee Relief Fund.[60]

One minority group of special interest is the French community of Winnipeg and St. Boniface, since the conscription crises of 1942 and 1944 posed a particular threat to French-English unity on a national scale. A detailed examination of the Franco-Manitoban response to the war is beyond the scope of this work, but the French Canadians of metropolitan Winnipeg generally did not display strong ethnic cohesion, if their voting behaviour is any indication. Franco-Manitobans did not automatically elect French candidates during elections in the 1930s and 1940s, but voted on the issues of the day.[61] The 1942 conscription plebiscite was an obvious exception, but we have seen that opposition was not limited to the French-speaking community. Political scientist Murray S. Donnelly has gone as far as to say that as a distinct community, "Winnipeg ... has never been particularly conscious of the existence of St. Boniface."[62] Winnipeg's most prominent historian, Alan Artibise, ignores the French community as a factor of any significance in his treatment of this period.[63] Although they differed on the conscription issue, Franco-Manitobans appear to have responded to the war effort's other demands in many of the same ways that other residents did. They too bought Victory Bonds, collected salvage, and donated blood. Like other towns across

Canada, St. Boniface adopted the Royal Canadian Navy minesweeper that was its namesake and raised money for comforts and supplies to support her crew. One group, the Free French Association, took a strong stand against Vichy France and raised money to support the resistance led by Charles De Gaulle.[64]

There are other indications that it was not just members of Winnipeg's Anglo-Saxon majority that invested their time in voluntary war work. Beyond the very wide range of direct services it provided for armed forces personnel, the Greater Winnipeg Coordinating Board acted on behalf of the Department of National War Services in handling applications for war charities fundraising permits. The list of permits issued gives an indication of the number of groups doing voluntary war work, and of the ethnic community's participation. In 1942–43 alone, there were sixty-one Winnipeg organizations registered as War Charities. The list included, among others, the Jewish Women's Organization, Jewish People's Committee, Lutheran Church Soldiers' Welfare Club, Polish Gymnastic Association Sokol, and the Ukrainian Young Women's Club. Ukrainian women, for example, sent comforts and cigarettes to servicemen at home and overseas, visited wounded veterans at Deer Lodge hospital, volunteered for the Red Cross, and raised money to buy two ambulances.[65]

Perhaps the most intriguing question is not who performed voluntary service, but why people did so. Motivating factors were as varied as the community from which volunteers were drawn. Concerning the members of Winnipeg's elite who led the voluntary effort, a tradition of public duty prevailed among educated Protestants of their era. Mary Kinnear explains, in her biography of Winnipeg feminist Margaret McWilliams, that this tradition derived from liberal philosophies that saw individual fulfilment as a function of the individual's "full participation in society."[66] Such views were disseminated to Canadian university students in the late Victorian period by scholars like Professor John Watson at Queen's University, who repudiated the narrow individualism of classical liberalism and insisted, in his 1898 *Outline of Philosophy*, that "the individual man...must learn that, to set aside his individual inclinations and make himself an organ of the community is to be moral, and the only way to be moral." Watson's career at Queen's spanned fifty years; his students—including a young Margaret McWilliams—spread the word "from the pulpit, in publications, and over the various lecture circuits" to the associations of university women to which McWilliams belonged during her long tenure of community activism in Winnipeg, a period which spanned both the First and Second World Wars.[67]

As Kinnear explains, some form of volunteer work was a routine activity for educated and financially secure women at a time when working women were expected to give up their careers upon marriage.[68] Such women filled a crucial role in a society that could not yet count on the provision of mass welfare services by the state. During the 1918 influenza epidemic in Winnipeg, for example, the most effective measures to fight the disease were taken not by the unprepared civic health authorities but by laypersons, particularly the community of middle-class Anglo-Canadian women to which McWilliams belonged.[69] It was the same class of women and sometimes, as in the case of Edith Rogers, some of the same individuals that would later organize the Central Volunteer Bureau.

Volunteers, of course, came from all social classes and the elite's tradition of public duty was not the driving factor for everyone. It is likely that some who volunteered their services were driven along by social pressure or caught up in a moment's enthusiasm. One woman wrote to a friend, "it seems it will be necessary for me to take in a refugee (having offered to do so in a rash moment when I registered with the V.R.C.W.)"[70] For those with loved ones serving overseas, motives were much more profound, especially as the war dragged on and casualties mounted. The War Service Unit of the Westminster United Church Woman's Association met every Wednesday to perform voluntary work such as sewing and knitting for V-Bundles. Members worked at the Red Cross parcel-packing plant, contributed money to the Aid to Russia Fund, bought War Savings Certificates that they donated to the church, and sent Christmas parcels to men and women overseas.[71] They shared sentiments that bound them together with women in regimental and unit associations across the country. As the church's annual report testified, "Sadness and loss are seldom mentioned but they cannot always be ignored. Grief at the death of Mr. George Morrow, beloved friend, gay companion, and of Wallace McKay, both 'lost at sea' from the same transport; anxiety for the safety of Wilson Caldwell, posted 'missing'; deep concern for our men at Hong Kong; love and sympathy for our boys, 'prisoners of war' in France, or Poland, or Germany—these are some of the experiences that unite all in a common sympathy, and spur to further effort."[72] Anxieties increased when the fighting intensified overseas during the defence of Hong Kong or the invasions of Sicily and Normandy. As the president of the Fort Garry Horse Women's Auxiliary recorded, "Courage ran high" on 24 June 1944, the day of their summer picnic at City Park, "as our Regiment was in action in France and it wasn't too easy to rise above concern. At the end of the day we sent a cable to our Commanding Officer, expressing our pride and hope."[73] Many women joined such associations and offered their time as a way to keep their minds off worries about their men overseas, commiserate, and make a material contribution to the welfare of soldiers, sailors, and airmen.

There was also a sense that the home front must prove itself worthy of the sacrifices made by those offering themselves for active service at the battle front. One way to do that was to improve social services to ensure that servicemen's families and those less fortunate did not fall through society's cracks. As the Central Volunteer Bureau's chairman reported in September 1940, "we must keep those social services up in war time because we want our Canadian boys to come back and find that their children have been cared for, their old folks looked after, and we want them to find Winnipeg ready and willing to help them in the difficult years of demobilisation and the return to civilian life."[74] These comments suggest a cognizance of the disaffection among returned soldiers in 1919 and a determination to make sure that few would have cause to ask once more what they had been fighting for.

There is sufficient evidence to conclude that there was a substantial degree of consensus in supporting Canada's war effort despite the centrifugal tensions that divided Winnipeggers. This is not to say that the war erased divisions and prejudice, for there were still plenty of examples of both. As the president of the Association of Canadian Clubs told a Winnipeg audience, "the intolerance on the part of the Anglo-Saxon toward anyone with a foreign-sounding name has been infinitely more harmful" than the supposedly subversive behaviour of a few members of the ethnic minority.[75] Whatever the degree of acceptance felt by the British-stock majority toward the city's other ethnic communities, those with "foreign-sounding" names did their bit alongside those from the majority. When a group of local Royal Canadian Naval Volunteer Reserve trainees left for the east coast in June 1941, the newspapers estimated that 2,000 people turned out to see them off. One of those trainees, Paul Verdeniuk, "had a large group singing him goodbye in Ukrainian."[76] Among the members of the Winnipeg Grenadiers dispatched to Hong Kong in the autumn were 104 Ukrainian-Canadians, thirty-eight of whom were killed in action.[77] And when Canadian soldiers returned to France in 1944, the commander of the Royal Winnipeg Rifles reportedly told the Winnipeg *Tribune* that "I have got a grand, remarkable bunch of boys; I estimate [that] forty percent of this unit is made up of lads of foreign extraction" representing eleven nationalities.[78] Their families thus had much the same hopes invested in the war's outcome as any other residents, and they were just as willing to contribute by volunteering.

Winnipeggers of all stripes demonstrated great commitment to the numerous war and community service initiatives mounted in the city: the upper class along with the working class; the Anglo-Saxon majority and the various ethnic minorities; Catholics, Protestants, and Jews; men and children as well as the women who did so much of the organizational work. Groups that may not have associated in peacetime shared in wartime a practical sort of unity, a spirit of service. Their voluntary efforts helped maintain a high level of morale because they allowed contributors to organizations like the Central Volunteer Bureau or the Greater Winnipeg Coordinating Board for War Services to feel that they were making an important contribution to the nation's war effort. Indeed they were, for the state was not equipped to assume the responsibilities for community service provision that it would develop after the war.[79] A key responsibility that both state and civil institutions shared, to which our attention will now turn, was the welfare of servicemen's families. Theirs was the most vulnerable component of home front morale and the most important to cultivate, yet the one that was most difficult to nourish.

5

THE FAMILY'S MATERIAL WELFARE

Canada accepted more than 1.1 million men and women into its armed forces during the Second World War. Given the size of the population—11.4 million in 1941—this amounted to nearly one in every ten citizens of all ages and an even higher proportion of those in the age range eligible for military service. More than 41 percent of the male population between eighteen and forty-five years of age enlisted in the three services.[1] Most Canadians, if they did not join the military themselves, knew or were related to someone who did. The war thus touched virtually every family in immediate and personal ways. It meant separation from loved ones, loneliness, and fears for their safety and well-being. For those remaining in Canada, there were difficulties procuring adequate housing in major cities, economic hardships for many families whose chief breadwinner had joined up, and forced adaptation to new roles for family members during the absence of service personnel. All of these material and emotional aspects of family welfare directly affected the morale of those left to hold the home front. Social workers and those concerned with providing war services shared a generally acknowledged belief in the corresponding impact of these family issues on the fighting men overseas. The effectiveness of the war effort, both at home and on the battlefields, thus depended to a certain degree on the maintenance of family morale.

In mid-1942 the Canadian Welfare Council sent a "Questionnaire Relating to Morale and Security Problems Among Families of Service Men" to social welfare agencies and municipal governments across the country. The council sought feedback on the common welfare problems faced by these families and suggestions about remedial measures. Responses poured in from dozens of agencies in Vancouver, Calgary, Edmonton, Regina, Hamilton, Montreal, and many other towns and cities. At this mid-point of the war, social workers most frequently cited concerns about housing, payment of dependents' allowances, and difficulty in coping with family illness. Other worries centred on wives' loneliness and infidelity, their ability to manage family finances, children's disciplinary problems and juvenile delinquency, and lack of transportation allowances for men going home on leave, which often required wives to pay for train tickets out of their monthly budgets.[2] Maintaining the energy and confidence with which Canadians confronted war on the home front required effective responses to these sorts of challenges to family welfare.

Government action to provide material support for soldiers' families was, however, uneven. The "breadwinner norm" that influenced thought in welfare circles during the period 1900 to 1945 held that it was the male breadwinner's responsibility to provide for his family's subsistence. This view had to be modified in wartime in response to the pressing need for military manpower. During the First World War, and to a greater extent in the Second, the state became a "surrogate for absent husbands" in that it assumed partial responsibility for family support through its provision of dependents' allowances.[3] Stepping in to bolster family incomes during the war was one step in the progressive extension of the state's reach into Canadian society, but the belief in private initiative and self-sufficiency that characterized the breadwinner norm precluded comparable government intervention to meet the wartime housing crisis affecting families across the country. The government's role in housing provision was limited at best until the post-war period, and families of both servicemen and low-income earners suffered as a result. Preservation of suitable family living conditions continued to depend largely on the efforts of private welfare agencies and, of course, the resources of the family itself.

Paying the Bills

We turn our attention first to matters related to income and the cost of living, since ability to pay the monthly bills is often the first concern of any family. For many Canadians, economic circumstances during the Second World War were a definite improvement over those in the preceding decade. Despite exponential tax increases, there was nearly full employment and the average annual salary before taxes rose from $956 in 1938 to $1525 in 1943. Although the consumer price index rose seventeen points from 1939 to 1944, wages rose thirty-eight points during the same period. And despite shortages and rationing of consumer goods, total grocery sales grew by 48 percent and retail sales by 58 percent in the first four years of the war.[4] Yet despite this apparent prosperity, many Canadians still struggled to make ends meet. Over 33 percent of male heads of families living in urban areas in 1941 earned less than $1,000 per year and another 32 percent earned between $1,000 and $1,500 annually. Most families were unable to greatly supplement this income, according to a study by the Dominion Bureau of Statistics. In 1937–38, male family heads earned an average of 92.4 percent of total family income in all wage ranges—and an even higher proportion, from 93 to 95 percent, in the $1,000 to $1,500 wage range.[5] Demographics obviously changed and wages generally increased under wartime conditions, but this is a useful benchmark to measure the condition of a majority of families.

With two-thirds of Canadian wage earners bringing home less than $1,500, it was obviously those more prosperous workers in the upper third who drove up the national average cited for 1943. But what is the significance of the $1,500 threshold? Leonard Marsh's 1943 *Report on Social Security for Canada* presented the findings of a 1939 examination of family budgets by the Welfare Council of Toronto, "covering all the items necessary to ensure health, reasonable living conditions and general self-respect." The results, though specific only to the Toronto area, could be considered a "gauge for metropolitan conditions" in other cities. The study defined a "desirable living minimum" budget which would be generally sufficient, and an "assistance minimum" which could suffice during brief "emergency periods" but would compromise health, morale, and employability if sustained over a longer term. With figures adjusted to reflect conditions in 1940–41, the study con-cluded that the minimum adequate annual budget for a family of five which included three children, deemed the average size, was $1,577.40. This left most families with children below what has come to be called the "poverty line," with one-third of Canadian households barely able to earn the $1,134.48 nec-essary to supply the emergency "assistance minimum."[6] The Marsh Report's "most startling conclusion" was the effect of children on a family's ability to make ends meet.[7] Added costs for even one child could push average urban working-class families below the poverty line, and this was one justification for the eventual implementation of Family Allowances in 1945.

The wartime cost-of-living index helps us evaluate the impact of changing prices on a family's budget. The index was based on the changing

Table 5.1. Family Budget Requirements Specified in Marsh Report

Standard Budget, Family of 5 (3 Children)	1939 (per month)	1940–41 (per month)	1940–41 (annual)
Desirable Living Minimum	$122.85	$131.45	$1,577.40
Assistance Minimum	$88.36	$94.54	$1134.48

Standard Budget, by Family Units	Man and Wife (per month, 1939)	1 Child (average, per month, 1939)
Desirable Living Minimum	$69.29	$17.85
Assistance Minimum	$44.46	$14.63

Source: Marsh, *Report on Security,* 39.

expenditures of 1,439 urban wage-earning families selected as representative of the Canadian average, according to census data. These families, with incomes ranging from $450 to $2,500 per year, comprised on average 4.6 members; in other words, a married couple with two or three children. The index tracked increases in prices for about 150 items in six major groups: food, which accounted for 34.6 percent of average budgets, rent (17.8 percent), clothing (12.1 percent), home furnishings and services (8.9 percent), fuel and light (5.7 percent), and a miscellaneous category (20.9 percent).[8] In its 1945 edition, the *Canada Year Book* reported that the total index had increased by only 17.6 percent over pre-war values, but there are some important caveats to these statistics. Although prices for bread and milk remained close to pre-war levels, food prices in general rose more than 31 percent to December 1944; and while rent controls helped slow increases in total living costs by limiting increases to 7.9 percent on average, a severe housing crisis affected most Canadian cities, adversely impacting living conditions.[9] Members of organized labour argued that the index failed to account for the disappearance of sale prices in retail stores, the elimination of low-cost items as production of consumer goods was curtailed, and "the declining quality of many consumer durables, necessitating their more frequent replacement." An opinion poll in September 1943 showed that only 62 percent of Canadians believed the index was accurate.[10]

However much faith one places in the accuracy of the cost-of-living index, keeping afloat financially during the war years was a struggle for many families, particularly if the husband served overseas. The main source of income for these families came from the serviceman's assigned pay and government dependents' allowances. Such state support, regardless of its limitations, was an innovation that greatly improved on provisions for families in previous conflicts. During the War of 1812 and the Boer War, families depended on private charities like the Canadian Patriotic Fund for their maintenance because a soldier's pay was too low to enable his family to survive without additional income. The federal government paid separation allowances during the First World War to dependents of Canadian soldiers serving overseas, but the amount—twenty dollars per month until 1917 and twenty-five dollars thereafter—was only intended to support one dependent. A soldier could assign a proportion of his monthly pay (fifteen dollars) to his family, though initially this practice was not mandatory.[11] Larger families counted on supplementary allowances from the Canadian Patriotic Fund.

Wages for soldiers of the Great War were based on the rates commanded by unskilled labour in 1914, and according to Desmond Morton and Glenn Wright, public policy made soldiers (and their families) poor because whatever they had earned before the war, an ordinary private's wage of $1.10 a day placed him "at the bottom of the income scale." Rates did not increase to account for wartime inflation, unlike civilian wages, so as early as 1915 privates were earning only half the pay of a common day-labourer.[12] Home service troops and their families had a difficult time, because they did not receive separation allowances or support from the Canadian Patriotic Fund. The Dominion government provided pensions for widows, orphans, and crippled veterans but, like service pay, they were based on the rate for manual labour. At the end of the war, the maximum award was $600 per annum plus an additional cost-of-living bonus. The bonus was increased to 50 percent in 1920, thus making a total disability pension worth $900 each year. Few pensioners received the maximum, however, and there was no increase in rates until 1948. Entitlement was assessed without regard to the recipient's civilian occupation or earning potential.[13] These provisions appear rather miserly decades later, but pension authorities shared the concern of CPF and welfare officials that overly generous support payments would risk "demoralizing" recipients by eroding their will and initiative to provide for themselves.[14]

One legacy of the Great War was a new sense of entitlement to state support for families of men joining the armed services. Herbert Ames, honorary secretary of the Canadian Patriotic Fund, had repeatedly insisted that the CPF was "not a charity" and "that allowances from the Fund were a right—at least to those who deserved them." But a 1915 court challenge in Montreal "established that the Patriotic Fund was a private charity, whose specific judgments could not be successfully appealed to the courts." The CPF was thus able to impose certain standards of behaviour; although the government could not discriminate against those whose lesser morality might classify them as undeserving, a private charity could. Patriotic Fund "visitors" accordingly investigated applicants, to determine need, and recipients, to provide "moral regulation."[15] Nevertheless, in part because of Ames' pronouncements, women increasingly came to view CPF and government support as a right which they merited because they had released their husbands to serve. They had thus sacrificed their standard of living, and they too claimed to have served the country by raising the next generation of citizens.[16]

During the interwar years, veterans' groups like the Canadian Legion had mobilized and their aversion to being treated as objects of charity led to persistent demands for benefits as of right.[17] By the autumn of 1939, their efforts had brought the issue of support for military families into the public's consciousness. Dean Oliver writes that "allowances for military dependants and job protection for volunteers provoked major public debates over society's responsibility for veterans and their families. Rumours of harsh or impersonal treatment by Ottawa's over-worked bureaucrats spawned myriad stories of starving mothers and bereft veterans unable to collect what was rightfully theirs, or of individuals whose particular circumstances failed to meet the existing legislation's often stringent requirements. Such tales found their way into Mackenzie King's letter box, MPs' constituency offices, and the briefing notes of Opposition Members of Parliament and were indicative of widespread popular concern."[18] Public opinion thus demanded that families of those volunteering to serve their country would not be made paupers or left dependent on charity for their welfare. Service pay had not increased greatly since the First World War, but the system of allowances helped pay for necessities.

Basic pay for an army private (pay and allowance rates were comparable in the navy and air force) in 1939 started at $1.30 per day, and increments were added for specialized trades like mechanics. The rate for higher ranks ranged from $1.50 for lance-corporals to twenty-four dollars for generals and senior staff officers (see Table 5.2). Upon enlistment, each man signed a declaration indicating whether or not he wanted to apply for a dependents' allowance (DA). If so, he would send appropriate documents, including marriage and birth certificates, to his unit paymaster. In certain cases an investigation would then be made into his family circumstances by local social agencies working in cooperation with the Dependents' Allowance Board that administered the system, just as CPF visitors had done a generation earlier. Investigations were done for all Aboriginal applicants; wives who did not reside with their soldier-husbands; wives whose behaviour was suspect on grounds of sexual impropriety, child neglect, or financial improvidence; and for all applications to support any other family members, such as mothers or siblings. Wives living with their husbands before enlistment did not normally require investigation.[19] Allowances were still not granted as of right; they could be denied or discontinued if a wife was, "in the opinion of the Board, morally unworthy of public assistance," or in the event of a serviceman's detention or absence without leave. To be eligible for an allowance, dependency before enlistment had to be shown and a man had to demonstrate responsibility for his dependents by assigning to them fifteen days' pay (a minimum of twenty dollars) each month.[20] With these conditions satisfied, a monthly DA would be granted amounting to thirty-five dollars for his wife plus twelve dollars for each of their first two children. Beginning in December 1941, supplements of nine and six dollars respectively were added for a third and fourth child. These supplements were increased in January 1943 to ten dollars for a third child and eight dollars each for a fourth, fifth, or sixth child. Child supplements were payable up to the age of sixteen for boys and seventeen for girls, or up to nineteen for children enrolled in an approved course of study.[21]

The basic allowance for a wife with no children added up to $660 per year, including assigned pay. *Chatelaine* magazine proclaimed in 1941 that this amount "compares favorably with the average income per capita, which is between $400 and $500 per annum in Canada," and offered sample budgets for a variety of income levels.[22] This argument was hardly accurate given urban living conditions. A per capita calculation would include housewives and others who did not earn a wage, thus lowering the average. In Winnipeg, the *minimum* wage for workers in the city, twenty-five cents an hour in 1941, translated into about $550 a year. Meanwhile, the rate for unskilled factory labour in Winnipeg ranged between approximately $800 and $1,700 per year. The basic DA rate was, therefore, substantially less than the average wage for unskilled labour.[23]

Still, the allowance was adequate for young wives without children, more so if they continued working. There had been little need in 1939 to encourage women to join the industrial work force, and it had been customary, even

Table 5.2. Army Pay Scale

Rank	Daily Rate (1939)	Daily Rate (1944)
Lieutenant-General		$24
Major-General		$20
Brigadier		$16
Colonel	$10.50	$12
Lieutenant-Colonel	$10	$10
Major	$7.75	$7.75
Captain	$6.50	$6.50
Lieutenant	$5	$5
2nd Lieutenant	$4.25	$4.25
Regimental Sergeant-Major	$4.20	$4.20
Warrant Officer 1	$3.90	$3.90
Sergeant-Major	$2.50	$3
Staff Sergeant	$2.50	$2.50
Sergeant	$2.20	$2.20
Lance-Sergeant	$1.90	$1.90
Corporal or Bombardier	$1.70	$1.70
Lance-Corporal or Lance-Bombardier	$1.50	$1.60
Private, Trooper, Gunner, Driver, etc.	$1.30	$1.30
-after 4 months	-	$1.40
-after 6 months	-	$1.50

Source: Winnipeg *Free Press*, 29 Sept. 1939. Rates for members of the Royal Canadian Air Force were comparable; see *Financial Regulations and Instructions for the Royal Canadian Air Force on Active Service* (Ottawa: King's Printer, 1940 and 1944 editions), 44–50.

obligatory, for working women to give up their jobs when they married. The growth of wartime industry soon caused a relaxation of pre-war restrictions. The depletion of the labour pool by 1942 due to male enlistments made it imperative to bring even wives and mothers into the workforce. Those who could combine a government allowance with a working wage were undoubtedly fairly comfortable. One Winnipeg *Free Press* article, following Canada's declaration of war, agreed with *Chatelaine* that the DA was adequate, and asserted that the war was bringing economic security to those who previously had none by offering the prospect of $1.30 per day for a husband in the army—almost forty dollars per month before his assigned pay was deducted—and a total of fifty-five dollars per month in assigned pay and DA for a wife: "Many young women have been forced to live on a lot less than $55 so, job or no job, they can get along."[24]

The situation was quite different for mothers who could not work, as the Marsh Report would clearly argue. It estimated that the monthly costs of raising one child, for example, added $14.63 to the monthly budget at the emergency minimum level, and $17.85 at an adequate minimum, based on 1939 prices.[25] With child supplements starting at only twelve dollars per month, the total government allowance was clearly inadequate for the maintenance of an average family with three children if the husband served in the ranks. The wife of an army private earning basic pay received approximately $948 (including assigned pay, DA, and child supplements) in his first year of service up to December 1941, or $79 per month. For the next year, additional child supplements increased the total to $1,056, or $88 monthly. Further increases in DAs and child supplements from January 1943 continued to improve the bottom line, but still not enough to meet the adequate minimum ($1,577.40) specified by Marsh. Although some welfare agencies considered the DA to be "quite adequate when used with care and strict economy,"[26] the Canadian Welfare Council suggested otherwise. It recommended a twenty-five-dollar weekly food budget for a mother and two children—not the average three; this was believed adequate to buy 13.5 quarts of milk, seven loaves of bread, 4.5 pounds of meat, fish, and cheese, eighteen eggs, 3.5 pounds of butter, 25.5 pounds of vegetables and five pounds of fruit, as well as "general groceries such as cereal, sugar, beverages and seasoning."[27] With rents in Winnipeg averaging twenty-eight dollars, a monthly budget for this sample family would have greatly exceeded the allowance once utilities, transportation, and other costs were included—even though enlistment meant that expenses for a husband's food, shelter, and clothing were largely covered by the armed forces. In fact, the *Labour Gazette* estimated that "clothing and sundries" alone added 50 percent to the budget.[28] Given this financial reality, many families had no choice but to double-up in shared houses or settle for rented rooms, an alternative that caused additional problems that will be explored below.

By Christmas 1943, the country boasted virtually full employment but families with young children could not enjoy the economic benefits if the mother did not work outside the home. Hope Wilmot, the wife of military chaplain Laurence (Laurie) Wilmot, bore witness to the dichotomy: "I have never seen the shops so full of expensive things, and there are plenty of people with plenty of money to buy $50.00 handbags and so on. Practically all the women one sees are married and working." For the "tired" and "shabby" mothers raising young children like herself—she had three children under eleven years—the budget "does not allow for clothes, [doctor, dentist, or] entertainment."[29] One might expect the Wilmots to have been relatively comfortable on an officer's pay,[30] but Hope was then paying $42.50 a month for two rented rooms in a Canora Street boarding house with a shared kitchen and a single bathroom used by thirteen people. This was hardly luxurious living and, within a week of taking possession, Hope was so discouraged that she was ready to continue her search for better accommodations although Winnipeg's low vacancy rate meant that there were virtually none available.[31]

Table 5.3. Dependents' Allowance Rates By Rank, Exclusive of Assigned Pay

Rank	Monthly DA (1939)	Monthly DA (1944)
all ranks above Major	$60	$62.20
Major	$55	$57.20
Captain	$50	$52.20
Lieutenant	$45	$47.20
Warrant Officer, Class I	$40	$42.20
all other ranks	$35	$37.20

Source: LAC, RG 24, vol. 13304, War Diary, Directorate of Special Services, July and Oct. 1942; *Financial Regulations and Instructions for the Canadian Active Service Force* (Ottawa: King's Printer, 1940 and 1944 editions); and LAC, RG 36, series 18, vol. 25, file 2-5, Cost of Living.

Table 5.4. Supplements to Dependents' Allowance for Children

Number of Children	To 31 Nov. 1941	1 Dec. 1941 – 31 Dec. 1942	From 1 Jan. 1943
first child	$12 / month	$12 / month	$12 / month
second child	$12 / month	$12 / month	$12 / month
third child	n / a	$9 / month	$10 / month
fourth child	n / a	$6 / month	$8 / month (applicable also to fifth and sixth child)

Source: *Financial Regulations and Instructions for the Canadian Active Service Force* (1940 and 1944 editions).

If money was tight for the Wilmots, there can be little question about the hardships experienced by families of the lower ranks, particularly given the routine delays in starting payment of allowances. The DA was paid in arrears—at month's end—and delays of about three weeks after enlistment, to complete investigations and process paperwork, were considered normal. Wives therefore had to wait a considerable period of time to receive their first payment, some as long as three months after their husbands left home.[32] Emergency expenses such as medical bills could impose a crippling additional burden. Frequent complaints early in the war concerned the lack of provision to pay for medical expenses, though the issue was addressed early in 1942 with the creation of the Dependents' Board of Trustees. This body administered a Supplementary Grants Fund which could add a maximum 25 percent to the regular DA to help families cope with illnesses and other emergencies, though it was not available to officers.[33] A family's budget could also be painfully stretched if the husband came home on leave. With no provision for his travel costs or subsistence allowance, a wife often had to pay for transportation, food, and other expenses out of her allowance. The resulting hardship may have made some men hesitant about visiting their families during leave periods, which likely took a toll on morale.

Higher prices due to inflation ate into monthly budgets as well, a problem that was not completely eliminated when Ottawa imposed a wage and price freeze, effective 1 December 1941. The freeze was followed by a cost-of-living bonus paid to certain classes of workers, and armed forces unit morale reports featured complaints from the ranks because their dependents did not receive the bonus. This did nothing to alleviate a general feeling among servicemen that civilians working at home were making large salaries, which fuelled a sense of injustice.[34] Groups like the Canadian Legion were quick to demand better conditions for servicemen's families, and so were some populist politicians. Bill Kardash, a communist member of Manitoba's legislative assembly, argued in December 1941 that "families of the armed forces [should] receive increases in their allowance, free medical attention and accommodation quarters, which is a very urgent problem. A wife with small children is unable to get living quarters. This has a demoralizing effect on the husband in the armed forces. We expect him to make a supreme sacrifice, to keep a high morale, and yet we do nothing to help his family. Increased allowances to meet the high cost of living should be given everyone on the allowance payroll.... This is just as important as providing the men with fighting equipment."[35]

In fact the Dominion government was working to keep the cost of living down as part of its general campaign against inflation. This was a difficult task given the expansion of consumer spending power due to full employment. From April to September 1941, the index rose at over three times the rate during the preceding year. Following the introduction of wage and price controls, the index rose by another 2.4 points by the summer of 1942. To bring prices back down, Ottawa paid subsidies on goods like milk and butter, and removed import taxes on others, such as oranges and bananas. In January 1943 the cost-of-living bonus was added to dependents' allowances, giving wives with children an additional twenty-five cents per week for each 1 percent increase in the index since October 1941; wives without children received a percentage increase in the allowance. By that time, however, the index was back to 116.2, only 0.8 points above the level in October 1941.[36] Rationing was another important measure implemented to prevent greater demand for goods from driving up prices, since consumers generally had more money to spend than previously. Food rationing began in February 1942, with sugar limited to three-quarters of a pound per person weekly. Following sugar were other scarce imported goods like tea, coffee, gasoline, and rubber. Butter was rationed from December 1942, and meat from May 1943. Housewives learned to adapt their culinary routines. For example, when the supply of dairy products became strained, retail sales of coffee cream and whipping cream were discontinued in Manitoba as a conservation measure. Soon after, they also had to do without bread wrappers.[37]

Public reaction to government controls was initially cool, but Canadians began to see their positive effects by the war's latter stages. The Wartime Information Board (WIB) sent weekly "observations on Canadian public opinion" to the cabinet, based on reports from selected observers such as business men, journalists, ministers, and social workers. One report in May 1943 noted a "widespread belief that living costs are rising more rapidly than appears in Government figures." It quoted similar responses from a number of cities and towns, including Winnipeg, where one witness believed that the "cost of living has risen very greatly, despite the so-called ceiling, and every woman knows it."[38] A few weeks earlier, concerns about rising costs had prompted the Winnipeg Trades and Labour Council to establish a "fact-finding committee to study the whole matter of price control, as it affects rising cost of living and wages."[39] Six months later, the tide of opinion had begun to turn. One poll in October 1943 indicated that only 5 percent of Canadians wanted to abandon wage and price controls and, by the first quarter of 1944, complaints about the high cost of living were markedly reduced compared to the previous year. It also appears that there was a general acceptance of rationing, despite some complaints about the lack of necessity.[40] A February 1945 cut in the sugar ration produced little reaction in Winnipeg, where one observer claimed that "the public have such confidence in the rationing system that they will accept whatever is suggested." Reports advised that people were willing to accept the restrictions because "it is the same for everybody" and they believed that the Wartime Prices and Trade Board dealt with violators appropriately.[41]

Public acceptance of controls was important because grumbling about living conditions could adversely affect home front morale. A key factor in securing that acceptance was the effort to educate the public about the need to control inflation and the measures that could be taken to fight it. The complete range of government anti-inflationary tools included wage, price, and rent controls, rationing, taxes, Victory Bonds, and War Savings certificates. Getting people to recognize the role of these measures in strengthening the economy took time. By the latter half of 1944, thanks largely to advertising and War Savings publicity, most people had received the message. A national survey done for the WIB in August showed that 70 percent of respondents understood that inflation would have an "adverse effect" on themselves or the country. Although only 46 percent of respondents could name a government measure against inflation other than price control, 78 percent could name an action the public itself could take to help control inflation. These included responses like "Refrain from unnecessary spending," "Refuse to pay higher than ceiling prices," "Cooperate with rationing," "Save money," and "Buy Bonds."[42] Whether or not consumers fully complied with the government's message—the increase in retail sales figures suggests that there was some resistance—by 1945 the various anti-inflationary measures had succeeded in keeping down the cost of living. The index had risen only about 3 percent from the end of 1941, when the wage and price freeze took effect, to the end of the war, compared to a ten-fold increase in prices during the last two years of the First World War. The cost of living in Winnipeg, when compared to other major Canadian cities—specifically Halifax, St. John, New Brunswick, Montreal, Toronto, Saskatoon, Edmonton, and Vancouver—had shown the smallest increase: 16.2 percent from August 1939 to April 1945.[43]

"An Open, Festering Sore": Housing in Winnipeg

Controlling increases in the cost of living was obviously crucial to home front stability and morale, and government policy in this sphere was distinctly successful. The same cannot be said for another area of policy that was perhaps even more important. The housing crisis that affected major cities across Canada took a definite toll on morale, it hit servicemen's families and renters with children particularly hard, and it was a problem of long standing in Winnipeg that would not be solved with the end of the war. A shortage of available dwellings, owing to population expansion and the inability of new construction to keep pace with demand, was at the heart of the crisis. It impacted people in two basic ways. First, anyone who had to change residences confronted an exceptionally low vacancy rate, which prompted families to double-up and caused overcrowding. Second, many had to pay more than they could afford for even substandard dwellings. For low-income residents, staving off poverty was harder because of a long-standing lack of interest exhibited by both federal and provincial governments in encouraging construction of low-cost or publicly subsidized housing. The crisis was, at least, democratic: there were almost no alternative accommodations available, whether people struggled to pay the rent or could afford to buy their own home. Overcrowding and slum formation, moreover, were social problems that affected the city as a whole during the war years and for some time thereafter.

Winnipeg's housing woes stemmed from its history as a frontier boomtown. The city's population had increased by nearly 100,000 in the decade 1901–1911, the "most spectacular increase" in its history. Expansion was uneven, with the city's bisection by the Canadian Pacific Railway's main line creating a large working-class enclave north of the tracks that became home to most of the foreign-born and least-affluent residents. Land developers seeking to house the influx of immigrants had "pinched" on lot sizes in order to maximize profits, and houses were therefore cramped together on streets that lacked playgrounds or other such "wasted" space. Sanitation was an afterthought, not just in the North End, and it took serious typhoid epidemics in 1904 and 1905 to prompt measures to expand sewer and water connections throughout the city and eliminate outdoor privies. Scarlet fever, diphtheria, and tuberculosis were common, and the mortality rate in the North End during the 1919 influenza epidemic was substantially higher than in more affluent quarters. The natural product of these various factors was considerable overcrowding and urban decay.[44]

Housing conditions were made worse by the Depression, and many of Winnipeg's problems were shared by other cities.[45] Large numbers of families on relief meant that rents had to be lowered, in turn reducing the ability and inclination of landlords to perform necessary repairs. Loss of income compelled many families to room together, thus increasing crowding, or to move to accommodations that were cheaper and perhaps ill-maintained. With fewer people able to buy, the number of new houses constructed fell dramatically, such that Winnipeg had experienced a seven-year period of minimal building by 1939. From 766 new units built in 1930, the number fell to 191 in 1932 and bottomed out at only eighty-three in 1936. New home construction throughout the decade failed to keep pace with losses by fire or demolition, so that in 1939, despite a larger population, there were fewer homes in the city than in 1930. Even when the war brought improved economic conditions, shortages of building materials and labour kept construction from rebounding. Those in a position to consider buying a house had to face higher building costs due, in part, to the city's harsh climate and higher interest rates for mortgages than in other major cities.[46]

Winnipeg's housing problems were therefore serious years before the war. Alexander Officer, the city's chief housing inspector, testified before the Parliamentary Committee on Housing in 1935, describing deplorable overcrowding and unhealthy sanitary conditions endured by tenement dwellers. As contributors to these problems, he identified speculative home builders who used substandard construction methods, and "house farmers" who converted larger single-family dwellings into multiple low-cost rental units equipped with poor-quality plumbing and improperly vented gas stoves. In some of these multiple-unit conversions, Officer found families occupying cramped attic rooms that were suitable only for storage because they posed a fire hazard, lacking functional windows and adequate ventilation. Officer argued that a public, low-rent housing solution was needed to remedy the living conditions he described. Until such a plan was at hand, he added, "I have not the soul or the conscience to throw these people out, because there is no place for them to go."[47]

Nothing of consequence had changed by 1941 except to make the situation worse. According to that year's census data, 19 percent of Winnipeg households were crowded—that is, they had less than one room per resident. The city's Health Department and the newspapers sounded alarms about the depth of a problem that linked overcrowding and poverty. Reports about dwellings like the following were not unusual:

It has 13 two-room suites. The rooms average about 12 feet square.

In one suite was living a family of nine. They slept in two beds. Plaster was off the walls and ceilings in huge chunks. The rooms ... were heated with small tin stoves.

Children were scampering around the suite in bare feet. They were filthy. There was no closet space. One battered dresser served the family....

Common bathroom facilities were used by the tenants. The bathrooms were littered with paper, dirt and grime. In places the floors sagged dangerously with the weight of a person.[48]

Officer estimated that 9,000 additional houses or suites were immediately required, plus about 3,000 more each year for some time to come. This number was so far beyond what was being accomplished in Winnipeg—there was a net gain of fewer than 600 new units in 1941, for example, including both houses and suites (see Table 5.5)—that one may wonder whether his impending retirement was motivated by a feeling of utter helplessness to improve the situation. His frustration was clear in the last report he wrote for the city, presented in January 1942:

The shortage of accommodation for the low-income group has been acute for years and I have referred to this over and over again in these [annual] reports. The present plight of the average working man to find moderate but satisfactory living quarters for his family is lamentable. The health and physical being of his children are endangered by the unnatural surroundings in which they are compelled to exist. And all because our various governing bodies shirk the responsibility of providing healthy dwellings suitable for family life.

Surely our present housing shortage cannot continue much longer. The risk to health of our sub-standard housing, not to mention that of the fire hazard in our non-de-script [sic] tenements, may be brought home to us with painful remorse. Already, we have much evidence of the toll in moral and mental standards, also the cost of crime, in our blighted districts. Children are denied the elementary, innocent amusements of youth, and are indeed, often exposed to health and moral hazards. There is also the danger of fire from leaky gas pipes, and defective cooking apparatus and heaters in individual rooms. The health and moral tone of whole families has been debased by close association with those of unclean and loose habits.[49]

Officer offered a bitter warning for authorities, arguing that if governments did not take action, "our slum conditions will grow...to a point where future generations will curse our apathy." His concerns about health and morality were later borne out by a survey of two crowded downtown areas of the city which showed higher than average incidences of scarlet fever, diphtheria, death from tuberculosis, and juvenile crime.[50]

Table 5.5. Assigned Pay and Dependents' Allowance, Basic Rates, No Children

Basic Service Pay	AP (min. 15 days/month)	DA	Total Income (AP+DA)
@ $1.30/day	$20/month ($240/year)	$35/month ($420/year)	to 31 Dec. 1942: $660
@ $1.50/day	from 1 Feb. 1943: $23/month ($276/year)	$35/month ($420/year)	from 1 Feb. 1943: $696 plus cost-of-living bonus

Source: Based on rate of pay for army privates. See *Financial Regulations and Instructions for the Canadian Active Service Force* (1940); and LAC RG 36, series 18, vol. 25, file 2-5, Cost of Living.

Officer's successors as chief housing inspector echoed virtually all of these observations in their annual reports. They noted the same problems of overcrowding, unsanitary plumbing and heating facilities, and generally poor environments for raising children.[51] Percy Pickering's November 1943 report cited a few representative examples, including a ten-room house inhabited by four families with one sink, one toilet, one bath, and one washbasin to serve eleven people, with unvented gas ranges in each suite. In another case, a dilapidated store converted into a two-room suite housed a family of nine. A 1943 study conducted by the Council of Social Agencies (CSA), *Housing in Winnipeg*, considered the effect on day-to-day living. It observed that the general inconvenience and reduced comfort of living in a crowded home had a significant impact on the well-being of residents, and the lack of privacy contributed to family tension.[52] Hope Wilmot wrote her husband about the constraints on her family life imposed by living in a crowded boarding house. Once they moved to roomier accommodations, she imagined, there would no longer be any worries that "the children will invade downstairs at the wrong time," no need to accompany them at wash-time "to see they do not hold up other people," no need to line up for use of the house's facilities.[53] The Wilmot children articulated their inconvenience in simpler terms. "Louise and Hopie were playing house to-day—'with no one upstairs or downstairs but *us*!' Oh happy Day!"[54]

More than a quarter of single-family dwellings in Winnipeg were occupied by two or more families by the end of 1943. Only Halifax and Toronto reported worse conditions. Although crowding was not exclusive to the poor, the CSA report found that the average income of those living in Winnipeg's crowded households, $942 per year, was lower than in all other cities except Hull and Saskatoon. Crowding, residence in run-down buildings, and poverty thus went hand-in-hand. Taking the position that a wage earner should expect to spend 20 percent of income on rent, most families with this level of income should have paid an average of $15.66 per month, which the study declared was "an impossibility." Only 14.4 percent of housing units in the city rented for less than fifteen dollars in 1941, but the report concluded that this amount would "not obtain decent housing for a family in Winnipeg." Surveys of 4,559 homeowners and 4,871 renters in varying income brackets found that about two out of three paid more than the benchmark 20 percent of income for shelter. Almost 46 percent paid more than twenty-four dollars per month. Even at the higher rents, many did not enjoy "decent" shelter. What these figures meant was that those earning less than $125 per month found it "almost impossible to get decent housing at the rent which [they] can properly afford."[55] This income bracket included two thirds of the population, according to the Marsh Report, and all families of average size dependent on servicemen below officer rank. Officer had written that "health and housing are intimately related; there can be no doubt of that. The health of the community is bound up with that of the individual and his home."[56] If this was true, a significant proportion of the community, about 6,000 families, required some form of financial assistance to improve their housing conditions if Winnipeg were to be considered a healthy place for all to live.

The city tried to ameliorate slum conditions in 1945 by creating a Dwelling Rehabilitation Commission to enforce repairs on run-down homes, but it was a half-hearted endeavour. The chief housing inspector recommended that it overlook sub-marginal properties in order to focus on those reasonably worth saving. That year, 197 dwellings were reported to the Commission as unfit for habitation, but it was only able to inspect ninety-two of them. The city directed owners to repair sixty-eight, but only a fraction of the orders

Table 5.6. Total Annual Family Service Income, Basic Rates, No Children

Total Service Pay[1]	Less AP Amount	Serviceman's Remainder*	Plus Family's DA and AP‡	Total Family Service Income (* plus ‡)
@ $1.30/day = $511/year	$240/year	$271.00/year	$660/year	$931.00, plus cost-of-living bonus after 1 Jan. 1943
@ $1.50/day = $547.50/year	from 1 Feb. 1943: $276/year	from 1Feb. 1943: $271.50/year	from 1 Feb. 1943: $696/year	from 1 Feb. 1943: $967.50 plus cost-of-living bonus

Source: Based on rate of pay for army privates. See *Financial Regulations and Instructions for the Canadian Active Service Force* (1940); and LAC RG 36, series 18, vol. 25, file 2-5, Cost of Living.

[1]   Annual rate given at $1.30 per day includes pay increase to $1.50 per day after six months' service.

had been obeyed by the end of the year. The Commission ceased to operate in 1946, recognizing the futility of its efforts owing to the shortage of building materials to effect repairs and the absence of alternative accommodations for people who might be displaced while work proceeded.[57]

The demobilization of servicemen would put further strain on an already intolerable situation. There were more than 35,000 Winnipeg residents enlisted in the armed services, excluding those from satellites like Transcona or St. Boniface, so the potential for the housing crisis to worsen was considerable.[58] The army's Directorate of Special Services studied the housing situation through unit morale reports and interviews with more than 1,400 veterans returned from overseas between October 1944 and April 1945. It found that problems securing shelter affected more than 30 percent of respondents, and that the problem extended to "almost every city and industrialized town in all areas of Canada."[59]

The problem of finding shelter upon return was especially significant for veterans because "to the repatriate, living accommodation is more than physical shelter, ... it is HOME." The idealized concept of "HOME is a fundamental consideration in the dreams, hopes and plans of most servicemen. It is the basic point of focus in their dominant desire for security. HOME symbolizes both economic security (a job, a good living, physical comfort) and the spiritual security (love, family, emotional satisfaction) which they have been so long denied and in anticipation of which they have built up a rose-hued

Table 5.7. Housing in Winnipeg, 1939–1946

Year	Population	New Houses	New Suites	Total Units Demolished	Total Units	Vacancies
1939	223,735	202	169	51	47,201	704
1940	224,252	307	116	30	47,594	337
1941	225,437	602	52	72	48,176	111
1942	227,004	390	47	44	48,569	94
1943	228,548	438	221	29	49,199	67
1944	229,208	510	87	36	49,760	27
1945	231,203	744	178	35	50,598	13
1946	231,414	1345	163	34	52,072	43

Source: AM, GR1609, Public Works, G8029, Winnipeg General, City of Winnipeg Health Department, annual housing surveys, 1942, 1943, 1946,1947. Figures given are as of December in the year indicated.

imaginative prospect while overseas." The report suggested that most veterans interviewed had been unaware of the extent of the housing problem and were shocked by the conditions to which they had returned. Many found their wives and children occupying temporary, cramped dwellings that were inadequate for a reunited family, while others were forced to live with relatives. One couple seeking accommodation in Winnipeg included a soldier who had lost a leg in the Rhineland and was currently sharing a five-room house with his wife, their child, and two other families. For many demobilized men, finding a home was the overriding priority upon their return to civilian life and frustration of their desire to do so caused anger and resentment, contributing to family, health, or marital problems.[60]

Some veterans criticized civilians for allowing the housing crisis to develop, and some directed their wrath at landlords who had not treated their families with appropriate consideration. Some landlords considered soldiers' wives undesirable tenants, perhaps because they moved more frequently, and many refused to rent to families with children. One woman expressed her frustration with the difficulties of finding accommodation in a letter to the *Free Press* in December 1942. The wives of servicemen, she wrote, "expect deprivations, hardships, loneliness and worry." All these they could stand and "keep our chins up, but what we can't and won't take any more is the treatment meted out to us by the people who have places to rent that our boys are fighting to preserve.... It is almost impossible for us to find respectable household accommodation" because "if one applies for a suite in a block or a house, the answer is: sorry, no soldiers' wives; if there are children, it is: sorry, no children."[61] Three years later, the Winnipeg *Tribune* printed a letter showing that nothing had changed. The writer claimed that "the only landlords who will accept children have cockroaches and bed bugs in their houses." Another woman complained, "you'd think children had smallpox." She and her children were forced to stay with her mother while her husband lived in a separate residence downtown.[62]

Although the Wartime Prices and Trade Board (WPTB) had authority to fix rental rates, set lease conditions, and control evictions, rent profiteering was common. Landlords overcharged on rent, illegally demanded "key money," or forced tenants to purchase supplied furniture. People hesitated to report such defiance of rent controls for fear of eviction.[63] Unscrupulous behaviour of this sort seems to have been a fairly common response to the swelling population in urban areas proximate to war industries or armed forces camps across the country. Issues were similar in the United States, where landlords advertised vacancies specifically for couples or adults only. Some delayed making necessary repairs or exterminating pests in the hope of encouraging tenants with children to leave.[64] Single tenants apparently paid as well but with less disruption.

Some wives shared a measure of responsibility for their difficult housing situations. Many of the social agencies responding to the Canadian Welfare Council's 1942 questionnaire on morale agreed that following a husband in the armed services from posting to posting was not good for a family's welfare because of the housing problem, moving expenses, the disruption to children's routines, and the loneliness that came from moving away from friends and family. A respondent from Calgary's Council of Social Agencies appreciated "the desire of wives to be near their husbands for as long as possible," but argued that since the family would eventually be separated anyway, it would be better to remain in their homes than trade a few weeks or months together for indefinite upheaval afterward. In many cases, families left "comfortable homes" in smaller towns to move to cities where they were "crowded together in one or two small rooms in a private home, block or rooming house." The writer guessed that "on the whole the dependents would have been much healthier, happier and their allowances would have gone much further if they had remained in their homes in the smaller towns."[65] For their part, military officials in Winnipeg discouraged soldiers' dependents from following them from posting to posting.[66] The soundest advice for many women may have been to stay in their pre-war homes, but for some the emotional difficulties of separation from their husbands were more pressing.

By the spring of 1945, the housing crisis was coming to a head. An almost complete absence of vacant dwellings in Winnipeg prompted some desperate behaviour. Because the WPTB had prohibited winter evictions, the first of May was a compulsory moving day for over 800 families that had been served with notices to vacate their premises by that date. The city opened an Emergency Housing office and mailed cards to every householder in Greater Winnipeg, asking owners to rent out spare rooms to help meet the shortage. The housing registry had on file 583 applications, but only 270 landlords listed vacancies, most for adults only. Many offered only sleeping quarters, rooms shared with strangers, or rooms in the country. With so few alternatives, many tenants refused to budge in defiance of their eviction orders. Some landlords took matters into their own hands, trying to use force in attempts to evict their tenants. Two men were charged following incidents on 2 May and faced court action: one had thrown his tenant's belongings into the street and then tried to choke her; the other broke down a door trying to get into the house. The *Tribune* warned readers against taking such action, noting that landlords had no power to evict without a court order.[67]

The depth of the wartime housing problem represented a profound social crisis that was fundamentally unaffected by the measures implemented by various levels of government to try to cope with it. Federal restrictions on the use of materials and labour for new home construction, repairs, or alterations constrained the latitude for action by provincial or civic governments. Ironically, federal government policies meant to ease the shortage of accommodations contributed to overcrowding. Finance Minister J.L. Ilsley announced, in late August 1942, a home extension plan to provide loans for homeowners to divide their residences into multiple units. The government also announced that if homeowners did not voluntarily open up rooms for war workers, it would enforce compulsory billeting. Wartime Prices and Trade Board regulations allowed any person to sublet in any way agreeable to the tenant and owner, thus permitting rental of unfit premises contrary to local zoning by-laws. The Board also stipulated that sale of rented premises required twelve months' notice to the tenant, who could only be forced to vacate if the owner wished to live on the property. Apparently, many owners preparing to sell thus chose to keep houses vacant even when there was no immediate buyer.[68] The number of vacant dwellings in Winnipeg declined year-by-year throughout the war, from 704 in 1939 to a low of only thirteen in 1945, including both houses and apartments. Of the eleven houses vacant in Winnipeg at the end of 1945, five were considered "dilapidated and unfit for occupation," and the other six required extensive repairs before they could be occupied. Only three had furnaces installed.[69] The number of vacancies, moreover, was always somewhat smaller because some premises were listed for sale or were considered uninhabitable pending repairs, and a proportion of vacant apartments had only one or two rooms, too small for a family. The city's annual housing survey noted that many people who had adequate homes before the war had been forced by circumstances to live in stores, tenements, attics, and cellars. Some of these people had the means to pay for better accommodations but there were simply none available.[70]

Ottawa hoped to stop the migration of additional people into cities hardest hit by the housing shortage by designating them "congested areas." In January 1945, the Wartime Prices and Trade Board proclaimed the Emergency Shelter Regulations to prevent the "congestion" from worsening. The regulations required anyone wishing to take up residence in one of the designated areas to obtain a permit, and prohibited private owners from leaving housing units vacant. Permits were only issued to "those whose presence was indispensable to the war effort," though exception was made for discharged servicemen and their families. These restrictions were abolished at the end of the war, but the WPTB remained responsible for converting unused public buildings into temporary living quarters.[71] In Winnipeg, the Canadian National and Canadian Pacific Railways' immigration sheds were turned into emergency shelters and, as the war effort wound up, so were surplus military establishments. The RCAF facilities at Stevenson Field (No. 8 Repair Depot and No. 5 Release Centre) and the Manitoba School for the Deaf in Tuxedo (No. 3 Wireless School), as well as the Royal Canadian Naval Volunteer Reserve drill hall on Ellice Avenue, were also converted to house families facing eviction. For the most part, the accommodation provided as emergency shelter was substandard and reproduced "all the social and environmental factors ... that mitigate against the welfare of the family," such as overcrowding and communal use of washrooms.[72] The walls erected in the former military barracks were often mere partitions, so there was a distinct lack of privacy. Children's health may have been at higher risk in the shelters, which exhibited a high incidence of infectious diseases like diphtheria, measles, and chicken pox.[73] These conditions were little better than those cited in Winnipeg's annual housing surveys.

Ottawa's most effective policy response to the need for housing was the creation in 1941 of a crown corporation, Wartime Housing Limited, for the purpose of building temporary accommodations for workers in war industries. Nonetheless, WHL was more a band-aid than a cure for the housing situation, especially in Winnipeg. Until 1944 the corporation focused on building temporary, "demountable" rental housing—lacking basements and heated by stoves rather than furnaces—specifically in areas where the location of war industries had drawn in large numbers of workers. Winnipeg had two major industries producing war materiel, the Defence Industries Limited cordite plant in Transcona and the aircraft repair and assembly plants concentrated near Stevenson Field in St. James, but neither was large enough to merit the construction of wartime houses under WHL's original mandate. The Canadian Legion had called for WHL to build homes for servicemen's families in 1942, but Mayor John Queen denounced any such plan at a conference of the Canadian Federation of Mayors and Municipalities in Ottawa, out of concerns over the quality of the houses: "I've seen some of that wartime housing and there isn't a thing to commend it. Why in the face of the great housing shortage should we sanction construction of houses to be pulled down in a couple of years?"[74] From the spring of 1944, however, the depth of the housing crisis and the impending demobilization of thousands of Canadian service personnel prompted WHL to begin providing better-quality houses of a more permanent nature, and priority in allocation was indeed given to servicemen's families.[75]

This policy reorientation offered some hope of alleviating Winnipeg's shortage of dwellings, but the construction of wartime houses was not without substantial controversy. When the prospect of building them in Winnipeg was raised again in January 1945, City Council approved a housing committee recommendation to secure at least 100 WHL homes. Garnet Coulter had replaced Queen as mayor, but there was significant opposition to the plan from six dissenting aldermen who argued that the homes were "bleak and drab," inferior types that "stand out like a sore thumb" and would quickly add to the slums. C.E. Simonite preferred trying to get more building materials allotted to contractors for private construction. Former housing committee chairman James Black, arguing for the motion, promised that returning veterans would hold his colleagues accountable if they could not get homes for their families.[76] Within a few months, Black had changed his mind. In May, after inspecting WHL homes in Toronto, he compared them to "woodsheds" and agreed that the "houses are going to be slums in five years."[77] Such concerns were shared by officials in other cities, such as Vancouver and Hamilton.[78]

The debate carried on throughout the summer of 1945, with various sides argued by council members, neighbourhood associations, and the newspaper editorial pages. Aldermen continued to argue against building houses without basements that would reduce property values, members from Ward 3 protested the proposed concentration of WHL houses in the North End, and City Council quibbled about paying for lot preparations that were required before construction. Public meetings of Elmwood and North End residents in June called for "proper homes or none at all," and objected to the lack of basements, furnaces, and adequate wiring for electric ranges and water heaters in WHL houses. But such additions, the meetings suggested, would make them acceptable permanent residences. City Council ultimately ratified an initial deal with WHL for 100 homes in north Winnipeg after the city engineer, W.D. Hurst, reported that although they lacked the refinements normally expected in new houses, they would nonetheless prove adequate given the urgent situation. The *Tribune*'s editorial page agreed: "Homes are needed—homes with 'refinements' if possible or just plain 'adequate' homes if not."[79]

Once the ball was rolling, it picked up speed. With the first deal concluded, the city negotiated for additional projects, subject to the addition of basements and furnaces. Opposition continued in the House of Commons from Alistair Stewart, the Co-operative Commonwealth Federation representative for the riding of Winnipeg North, but applications from veterans for WHL homes were coming in faster than the houses could be built. With 880 already on file by the beginning of November 1945, Winnipeg's housing registry was receiving new applications, according to WHL's general manager, at the rate of about 250 per month exclusive of civilian families. Four projects totalling 550 houses had already been approved in Winnipeg, while the surrounding municipalities of Transcona, St. James, St. Boniface, and Fort Garry had also secured commitments from WHL. Additional projects were negotiated over the next two years.[80] WHL had built 994 units in Winnipeg by late June 1947, with 106 more under construction. The city had applied for another 1,000 but still could not keep pace with applications, of which there were 3,000 more than WHL could accommodate even with the additional units approved.[81]

The city's chief housing inspector, Fred Austin, estimated a deficit of 10,000 dwellings in 1947 but the number of new houses being constructed was still just a fraction of the requirement. The doubling-up problem had not eased in 1946, and only 1,317 of the 16,482 families that had applied to the city's housing registry could be placed.[82] With a vacancy rate of virtually zero and too few new houses being constructed, 1,413 people continued to live in emergency shelters with an additional 4,818 families of two or more people waiting to get in as of late June 1947. To make matters worse, the housing crisis was about to be exacerbated by the expiry of the leases on the railway immigration sheds later that summer.[83] The numbers were still alarming a year later, with more than 1,500 people continuing to live in the shelters. Almost 2,000 were waiting for wartime houses, with about 100 new applications coming in to WHL every month. And only about 10 percent of applicants to the housing registry could be placed.[84]

Although WHL added to the housing stock and construction generally rebounded after the war, years of stagnation in the housing market meant that the lack of units could only be redressed slowly. The vacancy rate remained negligible for a number of years and there continued to be a lack of adequate rental housing.[85] There was little prospect of solving the problem of affordable housing for low-income residents. Of the forty-three vacant houses in December 1946 (there were no vacant apartments), twenty-one were in more affluent Fort Rouge. In any case, forty of these houses (thirty-three newly built) were being held for sale, so were unavailable for rent. The three that were available all needed extensive repairs to make them fit for habitation.[86] Despite the previous reports and recommendations, the city still had not determined a policy regarding slum clearance and low-cost housing construction. The Council of Social Agencies' 1943 housing report had recommended creating an active city planning organization, extending amortization periods to reduce the monthly cost of home ownership, eliminating down payments in certain cases of need, reducing municipal taxes and mortgage interest rates, licensing contractors to prevent substandard work, and creating municipal, provincial, and federal housing boards to foster cooperation among the three levels of government in securing, financing, and administering housing programs.[87]

This sort of cooperation did not materialize, and the federal government's measures to alleviate the housing shortage were inadequate because they merely provided answers for those who could afford to buy their own home. Little was done to help those who had to rent. As far back as 1935, Alexander Officer had stressed the need for low-rent public housing, and three years after the war this issue had degenerated from "an immediate, potential, public health menace" to "an open festering sore in the body politic."[88] The city's fact-finding board studying the housing problem in 1947 recommended asking Ottawa "to restrict the rental of Wartime Houses to low income families, with preference to veterans." The board also wanted City Council to create a "Winnipeg Housing Administration" to build 1,000 low-rent houses for families over a two-year period, with Ottawa's assistance.[89] These proposals stood little chance of accomplishing anything. Wartime houses, for example, leased for twenty-two to thirty dollars per month and had never been intended to supply the low-rent category of tenants able to pay less than twenty dollars. Still, some Members of Parliament mistakenly and misleadingly referred to them as such, including C.D. Howe, Minister of Munitions and Supply, the department responsible.[90] Nor were the emergency shelters low-rent, with more than half of them at thirty dollars per month in 1948.[91]

Neither the federal nor provincial government was committed to public housing. The Canadian Welfare Council contacted Monica McQueen, chair of Winnipeg's Council of Social Agencies, in October 1947 to propose sending a delegation to brief the municipal and provincial governments on its recent study of the national housing problem. McQueen's response was not encouraging. She explained that the CSA's own 1943 housing report, with which the CWC's report hardly differed, had already been formally presented to both governments, with copies distributed to the federal finance minister, the National Housing Administration, and "all the major cities in Canada." The CSA had also submitted a plan for a local housing authority. Two other housing reports had been brought before City Council, one by its own fact-finding board and the other by the Federation of Mayors and Municipalities. A house-to-house survey of overcrowding was expected to produce yet another report. McQueen advised against sending any delegation since "Winnipeg is well aware of the need for subsidized housing," and although Mayor Coulter was sympathetic to creating a locally subsidized housing scheme, the provincial government had "always been uncooperative with Winnipeg's welfare problems and have shown little general interest in housing."[92]

The province was little disposed to work around federal constraints to solve Winnipeg's housing problems. The city had only ten of fifty-five seats in the Legislature though it was home to 30 percent of all Manitoba residents (and 69 percent of the total urban population). Urban problems were not a priority for an assembly dominated by "farmers who seemed to feel that reticence was a virtue,"[93] nor for a government that had been philosophically shaped during the interwar years by John Bracken's minimalist approach to public administration, which made economy its chief goal. Bracken and Stuart Garson, his successor as premier from late 1942, successfully co-opted political opposition through the formation of non-partisan coalitions. This form of government, ostensibly adopted in order to broaden consensus, in practice stifled debate over public issues and made the cabinet little more than a regulatory board. The wartime coalition Bracken and Garson forged enacted almost no new legislation to 1945, and the government's relative inaction was made clear by the fact that most measures it passed were simply amendments to existing laws.[94] There were few champions in this political arena for activist measures such as the CSA and other advocates of public housing proposed.

Meanwhile in Ottawa, a private-industry mindset had always precluded any serious consideration of plans for public housing. Finance Minister J.L. Ilsley saw direct government provision of permanent housing as the thin edge of a socialist wedge that would produce disastrous results for private industry and the economy in general. When WHL President Joseph Pigott proposed to build low-income housing in Halifax and Hamilton in 1942, he "had his wings clipped" by Ilsley, who saw Pigott's plan as a "dangerous and far-reaching" precedent that would result in the "socialization of all our housing."[95] Because the provinces held constitutional jurisdiction over housing, the federal government could limit its involvement to financial assistance to promote new construction. This policy orientation accorded well with those who preferred leaving housing provision to private enterprise. Ottawa believed that the market would solve the problem of low-cost housing: as new houses were built, the units vacated by buyers would "trickle down" to lower-income buyers or renters. Legislation thus focused on providing loans at reduced mortgage rates to encourage new construction rather than creating a large federal involvement in public housing projects. The first comprehensive piece of federal housing legislation, the 1935 Dominion Housing Act, reduced the necessary down payment from 40 to 20 percent and permitted a twenty-year mortgage at 5 percent interest. Such measures were inadequate for the many people who could not afford a new home, even under these provisions, and only 4,903 units were built under the Act. Similarly, the 1938 National Housing Act catered less to prospective low-cost homeowners than to those in the mid-range. The average value of homes built under the Act was $4,000, about $1,500 more than the price of a low-cost home.[96]

W.C. Clark, who drafted the legislation, was the main influence on the character of Ottawa's housing policy during his tenure as Deputy Minister of Finance, from 1935 to 1952. Clark opposed government involvement in providing low-cost or public housing. He incorporated restrictive provisions in the legislation that discouraged the provinces and municipalities from building low-rent housing by maximizing red tape, setting unrealistic cost ceilings, limiting municipal taxation of housing projects, and generally setting "standards that [he] was fully aware could not be met." F.W. Nicolls, the head of the National Housing Administration which put the legislation into practice, was in step with Clark's policy. To cite one example, Nicolls reported that he had "accomplished a great deal of 'stalling' of Winnipeg public-housing proposals," which were "rejected because their costs per unit violated the Department of Finance's limits." Not all of the roadblocks were set in Ottawa. A proposal for a limited-dividend housing project, brought to Clark for discussion by Winnipeg alderman R.A. Sara in the summer of 1937, ultimately came to naught because of opposition from local mortgage and realty interests to what they saw as a "dangerous socialist experiment." They argued against building any publicly assisted housing in Winnipeg until every house on the market had been "sold to a satisfactory purchase."[97] The mindset was similar across the country. Other pre-war plans for low-rent housing in Vancouver were similarly opposed by building, finance, and property-owners' groups, and Pigott's 1942 scheme for Hamilton was opposed by the Ontario housing industry.[98]

During the war, Clark essentially ignored the realities faced by urban working-class Canadians living in substandard housing conditions. He argued that house construction and "unessential repair and improvement work" were a drain on the war effort. He saw overcrowding and lowered housing standards as part of "the price of war," and believed that deferring new housing construction would stabilize the market and encourage employment during the period of demobilization.[99] The economics of war and reconstruction may have offered some rationale for Clark's perspective, however harsh its implications for ordinary Canadians. For those like Alexander Officer or Monica McQueen, who dealt with the very personal realities of poverty, government inertia must have been doubly hard to accept when it appeared to derive from a complete ignorance of the facts. Against years of evidence to the contrary, C.D. Howe proclaimed in the House of Commons on 10 November 1941 that "Winnipeg was a city where there were many vacant houses. I suppose that before the war there was no city which had as large a number of vacant houses as had Winnipeg. I have heard of no shortage there, but if a shortage occurs, we will meet it. We have been building houses only in cities where there is a shortage of houses." The CSA's housing committee sent a "suitable representation" to correct Howe's erroneous perception, although it soon learned that "no action would be forthcoming."[100]

The 1943 housing report of Ottawa's own Advisory Committee on Reconstruction (the Curtis Report, after its chairman), was yet another body that recommended construction of low-rent projects, creation of local housing authorities, and rent-reduction subsidies. The federal government rejected most of these recommendations in passing the 1944 National Housing Act, which favoured augmented mortgage-assistance plans for home owners.[101] These provisions still did little to address the need for low-cost housing or rental units for those who could not afford to buy, since most loans made under the Act continued to finance homes of moderate value.[102] One project that did go ahead in Winnipeg was the Flora Place development at the Old Exhibition Grounds, where 100 temporary units were built in 1948. It was intended to rehouse veterans' families staying in emergency shelters but failed to resolve the problem of crowding. Each house had a mere two bedrooms, though at least twenty-four of these families had four or more children. This was accommodation at its most basic for twenty-two dollars a month. The houses were set on concrete blocks and measured only twenty by twenty-four feet, with ply-board walls. They were heated by stoves, wired for electricity, and featured bathrooms equipped with a sink and toilet but no bathtub.[103]

Although the 1949 amendment to the National Housing Act provided for joint federal-provincial funding, public housing projects continued to be held back in Manitoba because the provincial government passed on to municipalities much of its share of the cost. The housing shortage in Winnipeg was still described as "very acute," if not as severe, in 1950; the vacancy rate was 0.198 percent, while 2 percent was considered the desirable minimum. Even as late as 1954, Winnipeg had 199 families in emergency shelters.[104]

Winnipeg's housing problems were shared by other western cities after the Second World War, just as they had been during the inter-war period. Vancouver, which had a shortage of 10,000 dwellings in 1941, suffered during the 1950s from "a continuing, worsening scarcity of decent, low-income rental accommodation," as well as occasional shortages of units in the middle-income range. Vancouver's problems, like Winnipeg's, pre-dated the Depression but were exacerbated by the deferral of new construction during the 1930s.[105] In Alberta, the provincial government was no more enthusiastic about building public housing under the National Housing Act than was Manitoba, and Alberta likewise passed along to municipalities its 25 percent of the federal-provincial shared-cost program. Only 10,000 to 12,000 social-housing units were built in all of Canada between 1945 and 1960. The post-war economic boom may have facilitated house construction and the growth of suburbia, but those in need of low-income housing continued to be the last to enjoy any improvement in their situations. Winnipeg's first dedicated low-income housing development, Triangle Gardens on Herbert Avenue in Elmwood, was not completed until 1957.[106] The city's housing shortage was not resolved quickly, and the problems associated with slum neighbourhoods and poverty would persist throughout the post-war decades.

As they waited out the war years, families contended with all of the symptoms that attended the housing shortage: discomfort, lack of privacy, reduced standards of safety and sanitation, discrimination from landlords, rent gouging, and lack of alternatives in choosing accommodations. All of these took their toll on family morale during the war and some delayed the process of civil re-establishment for veterans when they returned home. It is impossible to measure the impact of the housing crisis on the community's war effort, but the fact that Winnipeggers endured it without splitting open the social fault lines may be indicative of their commitment to the national cause. People no doubt carried on despite their housing problems because there was little choice, but it is not inconceivable that they also saw the need to double-up or delay repairs and new construction for the benefit of the war effort in general.

Although the state acknowledged its duty to provide financial support to servicemen's families, the government's private-sector mentality concerning housing policy made it reluctant to assume greater responsibility for social welfare in this area that was so crucial to home-front morale. The state had expanded significantly for the purpose of fighting the war, but it was by no means clear that its encroachment into the family's private sphere was anything but a temporary expedient. Even its institution of Family Allowances in 1945 was more the result of a desire to stabilize post-war employment by maintaining consumers' spending power than any intention to hasten the arrival of a comprehensive welfare state.[107] It is not surprising, then, that the cultivation of non-material aspects of family morale was largely left to private welfare organizations, regimental associations, or the family itself.

6

RESPONSES TO FAMILY SEPARATION

*I send greetings from us all to your loved ones and friends in
your homelands; they are, indirectly, part of this great Army
in that their courage and fortitude is essential to the morale of
the Army itself.*

General Bernard L. Montgomery[1]

*Every attempt to advance the health and strength of our
fighting forces comes back to the health of the family. The vital
problem of morale turns out to be a question of the family and
its workings.*

Sidonie Gruenberg, *The Family in a World at War*[2]

The previous chapter outlined some of the most important material factors
contributing to family welfare—income, cost of living, and accommodations—but what about the intangible factors that shaped one's outlook and
thus influenced morale? How did servicemen's families cope with and
preserve long-distance relationships? How did they adapt to wartime disruptions of family roles and routines? Our attention turns now to the impact
on families of wartime separation, their strategies for coping, and some of
the emotional and social supports offered by organizations concerned with
family welfare. The family, like the state, would not emerge from six years of
war untouched. The war left a lasting impression on gender roles, on child
development, and on the stability of marital relationships. Concern for servicemen's families was not centred solely on the links between morale and
the war effort; there was also apprehension that the changes to the nature of
family life that the war accelerated would erode accepted social norms.

Family Responses to Separation

An eloquent expression of the hardships endured by wives and mothers on the home front was offered by Queen Elizabeth in a radio broadcast on Armistice Day, 11 November 1939. The queen and her husband, King George VI, earned the love and admiration of the Empire by remaining in London with their daughters, Princesses Elizabeth and Margaret, to bolster morale despite the German blitz and mounting public pressure to seek refuge in Canada. Her address to the women of the Empire is worth recalling in some detail:

> Wives and mothers at home [during the First World War] suffered constant anxiety for their dear ones, and too often, the misery of bereavement. Their lot was all the harder because they felt that they could do so little beyond heartening, through their own courage and devotion, the men at the front. Now this is all changed, for we, no less than men, have real and vital work to do.... The tasks that you have undertaken, whether at home or in distant lands, cover every field of national service.... The novelty, the excitement of new and interesting duties have an exhilaration of their own. But these tasks are not for every woman. Many of you have had to see your family life broken up, your husbands gone off with allotted tasks, your children evacuated to places of greater safety. The King and I know what it means to be parted from our children, and we can sympathize with those of you who have bravely consented to this separation for the sake of your little ones. Equally do we appreciate the hospitality shown by those of you who have opened your homes to strangers and to children sent from places of special danger. All this, I know, has meant sacrifice. And I would say to those who are feeling the strain: be assured that in carrying on your home duties, and meeting all these worries cheerfully, you are giving real service to the country. You are taking your part in keeping the home front ... stable and strong. It is, after all, for our homes and for their security, that we are fighting. And we must see to it, that despite all the difficulty of these days, our homes do not lose those very qualities which make them the background as well as the joy of our lives.[3]

The queen's address sought to encourage women because they were seen as the family linchpin, and the family's well-being was the keystone of national morale. But wartime separation threatened to undermine the stability of familial bonds. Sociologist Reuben Hill's 1949 study *Families Under Stress* revealed that reactions to separation were many and varied. Of the 135 American families separated by wartime service comprising his sample, twenty-two had not prepared for the prospect and suffered shock. Fifteen welcomed enlistment "as a release from an intolerable marital situation." Eleven "faced their emotional crisis in advance, cried it out, and were ready to go through with the separation when the time came." It is often said that a proportion of veterans took the attitude that they had a job to do in defeating the Axis powers, and seven of Hill's families repeated that view. To offset the loss of their husbands' income, four wives started working to put money away before their husbands left. Six families moved in with in-laws and four left their house for an apartment. In four cases where couples had gradually drifted apart over time, "the impending separation brought them closer together, made them more aware of the values of family living."[4] No doubt the range of reactions was similar among Canadian families.

One common response to war by people everywhere was the impulse to start a family while they had the chance. The uncertainties of wartime spurred many couples to marry much sooner and perhaps younger than they otherwise would have done. The number of marriages in Canada in 1939 increased by 17 percent over the number for 1938, followed by an additional increase of 20 percent in 1940. One article in *Chatelaine* asked, "Are They Too Young to Marry?" The author, coming down in favour of the decision, explained the point of view of young couples facing imminent separation as new husbands prepared to go overseas: "Precious moments of happiness have to be snatched as one crisis follows another." Who knew what fate the war had in store, or whether there would be time later for a traditional courtship? As for the emotional difficulty of long-distance relationships for couples still getting to know each other, this need not create an overwhelming obstacle since wives could take up voluntary or paid war work. Keeping busy was considered one of the best ways of dealing with the strain: Canadian women supposedly "know that hard work keeps anyone from too great worry and excessive loneliness."[5]

The author made it sound very easy, but coping with separation was not as simple as that. The emotional difficulties were probably as taxing as the financial. Social agencies reported problems resulting from hasty marriages where a couple's relationship lacked the foundation necessary to withstand the separation.[6] Loneliness in the absence of one's spouse could be difficult enough for both men and women, but the strain on a relationship was even greater when loneliness prompted infidelity. If the family broke up as a result of unfaithfulness, emotional anguish could turn into financial ruin as well. A wife's misconduct could lead to cancellation of her allowance, and service-men could request such action by the DA Board. The dependents' allowance investigations likely did not reveal every instance of adultery, but wives who became pregnant by other men often provided the evidence themselves.[7] Apart from this official surveillance, wives' behaviour in the absence of their husbands was also scrutinized unofficially by their neighbours. Married women going out with male friends or frequenting dance halls or bars met with disapproval. One woman whose husband served overseas went to live with her mother-in-law in a small town where "if you went out and your hus-band was overseas, ... the neighbours would talk and talk and point at you in the streets and you were ... lowest of the low."[8] But that did not stop everyone. Western Canada was home to a majority of the training schools established under the British Commonwealth Air Training Plan, and the airmen's danc-es attracted local girls, both single and married. One pilot recalled that in Lethbridge, "all these married girls would take their rings off and come to the dances when their old man was overseas. There was a lot of that."[9]

The papers of Laurence (Laurie) Wilmot, a chaplain from Swan River, Manitoba, who served with the West Nova Scotia Regiment in Italy, are an important source of primary evidence for an inquiry into how separation affected families, for two reasons. First, his work as a regimental chaplain en-tailed regular counselling to men with domestic problems and his comments offer insight into the difficulty of maintaining morale during a period of pro-longed separation and high anxiety. There may have been no one better placed to comment on morale because, as one Wartime Information Board memo put it, "the padre resides with the troops at all times. He gets up with the ser-vicemen in the morning, he goes into the field with them, he eats with them, plays with them, and is at their disposal at all times.... Any one will admit that the padre, by the fact of his presence amongst the troops has an enormous influence on [their] behaviour."[10] Second, Wilmot's papers contain a set of wartime letters exchanged with his wife Hope, who spent much of the war in Winnipeg. This particular collection is unique because most servicemen in combat units, lacking storage facilities, were unable to preserve significant volumes of correspondence from home. As an army chaplain, Wilmot usually had the use of an office or caravan where he could keep his papers. Laurie and Hope Wilmot wrote to each other almost every day during a two-year separation that lasted from September 1943 until the end of the war in August 1945. By education and economic class part of society's elite, the Wilmots were hardly representative of average Canadians. Nonetheless, the frequency and depth of their correspondence illuminate in a very rare manner the character of some family problems that would have been familiar to others.

In the spring of 1944, Wilmot reported his observations about the effects of family problems on morale in his regiment. His comments were generally applicable to other front-line units with long service overseas: "Many of the men who have been away from home for three and four years or more have very serious domestic problems at home which are sapping their morale. The apparent hopelessness of the appeal for compassionate leave for men who have serious home problems tends to create the impression in the mind of the soldier that the army is not interested in him or his problems. This not only knocks the bottom out of him as a soldier but is also damaging to the morale of his friends." Wilmot cited one example where a man suspected his wife of infidelity, but the DA Board told him that an investigation revealed his accusation to be groundless—despite the fact that he had a letter from her admitting having a two-year-old child, though he had been away for over four years. In cases like these, there was little a chaplain could do beyond writing to the man's wife. A group of chaplains, including Wilmot, recommended a system of home leaves for men with long service overseas in order to boost morale and reinforce marriages. Wilmot believed that "if there could be some assurance given to soldiers and their families that after three or four years away from home they would be given a two month furlough home, both would have something to look forward to and to live for."[11] Manpower needs in the armed services limited such prospects. The army, for example, instituted a "tri-wound" plan only in September 1944, later revised to a six-month tour of duty in Canada for veterans of three years who had been wounded twice, and one month home leave for those posted outside Canada for five years. The quota was only three men per battalion, and fewer than 10,000 men in total were able to take advantage of the scheme.[12]

Wilmot and his wife Hope had a remarkably strong bond that helped them endure their separation. From their home in Swan River, Manitoba, Laurie volunteered for the Chaplains Service in the summer of 1942 and was posted to his first unit, the Black Watch (Royal Highland Regiment), in Montreal. His letters show that he enlisted out of a profound sense of duty to provide spiritual support to the men risking their lives in the armed forces, and he recognized the burden he was placing on Hope by leaving her to raise their three small children on her own. Like many other couples, their efforts to seize every last possible moment together were complicated by the uncertainties imposed by frequent moves while Laurie's unit trained in preparation for embarkation overseas and by the difficulties of finding accommodations in each new town. They both hoped that the family would be able to join him but nothing was then certain about the duration of his posting with the regiment or whether it would stay in Montreal, so they were forced to wait until the situation clarified. Laurie agreed to send his daily letters by airmail in the meantime, so they would reach home without delay. By late July, he had learned that the regiment was to leave Montreal though the destination, Sussex, New Brunswick, was not known until early August. With continued uncertainty about the duration of his time in Sussex, available off-base housing, and a belief that it would not be logical to incur the expenses of moving east for just a short period of time, Laurie advised Hope to look for accommodations in Winnipeg. It was clearly an agonizing question for them both, and they found being apart a definite hardship. But shortly after he reached Sussex with his battalion on 18 August, he decided to have Hope join him and began to look for accommodations.[13] They were reunited in early September, but she was forced to remain in Sussex while Laurie was posted to Halifax in December. He soon recommenced the process of looking for family quarters there, with the same uncertainty about the duration of his stay but with more housing difficulty, due to the busy port city's congestion. For the next six months the couple made do with seeing each other for a few days or weeks at a time, with Hope moving to the Halifax area and then to Brockville, Ontario in response to Laurie's subsequent postings. In mid-September 1943, Laurie was sent overseas, and Hope went back to Winnipeg.[14]

The intermittent separation was very difficult for them both, though it may have given them some additional time to prepare for the inevitable. When Laurie left Hope in Halifax, she wrote: "Sometimes I cannot bear the thought that this past year is not the end of loneliness but only the beginning." To keep their bond strong while apart, they wrote constantly and observed a simple daily ritual: both kept a "noon watch" wherever they happened to be, during which time they paused to think of the other. Hope regularly sent Laurie parcels containing chocolates, chewing gum, cigarettes, as well as socks she had knitted and photographs of herself and the children. She also sent a diary and asked him to record all "the things you would come home and tell me at the end of a day's work" so that "when we get to-gether [sic] again, the years will not be completely lost." Laurie sent back photos and souvenirs from England, North Africa, and Italy as a way of sharing his experiences with her. Their religious faith was crucial to maintaining emotional stability because it gave them a certain peace of mind, a belief that all would unfold as it should. In his first letter from overseas, Laurie wrote: "I find you very near to me and I shall always carry in my mind the picture of you as on our last day together. God was very near to us on that day and will go with us to uphold us throughout the days which lie ahead. I think the best way is just to live one day at a time and not try to visualize the length of separation."[15]

Regular correspondence by mail was not just a lifeline for the Wilmots, it was absolutely crucial to the maintenance of morale for everyone on both the home and battle fronts. Hill's study of families reunited after wartime service found that the frequency and tone of letters, and the range of topics included in correspondence, could significantly affect the relative success of a family's adjustment to separation. Wives, the author suggested, could "pour out [their] affection and troubles into [their] letters" to vent their own domestic tensions. And including the husband or father in family issues by asking his advice in turn helped maintain his presence and eased reintegration upon demobilization.[16] Some couples may even have found their relationships strengthened by a new sort of intimacy developed through correspondence, if the lack of a physical connection prompted them to share their thoughts and feelings to a greater extent. Hope felt this way, telling Laurie:

> I think, when all this is over, if we are spared to one another, we shall decide that these months of separation have woven something enduring for us. You have been grand in your letters, pouring out your thoughts, and hopes, and never a lack of what to write about in spite of the fact that most of the time you could not mention *what* you were doing. And then I have surely kept you posted on all we did, on our little trials, and sometimes big ones...and on our victories, and also on my feelings, for I cannot put away feeling, where you are concerned. I cherish you completely.[17]

Newspapers, magazines, and radio programs included regular features on the importance of letter writing, as well as advice on how to write a good letter. *Chatelaine* urged its readers to write letters—cheerful ones—to the men overseas because the only thing as detrimental to their morale as bad news from loved ones at home was no news at all.[18] Their need was shared equally by families living with the daily fear of receiving the dreaded government telegram which always began with the words "Minister of National Defence deeply regrets to inform you...." Once a unit went into action, friends and relatives at home figuratively held their breath and waited for news that could be a long time coming. As the Allies fought through northwest Europe at the end of January 1945, the secretary of the Fort Garry Horse Women's Auxiliary wrote to the regiment's commanding officer, conveying thanks for efforts to maintain often tenuous lines of communication. "The distance is so great," she wrote, "the years so long[,] and mail so precious, you can readily understand the anxiety of loved ones."[19] Hope's letters to Laurie contained many pleas like the following: "If you don't write a lot & every day, I'll die." His replies echoed the sentiment: "Keep the letters coming, they mean everything at this end. Life goes very flat without news of you, for once I am off work my mind returns always to you, dear. You are my relaxation & my continual interest & I need to hear from you regularly."[20] The United States Post Office Department's annual report for 1942 summed up the importance of its work, observing that "frequent and rapid communication with parents, associates, and loved ones strengthens fortitude, enlivens patriotism, makes loneliness endurable, and inspires to even greater devotion the men and women who are carrying on our fight far from home and friends. We know that the good effect of expeditious mail service on those of us at home is immeasurable."[21]

Mail delivery to or from troops overseas was generally swift but could be erratic owing to a unit's frequent moves or the vicissitudes of war. Laurie's letters got through to Hope fairly regularly, though not in sequence, during his moves from England to Italy via North Africa in November and December 1943. The popular blue air-mail letters took about a week to cross the Atlantic, sometimes as quickly as five days. They were apparently rationed to one a week for servicemen during Laurie's stay in the United Kingdom, though there were obviously ways around the restrictions since he occasionally managed to send more. Reception of mail overseas was also timely, as long as the men did not move too frequently. When they did, it could take weeks to catch up, letters arriving a month or more after they were written. A Christmas parcel Hope sent to Laurie in October 1943 finally reached him the following April, having been repeatedly redirected following his move to the Mediterranean theatre.[22]

Such delays were understandable but they could make a hard job even harder for men in combat. During Laurie's interviews with members of his new unit, the West Nova Scotia Regiment, "one of the questions which always comes out is[,] Why is our mail not coming through? Some of them have not had mail for months."[23] Reports written by the army's Directorate of Special Services echoed the theme. As one corporal who served in Italy with the Royal Canadian Army Service Corps wrote, "We felt pretty lost and after a while the only thing we cared about was our mail." An infantry sergeant agreed: "When we are far from home we want to get news from our people and we don't bother much about the rest."[24] When that news did not get through, the result could be devastating to their morale and that of the family at home. One soldier in Wilmot's unit "gave me his home address that I might write on his behalf. He was getting no mail at all, no answers to letters he had written, no gifts of cigarettes, and his children had been placed in an orphanage."[25] In some cases like this, discouragement caused them to "stop writing home and I receive letters from wives and relatives asking me to try and locate them." He had no difficulty empathizing with these men because Hope's letters took more than a month to be redirected following his move to Italy. After weeks of waiting in vain for mail-call, in January 1944 he began receiving bunches of back-mail all at once. "What a difference it has made to me," he told Hope. "I feel like a new person; I sat down this a.m. & had a real picnic reading the letters & clippings, etc. which arrived yesterday." He was then just getting over a bout of dysentery, so the news from home cheered him considerably.[26]

Receiving mail could definitely have a tonic effect for men serving in a combat zone, with all its attendant dangers and discomforts. As one American airman wrote his wife, "You'll never know what a boost to morale it is to come back from a 3½ hour mission and find a pile of letters on my cot waiting for me—Pulling off my heavy shoes and jacket, I stretch out on my cot to read and relax—before I've read more than a page, I have forgotten all the tenseness and fear which had confronted me a few hours before as the formation approached the target."[27] Part of Wilmot's job as an army chaplain was conducting burials, a task that was shared by anyone assigned to a burial party. After one major battle, Wilmot and a group of men worked to gather the dead who had been temporarily buried in slit trenches or shell holes, and re-inter them at the regiment's cemetery. It was a gruesome experience, and "it took weeks to get rid of the smell of death that seemed to cling to us long after.... The task continued well into the evening and we did not get back until 2300 hours, tired and hungry. I was cheered to find that four letters and a parcel of food had arrived from Hope." Another part of his job involved writing to the next-of-kin, and responding to their inquiries about where and how their men had died. Wilmot's letters thus helped comfort the bereaved, just as Hope's letters comforted him on occasions when his sad duties left him feeling dejected, "pondering the inhumanity of war."[28]

Hope made the family's home life vivid for Laurie in her letters, often describing what they all wore when going out visiting or to church, how the older two children, Laurence and Louise, were doing at school, or some amusing thing Hope Fairfield (then age four) had said. For example, just before Hope's birthday, she wrote Laurie: "Laurence phoned [from boarding school] to be sure he was coming home. Said Gran Wilmot had sent him 2.00 and he was going to buy me something, I said no, then thought, 'there are some things I had better not order, no matter how sensible['] so I withdrew my objection.... Hopie is quite amazed that *I* have birthdays, and in her prayers said she would tell God, though he probably knew because he heard everyt[h]ing!"[29] On another occasion, Laurie learned that "Louise [is] taking part in a concert next door, she is a pumpkin in a costume and … sings a really nice little song learned at school."[30]

Updates like these were crucial if an absent father were to maintain his connection with the family's activities, and his letters were equally important to family morale. One child-guidance expert recommended turning a letter from "Daddy" into a family event that the children could share, along with writing the reply. But as historian William Tuttle explains, "naturally, the most wonderful letters for children were those written to them only."[31] The Wilmots and other close-knit families hardly needed such advice. Sharing photographs, the latest progress at school, or details of the places a father visited overseas no doubt provided fodder for much correspondence. Hope's efforts seemed to pay off, at least to a certain degree. A year into their separation, she wrote a letter that must have warmed her husband's heart:

> It is remarkable to me how real you are to [Hope Fairfield], one would gather from her attitude that all she had to do was run to the next room and see you…. I think this is lovely dear…they do not feel an awayness from you except in the matter of sight and sound and touch…which of course is a pretty big *except*, but you are very much beloved, and the children are right up to date on all your doings, and very enthusiastic about you in their conversation,

and there certainly won't be any strangeness when you come home
... another reason why the trip east was justified, they got used to
military comings and goings, and each in his or her own small way
had to learn to give you back to the army when the time came each
day as you left us.[32]

In such circumstances, the worry of a husband and father about his family's
welfare in the event that he was killed in action cannot be understated, nor the
fears of loved ones for his safety. As Laurie reflected in his diary,

I don't think I had really contemplated the possibility that death
might come to me in this struggle until quite recently under shell-
fire & with shrapnel falling about one [sic]—upon reflection you
realize that one of these might snuff out your life. I do not want to
die just yet—I have so much to live for—and apart from myself there
is my family—Hope & the children. I owe them so much that I can
only repay to them by returning to them.... Am I to return? That is
in God's Hands! He alone can decide when my work is done.[33]

These fears were nearly realized on 23 May 1944 when the West Novas played
their part in the battle to break the German defences of the Hitler Line,
guarding the Liri valley and the approaches to Rome. Helping to bring out
casualties during the attack, Wilmot was nearly killed by an exploding shell
while leading a carrying party bearing a wounded man back to the regimental
aid post. Perhaps by divine intervention, the shrapnel that pierced his steel
helmet merely nicked his ear before passing out the other side, though the
concussion knocked him to the ground. A few weeks passed before he was
able to acknowledge, in a letter to Hope, the magnitude of the event. He sent
her a news clipping describing the unit's action at the Hitler Line and his own
work under fire to help the wounded. Though he admitted that it might sound
reckless "when read in print," he assured her that he was simply following
his conscience in responding to the needs of his comrades. Of the danger to
himself, he wrote:

"the contemplation of the possibility of death did not frighten me
personally.... But the thought of your need & of the childrens [sic]
need filled my mind continually.... It would have been a compara-
tively simple matter had I been single and with no one depending
upon me, but with you ... & our lovely children with such great

possibilities before them—it was a terrific ordeal to face, for I know what it would mean to you [if he were killed]."³⁴

A wife's own fears for her husband hardly need stating, but as Hope succinctly put it a few months earlier, "I think of you all the time. I try not to let my mind dwell on possibilities, of disaster, but the papers are full of casualties, and we know there will be a drive on Rome." Two weeks after Laurie's close call—but before she had learned of it—Hope told him about attending a church service on 6 June to offer prayers for the success of the Normandy invasion, and her letter provides a sense of the tension under which families like hers had to carry on: "Well The Great Day is come, the day of the Invasion. How our hearts all beat, one is thankful because we pray that it is the beginning of the end, and yet I am sure every woman concerned feels, 'just how soon is this great convulsion of fighting going to affect me' ... and of course I am among them." Meanwhile, newspaper accounts of Rome's capture focused her attention on the Italian front:

> Pictures of the Rome entry are beginning to be shown in the papers and I wonder how soon you yourself will see the great city? I know there must be danger all about, and it only takes one dangerous missle [sic] to create havoc, and not necessarily in the midst of a battle! But I do not fear, ahead of time, the unknown, though I do think of you continually, and I *do* pray for your safety... for tho' it is not my place to feel that you should be more protected than other men, yet I do not feel it is God's will for you to be killed, and every breath I draw has behind it the continuous prayer for you.³⁵

Children, the War, and Disruption

A serviceman's children often shared these fears for his safety, and they were affected in various ways by his absence. Family morale could depend on children's responses to separation and the war as much as those of any other member of the household, so it is important to consider their experiences. There has been too little research on children's issues in the Canadian context to draw definite conclusions, but American scholars have revealed patterns from which the Canadian experience likely did not differ greatly. One 1946 study of child development found that children had little comprehension of war before age five, but began to understand its ramifications once they

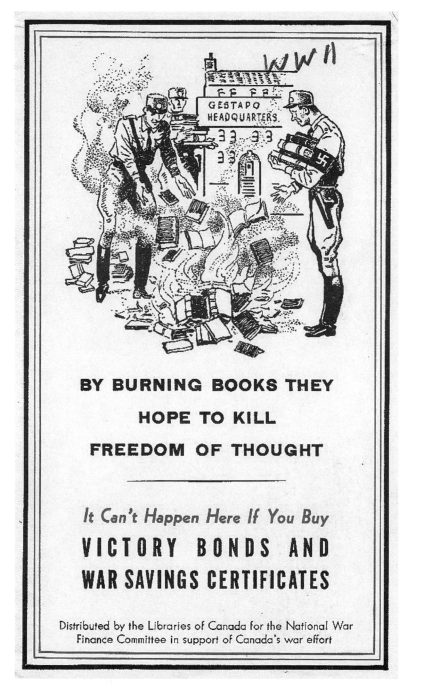

Figure 3.14. *It Can't Happen Here.*

Figure 3.15. If Day, 19 February 1942. Raising the Swastika at Lower Fort Garry.

Figure 3.16. If Day, 19 February 1942. Premier Bracken and Cabinet Ministers Interned at Lower Fort Garry.

Figure 3.17. If Day, 19 February 1942. Burning Books Outside the Carnegie Library.

Figure 3.18. If Day, 19 February 1942. "Nazis" Parade Down "Adolf Hitler Strasse"
(Portage Avenue).

Figure 3.19. 7th Victory Loan Pageant, 21 October 1944.

Figure 3.20. 8th Victory Loan Noon-gun Ceremony, 7 May 1945.

Figure 4.1. Red Cross Workers Packing Magazines.

Figure 4.2. Clothing Drive for Russian Relief, April 1944.

B U N D L E S of M A N I T O B A

215 Somerset Building

Winnipeg

telephone 28-153

Spring......and the bombs are falling.

Each raid sends more homeless children to the

nursery homes prepared for them.

Let's be up and helping NOW.

In these pages are practical, not costly, ways

to warm and cheer the brave women and children

of Britain.

·TODAY is the time to stoke up for next winter.

Bulletin Number 6   April, 1944

Figure 4.3. V-Bundles Newsletter.

The SCRAPPER

Published Monthly in the Interests of Volunteer
Salvage Workers Throughout Greater Winnipeg.
By The Patriotic Salvage Corps.
EDITOR: KEN W. PATTERN

Vol. 1, No. 13 — 24

March, 1944

RAGS ARE A "MUST" FOR APRIL

Once again, war needs have brought an urgent appeal from the Rag Controller for help from the Winnipeg Salvage Corps.

Rags are important in Canada's war effort and the supply is critically short. Roofing and building paper mills are closing down, or faced with the need for closing down as there is not enough roofing rags available to keep them running. War factories are in urgent need of wiping rags to keep their machinery running efficiently and are in a mad scramble for a share of the inadequate supply of rags coming out of the market. Manufacturers of uniforms and blankets for the armed forces need more and more woolen rags salvaged to keep up with war orders for these articles. Every scrap of material, large or small, is urgently needed. Factories and Winnipeg citizens will, we are sure, answer the appeal in their usual resounding manner and pro-

duce more than their quota of the rags necessary to meet the demand.

April is rag salvage month in Winnipeg for volunteer salvage workers. Every citizen of Winnipeg who has had the need explained to them is going to respond, and Winnipeg is going to produce, we are sure, seventy-five tons of rags as their contribution to Canada's need.

Now, district leaders, zone leaders and block captains must get behind this drive. Let's make it the most spectacular, most successful drive ever put on for rags in Canada. Talk rags for April; tell every one of your neighbors the need; impress on them the necessity for digging up every bit of material they have around their home they cannot find a use for and put it out on the boulevard for the salvage pick-up.

Once again, Salvagers, Winnipeg must and will go over the top.

WHERE TO LOOK FOR RAGS . . .

Attic, bedroom, kitchen, basement, garage, clothes closets, linen closets, wardrobes, dressers, chiffoniers, trunks, valises, and anywhere else rags may be.

REMEMBER . . . EVERY RAG IS WANTED NOW. DON'T OVERLOOK ANY PLACE THEY MAY BE . . . AND GET THEM OUT.

TAKE YOUR PLACE IN THIS TOTAL WAR . . . BACK THE RAG DRIVE OFFENSIVE . . . LET'S PUT IT OVER THE TOP!

WHAT RAGS ARE WANTED

Fabrics of linen, cotton, rayon, wool, old socks, stockings, shirts, dresses, underwear, suits, overcoats, gloves, table cloths, napkins, tea towels, etc., etc.

EVERY TYPE OF CLOTH IS VALUABLE AND NEEDED IN OUR WAR . . . GET IT ALL OUT.

Figure 4.4. "The Scrapper," Patriotic Salvage Corps newsletter, 1944.

Figure 4.5. Patriotic Salvage Corps, April 1942.

Figure 4.6. Winnipeg Ukrainians Hold a War Savings Concert, 19 October 1940.

passed that age. Around seven years, they became able to articulate fears about the war such as violence due to enemy activity, or the presence of spies. By eight or nine, they became curious about factual details like ideological differences between democracy and fascism, or the war's causes. They also became interested around this age in movies, games, or comic books depicting the war, and they participated in the home front effort by buying War Savings stamps, collecting scrap, or performing other patriotically motivated voluntary work.[36] Schools, news reporting, and domestic propaganda contributed to these responses as children learned to assimilate the information these sources provided.

Fear was a very real part of growing up during the war, whether fear of losing a father who might be killed in action, or fear engendered by blackouts and air raid drills. Fear was also conjured up by propaganda focusing on enemy cruelty and the destructiveness of war—the latter frequently employed to persuade the masses to enlist or buy war bonds. The psychological impact could be profound and life-long. Some small children separated from their fathers at a young age were prone to harbouring the fear of abandonment later on.[37] The erosion of domestic security was recognized as a key factor in developing such fears, and experts advised parents to adopt a calm and frank attitude in discussing issues related to the war with their children. Avoiding certain topics could make children uneasy in the knowledge that something was being kept from them. A 1942 study of family reactions to wartime conditions explained that "We have long known how foolish it is to try to deceive children.... We know too that it is not our words that convince, but rather the child's feeling that his parents have matters under control, that they know just what has to be done and can do it. The same is true even of serious disaster. When death comes to a family and grief seems for a time to overwhelm and destroy everything, the child who finds that his parents do, after all, go on again with life and living, nearly always finds that he can, too."[38] The authors advised parents to maintain familiar routines and a reassuring presence, and not to let children sense their own tension and fear.

Some children of servicemen reacted to the disruption of their home environment with behaviour that could be trying for the remaining parent. When Laurie Wilmot left his family to enlist, his youngest daughter, two-year-old Hope Fairfield, kept her mother awake at night for months, refusing to sleep. Nine-year-old Laurence Jr. took the changes less well, acting out with willful disobedience following the family's departure from Swan River and his

subsequent placement in the residence at St. John's College boarding school
in September 1942. He had been thriving up to that point, one year ahead of
his age group at school in Swan River. Laurie felt that his son's misbehaviour
resulted from a lack of discipline in his absence. At the same time, however,
Laurie recognized that the disruption to the family routine may have been
the cause of the difficulty: "I suppose he is just a child, and I have wondered
often if we arent [sic] expecting too much of him, and this is his unconscious
way of kicking back." Before the end of that summer, Laurence Jr. would have
to accept the departure of both his parents—since Hope followed Laurie to
New Brunswick in September—the loss of his home, and placement in a new
school. Once classes started, he would also have to cope with hazing and bullying at St. John's. As a new resident, younger and smaller than his classmates
since he remained one year ahead, he must have been an easy target for the
other boys. Hope brought him out to Halifax to spend the summer of 1943
with his parents and two sisters, but his behaviour during Laurie's absence
continued to trouble her. Nonetheless, he remained at boarding school until
1945, a decision Laurie later came to believe had been a mistake.[39] Whether
Laurence Jr.'s behavioural problems resulted from resentment at being left behind or were just a part of a normal boy's childhood, Hope's letters reiterated
her difficulties handling him:

> Laurence ... is a great problem ... perhaps with his day occupied
> at school, he will be different, I try so hard to be patient with him,
> but he is very demanding, and wants his own way insistently about
> every little thing, and has worn me down more the last week than
> the girls have all summer. He surely needs his Dad. I suppose that a
> boy senses that his Mother is continually occupied with a lot of little
> things, and can be ground down just because he sees so much of her,
> while his father will only stand so much infringement of the time he
> spends at home, and then clamps down.... oh to be a father![40]

Children's misbehaviour, in fact, spurred a moral panic over a perceived
rise in juvenile delinquency that was linked to two issues with which we are
fundamentally concerned: the absence from home of fathers in the services
and the adverse effects on family welfare of living conditions imposed by the
housing crisis. Delinquency was an issue of serious contemplation for social
agencies in all parts of Canada, and much of it stemmed from the belief—to
which the Wilmots subscribed—that mothers were unable to control their

children in the absence of the disciplinary influence of fathers and older brothers due to military service.[41] When mothers began entering the work force in significant numbers around 1942, social commentators proclaimed a harmful relationship between the resulting lack of adult supervision and juvenile delinquency. *Canadian Forum*, for example, urged the federal government to take steps to protect children and restrict employment of young mothers.[42] According to Christabelle Sethna, the wartime "working mother was caught in a Catch-22. If she did not contribute her labour to the war effort, she was unpatriotic. If she worked, she was deemed responsible for everything from her children's head lice to hookey to juvenile delinquency," especially the sexual delinquency of teenage daughters.[43] In Winnipeg, the chairman of the Council of Social Agencies, Mr. A.V. Pigott, outlined the problem this way: "Every growing individual has certain basic needs, such as a feeling of security, opportunity for growth, and a sense of achievement and of being appreciated. If he is frustrated and cannot have any of these needs fulfilled, he reacts to the situation—often through delinquent behaviour."[44] Children could be kept on the right path if they had good housing, sound educational and religious influences, and access to recreational programs. The key institution, though, was the home environment. With so many fathers serving away from home, the requisite guiding adult influence was lost to many children who, it was believed, turned to gangs or roamed the streets.[45] Juvenile delinquency was even claimed to impact the fighting efficiency of the armed forces, since delinquent girls were blamed for spreading venereal diseases to servicemen.[46]

The Canadian Welfare Council (CWC) echoed *Canadian Forum* in urging that mothers with children under two years should only be employed as a last resort. Its 1942 report "Day Care of Children in Wartime" favoured limiting working mothers to day shifts, preferably half-time, in order to minimize disruptions for their children. Although Ontario and Quebec took advantage of a federal-provincial Wartime Day Nurseries agreement to provide day care for mothers drawn into war industries, the CWC argued that such abdication of parental responsibility would be detrimental to family life. It claimed that "maintaining the all-important relationships which bind together mother and child" would be difficult if "full-time care is provided while the mother works." The report cited examples from the British context which showed that working mothers had an additional four to five hours of daily work, apart from their time at the factory, simply to keep their homes in order and prepare their children for the nursery or for bed.[47] In such circumstances, working mothers might have been happier to stay at home.

Winnipeg's Council of Social Agencies (CSA) set up a committee to make its own study of the issue. It conducted a survey to determine the number of working mothers and tried to ascertain the need for local day care facilities. The committee ultimately determined that because of the small proportion of Canadian war industry located in Winnipeg, said to be only 4 percent, the number of working mothers was insufficient to warrant the expense of providing day nurseries. The survey showed that a total of 3,963 children of school age or younger, or about 14 percent of the children attending Winnipeg schools, had working mothers. Only 374 of these children were of pre-school age, however, so it appeared that because most of these mothers worked while their children were in class, additional day care facilities were unnecessary. After-school drop-in clubs, where teachers or volunteers supervised athletics or crafts, were thought to be a better investment.[48]

There were significant shortfalls with the survey's methodology and findings, however. Although there was some useful commentary on mothers' work situations, such as place and type of employment, the surveys were done by classroom teachers, apparently by questioning their students about issues like lunch-time and after-school supervision. Aside from the obvious limitations of reporting on working mothers by relying on data furnished by their children, the survey was only designed to target the 2,100 mothers with kids in school. The needs of working mothers with only pre-school-age children were not taken into account; the 374 pre-schoolers noted above were included because they had older siblings in school. And although the CSA used the small proportion of war industry located here to deny the need for additional child care, the survey showed that most working mothers were employed in the service sector. They worked at retail stores like Eaton's and the Hudson's Bay Company, in restaurants, dry cleaners, the needle trades, or domestic service. Despite the small national proportion, by July 1943 there were 5,197 women in paid war work, most in the aircraft industry, which amounted to one-quarter of the city's war industry work force. In general there were "more women, and presumably more mothers," working for pay in Winnipeg than in Ontario cities like Hamilton and Windsor that set up nurseries under the federal-provincial agreement. Moreover, the National Selective Service had declared that all work done by women was vital to the cause of victory and should therefore be considered "war work."[49]

The day care issue did not die immediately following the CSA's November 1942 report. A Winnipeg School Board meeting generated publicity for problems of truancy and inadequate child care in June 1943, which prompted school trustee Joe Zuken to ask the province to reconsider creating day nurseries. Although a tentative budget for a thirty-space program was drafted, the $5,000 cost was too rich for the province and little more was subsequently heard on the issue. The CSA was likely glad to see the end of the debate since its members "were influenced by traditional ideals of motherhood" and maintained paternalistic attitudes regarding family affairs. Given the link forged by social welfare commentators between juvenile delinquency and the erosion of traditional home life and family roles, it is therefore not surprising that authorities were not prepared to take steps that could be perceived as weakening the family by encouraging mothers to work outside the home.[50] On this point they differed little from counterparts in Britain and the United States who only reluctantly made childcare provisions for munitions workers and similarly stressed the temporary wartime nature of such measures. The practical impact of this dominant attitude was that most working mothers in need of someone to watch their children turned to grandparents, older siblings, other relatives, neighbours, or borders in their homes.[51] The exigencies of war and paid work prompted the adoption of new family roles, however slow the corresponding changes to accepted notions about motherhood.

The widespread concern over juvenile delinquency inspired extensive newspaper coverage and at least five major studies of the problem in Canadian cities. In Winnipeg, attention was rivetted on the issue following the killing of a guard by three youths during their escape from the Vaughan Street detention home on 12 November 1943. All three were quickly returned to custody, but City Council was impelled to call upon the Council of Social Agencies to form a special committee of inquiry into the problem of delinquency. While the CSA studied the issue, *Free Press* editorials contemplated the causes of youth crime, suggesting that the problem festered in "distinct delinquent areas, characterized by poverty, alcoholism, immorality and adult criminality."[52] The CSA's 1944 report argued that, despite the depth of concern, the incidence of juvenile crime in Winnipeg had not reached the alarming proportions that some people seemed to believe it had. The problem was largely one of perception. As Jeff Keshen argues, "statistics indicate that the factor largely responsible for high delinquency rates, which continued until 1942—*before* mothers actually joined the paid workforce in record numbers—was demographics, namely the rising number of adolescents in the general population and the departure of eighteen- to thirty-year-old males for overseas." Men in this age category were more prone to criminal activity, so their removal left police with more time to focus on petty crimes such as those attributed to juvenile delinquency.[53]

The CSA report did stress the relationship between potential delinquent behaviour and the disruption of family life by the war. It attributed delinquency to "insecurity in the child's environment, lack of confidence in himself, a feeling that he is rejected by his family or society, too much or too little parental control, or a lack of affection. Among other contributing factors are bad housing, bad companions, lack of recreational opportunities and space to play." No one would deny that the war brought insecurity, Winnipeg certainly had housing problems, and there was a distinct need for additional recreational programs and facilities. The committee called for the creation of a civic Recreation Commission to develop organized leisure activities under the leadership of "men and women qualified to build character as well as healthy bodies—to teach responsibility and to develop good citizens." Keeping children busy with organized recreation would keep them out of trouble, but there were not enough skating rinks, summer playgrounds, or swimming pools—Winnipeg boasted only two of the latter. A "basketball hall" and an athletic stadium that could be used by the schools and the university were needed. So were proper playing fields on or near school grounds, since no city school had even a running track.[54] The city's Public Parks Board appointed another commission to study Winnipeg's recreational requirements in October 1945, and its recommendations to improve school and community club programs would be pursued in the post-war years.[55]

Of course not all children were seen as potential delinquents, their lives were not exclusively defined by family separation, and their activities did not turn just on the doings of absent fathers, uncles, or brothers in the armed forces. School and work were large parts of most children's upbringing then as now, but there were some subtle differences. Until 1943, the Winnipeg School Board did not offer kindergarten classes. In that year, it took responsibility for four trial kindergartens, and the number grew to twenty-one two years later. By 1947, there were thirty-four classes and the evident improvements in social adjustment of grade 1 students led to the perpetuation of what had been a trial plan.[56] Similarly, there had been no regular, tax-supported grade 12 classes offered in the city between 1932 and 1940. In the latter year, the school board filled the need over the objection of some trustees who argued that the new classes would be a costly burden for taxpayers and would take revenue away from institutions like the University of Manitoba which offered the courses for a fee.[57] Not all teens were eager to take advantage of the extra year of free education. The Winnipeg *Free Press* reported a trend among boys leaving school to take up full-time employment before turning eighteen so as to avoid being subject to certain National Selective Service restrictions once they reached the age of majority.[58] With the armed forces absorbing any surplus labour, social agencies were also concerned about increasing numbers of younger children working outside of school hours. The Child Health Services Board conducted a survey on out-of-school employment in January 1943, enlisting the cooperation of teachers who gathered information including the ages of working students, place and nature of employment, and hours worked per week. The survey found 2,532 boys attending Winnipeg public schools that worked at least ten hours per week out of school. Of that number, 494—including twenty-two boys under twelve years of age—worked fifteen hours per week or more, on top of 5.5 hours per day at school. Some of these boys were thus occupied from 43.5 to seventy hours a week, which allowed no time for homework. In response, City Council passed a by-law that required juvenile employees to hold permits signed by their school principals, and restricted the hours of work permitted to a maximum of fifteen per week during the school term.[59]

School children were also active in their free time. They could participate in recreation programs at the Young Men's or Young Women's Christian Associations, and there were groups to join like the Boy Scouts or Girl Guides, the Junior Red Cross, or Boys and Girls' Clubs. These groups taught them a variety of practical skills, citizenship, and the value of service to others.[60] Many helped out with voluntary work on behalf of the war effort. Children participated in Victory Loan publicity events, raised money for the various Allied relief funds, collected salvage, knitted comforts for servicemen, and more. Children who wanted to make a more martial contribution could join the army, air, or sea cadet corps organized through the schools. The Winnipeg Corps of Navy League sea cadets, for example, numbered 800 by June 1943, comprising three Ships' Companies, two of which were located at Kelvin High School and the third at Machray School. The cadets offered basic training for those aged fourteen to eighteen, hoped to foster an interest in the armed services, and instilled the "ideals of esprit de corps and good citizenship."[61]

Some children doubtless considered these activities a burdensome obligation mandated by parents, teachers, or government propaganda.[62] Yet in a time when people were bombarded with messages at the movies, at schools, the post office, the workplace, and on the radio, urging them to contribute in myriad ways to the war effort, "not being patriotic was unthinkable." Most children appear to have done what was expected of them, but on reflection, years later, some came to resent being taught to hate and fear through their wartime indoctrination.[63]

Military Family Welfare

Children's welfare was intimately bound up with the well-being of the family, and numerous organizations provided support to bolster the family institution during the war. Winnipeg's social agencies were key stakeholders in issues related to family welfare, and they worked alongside other groups concerned primarily with the special problems confronting servicemen's families, such as the Canadian Legion and the military's various unit auxiliaries. Social agencies fulfilled a key task, which they defined as working "to maintain morale by providing services which protect and build up family life." While the importance of this role was beyond dispute in peacetime, it was even more vital during a period of war when so many families were fragmented.[64] Social workers recognized the link between family welfare and armed forces morale, and they tried to ensure that home front living conditions were worthy of the sacrifices being made by Canadians fighting overseas. The Council of Social Agencies played a prominent role in public debates over issues like juvenile delinquency, the housing crisis, control of venereal disease, working mothers, and day nurseries. The CSA was also instrumental in establishing the Greater Winnipeg Coordinating Board for War Services in 1941 which, as we have seen, was concerned with providing auxiliary services to military personnel. The Coordinating Board's Dependents' Welfare Committee, in turn, served as a point of liaison for the various groups working on behalf of servicemen's dependents. One of the institutions that worked most intimately with struggling families was the Family Bureau of Winnipeg.

The Family Bureau was organized in 1936 as a private social agency to assist families encountering circumstances with which they could not cope, whether brought on by financial problems, illness, unemployment, or dysfunctional relationships. It was financed by the Community Chest, Winnipeg Foundation, the Junior League, and City Hall, and it worked closely with other community agencies, helping clients take advantage of the services they offered. The Family Bureau sometimes offered financial assistance to meet unforeseen expenses such as medical or moving costs, usually to be repaid. Early in the war, it contacted the Department of National Defence to object to the "undue delay" in payment of dependents' allowances, noting that payments were "not coming through as quickly as [they] should," and it provided support to families while they waited for their cheques.[65] More often, the nature of the Family Bureau's intervention focused on developing a strategy to help its client families work out their difficulties. Its case load grew more than fivefold during the war, from about 800 families in 1938–39 to over 5,500 in 1944–45. The steadily increasing number of men joining the armed forces was responsible for the growing case load, an indication of the special needs of servicemen's families. The proportion for which these families accounted grew from a low of nearly 30 percent early in the war to more than 70 percent by 1942–43.[66]

The Family Bureau's work brought it into contact with military families on routine matters as well as exceptional situations. It carried out investigations of family circumstances to assist the Department of National Defence in awarding dependents' allowances or making decisions regarding requests for leave, transfer, or discharge on compassionate grounds. It stepped in when infidelity was suspected or the husband had requested to have his assignment of pay, and thus the dependents' allowance, stopped. Its investigations were integral to the Dependents' Board of Trustees' procedures for awarding supplementary grants to a family's allowance in case of special hardship. The Family Bureau was often the point of contact for military chaplains who requested its help "when concern over the family at home is affecting the enlisted man's morale."[67] Counselling might be of help in such cases, and the Family Bureau offered advice on budgets, child-rearing, marital problems, and household management. In families where the mother had died, was absent, or was too ill to care for the house and children, it provided a "housekeeper" to perform such functions. The cooperation of social agencies like the Family Bureau, unit auxiliaries, the DA Board, and the Dependents' Board of Trustees was essential to the survival of some families when disaster struck. Such was the case when "Mr. K. went overseas early in the war and his wife became ill a few months later. The Regimental Auxiliary brought the matter to our attention and a housekeeper was placed immediately. On her death bed Mrs. K. asked our housekeeper, who had been in the home for several months, to care for the children until her husband returned. With the co-operation of the Dependents' Allowance

Board and the Special Grants Fund this plan has so far been carried out to the satisfaction of all concerned."[68]

Working to prevent family breakdowns helped prevent the erosion of wartime morale. Social agencies also cooperated in efforts to actively boost family morale, and a notable job was done in this connection by the Council of Social Agencies' Christmas Cheer Committee. Despite the name, this committee raised funds all year long to provide needy families with necessities like "surgical appliances, dentures, bedding, fuel, clothing, eye glasses, etc." Its main event was a three-night Christmas Carnival at the Auditorium that featured gambling and games of skill or chance; for example, in 1942 there was a "Bomb Berlin" game. There were booths for selling soft drinks, food, or candy. Carnival-goers could buy War Savings Stamps and Certificates, give blood, or dance to an orchestra. The committee distributed toys along with its Christmas hampers until 1942 when it opened a Toy Shop, staffed by volunteers, where parents could choose gifts for their children. The committee found that "the enjoyment that even the parent got out of this venture amply repaid the committee for this change in policy." The popular choices that year, apparently, were sleighs, wagons, and "large wooden scottie dogs." As increasing employment diminished the charge upon its services, the committee donated a portion of the proceeds to the Greater Winnipeg Coordinating Board for War Services to fund the United Services Lodge for personnel on leave.[69]

Supplementing the work of local social agencies, the Canadian Legion and numerous armed forces unit auxiliaries sought to provide for the welfare of troops on active service and their families. From its formation in 1925, the Legion had become by 1939 the most prominent advocate for veterans' issues in Canada, and it eagerly assumed the responsibility of assisting the new generation of servicemen and their dependents. The Legion's activities ranged from catering to the off-duty recreational requirements of troops at armed forces camps and stations to lobbying the Dominion government for better allowance and pension provisions. In one of its earliest initiatives, the Manitoba and Northwest Ontario Command set up a War Services Committee to act, in cooperation with a committee from the Legion's ladies' auxiliaries, as a liaison between enlisted personnel, government authorities, and families enduring financial hardship.[70] War Services officers worked with local social agencies to secure financial aid so that "the serving man's family would remain intact and free from other worries in addition to those for the safety of their loved one."[71]

The Legion pushed government authorities to justify their decisions when it felt that servicemen did not receive fair consideration. With roughly 150,000 members and half a million Great War veterans living in Canada, the Legion's voice carried significant weight.[72] For example, Legion pressure in January 1940 prompted the Manitoba government to include current volunteers for the armed services under the provisions of the Soldiers' Taxation Relief Act of 1922, which entitled pensioners and veterans' widows to remission of property taxes.[73] It held the federal government accountable for dependents' allowance provisions and other issues affecting servicemen and their families. In December 1939, the Manitoba and Northwest Ontario Command Council investigated the denial of an allowance to one soldier's widowed mother on the grounds that both had been on relief and his assigned pay alone exceeded the amount she had received before his enlistment. The Legion argued that "no man who enlists for service should be penalized because of his economic condition."[74] Three years later, Dominion Command President Alex Walker wrote the prime minister to assert the inadequacy of DA benefits. Walker objected to the process of investigating a serviceman's family before an allowance was authorized. He argued that allowances should be granted "as a statutory right."[75] While the Legion fought an uphill battle on this front—allowances continued to be considered a privilege that might be denied in certain cases—it continued its advocacy on behalf of servicemen and their families throughout the war and the decades to follow.

The Legion recognized that morale—and thus the calibre of Canada's armed forces—would suffer if the troops were distracted by worries about family hardships back home or lacked facilities for relaxation. The Canadian Legion War Services (CLWS) was thus established to see to off-duty requirements like concerts, movies, and other forms of entertainment. It provided troops at home and overseas with equipment for sports, ran over 1,000 canteens, distributed note paper and envelopes, sent cigarettes to men in hospital, and stocked lounges with reading materials. The CLWS hut in Shilo, Manitoba, for example, offered a "hostess service," essentially two Canadian National Railway caboose bodies furnished "to serve as a meeting place for the men and their relatives and friends," especially mothers, wives, and children.[76] Profits remaining from the operation of the CLWS at war's end were used, like the Canteen Funds left over from the Great War, to benefit ex-servicemen and their dependents through small grants in cases of distress.[77]

Like the Legion, armed forces units formed ladies' auxiliaries that were fundamentally concerned with the welfare of members' families. Many women joined these organizations in order to make a material contribution to the welfare of servicemen and military families through voluntary work. Some likely wanted to stay busy and keep their minds off worries about their men overseas. Perhaps some joined for social reasons. In any case, these auxiliaries provided important moral support. The Fort Garry Horse Women's Auxiliary divided its work among groups responsible for knitting comforts for the regiment, visiting veterans in hospital or the families of casualties, and meeting troop trains stopping in the city. They held dances, tag days, raffles, and teas to raise money, and then bought Victory Bonds, hampers for needy members, and hosted summer picnics and Christmas parties for their children.[78] Other units had similar auxiliaries. The Royal Canadian Naval Volunteer Reserve had a Women's Auxiliary and a Junior Women's Auxiliary that raised money to benefit the personnel of Winnipeg's Naval Division. They furnished the Chief and Petty Officers' Mess at HMCS *Chippawa*, and funded the construction of an outdoor skating rink. Meanwhile, the Winnipeg Women's Air Force Auxiliary operated an Airmen's Club that served over 100,000 meals in their canteen during 1944 alone, and arranged home hospitality for air force men. They held tag days and a Christmas bazaar, sent Christmas parcels overseas to No. 402 (City of Winnipeg) Squadron, which they had adopted, and sent cigarettes to Manitoba men taken prisoner of war and to men in hospital.[79]

Undoubtedly, the most difficult yet most essential task performed by members of unit auxiliaries was to visit the families of men killed or wounded on active service. Their commitment was conveyed by Mrs. R.B. Carter of the Fort Garry Horse Women's Auxiliary, who had the "privilege to write to the many mothers, wives and sisters of [those] Garry Boys who had been killed, were missing or wounded[,] to try to express to them a message of love, sympathy and friendship from us as members of the Auxiliary."[80] Miriam MacEwing, the president of the Women's Auxiliary, further reported that "for all its sadness, it was an unforgettable experience. To meet courage and faith and character in the face of despair, as we did most undoubtedly, is to be immeasurably strengthened. It fills you with determination to face any inevitability the same way—and to go on in this Auxiliary with even greater effort."[81]

Referring to all the "simple, quiet acts" performed by her friends and colleagues in the Fort Garry Horse—though her words could have applied equally to women in the other auxiliaries—Miriam MacEwing wrote in January 1945:

> It hasn't all been work. We have had our social gatherings and have reached out to one another in laughter and simple pleasures. But I · doubt if we have ever before been closer than we have been since June [1944] when we were drawn together in the bright face of danger. Our men were at last in the grip of conflict, and I feel with conviction that we have stood hand-in-hand ever since. To cry together creates even a stronger bond than the one of laughter, and we have wept in sympathy and pride for those of us whose husbands, fathers and brothers have made the supreme sacrifice. Just as deeply have we been touched with thankfulness and relief for those of our men who have returned.[82]

Reunion

Once the European war ended, families no doubt became impatient waiting for the men to return home. The job was not yet done, however, since occupation duties and the continuing war with Japan prolonged separation. As Hope Wilmot wrote a few weeks after the German surrender, "I'm afraid that from now on life takes on rather the aspect of an endurance test." Laurie had volunteered for the force being assembled for dispatch to the Pacific, and although Hope supported his decision, "these months ahead of us are among the very worst to wait through ... before you went overseas one knew that a long separation was looming; while you were fighting my mind was closed up tight as to possibilities of hurt coming to you, and now, you are so dear and life looms so precious after having been handed back again, that waiting is unbearable."[83] Japan's surrender made deployment of additional Canadians to the Far East unnecessary, but the struggle at home continued even after the Pacific war had ended. Putting a family's pieces back together was no easy task. Some couples that were fortunate enough to be reunited after the war found that lost time, new-found independence, or changed personalities as a result of wartime experience made reunification impossible. Partners were frequently changed by their wartime independence or the horrors of combat. Some wives found their husbands afflicted with nostalgia for the excitement of foreign people and places as opposed to the monotony of a repetitive civilian job. Sometimes couples found that the bonds of intimacy had been stretched too thin by the time apart. Loneliness had been a real problem for wives as well as husbands. Some succumbed to the temptation of new romantic possibilities offered by service overseas or new employment, or retaliated for a spouse's indiscretions.

Re-establishing his family had been the focus of many a serviceman's dream for the future while overseas, but reality did not always follow the script. Magda Fahrni argues, in her work on the post-war reunification of Montreal families, that "the moment of reunion, while it may have been the ending to one story, was the beginning of another. Suffering from wounds, illness, 'battle exhaustion,' or anxiety about the future, veterans and their advocates looked to the family as an agent of postwar healing. Women, as wives, girlfriends, or mothers, were to ensure the 'mental reestablishment of soldiers.' Yet veterans found that returning home was often difficult, and that readjusting to civilian status and family life required considerable work."[84]

The army's Directorate of Special Services reported on the problems encountered by 285 discharged servicemen when they returned home after prolonged absences overseas. Apart from the complications due to housing, the report found that a high proportion of the married men it surveyed experienced problems of "conjugal readjustment." One military district depot officer who interviewed returned men upon demobilization held the opinion that "50% of the married men have some problem when they come home. Cases are not always of infidelity but there is the financial, social, economic conditions they have to face. The big problem is their re-adaptation to living again with their wives." After four or five years apart, spouses might confront changes in their mate's personal habits or "irksome temperamental traits."[85] Wives had been forced to become more independent in their husbands' absence and both partners had to re-adapt to living together after years spent essentially reverting to life as single men and women.

Infidelity was a barrier to reunion that might be raised by either party. For some men, the memory of a wife back home could not satisfy their immediate desire for female companionship while overseas, and they often rationalized their behaviour by claiming that they were not cheating since their liaisons with the opposite sex were based solely on physical need rather than any real emotional attachment.[86] Wives might have been pardoned for using the same excuse, though they undoubtedly were held to more chaste societal expectations. In any case, as one Winnipeg woman recalled, "I knew what he was doing over there. I'd have been a fool if I didn't, so I had a right to live my own life too."[87] Reuben Hill found that the families most able to adapt successfully to separation were those who agreed in advance to permit "friendly contacts" with the opposite sex "in a mixed crowd," but no intimacy—as opposed to mutual sexual freedom or a double standard where one spouse was required to be faithful while the other was at liberty to indulge his or her desires.[88]

Military indoctrination and the lingering psychological effects of combat made the return to family life difficult for veterans. The Directorate of Special Services found that many "were clearly unprepared for the inevitable differences they encountered and they were too single-purposed and emotionally unadaptable to cope with even the normal every-day conjugal clashes of temperament and situation."[89] Returned men tended to be restless and disillusioned, unable to settle down into a civilian routine that often involved working in repetitive jobs that lacked the responsibility they had known in the armed forces. Also missing was the excitement of wartime life overseas, such as leave to historic European cities or the hospitality of people in liberated countries. Veterans might refer to civilians ignoring them or treating them coldly but, as one officer explained, the veterans had simply become accustomed to being treated like heroes overseas, so it was jarring now to be treated like everyone else. Still, a veteran's disillusionment could be profound for a number of reasons, as one man explained:

> No, I did not find things as I expected them to be. I found that the cost of living had gone up terribly. People unless they have someone close to their heart, do not care much about us. I found things at home in a terrible state. My wife had seemed to have lost me. I mean she was used to being alone and when I got back it was just as if I had been walking out of my grave after four and a half years. My baby is now five and a half. I had left my wife in a comfortable apartment and I found her living in a room.[90]

According to one Wartime Information Board correspondent in Edmonton, "there is an unrealistic attitude abroad that all returning men are alert, intelligent people who know exactly what they want, are entitled to anything they want, and that all we have to do is give it to them. My experience is that actually they are confused, restless and irritable—have a chip on their shoulder but don't know why."[91] Choosing a civilian role after years in the military could be difficult. Repatriated veterans were interviewed during the demobilization process by examiners who asked for three vocational preferences, but as one man determined, "it is a hard job to make them say what they want to do.... We have come to this conclusion that the men do not know what they want and when they have decided upon one thing they want that one and nothing else."[92]

There was a painful irony for men who had dreamt of coming home throughout their service overseas but were now nostalgic for the war years. One veteran who lost an arm in Sicily felt that "at least we were living then, we weren't mildewing like we are at home."[93] This sort of nostalgia could be debilitating to a marriage. One housewife whose story was told in *Chatelaine* found that her husband "John" had lost interest in the pre-war pastimes they had enjoyed, and had forsaken old friendships with men who had not shared the burden of service. He now preferred drinking with comrades from overseas and talking "about things I don't understand." Worse still, she continued, "John's attitude toward me is different. I guess he thought I was just about perfect when we got married and when he went overseas. But now, I'm sure, he sometimes thinks of me as a jailer.... He thinks my hair is all wrong and my clothes aren't smart enough. Well, I paid for the refrigerator with money I might have spent at the hairdresser." This woman was representative of the many wives—and children, siblings, or parents—who had to pick up the pieces of personal relationships that had been disrupted by the war. While they could sympathize with the dangers and discomforts endured by their men, it could be argued that veterans had at least seen a little more of the "fun and excitement" of foreign travel or leave, while they had "stayed home ... in Canada to take a war job by day, and knit, write letters and pack parcels by night."[94]

The changed personalities of returned men, perhaps resulting from what would be recognized today as Post-Traumatic Stress Disorder (PTSD), required patience and understanding from their loved ones. But PTSD was not officially recognized as a psychological disorder affecting veterans until 1980, and civilians had a difficult task responding appropriately when they could not be expected to really understand the brutalizing experience of combat. A Wartime Information Board correspondent wrote that "sometimes the man feels his people are strangers almost, and the families themselves frequently do not understand the man, and his need for a calm atmosphere for time to make the adjustments necessary."[95] One Winnipeg veteran who had been away for five years told a *Tribune* reporter about his difficulties adapting to civilian life. Upon arrival at the train station,

I looked at my brother, and he was a man. How strange, I thought. Everything's changed.

When I walked down the street, I felt stranger still. I met people who asked stupid questions, and didn't seem to understand what I'd been through. I ran into complacency—people considered war an adventure, a great experience, a lot of fun.

They asked me how it felt to fight in a war, and couldn't understand why I began to fidget. Then I would go out and get drunk to drown my despair. And when I came home, everybody was shocked that I was drunk.... I saw [men]...die. I saw things I can't talk about. And then they ask me questions like that.[96]

Reunification could cause conflicts in redefining family roles. A wife's new independence could be problematic for a returned husband trying to reassert pre-war authority. A father's relationship with his children could be even harder to reset. Many fathers who left young children at home when they enlisted were unrecognized by these children when they returned. Those who suffered from PTSD or alcoholism frightened children who were confused by their behaviour. A father's return might be seen as an intrusion after years away, during which time family roles had altered. Children who had grown up relatively pampered while living with their mother and grandparents may have resented a father's desire to impose discipline, particularly if his idea of discipline had been moulded by his time in the armed forces. In some families studied by Hill, the children had grown so close to the mother during his absence that they became jealous, resenting his competition for her attention and affection. Some accepted the father "as companion but refused to accept him as a disciplinarian."[97] Interpersonal dynamics could therefore put hurdles in the way of a family's successful reunion.

The government could not regulate a family's adaptation to separation, but it did offer a range of material supports that greatly assisted veterans in the process of re-establishing themselves in both career and community. The provisions for civil re-establishment were vastly improved, compared to the benefits to which veterans of the Great War had been entitled. Credits were offered to furnish a new home or for advanced education, and allowances were continued during the course of training. Loans or grants were available to buy land or start a business. A War Services Gratuity was paid to both men and women on discharge, which included fifteen dollars for every thirty days' service overseas and $7.50 for similar periods in the Western Hemisphere, plus a $100 clothing allowance. Regarding employment, many firms had guaranteed the positions of volunteers leaving work to enlist, and now preference in consideration for jobs in the civil service was given to veterans and widows whose husbands had died as a result of war service. The Returned Soldiers' Insurance Act provided lower rates for life insurance for veterans who could not get regular coverage because of their physical condition, so that they could protect their dependents.[98] These measures, collectively called the Veterans' Charter, offered Canadian ex-service personnel one of the most comprehensive veterans' benefits programs in the world, and it was a package that promised a measure of opportunity and security for their families in the post-war decades.

The war years were thus full of difficulties related to maintaining families financially, keeping them adequately housed, preserving the bonds of intimacy despite indefinite separations imposed by military service, and ensuring the emotional and developmental welfare of children in the face of grave disruptions to their lives. Wartime changes ultimately had lasting impacts on the family institution and produced considerable disquiet in welfare circles over issues like working mothers, juvenile delinquency, and the forced adaptation of gender roles in what were, for the duration, effectively single-parent families.

The future offered bright possibilities for veterans who managed to put their homes back together after the war, but some couples had simply changed too much during a husband's long absence. While some veterans prospered as a result of the wartime training they received or benefits that were well-earned, others found that victory was hollow. For families who lost their loved ones in the fighting overseas, the end of the war was nothing to celebrate—they merely breathed a sigh of relief that it was finally over. Mourning their losses cast a shadow over their lives. Some continued to receive letters from a father, husband, brother, or son even after being notified of his death. Some held out hope that it was all a mistake, that one day he would somehow walk up the street. Loved ones left behind scanned the newsreels and other photographs of returning troops, hoping to see that familiar face in the crowd. For eight-year-old Vicki Lacount in Minot, North Dakota, "there were shouts of joy, dancing in the streets, clanging of pots and pans" on VJ-Day, when victory was declared over Japan. "I was not rejoicing," she remembered. "The war never ended for me because my Dad never came home."[99]

CONCLUSION

This book is concerned with the ways that Winnipeggers experienced the Second World War at home, with particular focus on factors affecting unity and civilian morale. Investigating these issues reveals that popular perception of "the good war" as a crisis that brought Canadians together in a common struggle under the federal government's leadership does not fully recognize the nuanced experiences of smaller communities. At the same time that it points to variations in Winnipeg's response to war, it also permits some general observations about the character of war on the home front.

Similarities between the periods 1914–1918 and 1939–1945 in Canada were evident in the nature of domestic propaganda, military recruiting, the treatment of enemy aliens, and war loan appeals, to cite a few examples. Perhaps more significant were international similarities in urban living conditions and problems related to work, wages, consumption, and emotional well-being, as shown by Jay Winter and Jean-Louis Robert's study of European capital cities at war.[1] Canadians were not alone in feeling anxiety for the safety of loved ones in uniform, adapting to the necessity for state separation allowances, or coping with inflation, shortages of consumables, and increasing costs of living. In Canada as elsewhere, workers who did not secure high-paying jobs in munitions factories were, instead, impoverished. Rent controls led to tensions between owners and tenants. Working-class mothers could have shared similar stories about the difficulties of family separation and making ends meet.[2]

These examples allow us to generalize about home front living conditions in Europe and North America during the twentieth century's two great wars.

Comparisons within the more immediate geographical context reveal more specific commonalities between Winnipeg and American cities during the Second World War. Chicago was a much larger transportation hub but the difference was one of scale, not of kind. It contained half the population of Illinois and was "a city of ethnic and racial enclaves," making Chicago a "patchwork of attitudes." Chicago's Polish population had mixed feelings about the Soviet alliance, and the city received a large group of Japanese evacuees from the west coast.[3] Nashville, like Winnipeg, was not a war-boom town, but the small proportion of defence contracts it received produced full employment for a time. St. Louis, like Winnipeg, had seen urban decay progress in the absence of money for construction and repairs during the Depression, while wartime shortages of construction materials and skilled labour contributed to a housing crisis similar to that experienced across the continent. During the war, St. Louis too was home to blackout drills and victory gardens. Schools in Lowell, Massachusetts, were also focal points for salvage drives and Junior Red Cross work. American War Bond drives found a comparable level of support with patriotic appeals that were a virtual mirror-image of the type used in Canada. Residents of American cities shared the same concerns over juvenile delinquency and venereal disease as their Canadian cousins.[4]

Winnipeg's home front problems were not unique, but studying the response to these problems puts a much needed local spotlight on issues and events more often considered from the national perspective. The federal government's activities understandably loom large in Canadian histories of the conflict. Ottawa assumed broad new legal and regulatory powers, increased its control over the economy, mobilized material and human resources to unprecedented degrees, and became more involved in the field of social welfare. But the national war effort was also influenced by individual Canadians and non-state associations acting locally to give effect to federal policies. Public opinion had made Canada's belligerency a foregone conclusion; it scorned Mackenzie King's policies of "limited liability" and voluntary enlistment, and it demanded action against enemy aliens and Japanese Canadians. The federal government wielded considerable coercive power to prosecute the war, but individual citizens, newspaper editorials, and organizations like the Canadian Legion or the Imperial Order Daughters of the Empire had demanded that it do so. As the war effort required ever higher levels of mobilization, Ottawa depended on local institutions to take on much of the burden, whether that meant planning spectacles like If Day to sell bonds, fundraising for welfare agencies, or performing voluntary work to provide auxiliary services to the troops. Winnipeggers' engagement with such wartime issues within their non-state associations thus demonstrated the continued agency of civil society vis-à-vis state institutions. They also demonstrated a high level of morale—and a substantial measure of unity—through popular participation in various community efforts, and by sustaining that participation through six long years of war.

Jonathan Vance has observed that Canadian historians tend to be pre-occupied with the differences of religion, ethnicity, class, or gender that characterize the population. But he posits that we have underestimated the degree to which institutions, associations, and collective activity have "knit Canadians together, sometimes unconsciously, into larger communities at the regional and national levels."[5] He was not referring specifically to the war years, but he might have been. People in Winnipeg demonstrated their patriotism together at Victory Loan ceremonials. They demanded conscription together at affirmative-vote rallies. They marked significant events like the D-Day landings together at schools or churches. They pressed the government to adopt favourable policies. They leaned on each other for moral support in regimental associations and church groups. These activities demonstrated a basic unity that helped sustain morale.

Goodwin Watson stated in 1942 that high morale depended, in some circumstances, upon an awareness of evident danger, with morale stiffening as danger comes closer to home.[6] The British Ministry of Information found that morale improved once the Phoney War ended and the *Luftwaffe* began bombing London, perhaps because the waiting was finally over and there was now a sense of shared hardship for Britons to overcome.[7] Maintaining morale may have been more difficult in cities that were far removed from any real enemy threat. Winnipeg certainly lacked the atmosphere of immediacy that must have hung over a city like Halifax, a major naval base and the assembly point for transatlantic convoys. In some ways, the depth of Winnipeg's patriotic consensus was remarkable. The population was, and remains, highly polyethnic, with strong class divisions and a vibrant Leftist political tradition. Both factors meant a greater number of potential fault lines than in a city like Verdun which, according to Serge Durflinger, was united by its pre-dominantly working-class character despite a cleavage between English and French residents. But the large number of ethnic groups in Winnipeg and the

Left's relative lack of political power also meant that there was no dominant minority to seriously challenge the interpretation of the war expressed by the city's charter group.

Besides a preparedness to accept shared deprivations or work toward the achievement of common goals for the good of the community, high morale also depended upon the provision of "reasonable [economic] security, fair treatment, and honorable status in the group for all individuals."[8] In Winnipeg, these were threatened by the housing situation and attitudes toward ethnic minorities. But maintaining social cohesion also depended on the community's ability to keep its shared goal in view; although the experience of Winnipeg's Ukrainians or conscientious objectors betrayed an imperfect cohesion, centrifugal tendencies were mitigated by effective government propaganda that played on patriotism or fear of the enemy and constantly reminded people of the goals they were fighting for. Special efforts were also made to reach ethnic minorities, through the National War Finance Committee's foreign-language advertisements or newspaper articles featuring, for example, the Red Cross contributions of a Chinese women's group.

Was the war a unifying experience for the disparate communities of Winnipeg? For a lot of people, it was not completely so. Half of the Canadian population did not share British ancestry, but the public discourse about the war promoted the values of the Anglo-Canadian charter group that controlled the levers of political, social, and economic power.[9] Still, most of the ethnic minorities in Winnipeg came from homelands that were also at war with the Axis, conscientious objectors were themselves fragmented on the issue of participation, and the communists were eventually made into allies. Even the Japanese Canadians, despite the unfairness of their dispossession, proclaimed their loyalty and many backed up their words by enlisting at the first opportunity. The war fractured the wider community like it did individual families and it brought numerous examples of unjust treatment, supposedly for the good of the war effort; but at heart, the vast majority of Winnipeggers accepted the war's justice, its necessity, and they worked together to make sure that Canada ended up on the winning side.

ACKNOWLEDGMENTS

This book would never have seen the light of day without the contributions of many people who assisted in the process of researching and writing it. Without the encouragement of Stephen Harris at the Directorate of History and Heritage, National Defence Headquarters, and Carman Bickerton at Carleton University, I probably would not have started the research in the first place. The continued interest of my dissertation advisor at the University of Manitoba, Barry Ferguson, along with David Carr and Glenn Bergen at the University of Manitoba Press, kept this project alive when I was too busy trying to make a living to polish the manuscript. I am fortunate to have such understanding advisors.

Special thanks must go to the anonymous reviewers whose suggestions helped strengthen this book, and to Jeffrey Keshen at the University of Ottawa, Paul Thomas, Gerald Friesen, and Esyllt Jones at the University of Manitoba for their comments on the dissertation from which the book originated. Their advice has no doubt saved me some future embarrassment. Needless to say, any flaws that remain are my own.

My research was facilitated by generous financial support from a variety of sources, including the Social Sciences and Humanities Research Council of Canada; the Faculty of Graduate Studies, the Faculty of Arts, the Alumni Association, and the Departments of History and Economics at the University of Manitoba; Dr. James Burns; and Berdie and Irvin Cohen.

My gratitude goes to Barbara Kelcey, who brought Laurie Wilmot's papers to my attention. I also owe much appreciation for their assistance to the staffs at the Archives of Manitoba, the Manitoba Legislative Library, the University of Manitoba Archives and the Elizabeth Dafoe Library, the Fort Garry Horse Regimental Archives and Museum, Library and Archives Canada, the Bank of Canada Archives, the United Church Archives, the City of Winnipeg Archives, and the Winnipeg *Free Press* Archives for their assistance. There are others, no doubt, whom I have forgotten to mention. I beg their pardon.

Finally, I want to thank my family: Mom and Dad, Robin, Darrel, and Shelley, for all their support, free meals, and home repairs; and especially my wife Misty, who has had to endure the constant uncertainty of life with an academic.

APPENDIX I

Das Winnipeger Lügenblatt
Winnipeg *Tribune* If Day edition, 19 February 1942.

Source: Winnipeg Tribune collection, University of Manitoba Archives and Special
Collections, reproduced by permission.

This Is How Your Favorite Paper Might Look IF—

Das Winnipeger Lügenblatt

Published under the authority of Erich von Neurenberg.
Gauleiter for Hitler for the Provinz of
Manitoba by Das Lugenblatt Gesellschaft.

President: Erich von Neurenberg. Editor: Dr. Heinrich Seelheim.

Published at Himmlerstadt (Formerly Winnipeg)

A Great Day

THIS a Great Day is for Manitoba.

Everywhere the forces of the great and valiant Nazi army are bringing the New Order to the Provinz of the Greater Germany.

The great and valiant Nazi army is also bringing to the Provinz German Kultur and the blessings of German civilization.

Unfortunately, there are people who do not understand the blessings which we have brought them. THEY WILL BE MADE TO UNDERSTAND.

The Nazis, like Der Fuehrer, are patient, kind and tolerant, but THEIR PATIENCE IS RAPIDLY EXHAUSTED BECOMING.

There are still poor, blind dummkopfs who are protesting. They do not know it is too late to protest. They will learn [redacted] like it.

The former Lieutenant-Governor of Manitoba, the former Mayor of Winnipeg—these men have learned already what it is to obstruct. THEY HAVE ALSO LEARNED WHAT IT MEANS A CONCENTRATION CAMP.

It is intolerable that so many people in Manitoba fail yet to understand why the churches and synagogues are closed; why the labor halls and the union meetings are categorically forbidden; why the food has been comandeered for the glorious Nazi army.

LET THE PEOPLE OF MANITOBA UNDERSTAND ONCE AND FOR ALL. This is the New Order decreed by Hitler under his God-given all-under-one-ruling-people plan. There is no true freedom but the Higher Freedom.

There is freedom—for the Nazi rulers.
There is free speech—for the Nazi ruling class.
There is freedom of assembly—for the Nazi partei.
There is freedom of worship—for all, to worship Hitler.
Heil Hitler!

Our Platform Is Hitler's Platform

From Der Fuehrer's Own Words

HITLER ON HITLER

I, Hitler, am one of the hardest men Germany has had for decades, perhaps for centuries, equipped with the greatest authority [redacted] believe in it unconditionally.

CONQUEST

A clever conqueror will always, if possible, impose his demands on the conquered by instalments. For a people that makes a voluntary surrender saps its own character; and with such a people you can calculate, that none of these expressions in detail will supply quite enough reason for it to resort once more to arms. The more such extortions are suffered without resistance, the more unjustifiable it comes to seem to people to make any ultimate stand against pressures; which appear each to be new and isolated, though in fact there is perpetual recurrence of them.

CANADA

How can our people, its 360 per square mile, exist at all if they do not employ every ounce of brain power and physical strength to wrest from their soil what they need? This distinguishes us from the others. In Canada, for example, there are 2.6 persons per square mile; in other countries perhaps 16, 18, 20 or 26 persons.

PROPAGANDA

The task of propaganda lies not in a scientific training of the individual, but rather in directing the masses toward certain facts, events, necessities, etc., the purpose being to move their importance into the masses' field of vision.

The art now is exclusively to attack this so skilfully that a general conviction of the reality of a fact, of the necessity of an event, that something that is necessary is alsq right, etc., is created. Its effect has always to be directed more and more toward the feeling, and only to a certain extent to so-called reason.

All propaganda has to be popular and has to adapt its spiritual level to the perception of the least intelligent of those toward whom it intends to direct itself. Therefore its spiritual level has to be screwed lower, the greater the mass of people which one wants to attract.

GERMANIZATION

As the nationality, or rather the race, is not rooted in the language but in the blood, one could be permitted to speak of a Germanization only if one could succeed in changing, by such a procedure, the blood of the subjugated. But this is impossible. Except, perhaps, if by a blood blending a change were to take place which then, however, would mean the lowering of the standard of the higher race. Therefore the final result of such a procedure would be the destruction of just those qualities which once made the conquering people capable of victory.

ON THE JAPANESE

Immediately after the end of the war of 1914-18 the old American-Japanese mutual antagonism again began to manifest itself. Naturally, the great European world powers could not remain indifferent to this newly threatening danger of war. All the kinship connections, however, could not prevent a certain feeling of envious concern in England for the growth of the American Union in all fields of international economic and power politics. A new mistress of the world seemed to be growing out of the former colonial country, the child of the great mother.

The gigantic American State Colossus, with its enormous wealth of virgin soil, is more difficult to attack than the wedged-in German Reich. If some time here, too, the dice shall roll for a final decision, England would be doomed, were she to stand alone. Hence they anxiously reach out for the yellow (Japanese) fist and cling to an alliance which, viewed racially, is perhaps irresponsible, but which, nevertheless, politically offers the sole possibility of reinforcing the British world position in the face of the aspiring American continent.

Manitoba Looks At The Fuehrer

On The Record

What Hitler Did Not Say

By DOROTHY THOMPSON
—Exclusive to The Winnipeg Tribune

THE Hitler speech on Friday, Jan. 30, taken as a whole is significant—as important for what he did not say as for what he did.

[redacted]

Dorothy Thompson

It was under these conditions that Hitler spoke for one hour and fifty-three minutes to a mass meeting.

Of this time he devoted thirty-six minutes to his own version of the history of the last war. To prove what?

To prove

He then spoke for forty minutes on the history of the Nazi struggle for victory inside Germany.

To prove what? To prove

He then spoke for twenty-nine minut- on the history of the present war,

Finally, he devoted nine minutes to a report on the present situation of Germany in the war itself.

In this nine minutes he gave no figures on casualties.

From the speech, therefore, one can get some picture of the state of mind in Germany.

and such Nazi innovations as the Labor Front and Strength Through Joy are really popular.

An Explanation

THOUGH the glorious Nazi army Winnipeg and Manitoba with superb efficiency, today occupied it was manifestly impossible for our valourous forces to get everything for the glory of Hitler at once, operating.

For this reason, in taking over The Winnipeg Tribune it was necessary as much as possible the existing facilities to using, including with the members of the editorial redaction and printing room staffs.

For this reason, alzo, the new leader of this paper found it necessary some material to use for this page, already in type, as for example, the article by the accursed democratic journalist, Miss Dorothy Thompson. We have the precaution taken however of censoring the writing of this and other accursed freedom writers, as the reader above will see, so that nothing harmful to the new Nazi state may be dispersed.

When our next issue is coming out, the reader will note how completely the members of the staff of this paper have all cooperative become.

DR. HEINRICH SEELHEIM,
Editor, Das Winnipeger Lugenblatt.
Formerly Publisher of Das Deutsche Zeitung, Winnipeg.

Der Trumpeter

By HERMAN VON VERMIN

HEEL Hitler! It with great satisfaction is announced the name of this column has been changed. So has the writer. It is good. All citizens will think it is good, or else.

Before the present advance of Kultur to Winnipeg came, this column known was then as *Tribune Trumps*, a foolish name with card games associated and so no longer to the New Order agreeable.

Instead we have *Trumpeter* a name which associated with martial glory is. Heel Hitler.

Instead of the fat fellow who would the time waste daily of his unhappy readers with foolish sayings and nonsense yet, we have a new editor whose soul life purpose to spread German Humor is.

The former editor (whose name mentioned shall not be because it has offensive become to all admirers of the New Order) was a lazy usless misfit who unworthy was of the privilege of having his idle talkings in print put.

It is said the former so-called journalist, who this column was running, was ~~often~~ late.

So ~~comes a~~ joke, he is now the late journalist. (Joke).

Explained it should be that whenever the word (Joke) appears thus in this column from now on the reader is expected to laugh.

In this way there will be no need jokes to be looking for as they all plainly marked will be.

Such is German efficiency. Heel Hitler!

Orders are hereby given that *Der Trumpeter* must be read in each home, factory, hotel, or restaurant at six o'clock each evening, New German Time.

In homes the head of the family will read, yes, and at the appearance of each (Joke) he will raise his hand and the entire family will laught three times in unison.

Any person not laughing promptly, or loudly enough, must be reported at once by other members of the family, to the nearest agent of the Gestapo.

Children under two years of age are the only one permitted to be excused from sharing in this laughter.

It is also decreed that in future there will only be one kind of laughter, and that is official laughing. Any persons breaking into foolish giggles or loud guffaws at anything that is not an official joke, will be sternly dealt with.

They will be lodged in special prison camps where they will be required to laugh together for half-an-hour on the hour twelve times a day.

During their rest periods they will be engaged in digging holes in order to fill them up again.

Thus their sense of humor soon improved should be. (Joke) Ha! Ha! Ha!

In order to teach the new German laughter special practices will be held in each neighborhood for one hour each evening.

All citizens must attend. Those too sick to walk must be carried by relatives or friends.

At these gatherings an official German humorist will announce official jokes and count ein, zwei, drei, for the laughter which must follow.

Already the editor of this column has heard a Canadian joke to which he has consented to give official approval.

This joke must be told as follows:

Question: "Who was that lady last night I saw you out with?"

Answer: "That lady was my wife." (Joke) Ha! Ha! Ha!

Other official jokes will be released for public use from time to time.

As explained before no jokes, other than the official ones, will be permitted to written, told, or depicted in pictures or acting.

Thus the New Order brings proper regimentation to the department of humor, which must be used only sparingly as Der Fuehrer himself never laughs and regards this as senseless practice which is a waste of time.

Hereafter readers of this column will daily express gratitude over their good fortune in being able to read *Der Trumpeter*, instead of ridiculous and despised *Trumps*.

Let there be no mistake. Everybody must read this column from now on. It will be the only source of official jokes.

Storm Troopers and Gestapo agents will stop citizens on the street and ask them to repeat, and laugh at, the latest official joke.

If the citizen, has not read this column, or has forgotten the joke, or forgets to laugh after he has repeated it, he will be immediately arrested and his entire family penalized.

Thus Germany brings the blessings of true Nazi humor to the lucky Canadian people.

Everybody will agree with this statement, everybody will laugh loudly at all official jokes—or else.

Heel Hitler!

Illusions About Germany

By PROFESSOR FREDERICK H. CRAMER

[redacted] *and educated in Germany, is now a member of the history department of Mt. Holyoke College in Massachusetts. He has contributed articles to many North American periodicals.]*

And this task must be approached free from the illusion that there exists today, beneath the icy layer of Nazidom a democratic Germany, just waiting for liberation. There is no such democratic Germany. There never was. It will have to be created by the western world.

Bible Message

THE WINNIPEG TRIBUNE

It Must Not Happen Here—BUY VICTORY BONDS

This Is How Your Favorite Column Might Look IF—

BEHIND THE HEADLINES

Comment .... Interpretation
.... People .... Letters ....

THE WINNIPEG HAUS

Mein Kampf Vs. The Bible

New Nazi Religion Deifies Hitler And Warns Against Altering His Book One Jot Or Tittle

Drastic Changes In Meals Ordered By Der Fuehrer

By KATHARINE MIDDLETON

Our Guardian Angel

—Cartoon by Arthur Sayb

Hitler and His Nazi Gang Invaded Winnipeg

You couldn't fight them with old papers, old furniture and unwanted articles stored in your attic or garage.

Yet these things can be turned into effective weapons of war—IF you act now!

Practically every home has unwanted furniture, musical instruments, books, sports equipment, garden tools, bicycles and clothing which is no longer in use. All can be turned into cash and the cash into Victory Bonds to defeat the enemy before he reaches our shores.

Let The Tribune Classified Section find buyers for your unwanted useful articles, or a tenant for that empty room in your home. Tribune Want Ads can convert your frozen assets into Victory Bonds.

Let the Patriotic Salvage Corps turn your useless junk into munitions.

The time to act is NOW!

Tomorrow may be too late!

Phone 24 331 to insert a low cost Tribune Want Ad.

FROM Der Voelkischer Beobachter TODAY

Time Table For Occupation

U.S. Consul-General Discloses How Nazis Would Take Over City

A. W. KLIEFORTH
American Consul General

Nazis Revise Belgian Radio Regulations

YOUR OPINIONS

From now on you have no opinions of your own.
Der Fuehrer's are your opinions.

THE WINNIPEG TRIBUNE

It Must Not Happen Here—BUY VICTORY BONDS

What Nazi Occupation Has Meant To Lands Overseas

CZECHOSLOVAKIA

Nazis Seek To Erase Culture, Root And All

B. SLAVICEK
Czechoslovakian Vice-Consul, Winnipeg

By B. SLAVICEK

Before The Nazi Firing Squad

Four Poles, including a priest, face death in a suburb of Warsaw after the Nazi occupation.

POLAND

Nazis Martyr Nation, Seeking To Destroy It

By A. F. CHUDZICKI
Editor of the Polish Weekly, Czas, Winnipeg

A. F. CHUDZICKI

NORWAY

Faith In The Goodness Of Men Almost Destroyed

MAGNUS TALGOY

By MAGNUS TALGOY
Editor of The Norwegian Weekly News

These Were Russian Civilians

These pictures show Nazi soldiers hanging Russian civilians in the Smolensk region last September. Top: Executioners test ropes. Centre: Victims take their places. Bottom: Execution is completed.

GREECE

Now It's The Hungriest Place In All The Earth

By JOHN T. PAULOS
Secretary, Greek War Relief Fund

JOHN PAULOS

YUGOSLAVIA

Serbs And Croats Still Battle To Regain Unity

By PETER STANKOVIC
Editor, Croatian Voice

PETER STANKOVIC

News From Norway

BELGIUM

Looting On Huge Scale Follows Ruinous Hordes

By CAMILLE DeBUCK
Secretary, Belgian Club, St. Boniface.

CAMILLE DeBUCK

From Ghent

Nazis Plan Serfdom For Non-Nazis

HOLLAND

100,000 Die In Bombing In Hour In Rotterdam

By L. F. J. RIEMSDYK
Consul-General for The Netherlands

L. J. F. VAN RIEMSDYK

Bridges Blown Up

Go To England

IF Day

It Must Not Happen Here—BUY VICTORY BONDS

APPENDIX 2

Report of Public Relations Committee, Manitoba Division, Re: If Day.
Source: Archives of Manitoba, GR43, G76, file 112 (1942).

REPORT OF PUBLIC RELATIONS COMMITTEE
MANITOBA DIVISION

The Second Victory Loan objective is to raise in excess of $600,000,000.

There are four types of investors from whom this money must be obtained:

1. The financial institutions and industrial corporations.

2. Executives and high salaried employees.

3. Owners of small business and employees receiving a fair average salary from $3,000 to $4,000.

4. The wage earning class receiving less than $2,000.

In the subscriptions obtained in Victory Loan 1941, our large financial institutions and industrial corporations demonstrated by the size of their subscriptions that they are conscious of the absolute necessity of making these loans a success. But most of the people in the other three groups have not yet made the sacrifice to buy bonds to the extent evidenced by the people of England.

To make this loan a success we must secure a larger percentage of the money from the individual. We must reach and impress every man and every woman with the seriousness of the present and the necessity of each playing his or her part.

To properly reach the individual, the work of the Public Relations Committee must stress to the average man and woman what our present way of life means to him and to her and to make the average man and woman realize that our way of life can only be retained through personal sacrifice.

In previous loans the thrifty people bought bonds because they had savings. To a limited extent, people have purchased War Saving Certificates through salary deduction. Now people must be sold the idea of reducing their personal standard of living in order to buy bonds and at the same time to release their available savings bank deposits, for purchase of bonds.

The most difficult task before us seems to be in the field of promoting commitment of current earnings of the large mass of salaried employees and wage earners, to buy Victory Bonds on deferred payments.

This is a grim business and the public relations committee face up to it as such. No ordinary publicity measures would seem to meet this need.

We therefore propose to develop the theme of "Freedom" throughout the period of the campaign. At the moment our large scale plan is in formation, and it is only possible here to say that successive events will be devoted to each element

(2)

of freedom as we know it, in turn. Schools, churches, business, government, labor, sport, all the channels of democratic activity will be appropriately promoted on a scheduled day.

As an instance, we plan a gigantic sports convocation in honor of Manitoba champions, which will dramatize "Freedom to Play". Presentation of the Lou Marsh trophy to Theo. Dubois and Grey Cup to the Blue Bombers, prizes to skating competition winners and Bonspiel winners, a half hour junior all-star game coached by Dutton and Patrick - presentation of past Manitoba champions, etc by Foster Hewitt and various ancillary events promoted in Provincial centres and covered by radio and newspapers that day - gives a picture of one such unit.

The climax of the campaign will be reached on "V" day, on which honor will be paid to the Winnipeg Grenadiers at a ceremony in the Legislative chambers, or auditorium, with representations of the thirty allied nations taking part.

But in order that all these proposals have impact - and not mere lip service - we propose a preparatory event which we believe is without precedent on this continent.

It is planned to place Manitoba in the situation of occupied territory completely (for one day) and in reducing degree until the loan is fully subscribed.

This program is designed to color the whole campaign and to provide the "drive" necessary to propel all the subsequent events emphasizing our freedom and which will provide a cumulative effect as the campaign proceeds.

This plan provides a unique opportunity for a direct tie-in with daily progress during the entire period of the campaign. This phase will receive detailed attention later in the report.

It is emphasized that this interpretation is not intended as a spectacle, or a simple series of street incidents - but rather, an orderly demonstration (in normal channels) to provoke a deeper understanding of what would happen if Canada falters in her war effort.

The foreign occupation as conceived is revealed by the high-lights outlined in the ensuing section.

(3)

(a) A simulated "BLITZ" at 7-8 A.M. in Winnipeg, Brandon, Dauphin, and all possible centers consisting of:-

    1. Formation low flying with the maximum number of planes obtainable.

    2. Fire trucks and police cars and motorcycles with sirens throughout all residential areas.

    3. Bren gun carriers, military trucks and patrols operating throughout city - firing blanks, artillery rounds fired.

    4. Simulated anti-aircraft fire and bomb-explosions.

(b) Early morning RADIO REPORTS describing simulated attack all over Province and announcing final complete occupation by enemy forces. (Every Broadcast to contain frequent reference to the fact that this is simulation only).

(c) NEWSPAPERS:

    1. The co-operation of The Free Press and the Tribune be enlisted to publish their front pages in German and to present official arbitrary commands and proclamations issued by the head-quarters of the Army of Occupation.

    2. Department store advertising appear in foreign language quoting prices in reich marks, listing articles no longer available and emphasizing articles made in Japan and Germany. Smaller advertisements will carry the fiat by permission of occupation authority, etc.

    3. The Newspapers report in the same edition all the special events listed under other categories here and will suggest others of their initiative. All photographs and material of this sort should carry identifying slugs to designate the material as a facsimile of what would happen in Manitoba if the Victory Loan does not go over.

    4. Country papers and foreign language papers to be circularized and a special Committee be formed to assist editors in working out a program in consonance with the plan. Special meetings to be held to meet as many editors as possible. Special emphasis on expropriation of land, wheat, livestock, vegetables, etc.

(d) HEADQUARTERS OF ARMY OF OCCUPATION to be established by exterior treatment of Bank of Montreal at Portage and Main.

(e) SCHOOLS:

    1. Grade schools from Grade 4 up would teach the current rendering of a German or Japanese character. Special consideration of a suitable alternative program for schools in foreign extraction neighborhoods to be provided.

    2. High schools would receive token instruction in "geopalitiks" and be informed that only the top-ranking six in each class would be permitted to continue study. Remainder would be quizzed as to their experience in various heavy occupations.

    3. University program to be worked out in consultation with faculty.

CHURCHES:

    Church doors to be posted with proclamations closing them. Sermons and pastoral letter to be read the following Sunday.

(4)

(g) STORES:That a plan be developed with the co-operation of the large
   1. departmental stores and chains and packers and large whole-
      salers to enclose a notice with all parcels stating what
      rationing might result from occupation.

   2. Stores on Portage and Main and on arterial streets to display
      foreign language window cards and prices and to carry this
      throughout store as far as practical.

(h) BUSINESS:
   A direct mail piece be designed in the form of a letter of
   instructions from Army Headquarters which opens out to
   reveal Victory Loan message. This piece to be distributed
   through regular mailing lists of large institutions with
   appropriate copy changes for each class of business.

   1. Line elevator companies and packers.

   2. Banks and Insurance Houses.

   3. Customs Brokers and Importers, etc.

(i) RADIO: Two half hour programs to be arranged describing the installation
of foreign envoy on the floor of the legislative chamber and for gauleiter in the
City Hall. C. K. X. Brandon could duplicate, and C.F.A.R. at Flin Flon hourly
reports could be directed to various country points. All possible progress to be
preceded by permissive announcement.

(j) TRANSPORTATION: Street cards and buses to carry announcements that
soldiers of the Army of Occupation must not be permitted to stand and passengers
must immediately give them their seats. Transfers will be reprinted in German.

(k) HOMES: Complete coverage of Manitoba homes with official inventory
sheet, demanding list of garments and household effects that may be of use to
Army of Occupation or may be expropriated for use elsewhere.

(l) PROGRESS OF CAMPAIGN: and daily subscriptions to loan to be symbolized
in terms of the number of city blocks won back each day from the Army of
Occupation – in rural areas, the number of square miles. Section allotments, in
other words, would be translated into terms of blocks and square miles. Radio
and news releases would follow this progress with color stories and should be
able to provide a rising pressure as the campaign draws to a close. (Alternative
suggestions are being studied).

(m) MONEY: Facsimiles of reichsmark to be printed in newsprint. Reverse
side to carry message "that this is what we will have to use if we fail" etc.
Sufficient quantity to cover every pay envelope (for the week) and every
financial transaction in the Province for the day.

SUPPLEMENTARY ITEMS

These units comprise a list of smaller operations which can be controlled at will without latering the character of the main dramatization. They exist primarily as source material for "color" news stories and to promote national coverage in news, motion pictures, and magazines. It is believed that coverage by the Canadian Press, Minneapolis and St.Paul papers, Toronto Star, Montreal Herald and Weekly Star, The New World, Life, will be a reasonable possibility and that newsreels will find it of interest. News items can be released to N.B.C. Mutual and C.B.S.

On all these items, however, the tests must be applied of –

(a) Practicality within time limit.

(b) Coverage.

(c) Expense.

(d) Undesirable reactions either on the humorous or realistic side.

1. PICTORIAL SERVICE:

(a) The camera club will be given photos of refugees now available from News Services and asked to duplicate them as nearly as possible with Manitoba persons and locale. They will then be offered to the newspapers to be run in pairs with captions pointing out the moral.

(b) Special attention will be given to the creation of our own picture service in other directions.

2. POST OFFICE: To use cancellation stamps on local mail as apparently authorized by Army of Occupation Headquarters. "Censor"Stamp might be possible.

3. TELEGRAMS: Might also receive similar treatment.

4. TELEPHONES: We are interested in the suggestion outlined by Mr. Baker for a mass 'phone canvass of rural telephone subscribers. It would appear that an opportunity exists to "color" this canvass in consonance with the plan.

5. "IF" DAY: It is possible that some designation of the initial day of occupation would be needed to establish its character, point its meaning and to prevent too literal acceptance of it as fact.

6. MOVIES: A short subject might be made of a general of the enemy headquarters proclaiming what patrons will be allowed to see — and to laugh at.

7. MASS MEETINGS OF SERVICE CLUBS: To be arranged from 6 to 8 at the auditorium on Monday evening, Feb. 16th, to hear a speaker (Douglas Miller, author of "You Can't Do Business with Hitler" – or Alfred Keliforth, American Consul) on review of

conditions known by them to exist in occupied countries. Box lunch of black bread, etc., will be served.

8. RESTAURANTS:

    (a) Might serve sample ration menu.

    (b) An "incident" might be arranged between arbitrary enemy officers demanding service and displaced civilians.

9. EXECUTIVES: News shots could be arranged of selected executives carrying on business with gestapo agent overseeing contracts and interviews.

10. SWITCHBOARDS: In large organizations might refer in some way to reduced service conditions imposed by Army of Occupation. Conversations might be closed by the salutation "Heil Hitler".

11. BANKS: etc. Signs placed over tellers wickets in all financial organizations announcing the freezing of credit and deposits, etc.

12. LABOR: Trade Union Leaders might be subject to arrest and confinment in concentration camps - either in token operation or in news columns only.

13. DAIRIES AND BAKERIES: Milk bottle tops and bread inserts would be supplied in (a) German or (b) in English proclamation of ration imposed.

14. SCHOOLS: Photos could be arranged of selected classes waving German or Jap Flag.

15. MOBILE UNIT: Would patrol streets announcing arbitrary orders of Army of Occupation.

16. TRAFFIC: Foreign language signs and barricades erected at various points of arterial traffic.

17. RADIO: Could simulate announcement of curfew.

18. STORES: On Portage and Main could change their signs to a billingual form for temporary period.

19. NEWSPAPERS: Can warn of or publish lists of mass executions.

20. TAXIS: Can carry window banners "Official car - Army of Occupation.

21. JEWISH COMMUNITIES: To arrange interpretation with special reference to their problem in occupied territory.

22. MUSIC: Designated as "degnerate" will be barred from public performation.

23. POLICE: May be supplied with arm bands designating them as Gestapo.

24. TELEPHONE POLES: Might be posted as on election days with proclamation.

25. NEWSPRINT: 10 sheet calendar prepared - each sheet covering one day of campaign - and presenting positive and negative side of freedom in categories.

(3)

26. SCHOOL RADIO PROGRAM available at 3:30 to 4:00 p.m. Thursday for special
school program re occupation.

27. A TYPICAL TOTALITARIAN ELECTION BALLOT could be printed and distributed.

28. RATIONING NOTICE delivered to coal dealers customers.

29. TIMING OF MAIL arranged through Post Office.

30. "GALLUP POLL" tie up can be arranged.

31. R. D. COLQUETTE write special story for Country Guide.

32. SPECIAL STORIES in Free Press - Prairie Farmer.

33. RATIONING NOTICE for gasoline station customers.

34. R.C.M.P. STOP ALL CARS ENTERING or leaving City and ask for identification
cards.

Further suggestions arise with little provocation, but sufficient
material has received mention to indicate the scope of this plan.

ABBREVIATIONS

AM	Archives of Manitoba
AP	Assigned Pay
BCA	Bank of Canada Archives
BCATP	British Commonwealth Air Training Plan
BCSC	British Columbia Security Commission
CEC	Civic Election Committee
CLWS	Canadian Legion War Services
CO	Conscientious Objector
CPF	Canadian Patriotic Fund
CSA	Council of Social Agencies
CVB	Central Volunteer Bureau
CWC	Canadian Welfare Council
CWM	Canadian War Museum
DA	Dependents' Allowance
DHH	Department of National Defence, Directorate of History and Heritage
DND	Department of National Defence
DNWS	Department of National War Services
DOCR	Defence of Canada Regulations
FGH	Fort Garry Horse Regimental Archives and Museum
GWCBWS	Greater Winnipeg Coordinating Board for War Services
HMCS	His Majesty's Canadian Ship
IODE	Imperial Order Daughters of the Empire
LAC	Library and Archives Canada
MD	Military District
MJCCA	Manitoba Japanese Canadian Citizens' Association
MLL	Manitoba Legislative Library
NRMA	National Resources Mobilization Act
NSS	National Selective Service
NWFC	National War Finance Committee

OUN	Organization of Ukrainian Nationalists
PTSD	Post-Traumatic Stress Disorder
RAF	Royal Air Force
RCAF	Royal Canadian Air Force
RCMP	Royal Canadian Mounted Police
RCN	Royal Canadian Navy
RCNVR	Royal Canadian Naval Volunteer Reserve
SA	Separation Allowance
SPC	Social Planning Council of Winnipeg
UCA	United Church Archives
UCC	Ukrainian Canadian Committee
ULFTA	Ukrainian Labour Farmer Temple Association
UMA	University of Manitoba Archives
UNF	Ukrainian National Federation
USRL	Ukrainian Self-Reliance League
USSR	Union of Soviet Socialist Republics
WHL	Wartime Housing Limited
WIB	Wartime Information Board
WPTB	Wartime Prices and Trade Board
YMCA	Young Men's Christian Association
YWCA	Young Women's Christian Association

NOTES

Introduction

1 Winnipeg *Free Press*, 1 Sept. 1939.

2 Winnipeg *Tribune*, 5 Oct. 1940.

3 Robert A. Wardhaugh, "'Gateway to Empire': Imperial Sentiment in Winnipeg, 1867–1917," in Colin M. Coates, ed., *Imperial Canada* (Edinburgh: University of Edinburgh Press, 1997), 206–19.

4 Canada, Dominion Bureau of Statistics, Eighth Census of Canada, 1941 vol. II: Population by Local Subdivisions (Ottawa: King's Printer, 1944); Alan Artibise, *Winnipeg: An Illustrated History* (Toronto: Lorimer, 1977), Appendix.

5 W.L. Morton, *Manitoba: A History*, 2nd ed. (Toronto: University of Toronto Press, 1967), 167, 196; Alan F.J. Artibise, *Winnipeg: A Social History of Urban Growth, 1874–1914* (Montreal: McGill- Queen's University Press, 1975), 133, 158; Artibise, *Winnipeg: An Illustrated History*, Appendix.

6 G.W.L. Nicholson, *Canadian Expeditionary Force, 1914–1919: Official History of the Canadian Army in the First World War* (Ottawa: Queen's Printer, 1964), Appendix D; A.F. Duguid, *Official History of the Canadian Forces in the Great War, 1914-1919*, vol. 1 (Ottawa: KP, 1938), 50-51; C.A. Sharpe, "Enlistment in the Canadian Expeditionary Force 1914–1918: A Regional Analysis," *Journal of Canadian Studies* 18, 4 (Winter 1983–84), 15–29.

7 J.E. Rea, "The Politics of Class: Winnipeg City Council, 1919–1945," in Carl Berger and Ramsay Cook, eds., *The West and the Nation: Essays in Honour of W.L. Morton* (Toronto: McClelland, 1976), 232, 238.

8 Artibise, *Winnipeg: An Illustrated History*, 110–11.

9 C.B. Davidson, *Unemployment in Manitoba* (Winnipeg: Manitoba Economic Survey Board, 1938), 4, 31–32; T. Peterson, "Ethnic and Class Politics in Manitoba," in Martin Robin, ed., *Canadian Provincial Politics: The Party Systems of the Ten Provinces* (Scarborough: Prentice, 1972), 90; Ruben Bellan, *Winnipeg First Century: An Economic History* (Winnipeg: Queenston House, 1978), 219; A.B. McKillop, "The communist as Conscience: Jacob Penner and Winnipeg Civic

Politics, 1934–1935," in A.R. McCormack and Ian Macpherson, eds., *Cities in the West: Papers of the Western Canada Urban History Conference, University of Winnipeg, October 1974* (Ottawa: National Museums of Canada, 1975), 195–197; Mark E. Vajcner, "Stuart Garson and the Manitoba Progressive Coalition," *Manitoba History* 26 (Autumn 1993), 30.

10   Peterson, "Ethnic and Class Politics in Manitoba," 89, 114–15; Rea, "The Politics of Class," 243.

11   University of Manitoba Archives (hereafter UMA), MSS 73, box 1, file 4, interview with Mitch Sago and Michael Korol, May 1969, 18–19.

12   Jonathan F. Wagner, *Brothers Beyond the Sea: National Socialism in Canada* (Waterloo, ON: Wilfrid Laurier University Press, 1981), 62; Martin Robin, *Shades of Right: Nativist and Fascist Politics in Canada, 1920–1940* (Toronto: University of Toronto Press, 1992), 192; McKillop, "The communist as Conscience," 188, 192.

13   John E. Craig, "Public Opinion in Manitoba and the Approach to War, 1931–1939" (MA thesis, University of Toronto, 1952), xii, 42, 45, 121–23, 142.

14   Terry Copp, "Ontario 1939: The Decision for War," in Norman Hillmer et al., eds., *A Country of Limitations: Canada and the World in 1939* (Ottawa: Canadian Committee for the History of the Second World War, 1996), 111, 115n31.

15   Craig, "Public Opinion in Manitoba," 209; Copp, "Ontario 1939," 116.

16   Craig, "Public Opinion in Manitoba,"143–47.

17   J.L. Granatstein, *Canada's War: The Politics of the Mackenzie King Government, 1939–1945* (Toronto: University of Toronto Press, 1975 [rpt. 1990]), 19.

18   Copp, "Ontario 1939," 109.

19   Vancouver *Province*, 1 Sept. 1939, qtd. in Patricia E. Roy, "British Columbia in 1939," in Hillmer et al., *A Country of Limitations*, 85; Craig, "Public Opinion in Manitoba," 214.

20   Qtd. in Craig, "Public Opinion in Manitoba,"218.

21   Winnipeg *Free Press*, 28 Aug. 1939, 22, 23, 26.

22   Winnipeg *Free Press*, 8 and 11 Sept. 1939.

23   It has been more than thirty years since Alan Artibise published the only works of broad scope covering the city's post-Confederation history. Neither *Winnipeg: A Social History of Urban Growth, 1874–1914* (1975) nor *Winnipeg: An Illustrated History* (1977), focuses on the Second World War period. The same is true of the only general scholarly history of the province, W.L. Morton's *Manitoba: A History*, first published in 1957.

24   See, among others, C.P. Stacey, *Arms, Men and Governments* (Ottawa: Queen's Printer, 1970); J.L. Granatstein, *Canada's War: The Politics of the Mackenzie King Government, 1939–1945* (Toronto: University of Toronto Press, 1975); and W.A.B. Douglas and Brereton Greenhous, *Out of the Shadows: Canada in the Second World War* (Toronto: Oxford University Press, 1977).

25   Jeffrey A. Keshen, *Saints, Sinners, and Soldiers: Canada's Second World War* (Vancouver: UBC Press, 2004), 40.

26   Ian Miller, *Our Glory and Our Grief: Torontonians and the Great War* (Toronto: University of Toronto Press, 2001); Serge Marc Durflinger, *Fighting from Home: The Second World War in Verdun, Quebec* (Vancouver: UBC Press, 2006).

27   See, for example, Winnipeg *Free Press*, 16 May 1942.

28 Politics in Manitoba was a stagnant field during the war years, with coalition
    governments espousing a doctrine of non-partisanship that stifled debate over
    policy. Civic politics in Winnipeg were more lively, thanks to the radical Left's
    representation on City Council, but most areas of relevant wartime activity came
    under federal jurisdiction. Industrial growth in Winnipeg, as a result of the war,
    was not remarkable. Winnipeg factories did receive a variety of contracts for
    military production; but by 1942, they had amounted to only about 2 percent of
    Canadian and British government orders placed in Canada for war materiel. The
    city benefited from only two major war industries, the Defence Industries Limited
    cordite plant—which, in fact, was located east of the city in Dugald, Manitoba—
    and the aircraft assembly and refit plants clustered near Stevenson Field to service
    the British Commonwealth Air Training Plan. Structural changes to the economy
    were, nonetheless, temporary, and post-war industrial expansion was related to
    the general growth of the consumer economy and agricultural mechanization,
    rather than any ongoing need for industries created during the war. In 1943 the
    cordite plant reduced production of explosives and began to lay off workers. By
    the winter of 1945 the aircraft industry had also scaled back operations and cut
    jobs as the BCATP wound down. As for the military, while there was exponential
    expansion of the army, navy, and air force presence in Winnipeg and southern
    Manitoba, the city's contribution to the three services deserves a full study of its
    own. Winnipeg *Tribune*, 17 March 1942; AM, P641, Social Planning Council of
    Winnipeg, File 22, Minutes, 20 April 1942; Bellan, *Winnipeg First Century*, 223–24,
    258; Karen Wiederkehr, "Occupational Segregation and Macdonald Brothers
    Aircraft Ltd., 1940–1947" (MA thesis, University of Manitoba, 1994), 50; City of
    Winnipeg Archives, Special Committees, folder A-50, Coulter to Howe, 14 Jan.
    1943 and reply, 15 Jan. 1943.

29 John Keane, *Civil Society: Old Images, New Visions* (Stanford, CA: Stanford
    University Press, 1998), 6. Emphasis in original.

30 John Ehrenberg, *Civil Society: The Critical History of an Idea* (New York: New York
    University Press, 1999), 164.

31 Since French-English relations constituted the main threat to national unity
    during the war, one might expect a substantial consideration of the perspective
    of Greater Winnipeg's French-speaking minority, particularly the residents of
    St. Boniface. The local French community receives no such attention, however,
    mainly because with the exception of the conscription issue, which is examined in
    Chapter 2, the French appear to have experienced the war in much the same ways
    as the mainstream of Winnipeg residents. In other words, this community made
    no waves sufficiently turbulent to warrant detailed examination as a group apart
    from other Winnipeggers.

32 Ian McLaine, *Ministry of Morale: Home Front Morale and the Ministry of
    Information in World War II* (London: Allen and Unwin, 1979), 8–9.

33 Kurt Lewin, "Time Perspective and Morale," in Goodwin Watson, ed., *Civilian
    Morale: Second Yearbook of the Society for the Psychological Study of Social Issues*
    (Boston: Houghton, 1942), 70; Goodwin Watson, "Five Factors in Morale," in
    Watson, ed., *Civilian Morale*, 30–47.

Chapter 1: THE LIMITED CONSENSUS

1   Yet both Canadian and American writers have also recognized that the war had its darker side. For recollections of both, see Studs Terkel, *The Good War": An Oral History of World War Two* (New York: Ballantine, 1984); and Barry Broadfoot, *Six War Years, 1939–1946: Memories of Canadians at Home and Abroad* (Toronto: Doubleday, 1974).

2   John E. Craig, "Public Opinion in Manitoba and the Approach to War, 1931–1939" (MA, University of Toronto, 1952).

3   Marilyn F. Nefsky, "The Shadow of Evil: Nazism and Canadian Protestantism," in Alan Davies, ed., *Antisemitism in Canada: History and Interpretation* (Waterloo, ON: Wilfrid Laurier University Press, 1992), 202–204.

4   J.L. Granatstein, *Canada's War: The Politics of the Mackenzie King Government, 1939-1945* (Toronto: University of Toronto Press, 1975; reprint, 1990), 420.

5   Franklin D. Roosevelt, address to Congress, 6 January 1941, full text at www.americanrhetoric.com/speeches/fdrthefourfreedoms.htm (accessed 8 Aug. 2007).

6   Winnipeg *Free Press*, 1, 2, 4, 7, and 8 Sept. 1939.

7   Archives of Manitoba (hereafter AM), GR 43, Premier's Correspondence, G60, file 112 (1940), War – Enlistment and Service; Winnipeg *Free Press*, 4, 6, and 20 Sept. 1939.

8   Durflinger, *Fighting from Home*, 23.

9   Library and Archives Canada (hereafter LAC), RG 24, reel C–5290, file 8917-9, Directorate of Special Services, "What the Canadian Serviceman Thinks," 15 Sept. 1943; Jeffrey A. Keshen, *Saints, Sinners, and Soldiers: Canada's Second World War* (Vancouver: UBC Press, 2004), 22–23, 181.

10   Author's correspondence from Joe Hartshorn, Sarasota, Florida, 18 May 2005.

11   E.L.M. Burns, *Manpower in the Canadian Army, 1939–1945* (Toronto: Clarke, Irwin, 1956), 119. Ernie Kull, interview with author, Winnipeg, 29 July 2004.

12   Canada, *National Registration Regulations, 1940* (Ottawa: King's Printer, 1940); Michael D. Stevenson, *Canada's Greatest Wartime Muddle: National Selective Service and the Mobilization of Human Resources during World War II* (Montreal: McGill-Queen'sUniversity Press, 2001), 19–20.

13   Winnipeg *Free Press*, 22 Sept. 1939.

14   Winnipeg *Tribune*, 3 July 1941.

15   Winnipeg *Tribune*, 27 Oct. and 17 Dec. 1941.

16   Ottawa *Citizen*, 26 May 1942, clipping in AM, Chisick Collection, P2630, 1942 scrapbook.

17   Winnipeg *Tribune*, 16 Jan. 1942, clipping in AM, P2631, Chisick Collection, general scrapbook Jan. to July 1942.

18   Stevenson, *Canada's Greatest Wartime Muddle*, 52–53, 60.

19   David Fransen, "'As Far as Conscience Will Allow': Mennonites in Canada During the Second World War," in Norman Hillmer et al., eds., *On Guard for Thee: War, Ethnicity and the Canadian State, 1939–1945* (Ottawa: Canadian Committee for the History of the Second World War, 1988), 132–140; Thomas P. Socknat, *Witness against War: Pacifism in Canada, 1900–1945* (Toronto: University of Toronto Press, 1987), 238–251.

20   Fransen, 144–146; Socknat, 250–252; Winnipeg *Free Press*, 11 and 23 Oct. 1941; John Aron Toews, "Alternative Service in Canada during World War II" (MA, University of Manitoba, 1957), 68–71.

21   Fransen, "'As Far as Conscience Will Allow,'" 141–143.

22   AM, Howard W. Winkler papers, MG 14, B 44, box 4, file 1, J.E. Adamson, address to Blackstone Club of Winnipeg, 28 Jan. 1941, 7–8.

23   AM, Howard W. Winkler papers, MG 14, B 44, box 8, file 2, Toews to Winkler, 10 Dec.1941.

24   AM, Howard W. Winkler papers, MG 14, B 44, box 8, file 2, Winkler to Sobering, 26 May 1942.

25   AM, GR 43, Premier's Correspondence, G102, file 21, Conscientious Objectors, Adamson to Garson, 11 Nov. and 4 Dec. 1944.

26   AM, GR 43, Premier's Correspondence, G102, file 21, Conscientious Objectors, Westman to MacNamara, 31 Jan. 1945; MacNamara to Garson, 1 Feb. and 31 March 1945.

27   James W. St.G. Walker, "Race and Recruitment in World War I: Enlistment of Visible Minorities in the Canadian Expeditionary Force," *Canadian Historical Review* 70, 1 (1989), 1.

28   LAC, RG 27, vol.1486, file 2–162–9, Robertson to Deputy Minister National War Services, 15 Dec. 1941.

29   LAC, RG 27, vol.1486, file 2–162–9, "Minutes of a meeting to consider the position of men of oriental racial origin, held on December 18, 1941," 13 Jan. 1942.

30   LAC, RG 27, vol.1486, file 2–162–9, McPherson to Tache, 17 Nov. 1942 and reply, 30 Nov. 1942; DND memo, "Aliens and Canadians of Foreign Origin," 12 July 1943.

31   LAC, RG 27, vol.1486, file 2–162–9, Bjarnason to McLaren, 29 Nov. 1943; McPherson to Henry, 6 Dec. 1943; news clippings, Montreal *Star*, 29 Dec. 1943, and Montreal *Gazette*, 30 Dec. 1943; MacNamara to McPherson, 12 Jan. 1944.

32   Stevenson, *Canada's Greatest Wartime Muddle*, 44.

33   Emily Arrowsmith, "Fair Enough? How Notions of Race, Gender, and Soldiers' Rights Affected Dependents' Allowance Policies Towards Canadian Aboriginal Families during World War II" (PhD thesis, Carleton University, 2006), 128–129.

34   Stevenson, *Canada's Greatest Wartime Muddle*, 38–49.

35   Daniel G. Dancocks, *The D-Day Dodgers: The Canadians in Italy, 1943–1945* (Toronto: McClelland and Stewart, 1991), 225.

36   Arrowsmith, "Fair Enough?" 126.

37   Walker, "Race and Recruitment," 1; Arrowsmith, "Fair Enough?" 114.

38   W.R. Young, "Mobilizing English Canada: The Bureau of Public Information, the Wartime Information Board and a View of the Nation During the Second World War," in Sidney Aster, ed., *The Second World War as a National Experience* (Ottawa: Canadian Committee for the History of the Second World War, 1981), 198–200; Ninette Kelley and Michael Trebilcock, *The Making of the Mosaic: A History of Canadian Immigration Policy* (Toronto: University of Toronto Press, 1998), 273.

39   Norman Hillmer, "The Second World War as an (Un) National Experience," in Hillmer, et al., *On Guard for Thee*, xiv-xv.

40   "Low Morale," Wartime Information Board, Information Briefs 6, 19 April 1943, qtd. in W.R. Young, "Chauvinism and Canadianism: Canadian Ethnic Groups and the Failure of Wartime Information," in Hillmer et al., *On Guard for Thee*, 43.

41   Myrna Kostash, *All of Baba's Children* (Edmonton: Hurtig, 1977), 376–377.

42   Keshen, *Saints, Sinners, and Soldiers*, 14–18.

43   Paul Rutherford, *The Making of the Canadian Media* (Toronto: McGraw-Hill, 1978), 38, 64.

44   Timothy Balzer, *The Information Front: The Canadian Army and News Management during the Second World War* (Vancouver: UBC Press, 2011), 172.

45   Keshen, *Saints, Sinners, and Soldiers*, 17; Balzer, 79.

46   Hamilton *Spectator*, 24 Aug. 1940.

47   Manitoba Legislative Library (hereafter MLL), vertical file, "World War II – Manitoba," Manitoba War Speakers' Committee.

48   AM, P196, Patriotic Salvage Corps, scrapbook file 5, news clipping, n.d.

49   Keshen, *Saints, Sinners, and Soldiers*, 14–18

50   "Government's Propaganda Machine is Now in High Gear," Toronto *Telegram*, 26 July 1940, copy in Canadian War Museum, "Democracy at War: Canadian Newspapers and the Second World War," warmuseum.ca/cwm/newspapers (accessed 24 Sept. 2007).

51   Keshen, *Saints, Sinners, and Soldiers*, 15.

52   Earle Birney, "To Arms with Canadian Poetry," *Canadian Forum* (Jan. 1940); Fergus Glenn (pseudonym for McNaught), "The Conscription Build-Up," *Canadian Forum* (Oct. 1941); both qtd. in J.L. Granatstein and Peter Stevens, eds., *Forum: Canadian Life and Letters, 1920–1970* (Toronto: University of Toronto Press, 1972), 183–185 and 196–200.

53   Underhill expressed this opinion in 1932. Rutherford, 63.

54   Craig, "Public Opinion in Manitoba," vii.

55   UMA, MSS 3, Dafoe Papers, box 18, file 4, untitled memo by George Ferguson, n.d. On Dafoe's views on foreign policy during the 1930s, see, for example, Murray Donnelly, *Dafoe of the Free Press* (Toronto: Macmillan, 1968), 154–158; and Craig, *passim*.

56   UMA, MSS 3, Dafoe Papers, box 2, file 7, Dafoe to Ferguson, 3 Sept. 1939.

57   Arthur R. M. Lower, *My First Seventy-five Years* (Toronto: Macmillan, 1967), 270.

58   Ramsay Cook, "Canadian Freedom in Wartime, 1939–1945," in W.H. Heick and Roger Graham, eds., *His Own Man: Essays in Honour of Arthur Reginald Marsden Lower* (Montreal: McGill-Queen's University Press, 1974), 38.

59   Lester H. Phillips, "Canada's Internal Security," *Canadian Journal of Economics and Political Science* 12, 1 (Feb. 1946), 20–24.

60   Winnipeg *Free Press*, 12 Aug. 1941.

61   G.M.A. Grube, "Freedom and War," *Canadian Forum* (Nov. 1939), qtd. in Granatstein and Stevens, eds., *Forum*, 176–177.

62   Winnipeg *Free Press*, 2 Feb. 1940.

63   Winnipeg *Free Press*, 10 Feb. 1940.

64   Cook, "Canadian Freedom in Wartime," 48–49; Kelley and Trebilcock, *Making of the Mosaic*, 277.

65   Winnipeg *Free Press*, 9 Sept. 1939.

66   Larry Hannant, "Fifth-Column Crisis," *The Beaver* (Dec. 1993 - Jan. 1994), 25–28.

67   Winnipeg *Free Press*, 21 May 1940.

68   AM, GR 43, Premier's Correspondence, G60, file 112, War – Volunteer Reserve (1940), Moor to Bracken, 23 May 1940.

69   AM, GR 43, Premier's Correspondence, G60, file 112, War – Volunteer Reserve (1940). Bracken received resolutions from: the Winnipeg Board of Trade, 22 May; Russell Junior Chamber of Commerce, n.d.; Army and Navy Veterans in Canada, Fort Garry Unit No. 60, 24 May; Swan River Board of Trade, 31 May; Gladstone Legion, 10 June 1940; L.D.M. Baxter to Bracken, 22 May 1940; Edgerton to Bracken, 29 May 1940. Also, Winnipeg *Free Press*, 21 May 1940.

70   AM, GR 43, Premier's Correspondence, G59, file 112, War (1940), Cairns to Lockhart, 14 Sept. 1939, and Bracken to King, 22 Sept. 1939; also GR 43, G76, file 112, War (1942), Macdonald to Bracken, 11 June 1942.

71   AM, GR 43, Premier's Correspondence, G60, file 112, War – Volunteer Reserve (1940), "Employment of Veterans of the Great War, 1914–18," 13 June 1940.

72   AM, GR 43, Premier's Correspondence, G60, file 112, War – Volunteer Reserve (1940), Manitoba Committee Volunteer Reserve to Minister of National Defence, 15 June 1940; Riley to Major, 31 May 1940.

73   AM, GR 43, Premier's Correspondence, G59, file 112, War (1940), Bracken to Minister of National Defence, 2 July 1940; Power to Bracken, 3 July 1940.

74   *Statutes of Manitoba, 1940*, c.27 (Winnipeg: King's Printer, 1940); AM, GR 43, Premier's Correspondence, G69, file 112, War – Volunteer Reserve (1941), Flexman to Bracken, 26 April 1941 and Nicholson to Bracken, 12 Dec. 1941; "FGH (Reserve Army) 1942–1946," www.fortgarryhorse.ca (accessed 9 Oct. 2007).

75   Kelley and Trebilcock, *Making of the Mosaic*, 279. By the end of 1940 the number of internees had grown to about 1200.

76   Winnipeg *Free Press*, 8 Sept. 1939 and 16 May 1940.

77   Winnipeg *Free Press*, 30 Sept. 1939; *Canada Year Book, 1943–44* (Ottawa: King's Printer, 1944), 104. Only 21 enemy aliens in total were interned during the initial sweep.

78   Winnipeg *Free Press*, 21 and 22 May 1940.

79   Winnipeg *Free Press*, 26 Aug. 1939.

80   Oscar Ryan, *Tim Buck: A Conscience for Canada* (Toronto: Progress, 1975), 200.

81   Thomas M. Prymak, *Maple Leaf and Trident: The Ukrainian Canadians during the Second World War* (Toronto: Multicultural History Society of Ontario, 1988), 38; Watson Kirkconnell, *Canada, Europe, and Hitler* (Toronto: Oxford University Press, 1939), 147–149.

82   AM, MG 14, B35, Ralph Maybank Papers, box 5, file 89, correspondence 1937–46, "Memorandum for the Minister of Justice," 9 May 1942.

83   AM, GR 43, Premier's Correspondence, G69, file 112 (1941), War – Internment, United Garment Workers of America, Local No. 35, brief dated 16 Oct. 1941.

84   AM, GR 43, Premier's Correspondence, G59, file 112, War (1940), Williams to Bracken, n.d., March 1940.

85   B.K. Sandwell, "Growing Insecurity," copy in Winnipeg *Free Press*, 28 Nov. 1940.

86   Norman Penner, "Jacob Penner's Recollections, Introduction," in *Histoire Sociale / Social History 7*, 14 (Nov. 1974), 368.

87   Winnipeg *Tribune*, 6 June 1940, clipping in AM, Chisick collection, P2631, 1940-41 scrapbook; Doug Smith, *Joe Zuken: Citizen and Socialist* (Toronto: Lorimer, 1990), 71–80, 97–105; Ryan, 201–202. After the USSR entered the war and Canadian communists declared their support, Ross came out of hiding, was briefly interned, then later enlisted in the army.

88   AM, GR 43, Premier's Correspondence, G59, file 112, War (1940), Miller to Bracken, 19 June 1940.

89   See, for example, "Hearing Thursday for communists," 17 June 1940, 2; "Further Round-Up," 15 June 1940, 1; "More about communists," 14 June 1940, 7.

90   Winnipeg *Free Press*, 19 Sept. 1940, clipping in AM, Chisick collection, P2631, 1940–41 scrapbook.

91   Winnipeg *Free Press*, 18 and 25 Nov. 1940.

92   Winnipeg *Tribune*, 11 Dec. 1940, clipping in AM, Chisick collection, P2631, 1940–41 scrapbook.

93   AM, GR 43, Premier's Correspondence, G59, file 112, War (1940), Chairman, Ward 3 Unemployed Assn. to Bracken, 18 March 1940.

94   AM, GR 43, Premier's Correspondence, G69, file 112 (1941), War – Internment, Smith to Bracken, 3 May 1941 and Lysets to Bracken, 17 May 1941; Winnipeg *Free Press*, 10 Feb. 1942.

95   Winnipeg *Free Press*, 4 April 1941.

96   AM, Chisick collection, P2626, "Manitoba's Program for Total War," report of speech by W.A. Kardash in the Legislature, 16 Dec. 1941; UMA, Ed Rea collection, MSS 73, box 1, file 9, Norman Penner interview, 6 June 1969; Prymak, 50.

97   Winnipeg *Free Press*, 28 May 1942, clipping in AM, Chisick collection, P2630, 1942 scrapbook.

98   Winnipeg *Free Press*, 10 Feb. 1942, clipping in AM, Chisick collection, P2631, 1942 scrapbook.

99   AM, Chisick collection, P2631, 1942 scrapbook.

100 Winnipeg Free Press, 14 July 1942.

101 AM, Chisick collection, P2630, 1942 scrapbook.

102 Winnipeg Free Press, 6 March 1942, clipping in AM, Chisick collection, P2631, 1942 scrapbook.

103 Winnipeg *Free Press*, 10 June, 8 and 9 Sept. 1942.

104 AM, Chisick collection, P2626, "1942: Year of Victory," text of address by William Kardash to the National Workers' Conference for Total War, Toronto, May 30–31, 1942, 4–6, 29.

105 AM, Chisick collection, P2626, "Manitoba's Program for Total War," speech by W.A. Kardash in the Legislature, 16 Dec. 1941.

106 AM, Chisick collection, P2626, "1942: Year of Victory," text of address by William Kardash to the National Workers' Conference for Total War, Toronto, May 30–31, 1942, 27.

107 AM, Chisick collection, P2626, Leslie Morris, "Whose War? A Reply to the Liberal Party's Winnipeg Free Press," 8–11.

108 Winnipeg *Free Press*, 30 March 1942, clipping in AM, Chisick collection, P2631, 1942 scrapbook.

Chapter 2: US AND THEM

1   G.M.A. Grube, "Freedom and War," *Canadian Forum* (Nov. 1939), reproduced in J.L. Granatstein and Peter Stevens, eds. *Forum: Canadian Life and Letters, 1920–1970* (Toronto: University of Toronto Press, 1972), 176.

2   *Canada Year Book*, 1943–1944, 104–106; Thomas M. Prymak, *Maple Leaf and Trident: The Ukrainian Canadians during the Second World War* (Toronto: Multicultural History Society of Ontario, 1988), 38, 72; Paul Yuzyk, *The Ukrainians in Manitoba: A Social History* (Toronto: University of Toronto Press, 1953), 194–195; "Cross-Country," *Maclean's* (15 Jan. 1942), 34.

3   Watson Kirkconnell, *Canada, Europe, and Hitler* (Toronto: Oxford University Press, 1939), 79–84; Myrna Kostash, *All of Baba's Children* (Edmonton: Hurtig, 1977), 334; Library of Congress, "Revelations from the Russian Archives: Ukrainian Famine," www.loc.gov/exhibits/archives/ukra.html (accessed 20 Dec. 2007).

4   John C. Lehr, "Peopling the Prairies with Ukrainians," in Lubomyr Luciuk and Stella Hryniuk, eds., *Canada's Ukrainians: Negotiating an Identity* (Toronto: University of Toronto Press, 1991), 31, 48–49.

5   Oleh Gerus, "Consolidating the Community: The Ukrainian Self-Reliance League," in Luciuk and Hryniuk, eds., *Canada's Ukrainians*, 165, 172; Brian Osborne, "'Non-Preferred' People: Inter-war Ukrainian Immigration to Canada," in Luciuk and Hryniuk, eds., *Canada's Ukrainians*, 81–83.

6   Myron Gulka-Tiechko, "The Ukrainian National Federation, 1928–1945," unpublished paper, 1978, copy in UMA, Ed Rea collection, MSS 72, box 3, file 10; Gerus, 166–171.

7   Prymak, *Maple Leaf and Trident*, 44–46; Gerus, 174–175; N. Fred Dreisziger, "Tracy Philipps and the Achievement of Ukrainian-Canadian Unity," in Lubomyr Luciuk and Stella Hryniuk, *Canada's Ukrainians: Negotiating an Identity* (Toronto: University of Toronto Press, 1991), 340.

8   Winnipeg *Free Press*, 7 June 1940, clipping in AM, Chisick collection, P2631, 1940–41 scrapbook; Kelley and Trebilcock, *Making of the Mosaic*, 287.

9   Prymak, *Maple Leaf and Trident*, 33.

10 Bill Balan, "The Formation of the Ukrainian Canadian Committee, September 1938 - November 1940," unpublished paper, copy in UMA, Ed Rea collection, MSS 72, box 1, file 4.

11 Gerus, "Consolidating," 168; Marco Carynnyk, "Swallowing Stalinism: Pro-communist Ukrainian Canadians and Soviet Ukraine in the 1930s," in Luciuk and Hryniuk, eds., *Canada's Ukrainians*, 205.

12 Prymak, *Maple Leaf and Trident*, 26–28.

13 *Kanadiiskyi farmer*, 26 April 1939, qtd. in Kirkconnell, *Canada, Europe, and Hitler*, 142.

14 Kirkconnell, *Canada, Europe, and Hitler*, 140–150.

15 Prymak, *Maple Leaf and Trident*, 54; Kirkconnell, *Canada, Europe, and Hitler*, 152.

16 Winnipeg *Free Press*, 10 Jan., 14 Jan., and 5 May 1942.

17 Winnipeg *Free Press*, 7 Aug. and 21 Dec. 1943. After the ULFTA ban was lifted in October 1943, some of the ULFTA halls were subsequently reopened; Winnipeg *Free Press*, 15 Oct. 1943.

18 Bohdan S. Kordan and Lubomyr Y. Luciuk, "A Prescription for Nationbuilding: Ukrainian Canadians and the Canadian State, 1939–1945," in Norman Hillmer et al., eds., *On Guard for Thee: War, Ethnicity and the Canadian State, 1939–1945* (Ottawa: Canadian Committee for the History of the Second World War, 1988), 86–88.

19 AM, GR 43, Premier's Correspondence, G59, file 112, War (1940), Arsenych to Bracken, June 1940; Prymak, *Maple Leaf and Trident*, 37, 47.

20 Winnipeg *Free Press*, 29 Aug. 1941.

21 Prymak, *Maple Leaf and Trident*, 57–58.

22 Winnipeg *Tribune*, 31 Jan. 1942.

23 AM, Chisick collection, P2630, 1942 scrapbook.

24 Winnipeg *Free Press*, 12 Dec. 1941 and 18 Jan. 1943.

25 Prymak, *Maple Leaf and Trident*, 78.

26 Winnipeg *Free Press*, 30 March 1942. See also AM, Chisick collection, P2626, "Manitoba's Program for Total War," speech by W.A. Kardash in the Legislature, 16 Dec. 1941.

27 Prymak, *Maple Leaf and Trident*, 56–57, 96–97; Kordan and Luciuk, "Prescription for Nation Building," 92; Donald Avery, "Divided Loyalties: The Ukrainian Left and the Canadian State," in Luciuk and Hryniuk, eds., *Canada's Ukrainians*, 283–287.

28 Winnipeg *Free Press*, 17 Feb. 1942; Peter Melnycky, "Tears in the Garden: Alberta Ukrainians During the Second World War," in Ken Tingley, ed., *For King and Country: Alberta in the Second World War* (Edmonton: Reidmore, 1995), 332.

29 AM, Social Planning Council of Winnipeg (hereafter SPC), P666, file 4, program from Ukrainian Young Women's Club concert, 25 March 1945; Yuzyk, 193.

30 Winnipeg *Free Press*, 5 Nov. 1941.

31 UMA, Sheila Rabinovitch collection, TC74, Tape 17m, transcript of interview with James H. Gray, 1977.

32 See, for example, J.L. Granatstein, *Canada's War: The Politics of the Mackenzie King Government, 1939–1945* (Toronto: University of Toronto Press, 1975); and J.M. Hitsman and J.L. Granatstein, *Broken Promises: A History of Conscription in Canada* (Toronto: Oxford University Press, 1977).

33 André Laurendeau, "The Plebiscite," in J.L. Granatstein and Peter Neary, eds., *The Good Fight: Canadians in World War II* (Toronto: Copp Clark, 1995), 220–226; Frederick W. Gibson and Barbara Robertson, eds., *Ottawa at War: The Grant Dexter Memoranda, 1939–1945* (Winnipeg: Manitoba Records Society, 1994), 60, 161.

34 Winnipeg *Tribune*, 17 Dec. 1941.

35 Gibson and Robertson, *Ottawa at War*, 160–164, 242.

36 UMA, MSS 24, Winnipeg *Tribune* (hereafter cited as *Tribune* collection), file 1772, Conscription 1939–1944; Winnipeg *Tribune*, 23 Jan. 1942.

37 AM, Chisick collection, P2631, 1942 scrapbook; UMA, *Tribune* collection, file 1772, Conscription 1939–1944; AM, GR 43, Premier's Correspondence, G76, file 112 (1942), War, Litterick to King, n.d.

38 Winnipeg *Free Press*, 10 April 1942.

39 Winnipeg *Tribune*, 14 April 1942. Colin Gibson, Minister of National Revenue, had ordered government advertising proclaiming that, "As I see it – Hitler would vote 'No,' Quisling would not vote, and Canadians will vote 'YES.'"

40 Winnipeg *Free Press*, 3 April 1942.

41 Laurendeau, "The Plebiscite," 224.

42 Winnipeg *Tribune*, 28 April 1942; Winnipeg *Free Press*, 1 May 1942; Arnold Maydaniuk, "The 1942 Plebiscite Campaign in Manitoba and Its Results," unpublished paper, 1973, copy in UMA, MSS 72, Ed Rea (hereafter cited as Ed Rea collection), box 5, file 9. For population figures, see Canada, Dominion Bureau of Statistics, *Eighth Census of Canada* (Ottawa: KP, 1941), 446–447.

43 Winnipeg *Free Press*, "Where the 'No' Vote Lay Here," 29 April 1942; according to one account, the writer was James Gray; Prymak, 164.

44 Winnipeg *Free Press*, "Manitoba's 'No' Vote," 1 May 1942.

45 Prymak, *Maple Leaf and Trident*, 72.

46 Winnipeg *Free Press*, 2 May 1942.

47 Prymak, *Maple Leaf and Trident*, 78n37.

48 AM, Chisick collection, P2630, 1942 scrapbook.

49 Winnipeg *Free Press*, 16 May 1942.

50 Winnipeg *Free Press*, 5 May 1942, clipping in AM, Chisick collection, P2630, 1942 scrapbook.

51 Winnipeg *Free Press*, 23 May 1942.

52 Winnipeg *Tribune*, 1 May 1942; Winnipeg *Free Press*, 2 May 1942.

53 Prymak, *Maple Leaf and Trident*, 76–77.

54 Winnipeg *Free Press*, 9 May 1942.

55 Winnipeg *Tribune*, 4 May 1942.

56 Winnipeg *Free Press*, 2 May 1942.

57 "Ukrainian Canadian Protest," Winnipeg *Free Press*, 2 May 1942.

58 See, for example, Winnipeg *Free Press*, "National Selective Service," 19 Nov. 1941; "Australia's Experience," 29 Nov. 1941; and "Plain Talk," 16 Feb. 1942.

59 See, for example, "The Situation as it Stands," Winnipeg *Free Press*, 29 April 1942.

60 Winnipeg *Tribune*, 7 May 1942; E.L.M. Burns, *Manpower in the Canadian Army, 1939-1945* (Toronto: Clarke, Irwin, 1956), 119.

61 Winnipeg *Free Press* 8 May 1942.

62 Winnipeg *Tribune*, 28 and 30 May 1942.

63 Winnipeg *Tribune*, 26 March 1943.

64 Winnipeg *Tribune*, 22 June 1944.

65 Winnipeg *Free Press*, 14 July 1944.

66 Winnipeg *Tribune*, 2 Sept. 1944.

67 Winnipeg *Tribune*, 20 July and 26 Sept 1944.

68 Winnipeg *Tribune*, 4 Dec. 1944.

69 Winnipeg *Tribune*, 14 and 15 Sept. 1944.

70 Winnipeg *Tribune*, 19 Sept., 24 and 27 Oct. 1944.

71 Winnipeg *Tribune*, 25 and 27 Nov. 1944.

72 Winnipeg *Tribune*, 29 Nov. 1944.

73 See, for example, Ken Adachi, *The Enemy that Never Was: A History of the Japanese Canadians* (Toronto: McClelland, 1976); Ann Gomer Sunahara, *The Politics of Racism: The Uprooting of Japanese Canadians during the Second World War* (Toronto: Lorimer, 1981); Patricia Roy et al., *Mutual Hostages: Canadians and Japanese during the Second World War* (Toronto: University of Toronto Press, 1990); W. Peter Ward, "British Columbia and the Japanese Evacuation," *Canadian Historical Review* 57, 3 (Sept. 1976), 289–309; J.L. Granatstein and Gregory A. Johnson, "The Evacuation of the Japanese Canadians, 1942: A Realist Critique of the Received Version," in Norman Hillmer et al., eds., *On Guard for Thee: War, Ethnicity and the Canadian State, 1939–1945* (Ottawa: Canadian Committee for the History of the Second World War, 1988), 101–129.

74 Kelley and Trebilcock, *Making of the Mosaic*, 295.

75 John Ferris, "Savage Christmas: The Canadians at Hong Kong," in David J. Bercuson and S.F. Wise, eds., *The Valour and the Horror Revisited* (Montreal: McGill-Queen's University Press, 1994), 109–127; C.P. Stacey, *Official History of the Canadian Army in the Second World War, Vol. I: Six Years of War: The Army in Canada, Britain and the Pacific* (Ottawa: QP, 1955), 488–489.

76 Winnipeg *Tribune*, 23 and 26 Dec. 1941.

77 "Cross-Country," *Maclean's*, 15 Feb. 1942, 49.

78 Winnipeg *Tribune*, 24 and 27 December 1941.

79 UMA, Winnipeg Tribune collection, MSS 24, Canadian Army – Winnipeg Grenadiers.

80 Toronto *Globe and Mail*, 11 March 1942.

81 Winnipeg *Free Press*, 16 May 1945; Winnipeg *Tribune*, 21 May and 17 Aug. 1945.

82 UMA, Winnipeg Tribune collection, MSS 24, file 5486, Prisoners of War, 1941–45; Winnipeg *Free Press*, 1 Oct. 1942.

83 Harry P. McNaughton, *Shadow Lights of Shamshuipo* (n.p., 1945), copy in AM, Harry P. McNaughton collection, P2362, file 16.

84 Winnipeg *Free Press*, 26 June 1943; Winnipeg *Tribune*, 11 Sept. and 18 Oct. 1943.

85 UMA, Winnipeg Tribune collection, MSS 24, file 5486, Prisoners of War, 1941–45. Winnipeg *Tribune*, 24 April and 2 Oct. 1943.

86 W. Peter Ward, "British Columbia and the Japanese Evacuation," *Canadian Historical Review* 57, 3 (Sept. 1976), 289–291.

87 Ibid., 297–308; Roy Ito, *We Went to War* (Stittsville: Canada's Wings, 1984), 147–148.

88 Adachi, *The Enemy that Never Was*, 225; Roy et al., *Mutual Hostages*, 107; Ward, "British Columbia," 294, 300.

89 Granatstein and Johnson, "Evacuation," 105–107.

90 AM, GR 1609, Public Works, G8043, Japanese Nationals, Bracken to Crerar, 13 Feb. 1942.

91 AM, GR 43, Premier's Correspondence, G113, file 112, (1945), War – Japanese Nationals. See the following correspondence: Willis to Bracken, 20 Feb. 1942;

MacNamara to Lyons, 5 March 1942; Wright to Crerar and Pipes to Bracken, both 10 March 1942; Bracken to Pipes, 14 March 1942. See also AM, GR 1609, Public Works, G8043, Japanese Nationals, memo re: Japanese Nationals on Cranberry Portage Highway, 2 March 1942.

92 Winnipeg *Tribune*, 22 Feb. 1942.

93 AM, GR 43, Premier's Correspondence, G113, file 112, (1945), War – Japanese Nationals, Mitchell to Bracken, 24 March 1942 and reply, 25 March 1942; Bracken to Anderson, 26 May 1942.

94 LAC, RG 36/27, vol. 31, file 1721, Taylor to Alberta Beet Growers Association and to Beet Growers Association of Manitoba, 11 March 1942, cited in Louis Dion, "The Resettlement of Japanese Canadians in Manitoba, 1942–1948" (MA thesis, University of Manitoba, 1991), 30–31.

95 Winnipeg *Tribune*, 8 Dec. 1941.

96 Winnipeg *Free Press*, 9 Dec. 1941.

97 AM, Manitoba Japanese Canadians' Citizens Association oral history collection (hereafter MJCCA), C839, Alice Nakauchi interview, 2 Sept. 1987.

98 AM, MJCCA, C845, Sadako Mizobuchi interview, 14 Sept. 1987.

99 Winnipeg *Tribune*, 23 April 1942.

100 Peter Takaji Nunoda, "A Community in Transition and Conflict: The Japanese Canadians, 1935–1951" (PhD diss., University of Manitoba, 1991), 122–129.

101 Dion, "Resettlement," 41–48; British Columbia Security Commission, "Removal of Japanese from Protected Areas," March 4, 1942 to October 31, 1942, 28, copy in AM, GR 43, Premier's Correspondence, G113, file 112 (1945), War – Japanese Nationals.

102 AM, MJCCA, C851, Ken Nishibata interview, 28 Sept. 1987; C846, Matsue Nakai interview, 15 Sept. 1987; C852, Akira Sato interview, 28 Sept. 1987.

103 AM, MJCCA, C860, Harold Hirose interview, 20 Oct. 1987; C851, Ken Nishibata, C852, Akira Sato.

104 Winnipeg *Tribune*, 28 April and 8 May 1942.

105 AM, MJCCA, C840, Kanaye Connie Matsuo interview, 24 Aug. - 3 Sept. 1987.

106 AM, GR 1614, Public Works, G7250, Deputy Minister, Relief Assistance, Japanese Evacuees Case Files, 1942–1945; Roy et al., *Mutual Hostages*, 103.

107 AM, GR 1614, Public Works, G7250, Deputy Minister, Relief Assistance, Japanese Evacuees Case Files, 1942–1945; the analysis which follows is based on this restricted collection of confidential records, so specific source references are not possible.

108 Ibid.

109 Ibid.

110 Leonard Marsh, *Report on Social Security for Canada* (Ottawa: KP, 1943; reprint ed., Toronto: University of Toronto Press, 1975), 37.

111 AM, GR 1614, Public Works, G7250, Deputy Minister, Relief Assistance, Japanese Evacuees Case Files, 1942–1945.

112 Ibid.

113 Ibid.

114 AM, MJCCA, C862, Harold Hirose; C842, Eichi Oike interview, 10 Sept. 1987. See also Dion, "Resettlement," 99.

115   *Canada Year Book*, 1942, 712; Dion, "Resettlement," 112–114.

116   AM, MJCCA, C840, Connie Matsuo.

117   AM, MJCCA, C861, Harold Hirose.

118   AM, MJCCA, C861, Harold Hirose; Dion, "Resettlement," 123.

119   AM, MJCCA, C857, Nobu Sato Ellis interview, 9 Oct. 1987.

120   AM, SPC, P642, file 2, Board of Directors, Council of Social Agencies, Minutes, 21 Oct. 1942; Dion, "Resettlement," 102.

121   Winnipeg *Free Press*, 28 May 1942.

122   AM, GR 1609, Public Works, G8043, Japanese Nationals, Leitch to Willis, 18 May 1942; Winnipeg *Free Press*, 17 Oct. 1942.

123   Winnipeg *Free Press*, 7 May 1942.

124   Winnipeg *Free Press*, 27 May 1942.

125   AM, MJCCA, C860 and C861, Harold Hirose; C840, Kanaye Connie Matsuo; C864, Mas Nagamori interview, 27 Oct. 1987; C844, Shizuko Miki interview, 14 Sept. 1987; C841, H. Mitani interview, 9 Sept. 1987. See also Dion, "Resettlement," 124.

126   Roy et al., *Mutual Hostages*, 143; Nunoda, "Community in Transition," 3, 163; Dion, "Resettlement," 129, 143; AM, P827, Taichi Kato papers, file 4, Pickersgill to Chairman, Japanese Central Committee, Slocan City, BC, 9 April 1945.

127   AM, GR 43, Premier's Correspondence, G106, file 52 (1945), Japanese Canadians, draft memo by R.E. Moffat, 13 Nov. 1945.

128   AM, MJCCA, C845, Sadako Mizobuchi.

129   Winnipeg *Tribune*, 29 Aug. 1945; Roy et al., *Mutual Hostages*, 166–167; Dion, "Resettlement," 127–128, 145, 159.

130   UMA, Winnipeg Tribune collection, MSS 24, file 3847, Japanese Canadians; Winnipeg *Tribune*, 1 July 1944. See also Dion, "Resettlement," 148–153.

131   AM, GR 43, Premier's Correspondence, G106, file 52 (1945), Japanese Canadians, resolutions from the United Church's Winnipeg Presbytery, 13 Nov. 1945; Brandon East Presbytery, 5 Nov. 1945; and the church's Women's Missionary Society branches in Dauphin, 13 Dec. 1945; Portage la Prairie, 12 Dec. 1945; and Virden, 22 Nov. 1945.

132   AM, GR 43, Premier's Correspondence, G106, file 52 (1945), Japanese Canadians, Armstrong to Garson, 10 Jan. 1946.

133   UMA, Winnipeg Tribune collection, MSS 24, file 3847, Japanese Canadians.

134   AM, GR 43, Premier's Correspondence, G106, file 52 (1945), Japanese Canadians, Morton to Garson, 19 Oct. 1945; Garson to Morton, 20 Nov. 1945; Garson to Woodside, 17 Dec. 1945; press release, 20 Dec. 1945.

135   Winnipeg *Tribune*, 17 March 1945; AM, GR 43, Premier's Correspondence, G113, file 112 (1945), War – Japanese Nationals, Bracken to Mitchell, 25 March 1942 and Bracken to Taylor, draft, 16 June 1942; Dion, "Resettlement," 153.

136   UMA, Winnipeg Tribune collection, MSS 24, file 3847, Japanese Canadians. The particular orders-in-council were PC 7355, PC 7356, and PC 7357.

137   Winnipeg *Tribune*, 7 Jan. 1946.

138   Ito, *We Went to War*, 176–177, 302.

139   AM, MJCCA, C852 - C853, Akira Sato.

140 AM, MJCCA, C842, Eichi Oike; Ito, *We Went to War*, 241.

141 UMA, Winnipeg Tribune collection, MSS 24, file 3847, Japanese Canadians.

142 AM, MJCCA, C860 - C861, Harold Hirose; Ito, *We Went to War*, 166–188, 242.

143 Ito, *We Went to War*, 155–158.

144 Dion, "Resettlement," 145, 159; Roy et al., *Mutual Hostages*, 167.

145 Winnipeg *Tribune*, 17 Sept. 1946.

146 Ito, *We Went to War*, 246.

147 Kelley and Trebilcock, *Making of the Mosaic*, 304.

Chapter 3: INVESTING IN VICTORY

1 Canada, National War Finance Committee (hereafter NWFC), *Statistics and Information* on Dominion Government Public Borrowing Operations from September 1939 to *December 1945* (Ottawa: King's Printer, 1946), 10; *Canada Year Book*, 1942 (Ottawa: King's Printer, 1942), 757.

2 David W. Slater, *War Finance and Reconstruction: The Role of Canada's Department of Finance, 1939–1946* (Ottawa: Department of Finance, 1995), 274.

3 Slater, 77; NWFC, *Statistics and Information on Dominion Government Public Borrowing Operations*, 20, 81–88.

4 Slater, *War Finance*, 30--31.

5 C.P. Stacey, *Arms, Men and Governments: The War Policies of Canada, 1939–1945* (Ottawa: Queen's Printer, 1970), 6.

6 James J. Kimble, *Mobilizing the Home Front: War Bonds and Domestic Propaganda* (College Station: Texas A&M, 2006), 19–20.

7 Wendy Cuthbertson, "Pocketbooks and Patriotism: The 'Financial Miracle' of Canada's World War II Victory Bond Program," *Canadian Military History Since the 17th Century*, ed. Yves Tremblay (Ottawa: Directorate of History and Heritage, 2000), 178.

8 LAC, RG 19, vol. 3978, file F–1–11, Imrie to Ilsley, "Canada's War Loan Promotion," cited in Wendy Cuthbertson, "Popular Finance: Canada's World War II Victory Bond Programme as a Case Study in Social Marketing" (unpublished paper, University of Toronto, July 1999).

9 Slater, *War Finance*, 82–87.

10 NWFC, *Statistics and Information on Dominion Government Borrowing Operations*, 6.

11 LAC, RG 19, vol. 592, file 155–30, "NWFC Background for Operations," 26 Nov. 1941, 1.

12 Ibid., 9–10.

13 "NWFC Background for Operations," 19 Feb. 1942, 5–6.

14 Bank of Canada Archives (hereafter BCA), NWFC file 24–1, Executive Committee Minutes, Third War Loan, 18 March 1941, and National Committee Minutes, Third War Loan, 31 March 1941.

15 AM, P5005, NWFC – Manitoba Division, Analysis of Final Results, Second and Third Victory Loans, 1942; BCA, NWFC file 16–3, Conference of Provincial Chairmen, Payroll Savings Section, 22–23 Aug. 1944.

16   Desmond Morton, *Fight or Pay: Soldiers' Families in the Great War* (Vancouver: UBC Press, 2004), 188.

17   BCA, NWFC file 24–4, Executive Committee Minutes, 16–17 Aug. 1943; AM, GR 43, Premier's Correspondence, G69, file 112 (1941), War – Loans, Ilsley to Bracken, 13 Oct. 1941 and GR 43, G100, file 112 (1944), War – Loans, Garson memo 21 April 1943.

18   LAC, RG 19, vol. 592, file 155–30–0, NWFC, Meeting of National Executive Committee, 16–17 Aug. 1943, 3; BCA, NWFC file 13-B1.

19   BCA, NWFC file 4–3, "Poll of Canadian Public Opinion Upon Completion of Canada's Fifth Victory Loan."

20   AM, MG 14, C50, Ethel M. McKnight collection, box 3, file 18.

21   BCA, NWFC file 16–3, Meeting of Provincial Chairmen, Payroll Savings Section, 21–22 Feb. 1945.

22   AM, GR 43, Premier's Correspondence, G69, file 112 (1941), War – Loans.

23   AM, GR 43, Premier's Correspondence, G100, file 112 (1944), War – Loans, Brisbin memo 21 July 1943.

24   Keshen, *Saints, Sinners, and Soldiers*, 32.

25   LAC, RG 36, series 31, vol. 27, Field Reports, 12 May and 22 Sept. 1943.

26   Ibid.

27   BCA, NWFC file 16–3, Conference of Provincial Chairmen, Payroll Savings Section, 22-23 Aug. 1944.

28   Slater, 90; BCA, NWFC file 16–3, Meeting of Provincial Chairmen, Payroll Savings Section, 21–22 Feb 1945.

29   LAC, RG 19, vol. 592, file 155–30–0, NWFC, "Estimated Derivation of Subscriptions at Time of Issue," 11 Dec. 1943; and Meeting of National Executive Committee, 16–17 Aug. 1943; AM, P5005, NWFC – Manitoba Division, Analyses of Final Results, Second through Ninth Victory Loans; AM, GR 43, Premier's Correspondence, G100, file 112 (1944), War – Loans, Minister of Finance to Garson, 6 April 1944; NWFC, *Statistics and Information on Dominion Government Public Borrowing Operations*, 22.

30   BCA, NWFC file WSC – Circulars, *The Bulletin*, 12 Oct. 1940.

31   Slater, *War Finance*, 84.

32   Winnipeg *Free Press*, 5 Feb. 1941.

33   BCA, NWFC file WSC – Circulars, *The War Savings News*, 20 Feb. 1941.

34   Winnipeg *Free Press*, 7 Feb. 1941.

35   BCA, NWFC, WSC – Circulars, *War Savings News*, 20 Feb. 1941.

36   Winnipeg *Free Press*, 7 Feb. 1941.

37   BCA, NWFC file 24–4, Executive Committee Minutes, 2–3 Dec. 1943.

38   Ken Ford, "War's Brightlights," *Globe and Mail*, 8 Nov. 1943.

39   Victoria O'Donnell and Garth S. Jowett, "Propaganda as a Form of Cummunication," in Ted J. Smith, ed., *Propaganda: A Pluralistic Perspective* (New York: Praeger, 1989), 53.

40   Harold D. Lasswell, "Propaganda," in Robert Jackall, ed., *Propaganda* (New York: New York UP, 1995), 13, 18. The article originally appeared in R.A. Seligman, ed., *Encyclopaedia of the Social Sciences*, vol. XII (London: Macmillan, 1934).

41 BCA, NWFC file 2–8, "Summary of War Finance Press Advertising, January 1, 1941 to March 31, 1942."

42 Institute for Propaganda Analysis, "How to Detect Propaganda," in Jackall, ed., *Propaganda*, 217–22. This work was originally published in 1937.

43 BCA, NWFC file 4–12, "How to Make Posters That Will Help Win the War," n.d.(1942?).

44 LAC, HG 5155 02 1941, xxfol. Reserve.

45 BCA, NWFC file 16–3, "Conference of Provinicial Chairmen, Payroll Savings Section," 22–23 Aug. 1944.

46 Ibid.

47 BCA, NWFC file 16–3, Conference of Provincial Chairmen, Payroll Savings Section, 21–22 Feb. 1945; NWFC file 4–5, "Salesmen's Replies Regarding Public Attitude to the Eighth Victory Loan Campaign, August 1945."

48 Winnipeg *Free Press*, 5 May 1943.

49 BCA, NWFC file 16–3, Conference of Provincial Chairmen, Payroll Savings Section, 22–23 Aug. 1944.

50 BCA, NWFC file 16–3, Meeting of Provincial Chairmen, Payroll Savings Section, 21–22 Feb. 1945.

51 BCA, NWFC files 2–1 and 1–12, "Summary of Radio Activities, 4th Victory Loan."

52 BCA, NWFC file 1–1, War Finance Advertising Group, Second Victory Loan Campaign.

53 BCA, NWFC files 1–2 to 1–8, War Finance Advertising Group.

54 David Cannadine, "The Context, Performance and Meaning of Ritual: The British Monarchy and the 'Invention of Tradition', c. 1820–1977," in Eric Hobsbawm and Terence Ranger, eds., *The Invention of Tradition* (Cambridge: Cambridge UP, 1983), 104, 128–129.

55 Tori Smith, "'Almost Pathetic ... But Also Very Glorious': The Consumer Spectacle of the Diamond Jubilee," *Histoire Sociale / Social History* 58 (Nov. 1996), 335.

56 H.V. Nelles, "Historical Pageantry and the 'Fusion of the Races' at the Tercentenary of Quebec, 1908," *Histoire Sociale / Social History* 58 (Nov. 1996), 394.

57 Misty Rathert, "The 1939 Royal Visit to Winnipeg: Extensive Preparations" (unpublished paper, University of Manitoba, 26 November 2002).

58 Coincidentally, a 1918 Victory Loan poster had used virtually the same plea. BCA, NWFC file 24–1, National Committee Minutes, Third War Loan, 31 March 1941; Archives of Ontario, War Poster Collection, file C 233–2–0–1–8, "Let's Finish the Job."

59 Jonathan Vance, *Death So Noble: Memory, Meaning, and the First World War* (Vancouver: UBC Press, 1997), 67, 210; Alan R. Young, "'We throw the torch': Canadian Memorials of the Great War and the Mythology of Heroic Sacrifice," *Journal of Canadian Studies* 24, 4 (Winter, 1989–90): 16–17; Laura Brandon, "History as Monument: The Sculptures on the Vimy Memorial," Canadian War Museum, http://www.warmuseum.ca/cwm/vimy/ sculptures_e.html (accessed 20 November 2006).

60 Winnipeg *Free Press*, 30 May, 1941.

61 Dominion Publicity Committee, "Victory Loan 1941 Report," 10; AM, GR 43, Premier's Correspondence, G69, file 112 (1941), War – Loans, "Bulletin No. 1, Victory Loan – Dominion Torch Committee."

62 "Bulletin No. 1, Victory Loan – Dominion Torch Committee."

63 BCA, NWFC file 24–1, Executive Committee Minutes, Third War Loan, 15 April 1941.

64 "Bulletin No. 1, Victory Loan – Dominion Torch Committee."

65 Dominion Publicity Committee, "Victory Loan 1941 Report," 10–11.

66 LAC, RG 19, vol. 609, file 155–81–1–2, "1941 Victory Loan."

67 Dominion Publicity Committee, "Victory Loan 1941 Report," Appx. F.

68 AM, GR 43, Premier's Correspondence G69, file 112 (1941), War – Loans.

69 Winnipeg *Free Press*, 29 and 31 May 1941.

70 Winnipeg *Free Press*, 2 June 1941.

71 AM, GR 43, Premier's Correspondence, G69, file 112 (1941), War – Loans, Victory Torch Dedication Address, 1 June 1941.

72 Winnipeg *Free Press*, 2 June 1941.

73 Winnipeg *Free Press*, 2 and 3 June 1941.

74 Winnipeg *Tribune*, 4 June 1941.

75 Winnipeg *Tribune*, 4 and 5 June 1941. Shilo was home to the Canadian Army's A3 Artillery Training Centre and A15 (advanced) Infantry Training Centre.

76 Winnipeg *Tribune*, 5 June 1941.

77 Winnipeg *Tribune*, 19 June 1941.

78 AM, GR 43, Premier's Correspondence, G76, file 112 (1942), War – Loans, Lightcap to MacNeill, 19 Jan. 1942; NWFC, *Statistics and Information on Dominion Government Public Borrowing Operations*, 58.

79 LAC, MG 27, III B5, Ian Mackenzie Papers, vol. 48, file 501–63.

80 LAC, RG 19, vol. 609, file 155–81–1–2,Dominion Publicity Committee, "Victory Loan 1941 Report," 16.

81 AM, GR 43, Premier's Correspondence, G76, file 112 (1942), War – Loans, "Bulletin No. 1, Dominion Ceremonials Committee – Second Victory Loan," 26 Jan. 1942.

82 "Bulletin No. 1, Dominion Ceremonials Committee – Second Victory Loan," 26 Jan. 1942.

83 LAC, RG 19, vol. 592, file 155–30, and vol. 609, file 155–81–1–2, 1941 Victory Loan; AM, P5005, National War Finance Committee – Manitoba Division, Names List, 6th Victory Loan.

84 Winnipeg *Tribune*, 2 Aug. 1969.

85 AM, GR 43, Premier's Correspondence, G76, file 112 (1942) War – Loans, "Report of Public Relations Committee Manitoba Division."

86 AM, GR 43, Premier's Correspondence, G76, file 112 (1942) War – Loans, Waight to Bracken, 7 Feb. 1942.

87 Winnipeg *Tribune*, 18 and 19 Feb. 1942; Winnipeg *Free Press*, 19 Feb. 1942.

88 Winnipeg *Tribune*, 19 and 21 Feb. 1942.

89 Winnipeg *Free Press*, 19 Feb. 1942.

90 Winnipeg *Free Press*, 19 Feb. 1942.

91 Some of the measures planned by the Manitoba Division are listed in Appendix 2.

92 Winnipeg *Free Press*, 19 Feb. 1942.

93   For example, each person was permitted two ounces of bread per day and two ounces of meat every second day. Milk was limited to a half cup a week, and only for children five years and under. Soap was rationed at one half-tablet per person each month. Winnipeg *Tribune*, 19 Feb. 1942, supplement, "Das Winnipeger Lügenblatt."

94   Winnipeg *Tribune*, 19 Feb. 1942.

95   Winnipeg *Tribune*, 4 March 1980.

96   Winnipeg *Tribune*, 19 Feb. 1942.

97   UMA, Winnipeg *Tribune* collection, file 3637, "If Day."

98   Michael Newman, "February 19, 1942: If Day," *Manitoba History* 13 (Spring 1987), 27-30; Winnipeg *Free Press*, 19 Feb. 1942; UMA, Winnipeg *Tribune* collection, file 6921, Victory Loans.

99   Winnipeg *Tribune*, 26 Feb. 1942.

100   UMA, Winnipeg *Tribune* collection, file 3637, "If Day"; AM, GR 43, Premier's Correspondence, G76, file 112 (1942), War – Loans, Richardson to Bracken, 5 March 1942.

101   Winnipeg *Tribune*, 20 and 21 Feb. 1942.

102   Winnipeg *Free Press*, 14 Feb. 1942.

103   AM, GR 43, Premier's Correspondence, G76, file 112 (1942), War – Loans, Hughes to Bracken, 18 Feb. 1942, and Lightcap to Bracken, 20 Feb. 1942; Winnipeg *Tribune*, 19 Feb. 1942.

104   The first loan had 56,011 Manitoba subscribers. AM, GR 43, Premier's Correspondence, G76, file 112 (1942), War – Loans, Sellers to Bracken, 19 March 1942; Canada, National War Finance Committee (hereafter NWFC), *Statistics and Information on Dominion Government Public Borrowing Operations from September 1939 to December 1945* (Ottawa: KP, 1946), 59.

105   Bank of Canada Archives (hereafter BCA), NWFC file 24–1, Executive Committee Minutes, Third War Loan, 15 April 1941.

106   AM, GR 43, Premier's Correspondence, G76, file 112 (1942), War – Loans, radio address, Third Victory Loan, 14 Oct. 1942.

107   AM, GR 43, Premier's Correspondence, G76, file 112 (1942), War – Loans, "A Letter to the Ministers of Canada", circular publicity from the Religious Sub-Committee of the Third Victory Loan, n.d., attached to "Bulletin No. 1, Dominion Ceremonials Committee," Third Victory Loan, Sept. 1942.

108   AM, GR 43, Premier's Correspondence, G76, file 112 (1942), War – Loans, Ilsley to Bracken, 8 Oct. 1942; "Bulletin No. 1, Dominion Ceremonials Committee," Third Victory Loan, 25 Sept. 1942.

109   AM, GR 43, Premier's Correspondence, G76, file 112 (1942), War – Loans, "Bulletin No. 1, Dominion Ceremonials Committee," Third Victory Loan, 25 Sept. 1942.

110   Ibid.; Winnipeg *Free Press*, 20 Oct. 1942.

111   Winnipeg *Free Press*, 20 Oct. 1942.

112   "Bulletin No. 1, Dominion Ceremonials Committee," Third Victory Loan, 25 Sept 1942; Winnipeg *Free Press*, 19 Oct. 1942.

113   Winnipeg *Free Press*, 23 Oct. 1942.

114 Winnipeg *Free Press*, 6 Nov. 1942.

115 At least one Winnipeg resident later expressed the opinion that "the slogan used and the whole campaign [for the Fourth Victory Loan] has had a dignity sadly missing in the Third Campaign. The 'IV' symbol has something about it which appeals to men and women in the way a dagger never could.... It is sincerely hoped we will never again set out with such a symbol or slogan as was used in the Third Campaign." Exactly what was so appealing about a roman numeral as a campaign symbol, or so offensive about the dagger, the writer did not say. LAC, RG 36, series 31, vol. 27, Field Reports, 19 May 1943.

116 BCA, NWFC file 2–5, Meetings of the Public Relations Section, 26–27 Feb. and 23–24 Aug. 1943.

117 Winnipeg *Free Press*, 19, 24, and 27 April 1943.

118 Winnipeg *Free Press*, 16 April and 14 May 1943; Winnipeg *Tribune*, 25 April and 1 May 1944.

119 Winnipeg *Free Press*, 24 and 27 April 1943.

120 Winnipeg *Tribune*, 16, 18, 25, and 30 Oct. 1943.

121 Winnipeg *Tribune*, 25 April and 1 May 1944.

122 Winnipeg *Tribune*, 23 and 28 Oct. 1944.

123 AM, GR 43, Premier's Correspondence, G100, file 112 (1944), War – Loans, Fourth Victory Loan, "Noon-Day Ceremonial"; Winnipeg *Tribune*, 16 Oct. 1943, 24 April and 1 May 1944.

124 Winnipeg *Tribune*, 23 April and 5 May 1945.

125 LAC, RG 36, series 31, vol. 27, Field Reports, May 1944 and 1–7 May 1945.

126 BCA, NWFC file 13-B1, "Organizer's Note Book," 40.

127 BCA, NWFC file 2–1, "Summary of Public Opinion Reports of the 7th Victory Loan."

128 LAC, RG 36, series 31, vol. 27, Field Reports, 1–7 May 1945.

129 BCA, NWFC file 4–1, "Poll of Public Opinion Upon Completion of Third Victory Loan, Nov. 1942."

130 BCA, NWFC file 4–3, "Poll of Canadian Public Opinion Upon Completion of Canada's Fifth Victory Loan."

131 LAC, RG 2, vol. 12, file W–34–10, Memos to cabinet, 10 and 30 Oct. 1944.

132 Wendy Cuthbertson, "Pocketbooks and Patriotism: The 'Financial Miracle' of Canada's World War II Victory Bond Program," *Canadian Military History Since the 17th Century*, ed. Yves Tremblay (Ottawa: Directorate of History and Heritage, 2000), 178.

133 John J. MacAloon, "Olympic Games and the Theory of Spectacle in Modern Societies," in John J. MacAloon, ed., *Rite, Drama, Festival, Spectacle: Rehearsals Toward a Theory of Cultural Performance* (Philadelphia: Institute for the Study of Human Issues, 1984), 243–244.

134 Ralph H. Turner and Lewis M. Killian, *Collective Behavior*, 3rd ed. (Englewood Cliffs: Prentice-Hall, 1987), p. 296, cited in Robert Rutherdale, "Canada's August Festival: Communitas, Liminality, and Social Memory," *Canadian Historical Review* 77, 2 (July, 1996), 231.

135 Rutherdale, "Canada's August Festival," 221, 234–239. See also Victor Turner, "Variations on a Theme of Liminality," in Edith Turner, ed., *Blazing the Trail: Way Marks in the Exploration of Symbols* (Tucson: University of Arizona Press, 1992), 48–65.

136 Cuthbertson, "Pocketbooks and Patriotism," 177.

137 Goodwin Watson, "Five Factors in Morale," in Goodwin Watson, ed., *Civilian Morale: Second Yearbook of the Society for the Psychological Study of Social Issues* (Boston: Houghton, 1942), 30–47; Kurt Lewin, "Time Perspective and Morale," in Watson, ed., *Civilian Morale*, 58–60.

138 James J. Kimble, *Mobilizing the Home Front: War Bonds and Domestic Propaganda* (College Station: Texas A&M, 2006), 32.

139 BCA, NWFC file 16–3, Meeting of Provincial Chairmen, Payroll Savings Section, 21–22 Feb. 1945.

140 BCA, NWFC file 4–11, Canadian Opinion Company, "A Nation-wide Survey of Certain Diet and Buying Habits of the Canadian People," May 1942, 23–28.

141 NWFC, *Statistics and Information on Dominion Government Public Borrowing Operations*, 6.

142 Robert K. Merton, *Mass Persuasion: The Social Psychology of a War Bond Drive* (Westport, Conn.: Greenwood, 1946), 135.

143 LAC, RG 36, series 31, vol. 27, Field Reports, 17 Nov. 1943.

144 Kelley and Trebilcock, *Making of the Mosaic*, 273.

145 BCA, NWFC file 24–4, Executive Committee Minutes, 2–3 Dec. 1943, and file 16–3, Meeting of Executive Committee with the Provincial Vice-Chairmen, 17 Nov. 1942.

146 LAC, RG 36, series 31, vol. 27, Field Reports, 6 Oct 1943.

147 BCA, NWFC, W.S.C. circulars, *The Bulletin*, 30 Dec. 1940.

148 These included: *Hrvatski Glas* (Croatian Voice), *Der Nordwesten* (German), *Kanadai Magyar Ujsag* (Canadian Hungarian News), *Heimskringla* and *Logberg* (Icelandic), *Jewish Post* and *Western Jewish News*, *Norrona* (a Norwegian paper), *Czas* and *Gazeta Polska* (Polish), *Canada Posten* and *Canada Tidningen* (Swedish), *Kanadjiski Farmer*, *Tochylo*, and *Ukrainian Voice* (Ukrainian). BCA, NWFC file 1–1, War Finance Advertising Group, Second Victory Loan Campaign.

149 Winnipeg *Free Press*, 2 June 1941 and 22 Oct. 1942; Winnipeg *Tribune*, 2 May 1945.

150 John Porter, *The Vertical Mosaic: An Analysis of Social Class and Power in Canada* (Toronto: University of Toronto Press, 1965), 456–459.

151 Robert Rutherdale, *Hometown Horizons: Local Responses to Canada's Great War* (Vancouver: UBC Press, 2004), 61.

152 Porter, *Vertical Mosaic*, 302.

153 Rutherdale, *Hometown Horizons*, 104–105.

Chapter 4: THE SPIRIT OF SERVICE

1   LAC, RG 44, vol. 7, Citizens Committees Conference, Hill to Dir. Auxiliary Services, 10 Dec. 1941, and Memo re: Organization of Citizens Committees, n.d.

2   Gertrude Laing, *A Community Organizes for War: The Story of the Greater Winnipeg Co-ordinating Board for War Services and Affiliated Organizations,*

1939–1946 (Winnipeg: n.p., 1948), 3–6. I am grateful to Serge Durflinger for bringing this source to my attention.

3   AM, MG 10, C67, Royal Canadian Legion, box 33, Alex Cairns and A.H. Yetman, "The History of the Veteran Movement, 1916–1956," v. II, 12–13.

4   AM, Imperial Order Daughters of the Empire, P5513, "Minutes of the 44th Annual Meeting IODE 27 May–1 June 1944," 44–45, 99; IODE *Bulletin* 25 (May 1943), 11.

5   AM, Social Planning Council of Winnipeg (hereafter SPC), P666, file 5, VRCW and the origins of the CVB, 1939; LAC, MG 28, I 10, Canadian Council on Social Development, vol. 259 file 7, McQueen to Whitton, 27 Jan. 1940; Laing, 14–15.

6   LAC, MG 28, I 10, Canadian Council on Social Development, vol. 259, file 7, Monica McQueen, "A Year of Volunteers – Winnipeg's Newest Agency", n.d., 1.

7   AM, SPC, P666, file 5, VRCW and the origins of the CVB, 1939, clipping from *The Survey*, published Jan. 1941.

8   AM, SPC, P666, file 5, VRCW and the origins of the CVB, 1939; Winnipeg *Free Press*, 21 Sept. 1939.

9   LAC, MG 28, I 10, Canadian Council on Social Development, vol. 259, file 7, McQueen, "A Year of Volunteers" and memo, "Central Volunteer Bureau," n.d.

10   UMA, MSS 24, Winnipeg *Tribune* (hereafter Winnipeg *Tribune* collection), file 5486, Prisoners of War, 1941–45; Winnipeg *Tribune*, 25 Nov. 1942.

11   *Chatelaine* (March 1944), 72.

12   Laing, *Community Organizes*, 17, 21; AM, SPC, P666, file 5, VRCW and the origins of the CVB, 1939; file 9, CVB – annual meeting, 1942; and file 7, CVB annual report, 1940.

13   Laing, *Community Organizes*, 16–17; AM, SPC, P666, file 10, CVB – annual meeting, 1943.

14   AM, SPC, P666, file 9, CVB – annual meeting, 1942.

15   AM, SPC, P666, file 8, CVB annual meeting, 1941; Laing, *Community Organizes*, 55.

16   McQueen, "A Year of Volunteers," 3.

17   Laing, *Community Organizes*, 21, 83–85.

18   UMA, MSS 1, Margaret Konantz papers, Box 2, Folder 1, Incoming Correspondence 1940–1945, Richardson to Konantz, 7 Jan. 1943.

19   LAC, RG 44, vol. 7, Preliminaries to Salvage Campaign.

20   AM, Patriotic Salvage Corps, P196, scrapbook file 5, "Volunteer Drivers in White Take Pride in Strenuous Work," news clipping, n.d.

21   Laing, *Community Organizes*, 22–28; McQueen, "A Year of Volunteers"; AM, Chisick collection, P2631, 1942 scrapbook; AM, Patriotic Salvage Corps, P196, scrapbook files 3 to 5.

22   Winnipeg *Tribune*, 27 Feb. 1943; Department of National War Services, Office of the Director of Voluntary and Aux. Services, Bulletin #9, 27 June 1943, copy in AM, SPC, P664, file 10, Cdn War Service Cttee – various reports, 1940–45; AM, Patriotic Salvage Corps, P196, scrapbook files 4 and 5; Winnipeg *Free Press*, 28 June 1943; UMA, MSS 122, Laurence F. Wilmot collection (hereafter Wilmot collection), box 6, file 7.

23   Laing, *Community Organizes*, 25–28; AM, Patriotic Salvage Corps, P196, scrapbook file 5.

24 AM, Patriotic Salvage Corps, P196, scrapbook files 4 and 5; Laing, 28; UMA, MSS 1, Margaret Konantz papers, box 2, folder 1, clipping from Philadelphia *Inquirer*, Dec. 1943.

25 AM, SPC, P666, file 10, CVB – annual meeting, 1943.

26 Laing, *Community Organizes*, 18–19, 30–31; AM, SPC, P642, file 22, "Annual Report of the Secretary of the Council of Social Agencies, 9 June 1943," 8.

27 LAC, RG 44, vol. 7, Citizens Committees Conference, Memo re: Organization of Citizens Committees, n.d.; Pifher to Davis, 10 Nov. 1941; Thorson to Ralston, 18 Nov. and 10 Dec. 1941; Laing, 31–32.

28 AM, SPC, P664, file 3, Greater Winnipeg Coordinating Board for War Services (hereafter GWCBWS) minutes, 11 June 1941; LAC, RG 24, vol. 11457, file NDWG 1270–152 vol. 1, GWCBWS minutes, 11 May 1944; Ken Ford, "War's Brightlights," *Globe and Mail*, 8 Nov. 1943.

29 AM, SPC, P666, file 4, Publications, 1943–45, Second Annual Meeting, GWCBWS, 11 June 1943; LAC, RG 24, vol. 11457, file NDWG 1270–152 vol. 1, GWCBWS minutes, 24 Nov. 1944; Laing, 44–51.

30 Laing, *Community Organizes*, 38–42; LAC, RG 24, vol. 11457, file NDWG 1270–152 vol. 1, GWCBWS minutes, 11 May and 24 Nov. 1944; AM, SPC, P664, file 4, GWCBWS minutes, 1944.

31 Laing, *Community Organizes*, 67–69, 73.

32 LAC, RG 24, vol. 11457, file NDWG 1270–152 vol. 1, "Report of the War Services Conference, Montebello, Quebec, Jan. 22 to 26th, 1945," 6; Laing, 79, 92; AM, SPC, P664, file 4, GWCBWS minutes, 24 Nov. 1944.

33 Fort Garry Horse Regimental Archives and Museum (hereafter FGH), *Blue and Gold* 4, 11 (Dec. 1939), 8.

34 FGH, *Blue and Gold* 5:12 (Aug. 1940), 5; Regimental Association minutes, 11 Feb. 1943.

35 FGH, Women's Auxiliary, "Balance Sheet, 1945" and "Secretary's Report 1944"; Regimental Association minutes, 24 Oct. 1939.

36 Laing, *Community Organizes*, 53–58.

37 AM, SPC, P666, file 10, CVB – annual meeting, 1943, and file 4, Publications, 1943–45, "Second Annual Meeting, Greater Winnipeg Coordinating Board for War Services," 11 June 1943.

38 UMA, Wilmot collection, box 6, file 7, Hope to Laurence Wilmot, 28 Dec. 1943.

39 Laing, *Community Organizes*, 59. Laing was the Coordinating Board's executive secretary.

40 Ibid., 95; AM, Family Bureau of Winnipeg, P4651, Co-ordinating Board Reports, 26 April 1945; SPC, P664, file 5, GWCBWS minutes, 4 May 1945.

41 LAC, RG 44, vol. 7, file 9, Citizens Committees Conference, "Memorandum Re:Organization of Citizens Committees," n.d. [late 1941?].

42 LAC, RG 44, vol. 7, file 9, Citizens Committees Conference, Thomas-Peter to Thorsen [sic], 16 Sept. 1941.

43 LAC, RG 44, vol. 7, file 9, Citizens Committees Conference, "Memorandum Re:Organization of Citizens Committees."

44 James M. Whalen, "The Scrap That Made A Difference," *Legion Magazine* (November/December 1998), http://www.legionmagazine.com/features/canadianreflections/ 98–11.asp (accessed 16 January 2007).

45 LAC, RG 24, reel C5290, file 8917-3-7, Directorate of Special Services, Special Report 134, "Civilian-Army Relations," 30 June 1944.

46 Jay White, "Conscripted City: Halifax and the Second World War" (PhD diss., McMaster University, 1994), 307.

47 AM, SPC, P664, file 10, Canadian War Service Committee – various reports, 1940–45, "Great-West Life War Service Unit, Annual Reports for the Unit Year May 31, 1942 to May 31, 1943"; Laing, *Community Organizes*, 97.

48 United Church Archives, University of Winnipeg (hereafter UCA), "Westminster United Church Annual Report, 1941," 29–30.

49 Winnipeg *Tribune*, 4 Nov. 1944; AM, MG 14, B35, Ralph Maybank papers, box 6, newspaper clippings 1928–43; Winnipeg *Free Press*, 12 March 1942, clipping in AM, Chisick collection, P2631, 1942 scrapbook.

50 Durflinger, *Fighting from Home:*, Chapter 5, *passim*; Esyllt W. Jones, *Influenza 1918: Disease, Death and Struggle in Winnipeg* (Toronto: University of Toronto Press, 2007), 77–78.

51 AM, SPC, P666, file 5, VRCW and the origins of the CVB, 1939, McQueen to Hyndman, 27 Oct. 1939.

52 McQueen, "A Year of Volunteers," 1.

53 LAC, MG 28, I 10, Canadian Council on Social Development, vol. 259, file 7, McQueen to Whitton, 27 Jan. 1940; McQueen, "A Year of Volunteers," 3.

54 AM, SPC, P664, file 8, correspondence, 1941–45, memo by W.J. Major, chairman GWCBWS, n.d.

55 LAC, MG 28, I 10, Canadian Council on Social Development, vol. 258, file 4, Denne to Davidson, 6 Nov. 1942.

56 AM, SPC, P666, file 5, VRCW and the origins of the CVB, 1939; Winnipeg *Free Press*, 7 Oct. 1940 and 16 Aug. 1941.

57 Winnipeg *Free Press*, Tuesday 19 August 1941.

58 Winnipeg *Free Press*, 7 April 1942, clipping in AM, Chisick collection, P2630, 1942 scrapbook.

59 Winnipeg *Free Press*, Monday 7 and 11 Oct. 1940.

60 Verena Garrioch, "When There's Work To Do, We Do It With A Will," Winnipeg *Tribune*, 12 June 1943.

61 Roger E. Turenne, "The Minority and the Ballot Box: A Study of the Voting Behaviour of the French Canadians of Manitoba, 1888–1967" (MA thesis, University of Manitoba, 1969), 126.

62 Murray Donnelly, *Dafoe of the Free Press* (Toronto: Macmillan, 1968), 29.

63 Alan Artibise, *Winnipeg: An Illustrated History* (Toronto: Lorimer, 1977), 109–162.

64 The Naval Museum of Manitoba, "HMCS St. Boniface," http://www.naval-museum.mb.ca (accessed 24 April 2006); Winnipeg *Free Press*, 14 and 19 Aug. 1941; 11 Oct. 1941.

65 AM, SPC, P664, file 4, GWCBWS minutes, 1944; SPC, P666, file 4, Publications, 1943-45, "Second Annual Meeting," 11 June 1943, and program, Ukrainian Young Women's Club concert, 25 March 1945; Paul Yuzyk, *The Ukrainians in Manitoba: A Social History* (Toronto: University of Toronto Press, 1953), 193.

66 Barry Ferguson, *Remaking Liberalism: The Intellectual Legacy of Adam Shortt, O.D. Skelton, W.C. Clark, and W.A. Mackintosh, 1890–1925* (Montreal: McGill-Queen's University Press, 1993), 237–238.

67 Mary Kinnear, *Margaret McWilliams: An Interwar Feminist* (Montreal: McGill-Queen's University Press, 1991), 72–73, 158; A.B. McKillop, *A Disciplined Intelligence: Critical Inquiry and Canadian Thought in the Victorian Era* (Montreal: McGill-Queen's University Press, 1979), 199, 206.

68 Kinnear, *Margaret McWilliams*, 43–44.

69 Jones, *Influenza 1918*, 70–71, 168.

70 Voluntary Registration of Canadian Women. AM, MG 14 B 44, Howard W. Winkler papers, box 5, file 2, Booth to Winkler, 15 June 1940.

71 UCA, Westminster United Church annual reports, 1941–43.

72 UCA, "Westminster United Church Annual Report, 1941," 16.

73 FGH, Women's Auxiliary, "President's Report," 3 Jan. 1945.

74 AM, SPC, P666, file 7, CVB annual report, 1940.

75 Winnipeg *Tribune*, 19 June 1941.

76 The Naval Museum of Manitoba, "The Naval History of Manitoba," http://www.naval-museum.mb.ca (accessed 26 November 2004).

77 Yuzyk, *Ukrainians in Manitoba*, 193.

78 Qtd. in Thomas M. Prymak, *Maple Leaf and Trident: The Ukrainian Canadians during the Second World War* (Toronto: Multicultural History Society of Ontario, 1988), 109.

79 On the government's role in community service provision, see Shirley Tillotson, *The Public at Play: Gender and the Politics of Recreation in Post-War Ontario* (Toronto: University of Toronto Press, 2000).

Chapter 5: THE FAMILY'S MATERIAL WELFARE

1 Department of National Defence, Directorate of History and Heritage, "Statistics" file.

2 LAC, MG 28, I 10, Canadian Council on Social Development, vols. 133 and 134, file 600, Questionnaires, Servicemen's Families, 1942.

3 Nancy Christie, *Engendering the State: Family, Work, and Welfare in Canada* (Toronto: University of Toronto Press, 2000), 49, 314.

4 Keshen, *Saints, Sinners, and Soldiers*, 55. These are somewhat crude figures since they do not reflect *per capita* increases in spending and have not been adjusted for inflation, but they are nonetheless indicative of significant economic growth.

5 Leonard Marsh, *Report on Social Security for Canada* (Ottawa: King's Printer, 1943; reprint ed., Toronto: University of Toronto Press, 1975), 41–42.

6 Ibid., 36–39.

7 David W. Slater, *War Finance and Reconstruction: The Role of Canada's Department of Finance, 1939–1946* (Ottawa: Department of Finance, 1995), 183.

8 *Canada Year Book*, 1941, 722–723; *Canada Year Book*, 1945, 895–896; Wartime Information Board, "Wartime Controls: Questions and Answers on the Cost of

Living," 12 Sept. 1944, copy in AM, MG 14, B 44, Howard W. Winkler collection, box 12, file 5.

9   *Canada Year Book*, 1945, 897.

10   Keshen, *Saints, Sinners, and Soldiers*, 60.

11   Desmond Morton, *Fight or Pay: Soldiers' Families in the Great War* (Vancouver: UBC Press, 2004), 37–54.

12   Desmond Morton and Glenn Wright, *Winning the Second Battle: Canadian Veterans and the Return to Civilian Life, 1915–1930* (Toronto: University of Toronto Press, 1987), 223, 63–64.

13   Robert England, *Discharged: A Commentary on Civil Re-establishment of Veterans in Canada* (Toronto: Macmillan, 1943), 143; Clifford H. Bowering, *Service: The Story of the Canadian Legion, 1925–1960* (Ottawa: Canadian Legion, 1960), 169–170.

14   Morton, *Fight or Pay*, 91; Christie, *Engendering the State*, vii.

15   Morton, *Fight or Pay*, 72–73, 94, 102–103, 132.

16   Christie, *Engendering the State*, 79.

17   Morton and Wright, *Winning the Second Battle*, 224.

18   Dean F. Oliver, "Public Opinion and Public Policy in Canada: Federal Legislation on War Veterans, 1939–46," in Raymond B. Blake, Penny E. Bryden, and J. Frank Strain, eds., *The Welfare State in Canada: Past, Present and Future* (Concord, ON: Irwin, 1997), 195–196.

19   Emily Arrowsmith, "Fair Enough? How Notions of Race, Gender, and Soldiers' Rights Affected Dependents' Allowance Policies Towards Canadian Aboriginal Families during World War II" (PhD diss., Carleton University, 2006), 66–67.

20   *Financial Regulations and Instructions for the Canadian Active Service Force* (Ottawa: King's Printer, 1939 and 1944 editions); *Financial Regulations and Instructions for the Royal Canadian Air Force on Active Service* (Ottawa: King's Printer, 1940), 41; LAC, MG 28, I 10, Canadian Council on Social Development, vol. 283, file 31, Directory of Canadian Community Agencies Serving Dependents of the Forces, Feb. 1942. An additional allowance could be granted to dependent parents or siblings if he assigned another five days' pay ($6.50).

21   Winnipeg *Free Press*, 5 Feb. 1941; England, 150–151.

22   Adele White, "Are They Too Young to Marry?" *Chatelaine* (Sept. 1941), 9. Sylvia Fraser, ed., *A Woman's Place: Seventy Years in the Lives of Canadian Women* (Toronto: Key Porter, 1997), 78.

23   *Canada Year Book*, 1942, 712.

24   Winnipeg *Free Press*, 11 Sept. 1939.

25   Marsh, *Report on Social Security*, 39.

26   LAC, MG 28, I 10, Canadian Council on Social Development, vol. 133, file 600, Questionnaires, Servicemen's Families, 1942, Calgary Council of Social Agencies, response to questionnaire, 24 June 1942.

27   Winnipeg *Free Press*, 5 Feb. 1941.

28   *Labour Gazette*, Jan. 1940, 77–79; Marsh, *Report on Social Security*, 318.

29   UMA, MSS 122, Laurence F. Wilmot (hereafter Wilmot collection), box 6, file 7, Hope to Laurie, 3 Dec. 1943.

30   As a military chaplain, Laurie Wilmot held the honorary rank of captain. A captain's wage was $6.50 a day and Hope received $50 per month DA in 1942 in addition to Laurie's assigned pay, for an annual family income of over $3,300, plus a child supplement of $33 per month. The allowance and child supplements increased to $52.20 and $34, respectively, in 1943. LAC, RG 24, vol. 13304, War Diary, Directorate of Special Services, July and Oct. 1942; *Financial Regulations and Instructions for the Canadian Active Service Force* (1939 and 1944 eds.).

31   UMA, Wilmot collection, box 6, file 7, Hope to Laurie, 6, 11, 13, and 17 Oct. 1943.

32   LAC, MG 30, E 497, Mabel Geldard-Brown collection, vol. 2, "Directional Service for the Families of Enlisted Men," Feb. 1941; LAC, MG 28, I 10, Canadian Council on Social Development, vol. 133, file 600, Daniel to Vancouver Coordinating Council of Auxiliary Services, 6 June 1942; Arrowsmith, "Fair Enough?," 63.

33   LAC, MG 28, I 10, Canadian Council on Social Development, vol. 283, file 31, Directory of Canadian Community Agencies Serving Dependents of the Forces, Feb. 1942; Jeff Keshen, "Revisiting Canada's Civilian Women during World War II," in Veronica Strong-Boag, Mona Gleason, and Adele Perry, eds., *Rethinking Canada: The Promise of Women's History*, 4th ed. (Don Mills, ON: Oxford University Press, 2002), 253.

34   Keshen, *Saints, Sinners, and Soldiers*, 57; Slater, 157; LAC, RG 24, reel C–5290, file 8917–3–7, DAG (D) to Paymaster General, 9 Aug. 1942.

35   AM, Chisick collection, P2626, "Manitoba's Program for Total War," speech by W.A. Kardash in the Legislature, 16 Dec. 1941.

36   John English, "Politics and the War: Aspects of the Canadian National Experience," in Sidney Aster, ed., *The Second World War as a National Experience* (Ottawa: Canadian Committee for the History of the Second World War, 1981), 54–55; Slater, 157.

37   AM, Chisick collection, P2631, 1942 scrapbook.

38   LAC, RG 2, vol. 12, file W–34–10, Dunton to Heeney, 15 Nov. 1943; LAC, RG 36, series 31, vol. 27, Field Reports, 12 May 1943.

39   Winnipeg *Free Press*, 21 April 1943.

40   LAC, RG 2, vol. 12, file W–34–10, Andrew to Heeney, 22 Nov. 1943, and memos to cabinet, 24 Jan., 7 Feb., 21 Feb., 6 March, and 27 March, 1944.

41   Ibid., memo to cabinet, 26 Feb. 1945; LAC, RG 36, series 31, vol. 27, Field Reports, 17 Jan. and 20–26 Feb. 1945.

42   LAC, RG 2, vol. 49, file W–34–2–S, WIB Survey 47, 7 Oct. 1944. For an example of advertisements about the dangers of inflation, see "They're Talking About ... a Ten-Cent Dollar!" *The Canadian Unionist* (July-Aug. 1944) and "The Story of Inflation ... in One Easy Lesson," *Globe and Mail*, 14 April 1944, copy in "Democracy at War: Canadian Newspapers and the Second World War," Canadian War Museum on-line exhibit, http://www.civilisations.ca/cwm (accessed 21 March 2007).

43   Wartime Information Board, "Wartime Controls: Questions and Answers on the Cost of Living," 12 Sept. 1944, copy in AM, MG 14, B 44, Howard W. Winkler collection, box 12, file 5; *Canada Year Book*, 1945, 899.

44   Artibise, *Winnipeg: A Social History of Urban Growth*, 133, 158–161, 229–234; Jones, *Influenza 1918*, 61.

45   Donald G. Wetherell and Irene R.A. Kmet, *Homes in Alberta: Building, Trends, and Design, 1870–1967* (Edmonton: University of Alberta Press, 1991), 101–126,

176; Lynn Hannley, "Substandard Housing," in John R. Miron, ed., *House, Home, and Community: Progress in Housing Canadians, 1945–1986* (Montreal: McGill-Queen's University Press), 1993, 218; and Sean Purdy, "'It Was Tough on Everybody': Low-Income Families and Housing Hardship in Post-World War II Toronto," *Journal of Social History* 37,2 (2003), 460.

46   MLL, Council of Social Agencies of Greater Winnipeg, Report of Committee on Housing, *Housing in Winnipeg* (n.p., 1943), 18–19, 33–36; Winnipeg *Free Press*, 23 Sept. 1939; Ruben C. Bellan, "The Development of Winnipeg as a Metropolitan Centre" (PhD diss., Columbia University, 1958), 440–441.

47   Alexander Officer, qtd. in John C. Bacher, *Keeping to the Marketplace: The Evolution of Canadian Housing Policy* (Montreal: McGill-Queen's University Press, 1993), 77–78.

48   Winnipeg *Tribune*, 12 June 1943, cited in Council of Social Agencies of Greater Winnipeg, *Housing in Winnipeg*, 17–18.

49   City of Winnipeg Health Department, "Report of the Twenty-Fourth Annual Survey of Vacant Houses and Vacant Suites in the City," Jan. 1942, 5–6, copy in AM, GR 1609, Public Works, G8029, Winnipeg General.

50   AM, GR 1609, Public Works, G8029, Winnipeg General, "Report of The City of Winnipeg, Fact Finding Board on Housing in Winnipeg," 27 June 1947, 15–16.

51   City of Winnipeg Health Department, "Report of the Twenty-Fifth Annual Survey of Vacant Houses and Vacant Suites in the City," Jan. 1943, 5–6, copy in AM, GR 1609, Public Works, G8029, Winnipeg General.

52   Council of Social Agencies of Greater Winnipeg, *Housing in Winnipeg*, 17, 30–31.

53   UMA, Wilmot collection, box 6, file 10, Hope to Laurie, 11 Sept. 1944.

54   UMA, Wilmot collection, box 6, file 9, Hope to Laurie, 30 Aug. 1944.

55   Council of Social Agencies of Greater Winnipeg, *Housing in Winnipeg*, 18–22.

56   City of Winnipeg Health Department, "Report of the Twenty-Fourth Annual Survey of Vacant Houses and Vacant Suites in the City," Jan. 1942, 7.

57   City of Winnipeg Health Department, "Report of the Twenty-Eighth Annual Survey of Vacant Houses and Vacant Suites in the City," Jan. 1946, 6; "Report of the Twenty-Ninth Annual Survey of Vacant Houses and Vacant Suites in the City," Jan. 1947, 6.

58   Laurier Centre for Miltiary Strategic and Disarmament Studies, Wilfrid Laurier University, Department of Veterans Affairs, "Summary of Enlistments (All Forces) to 31 March 1945."

59   LAC, RG 24, reel C5290, file 8917-3-7, Directorate of Special Services, Special Report No. 186, "Study of the Housing Problem of Army Personnel Returned from Overseas," 11 May 1945.

60   Ibid.; Winnipeg *Tribune*, 1 May 1945.

61   Winnipeg *Free Press*, 5 Dec. 1942.

62   Winnipeg *Tribune*, 30 April 1945.

63   H. Peter Oberlander and Arthur L. Fallick, *Housing a Nation: The Evolution of Canadian Housing Policy* (Vancouver: UBC, Centre for Human Settlements, 1992), 26–27; Keshen, *Saints, Sinners, and Soldiers*, 81–84. For evidence of rent gouging, see responses from social agencies across Canada in LAC, MG 28, I 10, Canadian Council on Social Development, vol. 133, file 600, Questionnaires, Servicemen's

Families—Morale & Security; UMA, Wilmot collection, box 6 file 7, Hope to Laurie, 6 and 11 Oct. 1943.

64 William M. Tuttle, Jr., *"Daddy's Gone to War": The Second World War in the Lives of America's Children* (New York: Oxford University Press, 1993), 64.

65 LAC, MG 28, I 10, Canadian Council on Social Development, vol. 133, file 600, Questionnaires, Servicemen's Families—Morale & Security, Calgary Council of Social Agencies, response to questionnaire, 24 June 1942.

66 Winnipeg *Free Press*, 9 May 1942.

67 Winnipeg *Tribune*, 25 and 30 April, 1 and 3 May 1945; Keshen, *Saints, Sinners, and Soldiers*, 85; Desmond Morton and J.L. Granatstein, *Victory 1945* (Toronto: Harper, 1995), 93.

68 *Canada Year Book*, 1945, 444; AM, Chisick collection, P2631, Aug. 1942 scrapbook; LAC, RG 25, vol. 3034, file 4082–40, Wartime Information Board, Summary of editorial comment, 5–12 Oct. 1942; City of Winnipeg Health Department, "Report of the Twenty-Fifth Annual Survey of Vacant Houses and Vacant Suites in the City," Jan. 1943, 5–6, copy in AM, GR 1609, Public Works, G8029, Winnipeg General; Council of Social Agencies of Greater Winnipeg, *Housing in Winnipeg*, 17.

69 City of Winnipeg Health Department, "Report of the Twenty-Eighth Annual Survey of Vacant Houses and Vacant Suites in the City," Jan. 1946, 13–17.

70 City of Winnipeg Health Department, annual housing surveys, 1942, 1943, 1946, 1947.

71 LAC, RG 36, series 31, vol. 17, file 9–6–2–5, Housing, "Supplement to Housing and Community Planning," 15 Sept. 1945.

72 AM, GR 1609, Public Works, G8029, Winnipeg General, "Report on General Housing Conditions in the City of Winnipeg," 15 Nov. 1948, 47.

73 AM, GR 1609, Public Works, G8029, Winnipeg General, "Report of The City of Winnipeg, Fact Finding Board on Housing in Winnipeg," 27 June 1947, Appendix C.

74 AM, Chisick collection, P2630, 1942 scrapbook; Winnipeg *Tribune*, 29 May 1942.

75 LAC, RG 36, series 31, vol. 17, file 9–6–2–5, Housing, "Supplement to Housing and Community Planning," 15 Sept. 1945; Oberlander and Fallick, 24; Jill Wade, "Wartime Housing Limited, 1941–1947: Canadian Housing Policy at the Crossroads," *Urban History Review* 15:1 (June 1986), 44–46.

76 Winnipeg *Tribune*, 30 Jan. 1945.

77 Winnipeg *Tribune*, 4 May 1945.

78 Catherine Jill Wade, "Wartime Housing Limited, 1941–1947: Canadian Housing Policy at the Crossroads" (MA thesis, UBC, 1984), 127.

79 Winnipeg *Tribune*, 10 May, 18, 20, and 29 June 1945. In the event, WHL homes did in fact prove adequate and have stood the test of time in the decades since they were built. Many are still plainly visible today across Winnipeg.

80 Winnipeg *Tribune*, 17 July, 1 and 21 Nov. 1945; LAC, RG 28, vol. 344, file 196–46–9W-1, Gray to Sheils, 3 Nov. 1945; LAC, RG 28, vol. 526, file 64-W-5; City of Winnipeg Archives, Special Committees, misc. box 1.

81 AM, GR 1609, Public Works, G8029, Winnipeg General, "Report of The City of Winnipeg, Fact Finding Board on Housing in Winnipeg," 27 June 1947.

82 City of Winnipeg Health Department, "Report of the Twenty-Ninth Annual Survey of Vacant Houses and Vacant Suites in the City," Jan. 1947, 16.

83 AM, GR 1609, Public Works, G8029, Winnipeg General, "Report of The City of Winnipeg, Fact Finding Board on Housing in Winnipeg," 27 June 1947, Appendix C.

84 AM, GR 1609, Public Works, G8029, Winnipeg General, "Report on General Housing Conditions in the City of Winnipeg," 15 Nov. 1948, 22, 28, 48.

85 City of Winnipeg Archives, Special Committees misc. box 1; Canada, Department of Trade and Commerce, *Dwelling Units and New Buildings Containing Dwelling Units Reported by Municipalities and Other Areas as Completed in the Six Months Ending June 30, 1947* (Ottawa, 1947); and Canada, Department of Trade and Commerce, *Supplement to Housing Statistics 1946* (Ottawa, 1947).

86 City of Winnipeg Health Dept., 29th annual housing survey, Jan. 1947, 6–8.

87 Council of Social Agencies of Greater Winnipeg, *Housing in Winnipeg*, 35–40, 56–63.

88 City of Winnipeg Health Department, "Report of the Twenty-Ninth Annual Survey of Vacant Houses and Vacant Suites in the City," Jan. 1947, 14; "Report of the Twenty-Eighth Annual Survey of Vacant Houses and Vacant Suites in the City," Jan. 1946, 7.

89 AM, GR 1609, Public Works, G8029, Winnipeg General, "Report of The City of Winnipeg, Fact Finding Board on Housing in Winnipeg," 27 June 1947.

90 Wade, "Wartime Housing Limited," *Urban History Review* 15, 1 (June 1986), 49.

91 AM, GR 1609, Public Works, G8029, Winnipeg General, "Report on General Housing Conditions in the City of Winnipeg," 15 Nov. 1948, 22.

92 LAC, MG 28, I 10, Canadian Council on Social Development, vol. 55, file 471A, Housing Brief, McQueen to Davis, 16 Oct. 1947.

93 M.S. Donnelly, *The Government of Manitoba* (Toronto: University of Toronto Press, 1963), 96.

94 Ibid., 67, 96–104; Mark E. Vajcner, "Stuart Garson and the Manitoba Progressive Coalition," *Manitoba History* 26 (Autumn 1993), 29–35; John Kendle, *John Bracken: A Political Biography* (Toronto: University of Toronto Press, 1979), 248; Artibise, *Winnipeg: An Illustrated History*, 200.

95 Wade, "Wartime Housing Limited", 126; Michael Doucet and John Weaver, *Housing the North American City* (Montreal: McGill-Queen's University Press, 1991), 300–301; Jill Wade, *Houses for All: The Struggle for Social Housing in Vancouver, 1919–50* (Vancouver: UBC Press, 1994), 126.

96 LAC, RG 36, series 31, vol. 17, file 9–6–2–5, Housing, draft report, "Supplement to Housing and Community Planning," 15 Sept. 1945; Oberlander and Fallick, 16–20, 42; John Bacher, "W.C. Clark and the Politics of Canadian Housing Policy, 1935–1952," in Raymond B. Blake and Jeff Keshen, eds., *Social Welfare Policy in Canada: Historical Readings* (Toronto: Copp Clark, 1995), 280–282.

97 Bacher, "W.C. Clark and the Politics of Canadian Housing Policy," 277–285.

98 Wade, *Houses for All*, 28; Doucet and Weaver, *Housing the North American City*, 300–301.

99 Bacher, "W.C. Clark and the Politics of Canadian Housing Policy," 283–285.

100 AM, Social Planning Council of Winnipeg, P641, file 17, Housing Committee Minutes, 28 Nov. and 8 Dec. 1941.

101 Oberlander and Fallick, *Housing a Nation*, 30–37.

102 LAC, RG 36, series 31, vol. 17, file 9–6–2–5, Housing, Thwaites to Mignon, 19 Oct. 1945.

103 AM, GR 1609, Public Works, G8029, Winnipeg General, "Report on General Housing Conditions in the City of Winnipeg," 15 Nov. 1948, 22–24; The houses cost a mere $2,600 each to build; Winnipeg *Free Press*, 29 Sept. and 4 Nov. 1947.

104 City of Winnipeg Health Department, 33rd annual housing survey, 31 Dec. 1950; Bacher, *Keeping to the Marketplace*, 207, 311.

105 Wade, *Houses for All*, 94, 162.

106 Wetherell and Kmet, *Homes in Alberta,* 230; Doucet and Weaver, *Housing the North American City*, 302; David Burley, "Winnipeg's Landscape of Modernity, 1945–1975," in Serena Keshavjee, ed., *Winnipeg Modern: Architecture, 1945–1975* (Winnipeg: University of Manitoba Press, 2006), 61, 66; Purdy, "'It Was Tough on Everybody,'" 458.

107 Christie, *Engendering the State*, Chapter 7, passim.

Chapter 6: RESPONSES TO FAMILY SEPARATION

1 UMA, MSS 122, Laurence F. Wilmot collection (hereafter Wilmot collection), box 4, file 8, B.L. Montgomery, General, Eighth Army, Personal Message from the Army Commander, Christmas, 1943.

2 Sidonie Gruenberg, ed., *The Family in a World at War* (New York: Harper, 1942), 1–2.

3 Audio clip of radio broadcast, 11 Nov. 1939, from Canadian Broadcasting Corporation on-line exhibit "On Every Front: Canadian Women and the Second World War," http://www.archives.cbc.ca (accessed 3 Dec. 2004).

4 Reuben Hill, et al., *Families Under Stress: Adjustment to the Crises of War Separation and Reunion* (New York: Harper, 1949), 55–56.

5 Adele White, "Are They Too Young to Marry?" *Chatelaine* (Sept. 1941), 8–9.

6 LAC, MG 28, I 10, Canadian Council on Social Development, vol. 134, file 600, Questionnaires, Servicemen's Families, 1942, responses to questionnaire from Calgary Council of Social Agencies, 24 June 1942, and Hamilton Family Service Bureau, n.d.

7 Magda Fahrni, "The Romance of Reunion: Montreal War Veterans Return to Family Life, 1944–1949," *Journal of the Canadian Historical Association* 9 (1998), 192.

8 Barry Broadfoot, *Six War Years, 1939–1945: Memories of Canadians at Home and Abroad* (Toronto: Doubleday, 1974), 245.

9 Peter C. Conrad, *Training for Victory: The British Commonwealth Air Training Plan in the West* (Saskatoon: Western Producer Prairie Books, 1989), 58.

10 LAC, RG 36, series 31, vol. 12, file 8–2–2, "Canadian Women and Army Morale," 2 March 1943.

11 UMA, Wilmot collection, box 7, file 1, "Chaplain's Report to Officer Commanding, West Nova Scotia Regiment," 17 March 1944.

12 Keshen, *Saints, Sinners, and Soldiers*, 229.

13   UMA, Wilmot collection, box 6, file 1, Laurie to Hope, 6 and 9 July 1942, 6 Aug. 1942; and file 4, Laurie to Hope, 11 Nov. 1943.

14   UMA, Wilmot collection, box 6, files 2 and 3, misc. letters.

15   UMA, Wilmot collection, box 6, file 7, Hope to Laurie, 8 Aug. 1943, 13 and 15 Oct. 1943; box 6, file 4, Laurie to Hope, 19 Sept. 1943; box 7 file 1, Laurie to Hope, 20 Jan. 1944.

16   Hill, et al., *Families Under Stress*, 141.

17   UMA, Wilmot collection, box 6, file 9, Hope to Laurie, 9 Aug. 1944.

18   *Chatelaine* (Jan. 1944), 4; Fahrni, "Romance," 190.

19   Fort Garry Horse Regimental Archives and Museum (hereafter FGH), Women's Auxiliary, MacKenzie to Wilson, 30 Jan. 1945.

20   UMA, Wilmot collection, box 6, file 7, Hope to Laurie, 19 Aug 1943; box 7, file 1, Laurie to Hope, 18 Jan. 1944.

21   Qtd. in Judy Barrett Litoff and David C. Smith, "'Will He Get My Letter?' Popular Portrayals of Mail and Morale During World War II," *Journal of Popular Culture* 23, 4 (Spring 1990), 22.

22   UMA, Wilmot collection, box 7, file 1, diary entry, 12 April 1944.

23   UMA, Wilmot collection, box 6, file 7, misc. letters; box 6 file 4, Laurie to Hope, 21 Oct. and 29 Nov. 1943; box 7, file 1, Laurie to Hope, 20 and 27 Jan. 1944.

24   LAC, RG 24, reel C-5290, file 8917-3-7, Directorate of Special Services, Special Report No. 161, "Attitudes of Army Personnel Recently Returned from Overseas," 20 Nov. 1944, 4–6.

25   Laurence F. Wilmot, *Through the Hitler Line: Memoirs of an Infantry Chaplain* (Waterloo, ON: Wilfrid Laurier University Press, 2003), 39.

26   UMA, Wilmot collection, box 7, file 1, Laurie to Hope, 22 Jan. 1944.

27   Robert Zulauf to Frances Zulauf, 5 Nov. 1944, qtd. in Judy Barrett Litoff and David C. Smith, "'I Wish That I Could Hide Inside This Letter': World War II Correspondence," *Prologue* 24, 2 (Summer, 1992), 103.

28   Wilmot, *Through the Hitler Line*, 44, 54–55.

29   UMA, Wilmot collection, box 6, file 7, Hope to Laurie, 9 June 1944.

30   UMA, Wilmot collection, box 6, file 9, Hope to Laurie, 27 Aug. 1944.

31   William M. Tuttle, Jr., *"Daddy's Gone to War": The Second World War in the Lives of America's Children* (New York: Oxford University Press, 1993), 36, 44.

32   UMA, Wilmot collection, box 6, file 7, Hope to Laurie, 5 Aug. 1944.

33   UMA, Wilmot collection, box 4, file 10, Chaplain's Diary, Tues. 29 Feb 1944.

34   UMA, Wilmot collection, box 7, file 2, Laurie to Hope, letter 158, mid-June 1944.

35   UMA, Wilmot collection, box 6, file 7, Hope to Laurie, 26 Jan. and 8 June 1944.

36   Arnold Gesell et al., *The Child from Five to Ten* (New York: Harper, 1946), qtd. in Tuttle, *"Daddy's Gone to War,"* 16.

37   Tuttle, *"Daddy's Gone to War,"* 241.

38   Gruenberg, *Family in a World at War*, 255–56.

39   UMA, Wilmot collection, box 6, file 1, Laurie to Hope, 20 July, 4 and 10 Aug., 9 Dec. 1942; box 6, file 9, Hope to Laurie, 5 Aug. 1944; box 1, files 33a and 35.

40   UMA, Wilmot collection, box 6, file 10, Hope to Laurie, 7 Sept. 1944.

41   LAC, MG 28, I 10, Canadian Council on Social Development, vol. 134, file 600, Questionnaires, Servicemen's Families, 1942.

42   "If Women Must Work—What of the Children?" *Canadian Forum*, 22 May 1942, 37–38.

43   Christabelle Sethna, "Wait Till Your Father Gets Home: Absent Fathers, Working Mothers and Delinquent Daughters in Ontario during World War II," in Lori Chambers and Edgar-Andre Montigny, eds., *Family Matters: Papers in Post-Confederation Canadian Family History* (Toronto: Canadian Scholars' Press, 1998), 23.

44   AM, Social Planning Council of Winnipeg (hereafter SPC), P643, Council of Social Agencies, file 1, Annual Meeting, 19 June 1944, Chairman's Remarks.

45   Fahrni, "Romance," 202; Jeff Keshen, "Morale and Morality on the Alberta Home Front," in Ken Tingley, ed., *For King and Country: Alberta in the Second World War* (Edmonton: Reidmore, 1995), 156; D. Owen Carrigan, *Juvenile Delinquency in Canada: A History* (Concord, ON: Irwin, 1998), 113–116.

46   AM, SPC, P642, file 37, Council of Social Agencies, Health Division, "Report on Venereal Disease Control in Greater Winnipeg," Sept. 1943, 1; Ruth Roach Pierson, *"They're Still Women After All": The Second World War and Canadian Womanhood* (Toronto: McClelland, 1986), 170, 207.

47   LAC, MG 28, I 10, Canadian Council on Social Development, vol. 283, file 26, Canadian Welfare Council, "Day Care of Children in Wartime," Nov. 1942, Foreword, 2.

48   AM, SPC, P642, file 22, Minutes, "Annual Report of the Secretary of the Council of Social Agencies," 9 June 1943, 5; AM, SPC, P659 and P660, Survey of Working Mothers; Bob Hummelt, "Trouble on the Home Front: Perspectives on Working Mothers in Winnipeg, 1939–1945" (M.A., University of Manitoba, 2001), 114–117.

49   Hummelt, *Trouble oon the Home Front*," 88, 113–122; Karen Wiederkehr, "Occupational Segregation and Macdonald Brothers Aircraft Ltd., 1940–1947" (MA thesis, University of Manitoba, 1994), 46.

50   Hummelt, "Trouble on the Home Front," 34, 170.

51   Margaret Randolph Higonnet et al., eds., *Behind the Lines: Gender and the Two World Wars* (New Haven: Yale UP, 1987), 8; Tuttle, *"Daddy's Gone to War,"* 76.

52   Hummelt, "Trouble on the Home Front," 141–167; Winnipeg *Free Press*, 16 March 1944.

53   Keshen, *Saints, Sinners, and Soldiers*, 284.

54   Council of Social Agencies of Greater Winnipeg, *Youth Needs in Winnipeg: An Investigation into the Causes of Juvenile Delinquency*, n.d. [1944], 5–34.

55   Winnipeg, Public Parks Board, *Report of the Commission Appointed by the Public Parks Board to Report on Recreational and Youth Activity Needs of the City of Winnipeg*, 1 March 1946; LAC, MG 28, I 10, Canadian Council on Social Development, vol. 257, file 16, Winnipeg Board of Parks and Recreation, McEwen to Zimmerman, 16 Jan. 1950; Winnipeg *Tribune*, 7 May 1946.

56   W.G. Pearce, "Winnipeg School Days, 1871–1950," copy in AM, Alan Artibise collection, P2273, file 16.

57   AM, Chisick collection, P2631, 1940–41 scrapbook.

58 Winnipeg *Free Press*, 8 May 1942.

59 Hummelt, "Trouble on the Home Front," 133–138.

60 AM, SPC, P642, file 13, Group Work Division, Minutes, 1942–43; LAC, MG 28, I 10, Canadian Council on Social Development, vol.82, file 594, Miscellaneous Pamphlets.

61 AM, SPC, P666, Greater Winnipeg Co-ordinating Board for War Services, file 4, Publications, 1943–45.

62 Durflinger, *Fighting From Home*, 155–156.

63 Tuttle, *"Daddy's Gone to War,"* 125–127.

64 AM, SPC, P642, Council of Social Agencies, file 1, "Secretary's Report," 27 May 1942.

65 AM, Family Services of Winnipeg, P4650, file 24, Board of Directors Minutes, 12 Dec. 1939 and 16 Jan. 1940.

66 AM, Family Services of Winnipeg, P4650, file 24, "The Family Bureau of Winnipeg: How it Serves the Community", and file 3, 4, 5, and 7, annual reports.

67 AM, Family Services of Winnipeg, P4650, file 5, "Executive Director's Annual Report – 1942–43," 2–9.

68 AM, Family Services of Winnipeg, P4650, file 4, "Sixth Annual Report," Oct. 1942, 9.

69 AM, SPC, P642, file 22, "Report of the Christmas Cheer Committee," 29 April 1942 and 9 June 1943, and file 7, Christmas Carnival Committee Minutes, 1942; AM, SPC, P643, file 1, Annual Meeting, 19 June 1944, "Report of the Christmas Cheer Committee."

70 AM, MG 10, C67, Royal Canadian Legion, box 33, Alex Cairns and A.H. Yetman, "The History of the Veteran Movement, 1916–1956," v. II, 16.

71 Clifford H. Bowering, *Service: The Story of the Canadian Legion*, 1925–1960 (Ottawa: Canadian Legion, 1960), 129–130.

72 Membership figures provided by Dominion Command, Royal Canadian Legion, Ottawa. See also *The Legionary* (Dec. 1938), 10.

73 AM, MG 10, C67, Royal Canadian Legion, box 11, Provincial Council Minutes, Manitoba and Northwest Ontario Command, 2–3 Dec. 1939; Resident Members Committee Minutes, 3 Jan. 1940; *Revised Statutes of Manitoba, 1940* v.II, c.196 (Winnipeg, 1940).

74 AM, MG 10, C 67, Royal Canadian Legion, box 11, Provincial Council Minutes, 2–3 Dec. 1939.

75 *The Legionary* 18, 3 (Sept. 1942), 2.

76 *The Legionary* 16, 4 (Oct. 1940), 24; Frederick Edwards, "The Soldier and His Spare Time Problems," *Chatelaine* (March 1941), reproduced in Sylvia Fraser, ed., *A Woman's Place: Seventy Years in the Lives of Canadian Women* (Toronto: Key Porter, 1997), 151.

77 Bowering, *Service*, 130–134.

78 FGH, Women's Auxiliary, "Executive 1945" and "Balance Sheet, 1945."

79 LAC, RG 24, vol. 11457, file NDWG 1920–200/49 vol. 1, Commanding Officer HMCS "Chippawa" to Commanding Officer, Naval Divisions, 15 Feb. 1945; and file NDWG 1270–152 vol. 1, GWCBWS minutes, 24 Nov. 1944.

80 FGH, Women's Auxiliary, "Casualty Visitor's Report," 3 Jan. 1945.

81 FGH, Women's Auxiliary, "President's Report," 3 Jan. 1945.

82 Ibid.

83 UMA, Wilmot collection, box 6, file 12, Hope to Laurie, 2 and 7 June 1945.

84 Fahrni, "Romance," 188–192; Margaret Ecker Francis, "Nostalgia," *Chatelaine* (Nov. 1946), reproduced in Fraser, ed., *A Woman's Place*, 53–56.

85 LAC, RG 24, reel C–5290, file 8917-3-7, Directorate of Special Services, Special Report No. 161, "Attitudes of Army Personnel Recently Returned from Overseas," 20 Nov. 1944, 20–22.

86 Keshen, *Saints, Sinners, and Soldiers*, 232.

87 Broadfoot, *Six War Years*, 243.

88 Hill et al., *Families Under Stress*, 143.

89 LAC, RG 24, reel C–5290, file 8917-3-7, Directorate of Special Services, Special Report No. 161, "Attitudes of Army Personnel Recently Returned from Overseas," 20 Nov. 1944, 20.

90 Ibid., 19–23.

91 LAC, RG 36, series 31, vol. 27, Field Reports, 31 Jan. 1945.

92 "Attitudes of Army Personnel Recently Returned from Overseas," 20 Nov. 1944, 28.

93 Francis, "Nostalgia," 55.

94 Ibid., 53–56.

95 . LAC, RG 36, series 31, vol. 27, Field Reports, 20–26 March 1945; Tuttle, *"Daddy's Gone to War,"* 217.

96 Winnipeg *Tribune*, 8–9 Nov. 1944.

97 Hill et al., *Families Under Stress*, 85; Tuttle, *"Daddy's Gone to War,"* Chapter 12, passim.

98 Bowering, *Service*, 165; Walter S. Woods, *Rehabilitation (A Combined Operation)* (Ottawa: Queen's Printer, 1953), 24–27; England, *Discharged*, 100.

99 Tuttle, *"Daddy's Gone to War,"* 215; see also Emmy E. Werner, *Through the Eyes of Innocents: Children Witness World War II* (Boulder, CO: Westview, 2000), 169.

Conclusion

1 Jay Winter and Jean-Louis Robert, *Capital Cities at War: Paris, London, Berlin, 1914-1919* (Cambridge: Cambridge University Press, 1997).

2 Ibid., 283, 544; Durflinger, *Fighting from Home*, 143–147; William M. Tuttle, Jr., *"Daddy's Gone to War': The Second World War in the Lives of America's Children* (New York: Oxford University Press, 1993), 64.

3 Perry R. Duis and Scott LaFrance, *We've Got a Job to Do: Chicagoans and World War II* (Chicago: Chicago Historical Society, 1992), 33, 52–56.

4 Robert G. Spinney, *World War II in Nashville: Transformation of the Homefront* (Knoxville, Tennessee: University of Toronto Press, 1998), 32, 97–123; Betty Burnett, *St. Louis at War: The Story of a City, 1941–1945* (St. Louis: Patrice, 1987), 162; Marc Scott Miller, *The Irony of Victory: World War II and Lowell, Massachusetts* (Urbana, Illinois: University of Illinois Press, 1988), 180; James

J. Kimble, *Mobilizing the Home Front: War Bonds and Domestic Propaganda* (College Station: Texas A&M, 2006).

5   Review of H.V. Nelles, *A Little History of Canada* (Don Mills, Ontario: Oxford University Press, 2004), http://www.h-net.org (accessed 21 March 2005).

6   Goodwin Watson, "Five Factors in Morale," in Watson, ed., *Civilian Morale: Second Yearbook of the Society for the Psychological Study of Social Issues* (Boston: Houghton, 1942), 30–47.

7   Ian McLaine, *Ministry of Morale: Home Front Morale and the Ministry of Information in World War II* (London: Allen & Unwin, 1979), 59–63.

8   Gordon W. Allport, "The Nature of Democratic Morale," in Goodwin Watson, ed., *Civilian Morale: Second Yearbook of the Society for the Psychological Study of Social Issues* (Boston: Houghton, 1942), 10.

9   John Porter, *The Vertical Mosaic: An Analysis of Social Class and Power in Canada* (Toronto: University of Toronto Press, 1965), 286.

BIBLIOGRAPHY

Primary Sources

Archives of Manitoba

Government Records

GR 43 Premier's Office Correspondence

GR 1609 Public Works, general

GR 1609 Public Works, G8029, City of Winnipeg Health Department, Annual Surveys of Vacant Houses and Vacant Suites in the City

GR 1614 Public Works, G7250 and G7251, Deputy Minister, Relief Assistance: Japanese Evacuees Case Files, 1942–1945

Manuscript Collections

C839–865, Manitoba Japanese Canadians' Citizens Association

MG 6, E2, Canada – National Defence, Prisoners of War and Internment Operations

MG 10, C67, Royal Canadian Legion

MG 14, B35, Ralph Maybank

MG 14, C50, Ethel M. McKnight

P196, Patriotic Salvage Corps

P641–P666, Social Planning Council of Winnipeg
    Central Volunteer Bureau
      Greater Winnipeg Co-ordinating Board for War Services

P827, Taichi Kato

P2273, Alan Artibise

P2626–P2631, Ernest Chisick

P4650–P4651, Family Bureau of Winnipeg

P5005, National War Finance Committee – Manitoba Division

P5513, Imperial Order Daughters of the Empire

Manitoba Legislative Library

Manitoba Legislative Library, vertical file, "World War II - Manitoba"

University of Manitoba Archives

TC 74, Sheila Rabinovitch

MSS 1, Margaret Konantz

MSS 3, J.W. Dafoe

MSS 24, Winnipeg *Tribune*

MSS 59, Henry Kreisel

MSS 72 and 73, Ed Rea

MSS SC 101, Jack Ludwig

MSS 122, Laurence F. Wilmot

City of Winnipeg Archives

Special Committees

United Church Archives, University of Winnipeg

Westminster United Church Annual Reports

Library and Archives Canada, Ottawa

Government Records

RG 2, Privy Council Office

RG 19, Finance

RG 24, National Defence

RG 25, External Affairs

RG 28, Munitions and Supply

RG 36, series 31, Wartime Information Board

RG 44, National War Services

Manuscript Collections

MG 27, III B5, Ian Mackenzie

MG 28, I 10, Canadian Council on Social Development

MG 30, E 497, Mabel Geldard-Brown

Bank of Canada Archives, Ottawa

National War Finance Committee

Archives of Ontario, Toronto

War Poster Collection

Laurier Centre for Miltiary Strategic and Disarmament Studies, Wilfrid Laurier University, Waterloo, Ontario
Department of Veterans Affairs Library, "Summary of Enlistments (All Forces) to 31 March 1945"

Interviews and Correspondence

Dennis Brown, Winnipeg, 15 May 2005

Garry Brown, Winnipeg, 15 May 2005

Mary Elaine Critchley, Winnipeg, 15 May 2005

Reg Forbes, Brandon, Manitoba, 18 February 2005

Joe Hartshorn, Sarasota, Florida, 18 May 2005.

Lawrence Peter Klyne, Baltimore, ON, 15 March 2005

Eileen Kull, Winnipeg, 29 July 2004

Ernie Kull, Winnipeg, 29 July 2004

Neil Gerard Macphee, 1 April 2005

Paul E. Martin, Winnipeg, 27 March 2007

Carrol Perrun, Winnipeg, 15 May 2005

Maggie Morris Smolensky, Toronto, 27 Sept. 2007

Published Primary Sources

Statutes of Manitoba, 1940, c.27. Winnipeg: King's Printer, 1940.

Government Reports

Canada. Department of Labour. *Wartime Orders in Council Affecting Labour*. Ottawa: King's Printer, 1943.

_____. Department of Labour. *Wartime Work of the Department of Labour*. Ottawa: King's Printer, 1943.

_____. Department of Trade and Commerce. *Dwelling Units and New Buildings Containing Dwelling Units Reported by Municipalities and Other Areas as Completed in the Six Months Ending June 30, 1947*. Ottawa: King's Printer, 1947.

_____. Department of Trade and Commerce. *Supplement to Housing Statistics 1946*. Ottawa: King's Printer, 1947.

_____. Dominion Bureau of Statistics. *Eighth Census of Canada*. Ottawa: King's Printer, 1941.

_____. Dominion Bureau of Statistics. *Canada 1945: The Official Handbook of Present Conditions and Recent Progress*. Ottawa: King's Printer, 1945.

_____. Dominion Bureau of Statistics. *Canada 1946*. Ottawa: King's Printer, 1946.

_____. Dominion Bureau of Statistics. *Census of the Prairie Provinces, 1946*, 4 vols. Ottawa: King's Printer, 1949–51.

____. National War Finance Committee. *Statistics and Information on Dominion Government Public Borrowing Operations from September 1939 to December 1945*. Ottawa: King's Printer, 1946.

____. Special Committee on Social Security. *Health Insurance: Report of the Advisory Committee on Health Insurance Appointed by Order in Council P.C. 836 Dated February 5, 1942*. Ottawa: King's Printer, 1943.

Davidson, C.B. *Unemployment in Manitoba*. Winnipeg: Manitoba Economic Survey Board, 1938.

Financial Regulations and Instructions for the Canadian Active Service Force. Ottawa: King's Printer, 1940 and 1944 editions.

Financial Regulations and Instructions for the Royal Canadian Air Force on Active Service. Ottawa: King's Printer, 1940.

Marsh, Leonard. *Report on Social Security for Canada*. Ottawa: King's Printer, 1943; reprint ed., Toronto: University of Toronto Press, 1975.

Other Reports

Council of Social Agencies of Greater Winnipeg, Report of Committee on Housing. *Housing in Winnipeg*. 1943.

Council of Social Agencies of Greater Winnipeg. *Youth Needs in Winnipeg: An Investigation into the Causes of Juvenile Delinquency*. 1944?

Periodicals

Canada Gazette

Canada Year Book

Canadian Forum

Chatelaine

Hamilton *Spectator*

The Legionary

McKim's Directory of Canadian Publications

The New Canadian

Toronto *Globe and Mail*

Toronto *Telegram*

Winnipeg *Free Press*

Winnipeg *Tribune*

Contemporary Publications

Allport, Gordon W. "The Nature of Democratic Morale." *Civilian Morale: Second Yearbook of the Society for the Psychological Study of Social Issues*, ed. Goodwin Watson. Boston: Houghton, 1942. 3–18.

Dafoe, John W. *The Voice of Dafoe: A Selection of Editorials on Collective Security, 1931–1944*, ed. W.L. Morton. Toronto: Macmillan, 1945.

Edwards, Frederick. "The Soldier and His Spare Time Problems." *Chatelaine* (March 1941). Reproduced in *A Woman's Place: Seventy Years in the Lives of Canadian Women*, ed. Sylvia Fraser. Toronto: Key Porter, 1997. 151.

England, Robert. *Discharged: A Commentary on Civil Re-establishment of Veterans in Canada*. Toronto: Macmillan, 1943.

Francis, Margaret Ecker. "Nostalgia." *Chatelaine* (Nov. 1946). Reproduced in *A Woman's Place: Seventy Years in the Lives of Canadian Women*, ed. Sylvia Fraser. Toronto: Key Porter, 1997. 53–56.

Gruenberg, Sidonie, ed. *The Family in a World at War*. New York: Harper, 1942.

"If Women Must Work – What of the Children?" *Canadian Forum* 22 (May 1942). 37–38.

Ketchum, J.D. and J.S.A. Bois. "Morale in Canada." *Civilian Morale: Second Yearbook of the Society for the Psychological Study of Social Issues*, ed. Goodwin Watson. Boston: Houghton, 1942. 249–70.

Ketchum, J.D. "Psychology and Wartime Information." *Bulletin of the Canadian Psychological Association* 3, 2 (1943). 20–23.

Kirkconnell, Watson. *Canada, Europe, and Hitler*. Toronto: Oxford University Press, 1939.

_____. *Canadians All: A Primer of Canadian National Unity*. Ottawa: Director of Public Information, 1941.

Laing, Gertrude. *A Community Organizes for War: The Story of the Greater Winnipeg Co-ordinating Board for War Services and Affiliated Organizations, 1939–1946*. Winnipeg: n.p., 1948.

Lewin, Kurt. "Time Perspective and Morale." *Civilian Morale: Second Yearbook of the Society for the Psychological Study of Social Issues*, ed. Goodwin Watson. Boston: Houghton, 1942. 48–70.

Pidgeon, Mary Elizabeth. "Reconversion and the Employment of Women." *Public Affairs* (Winter 1946). 103–107.

Watson, Goodwin. "Five Factors in Morale." *Civilian Morale: Second Yearbook of the Society for the Psychological Study of Social Issues*, ed. Goodwin Watson. Boston: Houghton, 1942. 30–47.

Watson, Goodwin, ed. *Civilian Morale: Second Yearbook of the Society for the Psychological Study of Social Issues*. Boston: Houghton, 1942.

Electronic Sources — Collections

Canadian Broadcasting Corporation Radio archives, http://archives.cbc.ca.

Canadian War Museum, "Democracy at War: Canadian Newspapers and the Second World War," http://warmuseum.ca/cwm/newspapers.

Hong Kong Veterans Commemorative Association, http://www.hkvca.ca.

Library of Congress, "Revelations from the Russian Archives: Ukrainian Famine," http://www.loc.gov/exhibits/archives/ukra.html.

Naval Museum of Manitoba, http://www.naval-museum.mb.ca

University of Manitoba Archives and Special Collections, "The Canadian Wartime Experience: The Documentary Legacy of Canada at War," http://www.umanitoba.ca/libraries/archives/canada_war.

Secondary Sources

Addison, Paul. "Britain and the Politics of Social Patriotism." *The Second World War as a National Experience*, ed. Sidney Aster. Ottawa: Canadian Committee for the History of the Second World War, 1981. 38–51.

Adleman, Robert H. and George Walton. *The Devil's Brigade*. Annapolis: Naval Institute Press, reprint 2004, first pub. 1966.

Arrowsmith, Emily. "Fair Enough? How Notions of Race, Gender, and Soldiers' Rights Affected Dependents' Allowance Policies Towards Canadian Aboriginal Families during World War II." PhD diss. Carleton University, 2006.

Artibise, Alan F.J. *Winnipeg: A Social History of Urban Growth, 1874–1914*. Montreal: McGill-Queen's University Press, 1975.

_____. *Winnipeg: An Illustrated History*. Toronto: Lorimer, 1977.

Aster, Sidney, ed. *The Second World War as a National Experience*. Ottawa: Canadian Committee for the History of the Second World War, 1981.

Avery, Donald. "The Radical Alien and the Winnipeg General Strike of 1919." *The West and the Nation: Essays in Honour of W.L. Morton*, ed. Carl Berger and Ramsay Cook. Toronto: McClelland, 1976. 209–231.

_____. "Divided Loyalties: The Ukrainian Left and the Canadian State." *Canada's Ukrainians: Negotiating an Identity*, ed. Lubomyr Luciuk and Stella Hryniuk. Toronto: University of Toronto Press, 1991. 271–287.

Bacher, John C. *Keeping to the Marketplace: The Evolution of Canadian Housing Policy*. Montreal: McGill-Queen's University Press, 1993.

Bacher, John. "W.C. Clark and the Politics of Canadian Housing Policy, 1935–1952." *Social Welfare Policy in Canada: Historical Readings*, ed. Raymond B. Blake and Jeff Keshen. Toronto: Copp Clark, 1995. 277–292.

Balzer, Timothy. *The Information Front: The Canadian Army and News Management during the Second World War*. Vancouver: UBC Press, 2011.

Bellan, Ruben C. "The Development of Winnipeg as a Metropolitan Centre." PhD diss., Columbia University, 1958.

_____.*Winnipeg First Century: An Economic History*. Winnipeg: Queenston House, 1978.

Berger, Carl. *The Writing of Canadian History: Aspects of English-Canadian Historical Writing since 1900*, 2nd ed. Toronto: University of Toronto Press, 1986.

Bland, M. Susan. "Henrietta the Homemaker, and 'Rosie the Riveter': Images of Women in Advertising in *Maclean's* Magazine, 1939–1950." *Atlantis* 8, 2 (Spring 1983). 61–86.

Blue, Howard. *Words at War: World War II Era Radio Drama and the Postwar Broadcasting Industry Blacklist*. Lanham, Maryland: Scarecrow, 2002.

Blum, John Morton. *V Was For Victory: Politics and American Culture During World War II*. New York: Harcourt, 1976.

Boddington, Steven and Sean Moir. "'The Friendly Invasion': The American Presence in Edmonton, 1942–1945." *For King and Country: Alberta in the Second World War*, ed. Ken Tingley. Edmonton: Reidmore, 1995. 177–192.

Bowering, Clifford H. *Service: The Story of the Canadian Legion, 1925–1960*. Ottawa: Canadian Legion, 1960.

Braida, Jason R.H. "The Royal City at War: The Military Mobilization of Guelph, Ontario during the First 18 Months of the Second World War." *Canadian Military History* 9, 2 (Spring 2000). 25–42.

Brandon, Laura. "History as Monument: The Sculptures on the Vimy Memorial." The Battle of Vimy Ridge, Canadian War Museum, http://www.warmuseum.ca/cwm/vimy/sculptures_e.html (accessed 20 November 2006).

Broadfoot, Barry. *Six War Years, 1939–1946: Memories of Canadians at Home and Abroad*. Toronto: Doubleday, 1974.

Burhans, Robert D. *The First Special Service Force: A War History of the North Americans, 1942–1944*. Nashville: Battery Press, reprint 1996, first pub. 1947.

Burley, David. "Winnipeg's Landscape of Modernity, 1945–1975." *Winnipeg Modern: Architecture, 1945–1975*, ed. Serena Keshavjee. Winnipeg: University of Manitoba Press, 2006. 29–86.

Burnett, Betty. *St. Louis at War: The Story of a City, 1941–1945*. St. Louis: Patrice, 1987.

Burns, E.L.M. *Manpower in the Canadian Army, 1939–1945*. Toronto: Clarke, Irwin, 1956.

Cannadine, David. "The Context, Performance and Meaning of Ritual: The British Monarchy and the 'Invention of Tradition', c. 1820–1977." *The Invention of Tradition*, eds. Eric Hobsbawm and Terence Ranger. Cambridge: Cambridge University Press, 1983. 101–164.

Carbone, Stanislao. *The Streets Were Not Paved With Gold: A Social History of Italians in Winnipeg*. Winnipeg: Manitoba Italian Heritage Committee, 1993.

Carrigan, D. Owen. *Juvenile Delinquency in Canada: A History*. Concord, ON: Irwin, 1998.

Carter, David J. *POW—Behind Canadian Barbed Wire: Alien, Refugee and Prisoner of War Camps in Canada, 1914–1916*, 2nd ed. Elkwater, AB: Eagle Butte Press, 1998.

Carynnyk, Marco. "Swallowing Stalinism: Pro-communist Ukrainian Canadians and Soviet Ukraine in the 1930s." *Canada's Ukrainians: Negotiating an Identity*, eds. Lubomyr Luciuk and Stella Hryniuk. Toronto: University of Toronto Press, 1991. 187–205.

Chapman, James. *The British at War: Cinema, State and Propaganda, 1939–1945*. London: I.B. Tauris, 1998.

Christie, Nancy. *Engendering the State: Family, Work, and Welfare in Canada*. Toronto: University of Toronto Press, 2000.

Conrad, Peter C. *Training for Victory: The British Commonwealth Air Training Plan in the West*. Saskatoon: Western Producer Prairie Books, 1989.

Cook, Ramsay. "Canadian Freedom in Wartime, 1939–1945." *His Own Man: Essays in Honour of Arthur Reginald Marsden Lower*, ed. W.H. Heick and Roger Graham Montreal: McGill-Queen's University Press, 1974. 37–53.

Copp, Terry. "Ontario 1939: The Decision for War." *A Country of Limitations: Canada and the World in 1939*, ed. Norman Hillmer, et al. Ottawa: Canadian Committee for the History of the Second World War, 1996. 109–119.

_____. "The Defence of Hong Kong, December 1941." *Canadian Military History* 10, 4 (Autumn 2001). 5–20.

_____. "From the Editor." *Canadian Military History* 10, 4 (Autumn 2001). 3–4.

Craig, John E. "Public Opinion in Manitoba and the Approach to War, 1931–1939." MA thesis, University of Toronto, 1952.

Cuthbertson, Wendy. "Popular Finance: Canada's World War II Victory Bond Programme as a Case Study in Social Marketing." Unpublished MA research paper, University of Toronto, 1999.

_____. "Pocketbooks and Patriotism: The 'Financial Miracle' of Canada's World War II Victory Bond Program." *Canadian Military History Since the 17th Century*, ed. Yves Tremblay. Ottawa: Directorate of History and Heritage, 2000. 177–186.

Dancocks, Daniel G. *The D-Day Dodgers: The Canadians in Italy, 1943–1945*. Toronto: McClelland, 1991.

Dawe, Michael. "Community in Transition: Red Deer in the Second World War." *For King and Country: Alberta in the Second World War*, ed. Ken Tingley. Edmonton: Reidmore, 1995. 119–138.

Dempsey, James. "Alberta's Indians and the Second World War." *For King and Country: Alberta in the Second World War*, ed. Ken Tingley. Edmonton: Reidmore, 1995. 39–52.

Dion, Louis. "The Resettlement of Japanese Canadians in Manitoba, 1942–1948." MA thesis, University of Manitoba, 1991.

Donnelly, M.S. *The Government of Manitoba*. Toronto: University of Toronto Press, 1963.

Donnelly, Murray. *Dafoe of the Free Press*. Toronto: Macmillan, 1968.

Doucet, Michael and John Weaver. *Housing the North American City*. Montreal: McGill-Queen's University Press, 1991.

Dreisziger, N.F. "The Rise of a Bureaucracy for Multiculturalism: The Origins of the Nationalities Branch, 1939–1941." *On Guard for Thee: War, Ethnicity and the Canadian State, 1939–1945*, ed. Norman Hillmer, et al. Ottawa: Canadian Committee for the History of the Second World War, 1988. 1–30.

_____. "Tracy Philipps and the Achievement of Ukrainian-Canadian Unity." *Canada's Ukrainians: Negotiating an Identity*, ed. Lubomyr Luciuk and Stella Hryniuk. Toronto: University of Toronto Press, 1991. 326–341.

Duguid, A.F. *Official History of the Canadian Forces in the Great War, 1914–1919*, vol. 1. Ottawa: King's Printer, 1938.

Duis, Perry R., and Scott LaFrance. *We've Got a Job to Do: Chicagoans and World War II*. Chicago: Chicago Historical Society, 1992.

Durflinger, Serge Marc. *Fighting from Home: The Second World War in Verdun, Quebec*. Vancouver: UBC Press, 2006.

Ehrenberg, John. *Civil Society: The Critical History of an Idea*. New York: New York University Press, 1999.

English, John. "Politics and the War: Aspects of the Canadian National Experience." *The Second World War as a National Experience*, ed. Sidney Aster. Ottawa: Canadian Committee for the History of the Second World War, 1981. 52–67.

Epp, Frank H. "An Analysis of Germanism and National Socialism in the Immigrant Newspaper of a Canadian Minority Group, the Mennonites, in the 1930s." PhD diss., University of Minnesota, 1965.

Fahrni, Magda. "The Romance of Reunion: Montreal War Veterans Return to Family Life, 1944–1949." *Journal of the Canadian Historical Association* 9 (1998). 187–208.

Ferguson, Barry. *Remaking Liberalism: The Intellectual Legacy of Adam Shortt, O.D. Skelton, W.C. Clark, and W.A. Mackintosh, 1890–1925*. Montreal: McGill-Queen's University Press, 1993.

Ferris, John. "Savage Christmas: The Canadians at Hong Kong." *The Valour and the Horror Revisited*, ed. David J. Bercuson and S.F. Wise. Montreal: McGill-Queen's University Press, 1994. 109–127

Fine, Jonathan. "Anti-Semitism in Manitoba in the 1930s and 40s." *Manitoba History* 32 (Autumn 1996). 26–33.

Fransen, David. "'As Far as Conscience Will Allow': Mennonites in Canada During the Second World War." *On Guard for Thee: War, Ethnicity and the Canadian State, 1939–1945*, ed. Norman Hillmer, et al. Ottawa: Canadian Committee for the History of the Second World War, 1988. 131–150.

Fraser, Sylvia, ed. *A Woman's Place: Seventy Years in the Lives of Canadian Women*. Toronto: Key Porter, 1997.

Gaffen, Fred. *Forgotten Soldiers*. Penticton, BC: Theytus, 1985.

Gerus, Oleh. "Consolidating the Community: The Ukrainian Self-Reliance League." *Canada's Ukrainians: Negotiating an Identity*, ed. Lubomyr Luciuk and Stella Hryniuk. Toronto: University of Toronto Press, 1991. 157–186.

Gleason, Mona. *Normalizing the Ideal: Psychology, Schooling, and the Family in Postwar Canada*. Toronto: University of Toronto Press, 1999.

Granatstein, J.L. *Canada's War: The Politics of the Mackenzie King Government, 1939–1945*. Toronto: University of Toronto Press, 1975.

____. "Commentary." *A Country of Limitations: Canada and the World in 1939*, ed. Norman Hillmer, et al. Ottawa: Canadian Committee for the History of the Second World War, 1996. 288–291.

____. "The End of Darkness." *Legion Magazine* (May/June 2005). 14–22.

Granatstein, J.L., and Gregory A. Johnson. "The Evacuation of the Japanese Canadians, 1942: A Realist Critique of the Received Version." *On Guard for Thee: War, Ethnicity and the Canadian State, 1939–1945*, ed. Norman Hillmer, et al. Ottawa: Canadian Committee for the History of the Second World War, 1988. 101–129.

Granatstein, J.L., and Peter Stevens, eds. *Forum: Canadian Life and Letters, 1920–1970*. Toronto: University of Toronto Press, 1972.

Gray, James H. *The Boy from Winnipeg*. 2nd ed. Saskatoon: Fifth House, 1996.

Grenke, Arthur. "The Formation and Early Development of an Urban Ethnic Community: A Case Study of the Germans in Winnipeg, 1872–1919." PhD diss., University of Manitoba, 1975.

Hall, David Ian. "'Black, White and Grey': Wartime Arguments for and against the Strategic Bomber Offensive." *Canadian Military History* 7, 1 (Winter 1998). 7–19.

Hamelin, Christine. "A Sense of Purpose: Ottawa Students and the Second World War." *Canadian Military History* 6, 1 (Spring 1997). 34–41.

Hannant, Larry. "Fifth-Column Crisis." *The Beaver* (December 1993–January 1994). 24–28.

Hannley, Lynn. "Substandard Housing." *House, Home, and Community: Progress in Housing Canadians, 1945–1986*, ed. John R. Miron. Montreal: McGill-Queen's University Press, 1993. 203–219.

Haste, Cate. "The Machinery of Propaganda." *Propaganda*, ed. Robert Jackall. New York: New York University Press, 1995. 105–136.

Higonnet, Margaret Randolph, et al., eds. *Behind the Lines: Gender and the Two World Wars*. New Haven: Yale University Press, 1987.

Hill, Reuben, et al. *Families Under Stress: Adjustment to the Crises of War Separation and Reunion*. New York: Harper, 1949.

Hillmer, Norman, et al., eds. *On Guard for Thee: War, Ethnicity and the Canadian State, 1939–1945*. Ottawa: Canadian Committee for the History of the Second World War, 1988.

Hillmer, Norman. "The Second World War as an (Un) National Experience." *On Guard for Thee: War, Ethnicity and the Canadian State, 1939–1945*, ed. Norman Hillmer, et al. Ottawa: Canadian Committee for the History of the Second World War, 1988. xi–xx.

Hillmer, Norman, et al., eds. *A Country of Limitations: Canada and the World in 1939*. Ottawa: Canadian Committee for the History of the Second World War, 1996.

Hitsman, J.M. and J.L. Granatstein. *Broken Promises: A History of Conscription in Canada.* Toronto: Oxford University Press, 1977.

Hummelt, Bob. "Trouble on the Home Front: Perspectives on Working Mothers in Winnipeg, 1939–1945." MA thesis, University of Manitoba, 2001.

If Day: The Nazi Invasion of Winnipeg. Dir. Aaron Floresco. Past Perfect Productions, 2006, 21 mins.

Institute for Propaganda Analysis. "How to Detect Propaganda." *Propaganda*, ed. Robert Jackall. New York: New York University Press, 1995. 217–224.

Ito, Roy. *We Went to War: The Story of the Japanese Canadians Who Served During the First and Second World Wars.* Stittsville: Canada's Wings, 1984.

Jackall, Robert, ed. *Propaganda.* New York: New York University Press, 1995.

Jones, Esyllt W. *Influenza 1918: Disease, Death, and Struggle in Winnipeg.* Toronto: University of Toronto Press, 2007.

Jowett, Garth S. and Victoria O'Donnell. *Propaganda and Persuasion*, 4th ed. London: Sage, 2006.

Keane, John. *Civil Society: Old Images, New Visions.* Stanford, CA: Stanford University Press, 1998.

Kelley, Ninette, and Michael Trebilcock. *The Making of the Mosaic: A History of Canadian Immigration Policy.* Toronto: University of Toronto Press, 1998.

Kelly, John Joseph. "Der Deutsche Kriegsgefangener auf Alberta: Alberta and the Keeping of German Prisoners of War, 1939–1947." *For King and Country: Alberta in the Second World War*, ed. Ken Tingley. Edmonton: Reidmore, 1995. 285–302.

Keshen, Jeff. "Morale and Morality on the Alberta Home Front." *For King and Country: Alberta in the Second World War*, ed. Ken Tingley. Edmonton: Reidmore, 1995. 145–162.

_____. "Revisiting Canada's Civilian Women during World War II." *Rethinking Canada: The Promise of Women's History*, 4th ed. Veronica Strong-Boag, Mona Gleason, and Adele Perry, eds. Don Mills, ON: Oxford University Press, 2002. 249–267.

Keshen, Jeffrey A. *Propaganda and Censorship During Canada's Great War.* Edmonton: University of Alberta Press, 1996.

_____. *Saints, Sinners, and Soldiers: Canada's Second World War.* Vancouver: UBC Press, 2004.

Kimble, James J. *Mobilizing the Home Front: War Bonds and Domestic Propaganda.* College Station: Texas A&M University Press, 2006.

Kinnear, Mary. *Margaret McWilliams: An Interwar Feminist.* Montreal: McGill-Queen's University Press, 1991.

Kordan, Bohdan S., and Lubomyr Y. Luciuk. "A Prescription for Nationbuilding: Ukrainian Canadians and the Canadian State, 1939–1945." *On Guard for Thee: War, Ethnicity and the Canadian State, 1939–1945*, ed. Norman Hillmer, et al. Ottawa: Canadian Committee for the History of the Second World War, 1988. 85–100.

Kristjanson, Wilhelm. *The Icelandic People in Manitoba: A Manitoba Saga*. Winnipeg: Wallingford Press, 1965.

Lasswell, Harold D. "Propaganda." *Propaganda*, ed. Robert Jackall. New York: New York University Press, 1995. 13–25.

Laurendeau, André. "The Plebiscite." *The Good Fight: Canadians in World War II*, ed. J.L. Granatstein and Peter Neary. Toronto: Copp Clark, 1995. 220–226.

Lehr, John C. "Peopling the Prairies with Ukrainians." *Canada's Ukrainians: Negotiating an Identity*, ed. Lubomyr Luciuk and Stella Hryniuk. Toronto: University of Toronto Press, 1991. 30–52.

Leonard, David. "Popular Culture in Edmonton During the Second World War." *For King and Country: Alberta in the Second World War*, ed. Ken Tingley. Edmonton: Reidmore, 1995. 163–176.

Litoff, Judy Barrett, and David C. Smith. "'Will He Get My Letter?' Popular Portrayals of Mail and Morale During World War II." *Journal of Popular Culture* 23, 4 (Spring, 1990). 21–43.

_____. "'I Wish That I Could Hide Inside This Letter': World War II Correspondence." *Prologue* 24, 2 (Summer, 1992). 103–114.

Littman, Sol. *Pure Soldiers or Sinister Legion: The Ukrainian 14ᵗʰ Waffen-SS Division*. Montreal: Black Rose, 2003.

Loewen, Harry. "Mennonites, National Socialism and Jews 1933–1945: A Historical Reflection." *A Sharing of Diversities*, ed. Fred Stambrook. Regina: Canadian Plains Research Center, 1999. 231–244.

Lower, Arthur R. M. *My First Seventy-five Years*. Toronto: Macmillan, 1967.

MacAloon, John J. "Olympic Games and the Theory of Spectacle in Modern Societies." *Rite, Drama, Festival, Spectacle: Rehearsals Toward a Theory of Cultural Performance*, ed. John J. MacAloon. Philadelphia: Institute for the Study of Human Issues, 1984. 241–280.

McInnis, Peter S. *Harnessing Labour Confrontation: Shaping the Postwar Settlement in Canada, 1943–1950*. Toronto: University of Toronto Press, 2001.

McKillop, A.B. "The Socialist as Citizen: John Queen and the Mayoralty of Winnipeg, 1935." Manitoba Historical Society *Transactions* Series 3, no. 30 (1973–74), www.mhs.mb.ca/docs/transactions/3/queen1935.shtml#06 (accessed 26 November 2004).

_____. "The communist as Conscience: Jacob Penner and Winnipeg Civic Politics, 1934–1935." *Cities in the West: Papers of the Western Canada Urban History Conference, University of Winnipeg, October 1974*, ed. A.R. McCormack and Ian Macpherson. Ottawa: National Museums of Canada, 1975. 181–209.

_____. *A Disciplined Intelligence: Critical Inquiry and Canadian Thought in the Victorian Era*. Montreal: McGill-Queen's University Press, 1979.

Melady, John. *Escape from Canada! The Untold Story of German POWs in Canada, 1939–1945*. Toronto: Macmillan, 1981.

Melnycky, Peter. "Tears in the Garden: Alberta Ukrainians During the Second World War." *For King and Country: Alberta in the Second World War*, ed. Ken Tingley. Edmonton: Reidmore, 1995. 327–344.

Merton, Robert K. *Mass Persuasion: The Social Psychology of a War Bond Drive*. Westport, Conn.: Greenwood, 1946.

Milkman, Ruth. "American Women and Industrial Unionism during World War II." *Behind the Lines: Gender and the Two World Wars*, ed. Margaret Randolph Higonnet, et al. New Haven: Yale University Press, 1987. 168–181.

Miller, Ian. *Our Glory and Our Grief: Torontonians and the Great War*. Toronto: University of Toronto Press, 2001.

Miller, Marc Scott. *The Irony of Victory: World War II and Lowell, Massachusetts*. Urbana, Illinois: University of Illinois Press, 1988.

Milner, Marc. "Establishing the Naval Reserve." *Legion Magazine* (Nov./Dec. 2005). 47–49.

Miron, John R. "On Progress in Housing Canadians." *House, Home, and Community: Progress in Housing Canadians, 1945–1986*, ed. John R. Miron. Montreal: McGill-Queen's University Press, 1993. 7–21.

Miron, John R., ed. *House, Home, and Community: Progress in Housing Canadians, 1945–1986*. Montreal: McGill-Queen's University Press, 1993.

Modell, John, and Duane Steffey. "Waging War and Marriage: Military Service and Family Formation, 1940–1950." *Journal of Family History* 13, 2 (1988). 195–218.

Morton, Desmond, and Glenn Wright. *Winning the Second Battle: Canadian Veterans and the Return to Civilian Life 1915–1930*. Toronto: University of Toronto Press, 1987.

Morton, Desmond. *Fight or Pay: Soldiers' Families in the Great War*. Vancouver: UBC Press, 2004.

Morton, Desmond, and J.L. Granatstein. *Victory 1945*. Toronto: Harper, 1995.

Morton, W.L. *Manitoba: A History*. 2nd ed. Toronto: University of Toronto Press, 1967.

_____.*One University: A History of the University of Manitoba, 1877–1952*. Toronto: McClelland, 1957.

Naylor, James. "The Dilemma of the CCF in Bracken's Manitoba." Paper presented at "Manitoba, Canada, Empire: A Day of History in Honour of John Kendle," University of Manitoba, 15 Nov. 2002.

Nefsky, Marilyn F. "The Shadow of Evil: Nazism and Canadian Protestantism." *Antisemitism in Canada: History and Interpretation*, ed. Alan Davies. Waterloo, ON: Wilfrid Laurier University Press, 1992.

Nelles, H.V. "Historical Pageantry and the 'Fusion of the Races' at the Tercentenary of Quebec, 1908." *Histoire Sociale / Social History* 29, 58 (Nov. 1996). 391–416.

Newman, Michael. "February 19, 1942: If Day." *Manitoba History* 13 (Spring 1987). 27–30.

Nicholson, G.W.L. *Canadian Expeditionary Force, 1914–1919: Official History of the Canadian Army in the First World War*. Ottawa: Queen's Printer, 1964.

Nunoda, Peter Takaji. "A Community in Transition and Conflict: The Japanese Canadians, 1935–1951." PhD diss., University of Manitoba, 1991.

O'Donnell, Victoria, and Garth S. Jowett. "Propaganda as a Form of Cummunication." *Propaganda: A Pluralistic Perspective*, ed. Ted J. Smith. New York: Praeger, 1989. 49–64.

Oberlander, H. Peter, and Arthur L. Fallick. *Housing a Nation: The Evolution of Canadian Housing Policy.* Vancouver: UBC Centre for Human Settlements, 1992.

Oliver, Dean F. "Public Opinion and Public Policy in Canada: Federal Legislation on War Veterans, 1939–46." *The Welfare State in Canada: Past, Present and Future*, ed. Raymond B. Blake, Penny E. Bryden, and J. Frank Strain. Concord, ON: Irwin, 1997. 193–214.

Osborne, Brian. "'Non-Preferred' People: Inter-war Ukrainian Immigration to Canada." *Canada's Ukrainians: Negotiating an Identity*, ed. Lubomyr Luciuk and Stella Hryniuk. Toronto: University of Toronto Press, 1991. 81–102.

Penner, Norman. "Jacob Penner's Recollections, Introduction." *Histoire Sociale / Social History* 7, 14 (Nov. 1974). 366–78.

Peterson, T. "Ethnic and Class Politics in Manitoba." *Canadian Provincial Politics: The Party Systems of the Ten Provinces*, ed. Martin Robin. Scarborough: Prentice, 1972. 69–115.

Phillips, Lester H. "Canada's Internal Security." *Canadian Journal of Economics and Political Science* 12, 1 (Feb. 1946). 18–29.

Pierson, Ruth Roach. *"They're Still Women After All": The Second World War and Canadian Womanhood.* Toronto: McClelland, 1986.

Pope, Maurice A. *Soldiers and Politicians: The Memoirs of Lt.-Gen. Maurice A. Pope.* Toronto: University of Toronto Press, 1962.

Porter, John. *The Vertical Mosaic: An Analysis of Social Class and Power in Canada.* Toronto: University of Toronto Press, 1965.

Prymak, Thomas M. *Maple Leaf and Trident: The Ukrainian Canadians during the Second World War.* Toronto: Multicultural History Society of Ontario, 1988.

Purdy, Sean. "'It Was Tough on Everybody': Low-Income Families and Housing Hardship in Post-World War II Toronto." *Journal of Social History* 37, 2 (2003). 457–482.

Rathert, Misty. "The 1939 Royal Visit to Winnipeg: Extensive Preparations." Unpublished course paper, University of Manitoba, 26 November 2002.

Rea, J.E. "The Politics of Conscience: Winnipeg after the Strike." *Historical Papers*, Canadian Historical Association, 1971. 276–288.

____. "The Politics of Class: Winnipeg City Council, 1919–1945." *The West and the Nation: Essays in Honour of W.L. Morton*, ed. Carl Berger and Ramsay Cook. Toronto: McClelland and Stewart, 1976. 232–249.

Rich, S. George. "Metropolitan Winnipeg, 1943–1961." *Cities in the West: Papers of the Western Canada Urban History Conference, University of Winnipeg, October 1974*, ed. A.R. McCormack and Ian Macpherson. Ottawa: National Museums of Canada, 1975. 237–268.

Roberts, Lance W., and Barry Ferguson. "Civil Society, Social Capital and Trust." *Social Capital and Community in Canada and Germany*, ed. Barry Ferguson and Lance W. Roberts (Winnipeg: St. John's College Press, 2004)

Robin, Martin. *Shades of Right: Nativist and Fascist Politics in Canada, 1920–1940.* Toronto: University of Toronto Press, 1992.

Roy, Patricia E. "British Columbia in 1939." *A Country of Limitations: Canada and the World in 1939*, eds. Norman Hillmer, et al. Ottawa: Canadian Committee for the History of the Second World War, 1996. 74–93.

Roy, Patricia, et al. *Mutual Hostages: Canadians and Japanese during the Second World War.* Toronto: University of Toronto Press, 1990.

Roy, Reginald H. "Western Canada During the Second World War." *For King and Country: Alberta in the Second World War*, ed. Ken Tingley. Edmonton: Reidmore, 1995. 109–118.

Rutherdale, Robert Allen. "The Home Front: Consensus and Conflict in Lethbridge, Guelph and Trois-Rivières During the Great War." PhD diss., York University, 1993.

Rutherdale, Robert. "Canada's August Festival: Communitas, Liminality, and Social Memory." *Canadian Historical Review* 77, 2 (July, 1996). 221–249.

_____. *Hometown Horizons: Local Responses to Canada's Great War.* Vancouver: UBC Press, 2004.

Rutherford, Paul. *The Making of the Canadian Media.* Toronto: McGraw-Hill, 1978.

Ryan, Oscar. *Tim Buck: A Conscience for Canada.* Toronto: Progress, 1975.

Sarty, Roger. "Mr. King and the Armed Forces." *A Country of Limitations: Canada and the World in 1939*, ed. Norman Hillmer, et al. Ottawa: Canadian Committee for the History of the Second World War, 1996. 217–246.

Saywell, John T. *Housing Canadians: Essays on the History of Residential Construction in Canada.* Ottawa: Economic Council of Canada, 1975.

Schweyer, Robert. *Sights on Jarvis: No. 1 Bombing and Gunnery School, 1940–1945.* Nanticoke, ON: Heronwood, 2003.

Sethna, Christabelle. "Wait Till Your Father Gets Home: Absent Fathers, Working Mothers and Delinquent Daughters in Ontario during World War II." *Family Matters: Papers in Post-Confederation Canadian Family History*, ed. Lori Chambers and Edgar-Andre Montigny. Toronto: Canadian Scholars' Press, 1998. 19–38.

Sharpe, C.A. "Enlistment in the Canadian Expeditionary Force 1914–1918: A Regional Analysis." *Journal of Canadian Studies* 18, 4 (Winter 1983–84). 15–29.

Slater, David W. *War Finance and Reconstruction: The Role of Canada's Department of Finance, 1939–1946.* Ottawa: Department of Finance, 1995.

Smith, David E. "A Period of Waiting Over: The Prairies in 1939." *A Country of Limitations: Canada and the World in 1939*, ed. Norman Hillmer, et al. Ottawa: Canadian Committee for the History of the Second World War, 1996. 94–108.

Smith, Doug. *Joe Zuken: Citizen and Socialist.* Toronto: Lorimer, 1990.

Smith, Tori. "'Almost Pathetic . . . But Also Very Glorious': The Consumer Spectacle of the Diamond Jubilee." *Histoire Sociale / Social History* 29, 58 (Nov. 1996). 333–356.

Socknat, Thomas P. *Witness against War: Pacifism in Canada, 1900–1945.* Toronto: University of Toronto Press, 1987.

Spinney, Robert G. *World War II in Nashville: Transformation of the Homefront.* Knoxville, Tennessee: University of Toronto Press, 1998.

Stacey, C.P. "The Second World War as a National Experience: Canada." *The Second World War as a National Experience*, ed. Sidney Aster. Ottawa: Canadian Committee for the History of the Second World War, 1981. 16–23.

Stacey, C.P. *Official History of the Canadian Army in the Second World War Volume I, The Army in Canada, Britain and the Pacific.* Ottawa: Queen's Printer, 1955.

_____. *Official History of the Canadian Army in the Second World War Volume III, The Victory Campaign: The Operations in North-West Europe 1944–1945.* Ottawa: Queen's Printer, 1960.

_____. *Arms, Men and Governments: The War Policies of Canada, 1939–1945.* Ottawa: Queen's Printer, 1970.

Stevenson, Michael D. *Canada's Greatest Wartime Muddle: National Selective Service and the Mobilization of Human Resources during World War II.* Montreal: McGill-Queen's University Press, 2001.

Terkel, Studs. *"The Good War": An Oral History of World War Two.* New York: Ballantine, 1984.

Tillotson, Shirley. "Citizen Participation in the Welfare State: An Experiment, 1945–57." *Canadian Historical Review* 75, 4 (1994). 511–542.

_____. *The Public at Play: Gender and the Politics of Recreation in Post-War Ontario.* Toronto: University of Toronto Press, 2000.

Tingley, Ken, ed. *For King and Country: Alberta in the Second World War.* Edmonton: Reidmore, 1995.

Toews, John Aron. "Alternative Service in Canada during World War II." MA thesis, University of Manitoba, 1957.

Trachtenberg, Henry. "The Winnipeg Jewish Community and Politics: the Inter-War Years, 1919–1939." Manitoba Historical Society *Transactions* Series 3, Number 35 (1978–79), www.mhs.mb.ca/docs/transactions/3/jewishpolitics.shtml#220 (accessed 29 November 2004).

Trofimenkoff, Susan Mann. *Stanley Knowles: The Man From Winnipeg North Centre.* Saskatoon: Western Producer Prairie Books, 1982.

Turek, Victor. *Poles in Manitoba.* Toronto: Polish Alliance Press, 1967.

Turenne, Roger E. "The Minority and the Ballot Box: A Study of the Voting Behaviour of the French Canadians of Manitoba, 1888–1967." MA thesis, University of Manitoba, 1969.

Turner, Victor. "Variations on a Theme of Liminality." *Blazing the Trail: Way Marks in the Exploration of Symbols*, ed. Edith Turner. Tucson: University of Arizona Press, 1992. 48–65.

Tuttle, William M. Jr. *"Daddy's Gone to War": The Second World War in the Lives of America's Children*. New York: Oxford University Press, 1993.

Vajcner, Mark E. "Stuart Garson and the Manitoba Progressive Coalition." *Manitoba History* 26 (Autumn 1993). 29–35.

Vance, Jonathan F. *Death So Noble: Memory, Meaning, and the First World War*. Vancouver: UBC Press, 1997.

_____. Review of H.V. Nelles, *A Little History of Canada* (Don Mills, Ontario: Oxford University Press, 2004), www.h-net.org (accessed 21 March 2005).

Vipond, Mary. *The Mass Media in Canada*, 2nd ed. Toronto: Lorimer, 1992.

Wade, Catharine Jill. "Wartime Housing Limited, 1941–1947: Canadian Housing Policy at the Crossroads." MA thesis, University of British Columbia, 1984.

Wade, Jill. "Wartime Housing Limited, 1941–1947: Canadian Housing Policy at the Crossroads." *Urban History Review* 15, 1 (June 1986). 40–59.

_____. *Houses for All: The Struggle for Social Housing in Vancouver, 1919–50*. Vancouver: UBC Press, 1994.

Wagner, Jonathan F. "The Deutsche Zeitung für Canada: A Nazi Newspaper in Winnipeg." Manitoba Historical Society *Transactions* Series 3, Number 33 (1976–77), www.mhs.mb.ca/docs/transactions/3/deutschezeitung.shtml (accessed 29 November 2004).

_____. *Brothers Beyond the Sea: National Socialism in Canada*. Waterloo, ON: Wilfrid Laurier University Press, 1981.

Walker, James W. St.G. "Race and Recruitment in World War I: Enlistment of Visible Minorities in the Canadian Expeditionary Force." *Canadian Historical Review* 70, 1 (1989). 1–26.

Ward, W. Peter. "British Columbia and the Japanese Evacuation." *Canadian Historical Review* 57, 3 (Sept. 1976). 289–309.

Wardhaugh, Robert A. "'Gateway to Empire': Imperial Sentiment in Winnipeg, 1867–1917." *Imperial Canada*, ed. Colin M. Coates. Edinburgh: University of Edinburgh Press, 1997. 206–219.

_____. *Mackenzie King and the Prairie West*. Toronto: University of Toronto Press, 2000.

Wark, Wesley K. "Diplomatic Revolution in the West: 1939, the End of Appeasement and the Origins of the Second World War." *A Country of Limitations: Canada and the World in 1939*, ed. Norman Hillmer, et al. Ottawa: Canadian Committee for the History of the Second World War, 1996. 35–57.

Werner, Emmy E. *Through the Eyes of Innocents: Children Witness World War II*. Boulder, CO: Westview, 2000.

Wetherell, Donald G., and Irene R.A. Kmet. *Homes in Alberta: Building, Trends, and Design, 1870–1967*. Edmonton: University of Alberta Press, 1991.

Whalen, James M. "The Scrap That Made A Difference." *Legion Magazine* (November/December 1998), www.legionmagazine.com/features/canadianreflections/98-11.asp (accessed 16 January 2007).

White, Jay. "Conscripted City: Halifax and the Second World War." PhD diss., McMaster University, 1994.

Wicks, Ben. *The Day They Took the Children.* Toronto: Stoddart, 1989.

Wiederkehr, Karen. "Occupational Segregation and Macdonald Brothers Aircraft Ltd., 1940–1947." MA thesis, University of Manitoba, 1994.

Wilmot, Laurence F. *Through the Hitler Line: Memoirs of an Infantry Chaplain.* Waterloo, ON: WLU Press, 2003.

Winter, Jay, and Jean-Louis Robert. *Capital Cities at War: Paris, London, Berlin, 1914–1919.* Cambridge: Cambridge University Press, 1997.

Woods, Walter S. *Rehabilitation (A Combined Operation).* Ottawa: Queen's Printer, 1953.

Young, Alan R. "'We throw the torch': Canadian Memorials of the Great War and the Mythology of Heroic Sacrifice." *Journal of Canadian Studies* 24, 4 (Winter 1989–90). 5–28.

Young, W.R. "Mobilizing English Canada for War: The Bureau of Public Information, the Wartime Information Board and a View of the Nation During the Second World War." *The Second World War as a National Experience*, ed. Sidney Aster. Ottawa: Canadian Committee for the History of the Second World War, 1981. 196–212.

_____. "Building Citizenship: English Canada and Propaganda during the Second World War." *Journal of Canadian Studies* 16, 3–4 (Fall-Winter 1981). 121–132.

_____. "Chauvinism and Canadianism: Canadian Ethnic Groups and the Failure of Wartime Information." *On Guard for Thee: War, Ethnicity and the Canadian State, 1939–1945*, ed. Norman Hillmer, et al. Ottawa: Canadian Committee for the History of the Second World War, 1988. 31–52.

Yuzyk, Paul. *The Ukrainians in Manitoba: A Social History.* Toronto: University of Toronto Press, 1953.

Zwicker, Donna Alexander. "Alberta Women Join Up." *For King and Country: Alberta in the Second World War*, ed. Ken Tingley. Edmonton: Reidmore, 1995. 89–106.

_____. "Volunteer War Service in Alberta, 1939–1945." *For King and Country: Alberta in the Second World War*, ed. Ken Tingley. Edmonton: Reidmore, 1995. 269–284.

INDEX